MARLENE

rh

ALSO BY C. W. GORTNER

The Vatican Princess

Mademoiselle Chanel

The Tudor Vendetta

The Tudor Conspiracy

The Tudor Secret

The Queen's Vow

The Confessions of Catherine de Medici

The Last Queen

MARLENE

C. W. GORTNER

WILLIAM MORROW

An Imprint of HarperCollins*Publishers*

This book is a work of fiction. References to real people, events, establishments, organizations, or locales are intended only to provide a sense of authenticity, and are used fictitiously. All other characters, and all incidents and dialogue, are drawn from the author's imagination and are not to be construed as real.

HarperCollins books may be purchased for educational, business, or sales promotional use. For information please e-mail the Special Markets Department at SPsales@harpercollins.com.

FIRST EDITION

Library of Congress Cataloging-in-Publication Data has been applied for.

ISBN 978-0-06-240606-4 (hardcover)
ISBN 978-0-06-246587-0 (international edition)

16 17 18 19 20 ov/rrd 10 9 8 7 6 5 4 3 2 1

I am, at heart, a gentleman.
—MARLENE DIETRICH

MARLENE

SCENE ONE
SCHOOLGIRL
1914–1918

"I HAD NOTHING TO DO WITH MY BIRTH."

I

The first time I fell in love, I was twelve years old.

It happened at the Auguste-Viktoria-Schule in the suburban district of Schöneberg, southwest of Berlin. Here in a squat building defended by wrought-iron gates, whose extravagant plaster facade concealed a warren of icy classrooms, I studied grammar, arithmetic, and history, followed by homemaking skills and an hour of bracing calisthenics before ending the long day with a perfunctory French class.

I disliked school, but not because I was unintelligent. In my childhood, a series of governesses had overseen my education, although my year-older sister, Elisabeth, known in our family as Liesel, received most of their attention because of her poor health. English and French, deportment, dancing and music were our daily regimen, from which our mother demanded unimpeachable perfection. Though better prepared than most for the rigors of institutional learning, I disliked school because I didn't fit in with the jam-smeared fingers and confidences of my fellow students, all of whom had known one another since infancy and dubbed me *Maus* for my timidity, unaware that "timid" was the last word my mother would have used to describe me.

Not that Mutti would tolerate a word of complaint. When Papa died of cardiac arrest in my sixth year, the urgent need to economize had sub-sumed our grief. Appearances must be maintained. After all, the widow Josephine Dietrich was of the distinguished Felsings of Berlin, founders of the renowned Felsing Clockmaker and Watch Company, which had oper-ated under imperial patent for over a century. Mutti refused to accept her family's charity, though Papa had been a suburban police lieutenant whose death benefit stretched only so far. As soon as he was buried, the govern-esses vanished, deemed an unaffordable luxury. Because of Liesel's vaguely diagnosed indispositions, Mutti took employment as a housekeeper and set forth an educational schedule for my sister to follow at home. While Mutti squeezed me into the starched gray uniform, twined my strawberry blond hair into braids topped by a gigantic taffeta bow, and with patent-leather shoes pinching my toes, marched me to the Schule, where irreproachable spinsters could mold my character.

"You will behave," Mutti admonished me. "Mind your manners and do as you're told. Do I make myself clear? Don't let me hear you give your-self airs. You've had more advantages than many, but no daughter of mine should boast of her accomplishments."

She needn't have worried. At home, I was often reprimanded for my competitive spirit, always seeking to outdo Liesel, but once I entered the schoolyard, I realized it was preferable to act as though I knew as little as possible, overwhelmed by the tribal cliques and suspicious stares of my classmates. No one could suspect I had more than a rudimentary under-standing of anything, including French—a language which every well-bred girl must learn but no well-bred German girl should become too familiar with, carrying as it did a hint of the forbidden with its sharp r and seduc-tive s. Feigning ignorance, and to deflect attention, I assumed the last seat in the last desk at the back of the classroom and kept to myself, a mouse hiding in plain sight.

Until the day our new French teacher arrived.

Strands of chestnut-colored hair escaped her chignon, and her rounded cheeks were flushed, as if she'd been racing down the hall, late for her entrance—which she was. The class bell had rung and the girls, already passing scribbled notes torn from their primers, huddled across the aisles to exchange whispers.

All of a sudden she swept in, the long-awaited replacement for Madame Servine, who had suffered a sudden fall that precipitated her retirement. With sweat dappling her brow from the unseasonable July heat, our new teacher dropped the books she carried onto her desk with a resounding thump, making every girl jolt upright.

Madame Servine had not abided dawdling. Many here had felt the sharp rap of her ruler on their knees or knuckles for perceived insolence; this startling young woman with her disheveled air and collection of tomes might prove equally formidable.

From my habitual seat in the back of the room, I peered past the shoulders of those in front of me to where she stood, mopping her forehead with a handkerchief.

"*Mon Dieu,*" she said. "*Il fait si chaud.* I didn't think Germany got so hot."

A swirl of emotion stirred in my belly.

No one said a word. With a careless gesture, she stuffed her sodden handkerchief into her shirtwaist. "*Bonjour,* mesdemoiselles. I am Mademoiselle Bréguand and I'm your new instructress for the rest of the term."

The introduction was unnecessary. We knew who she was; we'd been expecting her for weeks. While the school sought a replacement for Madame Servine, we'd spent this hour in interminable study sessions overseen by caustic Frau Becker. Now, our new teacher's crisp accent thickened the hush. The unmistakable carol of Paris sang in her voice, and I could feel the girls around me cringe. They'd called Madame *l'Ancien Régime* for her lorgnette and the way her dentures clacked when she enunciated *accents graves* in toneless superiority and her high-necked black gown dating to the turn of the century. This woman wore a collared blouse with lace trim at her neck and wrists, her slim figure set off by a fashionable ankle-length skirt that showed off smart walking boots. Years younger than Madame, she was certain to be more energetic.

I inched up from my slouch.

"*Allez,*" she declared. "*Ouvrez vos livres, s'il vous plaît.*"

The girls sat motionless. As I reached for my primer, Mademoiselle sighed and explained in German, "Your notebooks, please. Open them."

I bit back a smile.

"We are conjugating verbs today, yes?" she said, surveying the class. No one responded. None of the girls had bothered to so much as glance at their primers since Madame had taken her opportune tumble. They didn't care. From the few conversations I'd overheard, their lifelong aspiration consisted of marrying as soon as possible to escape their parents. *Kinder, Küche, Kirche*: children, kitchen, church. It was the sole ambition inculcated in every German girl, like our mothers and grandmothers before us. What possible use could speaking French offer, unless one had the misfortune to marry a foreigner?

Mademoiselle Bréguand oversaw the anxious ruffling of pages, unaware of, or unwilling to comment on, the frantic edge in her students' movements. Delinquency in homework was an offense everyone courted yet feared. Madame had been known to keep a girl at her desk until nightfall, toiling until she either completed her assignment or dropped in exhaustion.

Then, to my disbelief, I saw Mademoiselle flash a mischievous smile. It was so unexpected in this place of restraint, where teachers brooded like ravens, that its warmth stunned me, turning the swirl in my stomach into whipped cream.

"Let's start with the verb 'to be.' *Être: je suis, je serai, j'étais. Tu es, tu seras, tu étais. Il est, il sera, il était. Nous sommes, nous serons, nous étions . . .*" As she spoke, she paced the narrow aisles between our desks, her head tilted, listening to the mutilated recital coming from the students. It was a pathetic display, evidence of truancy and utter disregard for the language, but she didn't correct a single one, repeating the conjugations as the girls followed her lead.

Then she came before me. She halted. Her hand lifted. The girls went quiet. Fixing her amber-green gaze on me, Mademoiselle said, *"Répétez, s'il vous plaît?"*

I wanted to sound as awful as the others to avoid being singled out. But my tongue disobeyed me and I found myself saying haltingly, *"Vous êtes. Vous serez. Vous étiez."*

A stifled giggle from a girl nearby sounded, in my ears, like a slap.

The warm smile returned to Mademoiselle's lips. This time, to my dismay and simultaneous joy, she directed it at me. "And the rest?"

In a whisper, I said, "*Vous soyez. Vous seriez. Vous fûtes. Vous fussiez.*"

"Now, use the verb in a sentence."

I gnawed my lower lip, considering. Then I burst out, "*Je voudrais être connue comme personne qui vous plaise.*" The moment I spoke, I regretted it. What had possessed me to say something so—so overt, so forward? So *unlike* me?

Although I didn't dare look, I could feel the others staring at me. They might not have understood my actual words, but the way I had spoken them was enough.

I had unmasked myself.

"*Oui,*" said Mademoiselle softly. "*Parfait.*"

She proceeded down the aisle, chanting the refrain and signaling to the girls to follow suit. I sat, frozen, until a finger jabbed my ribs and I turned to find a dark-haired, thin girl with an elfin face winking at me. "*Parfait,*" she whispered. "Perfect."

It wasn't the reaction I'd expected. I thought the other girls would wait until the closing bell rang, then accost me outside the gates on my way home, thrashing me for deceiving them and trying to ingratiate myself with our new teacher. But what I glimpsed on this girl's face was not resentment or anger. It was . . . admiration.

After Mademoiselle assigned our homework and the girls filed out, I tried to slip past her at her desk. I'd almost made it to the door when she said, "Mademoiselle. A moment, please."

I paused, glancing warily over my shoulder. The others pushed past me; one of them sneered, "Maria the mouse is about to get her first gold star."

Then I stood alone before the teacher's pensive gaze. The late-afternoon sunlight filtering through the dusty classroom window burnished her unkempt chignon with copper. Her skin was rosy, with a slight down on her cheeks. My knees weakened. I didn't understand why I'd said what I had, but I had the disquieting impression that she did.

"Maria?" she asked. "Is that your name?"

"Yes. Maria Magdalene." I forced my voice out of my knotted throat. "Maria Magdalene Dietrich. But I prefer . . . everyone in my family calls me Marlene. Or Lena, for short."

"A lovely name. You speak French very well, Marlene. Did you learn it here?" Before I could answer, she laughed. "But of course you did not. Those others: *C'est terrible, combien peu ils savent.* You shouldn't be in this class. You're too advanced."

"Please, Mademoiselle." I clutched my satchel to my chest. "If the headmistress finds out, she'll . . ."

"What?" She cocked her head. "What will she do? It's not a crime to know how to speak another language. You'll waste your time here. Wouldn't you prefer to use this hour for something you can actually learn?"

"No." I was close to tears. "I . . . like learning French."

"I see. Well. Then we must see what we can arrange. Your secret is safe with me, but I cannot vouch for the others. They might be negligent, but they're not deaf."

"*Merci,* Mademoiselle. I'll study very hard, you'll see. I only wish to please you." It was my standard avowal, accompanied by an awkward curtsy, as Mutti had taught me during social calls after church, when we went to visit other respectable widows for hot cocoa and strudel. Then I started for the door, desperate to escape her amused eyes and my own impulsiveness.

As I left I heard her say, "Marlene. You do please. You please me very much."

II

I skipped my way back home, swinging my satchel. Crossing the tram tracks and dodging street vendors shouting out the price of their wares, I ignored everything, hearing her voice in my head, like an echo in the soft rustle of the leafy linden trees lining the avenue.

You do please. You please me very much.

By the time I dashed up the cracked marble stairs to our flat at 13 Tauentzienstrasse, I was humming under my breath. Tossing my satchel onto the foyer table, I went into the immaculate parlor where my sister, Liesel, sat hunched over her books. She glanced up, looking as weary as if she'd been sitting there for weeks.

"Is *Der Gouverneur* here?" I asked, reaching to the plate at her side for a leftover slice of strudel.

The disapproving line between her eyebrows deepened. "You mustn't call Mutti that, it's so disrespectful. And you know on Thursdays she works late at the von Losch residence. She'll be here by seven. Lena, use a plate. You're dropping crumbs everywhere. The maid just left."

I bent to the threadbare carpet, dabbing up the few crumbs. "There." I licked my finger.

"Better use the broom."

I went into the kitchen for the broom, even if it was futile. Mutti would re-sweep the carpet after we went to bed, and scrub and wax the floors, too. She never tired of cleaning, despite the fact that she spent the entire day doing it for someone else. She had let four maids go in as many months, declaring them slovenly. It happened with such frequency that Liesel and I didn't even bother anymore to learn the current maid's name.

Still humming under my breath, I moved to the small fortepiano and violin in the living room. Both were in dire need of expert tuning; the violin had been my eighth-year birthday present, purchased by Oma, my grandmother, after my private music tutor had assured Mutti I had talent. The tutor had gone the way of the governesses yet I persisted in my practice. I loved music; it was one of the few interests I shared with Mutti, who was an accomplished pianist herself after years of her own childhood lessons. We often played together after supper and I now found waiting on the piano lid an étude by Bach that she'd left for me to rehearse.

As I settled the violin onto my shoulder, Liesel said, "You're in a rare good humor. Did something special happen at school today?"

"Nothing." I adjusted the tuning pegs, hoping to spare the worn strings. Mutti would buy new strings for my birthday, but December was still months away. I had to make the best of these until then. As I passed my bow over the bridge, releasing a discordant twang, Liesel added, "Nothing? You never come home with a smile. And you never start practicing as soon as you do. *Something* must have happened."

I began to play the sonata, wincing as the worn strings resisted my efforts. "I have a new French teacher. Her name is Mademoiselle Bréguand."

Liesel went quiet, watching me play. I glanced only once or twice at the sheet music; despite the poor quality of my strings, I had memorized this piece. Mutti would be proud.

Then my sister said, "You're happy because of a new teacher? I don't believe you. I know how much you detest that school. You're always saying the teachers are frumps and the girls chatter about nothing. Tell me this instant. Did you meet a boy?"

My bow slipped, ruining my concentration. I stared at her in disbelief before I snorted. "Where would I meet a boy? All my classmates are girls."

"You still walk home every day. You see boys on the street, don't you?" She sounded serious. And somewhat angry, too.

"The only boys I see are the ones who kick stray dogs and run around like hooligans. I don't meet them. I avoid them."

I wanted to add that if she was so interested in boys, she should go out more. But I bit back my retort because it wasn't Liesel's fault that she had weak lungs or phlegmatic bronchial tubes or whatever the current illness might be. Mutti fussed constantly over her, which, in my opinion, did her no good; but the fact remained that my sister was "delicate" and she embraced the condition wholeheartedly.

"I only ask because I'm concerned," she said. "I don't mean to pry, but you'll be thirteen this year, almost a woman, and boys—well, they tend to . . ."

Her voice faded into uncomfortable silence. Retuning the violin, I pondered what she'd said, and more important, what she had not.

Liesel's experience with the opposite sex mirrored my own. Since our father's demise, the only man we saw with regularity was our uncle Willi in Berlin. But I didn't point this out because Liesel and I weren't close, not as siblings should be. We weren't antagonistic, either—we shared a bedroom and rarely quarreled—but our temperaments were so disparate that even Mutti remarked on it. Physically, the differences were apparent. Liesel was thin and wan, like a faded lamp under a shade, with our father's sallow complexion. I'd inherited Mutti's plump build, her blue eyes, upturned nose, and near-translucent skin that turned as red as a beet if I stayed out in the sun for too long. But our differences ran deeper than that. As I'd grown older, I began to realize that my reticence in public was due to Mutti drilling into me that it was how girls ought to behave. She never had to remind Liesel, to whom it came naturally. Calling attention to herself terrified my sister; it was why she never left home except for our Sunday social calls, trips to the market, and monthly outings to Berlin.

"Are you saying boys might tease me?" I said, with a deliberate lift of my eyes. She went rigid on her chair, betraying the fact that it was precisely what she was trying to say.

"Do they?" she breathed.

"No. Or at least not that I've noticed." I paused. "Why? Should I— notice, that is?"

"Never." She was appalled. "If they ever tease you or say something improper, you must ignore them and tell Mutti at once."

"I will." I caressed my bow across the strings. "I promise."

I wasn't lying. No boy had paid me any mind. But today someone had. And I knew the way she'd made me feel wasn't something I should admit to.

Your secret is safe with me.

I'd never had a secret before. I intended to keep it.

MUTTI ARRIVED AT PRECISELY FIVE PAST SEVEN. We'd already cleared the table of Liesel's study materials and set it with our chipped ceramic dishware, as the Meissen porcelain was reserved for special occasions. I was heating up a pot of *weisse Bohnensuppe,* a white-bean potage I'd prepared the day before. Mutti refused to let the maid do any cooking and had put me in charge of our daily supper. I enjoyed cooking and was better at it than Liesel, who always ended up with a scorched sauce or an underdone roast. Much like playing music, I found a soothing orderliness in following a recipe, from mixing specific ingredients just so to create a desired result. Mutti had trained me herself, but as with everything else, she did not trust anyone's skills but her own, coming directly to the kitchen with her hat and gloves still on to peer into the pot.

"More salt," she pronounced. "And reduce the flame. Otherwise, it'll turn to mush." Turning away, she went to her bedroom. She emerged minutes later in her housedress and apron, her dark blond hair coiled at the nape of her neck. I'd never seen Mutti with her hair loose, not even when she used the washroom; unbound tresses were not something widows showed, it seemed.

"How was school today?" she asked as she directed me to bring the potage to the table.

"Good," I replied. She nodded. I wondered whether she'd notice if I told her the school had burned to the ground. I didn't think so. She made the daily inquiry only because it was the polite thing to do. My answer was superfluous.

We ate in silence, idle conversation discouraged at the table. When I wiped my plate with my bread (I had a hearty appetite), she clucked, "Lena, what did I tell you?" I could have recited her litany by heart: "Girls of good breeding don't sop up their food like peasants. If you want another helping, ask."

I never asked. If I did, she'd tell me that girls of good breeding didn't require second helpings. An uncontrolled appetite displayed a lack of suitable refinement.

We washed the plates and put them away in the cupboard. Before Papa died, this was the hour when we always made ourselves scarce so our parents could retire to the living room, where Mutti would play the fortepiano while he smoked his pipe and sipped an evening *Weinbrand*. But he was gone, and as we were of suitable age, my sister reclined on the sofa as Mutti oversaw my rendition of the Bach sonata.

As always, I was nervous. Mutti might not be experienced with the violin, but she had an unerring ear and I wanted to prove I was practicing every afternoon as instructed. She was not a disciplinarian in the physical sense; she had slapped me only once. I was ten years old and at dance class, where I refused to partner with a boy whose breath stank of onion. I'd never forgotten how she strode across the floor in full view of the other children and their parents to deliver her humiliating blow, along with a stern: "We never display our feelings in public. It's rude." I'd taken pains since then to never incite her again. Though she might spare the proverbial rod, her tongue could be just as lacerating, and she had even less patience for sloth than she did for dirt or rudeness. "*Tu etwas*" was her motto: "*Do something.*" We'd learned that idleness was the worst sin of all, one we must avoid at any cost.

I finished the sonata without errors. Mutti leaned back on the bench before the fortepiano. "That was excellent, Lena." She spoke with an affection she never showed unless I had surpassed her expectations.

Relief filled me. Her praise was so rare, it made me feel as if I'd accomplished a feat.

"You've been practicing," she went on. "It shows. You must continue. It shan't be long before we must arrange a scholarship audition to the Weimar music conservatory."

"Yes, Mutti," I said. The prestigious conservatory in Weimar was her ambition, not mine; she believed my talent could pave the way to a career as a concert soloist and had not solicited my opinion. Girls of good breeding did what their mothers told them to do.

"And you, my dear?" She glanced at Liesel, who had applauded at the end of my performance. "Would you like to play something on the piano for us?"

Apparently, I thought resentfully, my sister's opinion did matter, for when she demurred, "Forgive me, but I have a headache," Mutti sighed and closed the lid on the keys. "You must go to bed, then. It's getting late and we have to rise early tomorrow."

Earlier than usual? I groaned inside. It meant she had chores we must do before I left for school and she went to work. As I set my violin in its case, I wondered why we kept a maid at all. Between our daily chores and Mutti's nightly ritual—I could tell she was eager to see us to bed so she could attack the foyer parquet—surely paying a maid was another needless expense.

Then Mutti said, "Before we retire, I have important news."

I paused in surprise. News?

We waited as she glanced at her chafed hands, which no amount of lotion could relieve, visible proof that Wilhelmina Josephine Felsing, known in the community as the Widow Dietrich, had come down in the world. She still wore her gold wedding band, tight around her swollen knuckle. She fingered it. Something about her gesture made me nervous.

"I am getting married again."

Liesel sat frozen. Incredulous, I said, "Married? To whom?"

She frowned. As I braced for her retort that children did not question their elders, she replied, "To Herr von Losch. As you know, he is a widower, with no children; after careful consideration, I have decided to accept his proposal."

"Herr von Losch?" I was aghast. "The man whose house you clean?"

"I do not clean it." Though she didn't raise her voice, her tone turned sharp. "I oversee its upkeep. I am his *Haushälterin*. His maids do the cleaning and I supervise. Are you quite finished with your questions, Lena?"

I wasn't. A hundred more clamored in my mind but all I said was, "Yes, Mutti," and stepped toward my sister, thinking I had just earned my second slap.

"The wedding will take place next year." Mutti stood, smoothing her hands over her apron. "I've asked for sufficient time to prepare and he has granted it. I want to inform your grandmother and Uncle Willi first of course, as they must give their approval and present me at the altar. That is why we must rise extra early tomorrow. I've invited them to visit; before they arrive, we've much to do if we're to set this house in order."

Unless she intended us to switch out the furniture, I couldn't see what else needed doing. Every Saturday after market we scrubbed the entire flat, addressing each nook and cranny the maid had neglected. And no matter how much we cleaned, anyone could see that, unlike Oma and Uncle Willi, we lived in a rented flat that, while not mean, was hardly luxurious. But I didn't dare say another word, too shocked by her unexpected news.

She would marry again. Liesel and I would have a new stepfather—a man we did not know, who we'd be expected to respect and obey.

"We've not yet decided our living arrangements, but I assume after the wedding, we'll move to his house in Dessau. I'm going there next week to see if it's suitable. In the meantime, you are not to say a word to anyone. I don't want the neighbors gossiping out of turn or advising the landlord that we intend to give notice. Is that understood?"

"Yes, Mutti," Liesel and I said in unison.

"Good." She tried to smile, but it was such an infrequent occurrence for her, it came out as a grimace. "Now, wash your faces and say your prayers." As we turned to leave, she called out, "Lena, make sure you wash behind your ears."

Liesel didn't speak as we took our turns in the cramped washroom, undressed, and slipped into our narrow twin beds. A nightstand separated us; I could have reached across and touched her, but I didn't, lying on my back to stare up at the ceiling. When I heard Mutti in the foyer, on her knees with her rags and wax, I whispered, "Why would she do this, at her age?"

My sister sighed. "She's only thirty-eight. It's not so old. Herr von Losch is also a colonel in the Imperial Grenadiers, as Papa was. He must be an honest man."

"Thirty-eight seems old enough to me," I retorted. "And how do we know he's honest? She supervises his maids. What can she know about him, besides how much starch to use on his shirts?" My voice hardened. "And Dessau is so far away that I'll have to leave my school."

"Lena." Liesel turned to me, her eyes like two pinched holes in the gloom. "You mustn't try her. She only does what is best for us."

Somehow, I doubted that. Marrying a stranger and upending our existence didn't seem like what was best for anyone, save for her and Herr von Losch.

"A woman alone is a terrible thing," Liesel went on. "You cannot understand, but to be a widow with two daughters to raise—it's a test of perseverance." She turned away, pulling her sheet to her chin. Within minutes, she was snoring. Liesel would not protest. Whatever Mutti said or did, she always complied. A parlor here or there: It was all the same to her.

While I had other interests. I had my secret.

With my sheets bunched in my fists, I did not fall asleep for a long time.

III

I trudged through the weekend. Mutti couldn't help but notice, especially when Liesel whispered, "Stop glowering!" But she refrained from any chastisement, first having us clean the entire apartment, floors and windows included, before she received word that Uncle Willi couldn't visit. Instead, to my delight, Mutti said we would go see him in Berlin.

I loved Unter den Linden in the city, that sweeping boulevard with its luxurious shopping emporia; here, we visited the Felsing Clock and Watch Company run by Uncle Willi. Delighted to see us, he took us to a *confiserie* for vanilla cakes and marzipan, and then on to the Café Bauer on the Friedrichstrasse for hot chocolate to go with our cakes. I had an insatiable sweet tooth, and Mutti, for all her rigidity at the table, indulged my vice, as a girl with flesh on her bones proved she came from an upstanding family. I ate my share but also surreptitiously wrapped several marzipans in my handkerchief, pocketing them while Uncle Willi paid the bill, even as my sister eyed me in dismay.

Mutti did not mention her upcoming marriage again, at least not with us, though I assumed at some point she informed Uncle Willi. She didn't believe in debating her decisions with us, and of course we were in no position to challenge them. But rebelliousness seethed in me. By the following week, I felt so helpless before this momentous change in my life, I stopped pretending in class and vied openly for Mademoiselle's attention. I was the first to present my flawless assignments, the first to raise my hand and answer any question she posed, oblivious to the others' glares when she commended me for my diligence.

"Let Maria be an example," she told the class, giving me her coveted smile. "She has shown that with the proper attitude and diligence, anyone can learn to speak French."

As almost everyone suspected I had started out with an advantage they lacked, I didn't endear myself to my classmates and I didn't care. I wanted only to endear myself to her. The marzipan I'd taken became little gifts wrapped in scraps of lace, adorned with a single poppy, which I deposited on her desk every day before I left, my eyes downcast as she exclaimed, "How thoughtful of you," and I murmured, "*De rien*, Mademoiselle." That the marzipan was misshapen, soggy from being stored in my pocket, made no difference; it was my gesture of appreciation that mattered.

The very next week when Mutti went to Dessau to determine if the von Losch house would suit as our new residence, which meant she'd return home later than usual, Mademoiselle invited me to a stroll after school. Although I'd promised to go straight home to help Liesel with chores and supper—as predicted, our maid had been sacked—I waited for Mademoiselle outside the gates. She emerged with her satchel stuffed with books and a straw boater on her head.

"Shall we?" she said, and I found myself walking beside her to the boulevard, passing laced-up ladies with parasols and dogs on leashes, gentlemen in bowler hats and gold fob chains slung from vests, and tired governesses with protesting charges in tow. Any of them might know Mutti. Despite its proximity to Berlin, Schöneberg was still a garrison town, where the kaiser barracked his troops. Everyone knew everyone else. I kept my face lowered under my cap, hoping my uniform would hide my identity. To my relief, no one paid us particular mind, the men doffing their hats and the ladies murmuring their *guten Tags*.

"Let's have a coffee." Mademoiselle stopped at a corner café, taking one of the outdoor marble-topped tables. As I perched opposite her, I realized that in daylight, she was even lovelier than in the classroom, her hazel eyes flecked with green, her lips as pink as the ribbon on her hat. A few stray hairs from her chignon clung to her cheek. I had to clench my hands in my lap to stop myself from reaching over to peel them off her skin.

She ordered. The waiter frowned. "Coffee for the fräulein?"

"How silly of me." She laughed. "Marlene, would you prefer a chocolate or a lemonade?"

"No, thank you." I straightened my back. "Coffee is fine."

I'd never had coffee. Mutti drank tea. Proper ladies only drank tea. Regardless of its popularity, according to Mutti, coffee was a foreign predilection that soured one's breath.

While we waited to be served, Mademoiselle sighed and removed her boater, running her fingers through her hair, causing more strands to unravel about her face. Then without warning, she said, "Now, you must tell me what troubles you."

I was startled. "Troubles me? Nothing, Mademoiselle." Except that I was sitting at a café on the boulevard with her and was afraid someone who knew Mutti might see us.

"Oh, no." She wagged her finger. "I've sufficient experience to know when a student tries to hide something."

"Experience?"

"Yes." She nodded as the waiter set two cups of dark liquid before us, pouring cream from the pitcher into hers. She extended the pitcher. "It's less bitter this way. Add sugar, too." As I did, she went on, "Before I took this job, I worked as a governess in a large house. I had three charges. I know when a girl fears saying what's on her mind."

For a paralyzing instant, I thought she'd seen through me, my gifts of marzipan and eagerness for attention betraying me. But then I realized she didn't appear angry or upset, her candid gaze on me as she said, "I promise whatever you tell me will stay between us."

"Like . . . a secret?" I asked. I sipped the coffee; it tasted like sweet molten velvet.

"If you like. *Un secret entre nous.*"

My French might be good, but not good enough to describe my surge of emotion. I didn't want to impose on her astonishing informality, exciting as it was. No one had ever asked me what I felt, much less my innermost thoughts. As if Mutti were at my side, a sibilant shadow in my ear, I heard: *We never display our feelings in public.*

I tore my gaze from her face. "It really is nothing," I muttered.

Her hand slid over mine. Her fingers were so warm, the sensation speared all the way to my toes. "Please. I want to help you, if I can."

Was I so transparent? Or was it rather that until this moment, no one had ever deigned to see me as someone with feelings worth noting?

"It's . . . my mother. She's getting married again."

"Is that all? But I had the impression it must be something else."

"Such as?" I was terrified to learn what else she'd divined, prepared to be told that my affection, while flattering, was hardly appropriate between a student and her teacher.

Instead she said, "I thought there might be a boy you liked, perhaps, or some female trouble?"

I understood the euphemism and shook my head. I'd had my first menses three months before.

"Then it is only your mother getting married? But why? Do you not like her suitor?"

"I don't know him. My father died when I was six. Until now, it's just been Mutti, my sister, and me. . . ." Before I knew it, I was telling her all about Herr von Losch and the threatening move to Dessau, about my talent for the violin and Mutti's ambition to see me enter the conservatory. I curbed my outburst only when I was about to confess that she also troubled me, as I had no words to explain what she made me feel, but that I didn't want to go anywhere that might take me away from her.

She sipped her coffee. "I understand how frightening change can be," she said at length. "*Mon Dieu*, how I understand. But it doesn't seem as if you've reason to worry. Your mother sounds like a decent woman who has found a husband to care for her. You want her to be happy, don't you? And

Dessau isn't too far away. I'm certain there are schools there, with other girls." She paused. "You've not made friends here. That dark-haired girl who sits next to you in class, Hilde—she's always trying to catch your attention but you behave as if she's invisible."

She did? I hadn't noticed. But then I never noticed anything at school these days, except Mademoiselle.

"A girl like you," she said, "so pretty and intelligent. Why, you could have a hundred friends if you wanted them. But you never try, do you?"

The conversation had taken an awkward turn. I didn't want to talk about my lack of friends; I wanted—

She pointed at my cup. "You should drink that before it gets cold."

As I gulped down the now-lukewarm coffee, she regarded me with that disconcerting blend of sincerity and insight that made me think she could read my deepest thoughts.

"Have you ever been to a *cinématographe*?" she abruptly asked.

"A what?" Her question was so disconcerting, I had no idea what she meant.

"A moving picture. A flicker."

I knew the term but had never seen one. Mutti did not approve.

"You haven't. Marvelous! There's one near here. It's not grand like those in Berlin, but not as expensive, either. It's in a cabaret hall, where they show flickers on weekday evenings. Would you like to go? I adore the cinema. I believe it's the new entertainment for our modern age, which will make even the theater seem passé. They're showing *Der Untergang der* Titanic. Do you know what it's about?"

I nodded. "The *Titanic* sank after striking an iceberg." I remembered because when it happened two years earlier, every newspaper boy had blared the headline for days on end.

"Indeed. Many lives were lost. This moving picture is supposed to be amazing. Continental-Kunstfilm in Berlin produced it. They're building entire studios dedicated to the cinema." She gestured to the waiter for the check. "If we hurry, we can make the first showing."

I knew I should decline, thank her for the coffee and advice, and make my way back before it was too late. Liesel would worry. She'd tell Mutti I'd been late coming home, and—

Mademoiselle ladled coins onto the platter with the bill and stood, holding out her hand. "Quickly, Marlene. Before we miss the Stadtbahn!"

How could I resist? Grasping her hand, I let Mademoiselle Bréguand lead me astray.

I WEPT.

I couldn't help it, my sorrow and amazement overcoming me as the grainy images on the warped sheet hung on the wall as a screen came to life, depicting a titan lost at sea, the forlorn men waiting on deck while the orchestra played and the tragic women huddled in lifeboats, witnesses to catastrophe. At one point, I even grabbed Mademoiselle's knee, so over-whelmed that I forgot we were in public, albeit in a darkened hall that stank of beer and stale cigarettes, with others seated around us, their gasps and whispered commentary enhancing the mute display.

Afterward, I was in a daze.

"Wasn't it sublime?" Mademoiselle's face was luminous. "I want to be there one day."

"On the *Titanic*?" I managed to say, trying to shake off the sensation of being stranded on the open sea, watching my loved ones sink under cold black water.

"No, silly. Up there. On the screen. I want to be an actress; it's why I left Paris to come here. I'm working as a teacher until I earn enough to rent a room in Berlin. It's terribly expensive to live in Berlin these days—it's the fastest city in the world and I need extra money to pay for my rent and dramatic classes." She took my hand again as we waited for the overhead Stadtbahn tram. "Now, we both have secrets to keep. I've just told you mine."

I longed to ask her if there was someone she loved or missed, whom she'd left behind in France to pursue her dream. But I couldn't untangle the words from my mouth, and all too soon we reached the boulevard, where the new electrical lighting shed a sulfuric glow over the populace as they milled about the beer gardens and cafés.

We hurried toward the shuttered school.

By the gates, she halted. "I live this way," she said, motioning to a side street that wound between ramshackle older buildings. "But I can accompany you home and explain why you're late." Her mischievous smile crinkled her mouth. "We'll have to say you didn't finish your assignment in time. It might mean your mother will be displeased."

Displeasure, I thought, was the least I could expect.

"There's no need. She's working late today. She might not be home yet." Though it seemed as if an eternity had passed, the picture had lasted only forty minutes. I'd get a scolding from Liesel, no doubt, but Mutti wouldn't be back until nine at the earliest.

"Ah, yes. I forgot. She's in Dessau. Well, then. If you're quite sure you'll be safe?"

"I am." I began to curtsy, but she reached out and embraced me. She smelled of perspiration, with a faint trace of lavender water and coffee, and the acrid stink of the cabaret hall, which permeated her clothes. I melted against her. "*Merci*, Mademoiselle."

"*Mais non, ma fille.*" She cupped my chin in her hands, kissing both my cheeks. "You must call me Marguerite when we're alone. Women with secrets must also be friends, *oui?*"

Swirling around, she walked away. As the shadows of the encroaching buildings darkened her passage, she half-turned, raising her hand. "*À bientôt, mon amie* Marlene!"

I didn't want her to go. I might never bathe again, lest I erased her scent from my hands. On my way home, I kept lifting my palms to inhale her, ignoring the sharp chill in the air.

Our warm July had forsaken us.

I would never see Marguerite Bréguand again.

IV

She left," Hilde said. We were sitting outside in the courtyard after Frau Becker had informed us there would be no French lesson today or in the foreseeable future. "I don't know why."

Dismayed by Mademoiselle's unexplained absence, I'd accosted Hilde, the thin, dark-haired girl who'd told me *parfait* meant "perfect" and longed to catch my eye. She leaped at the chance to be my confidante, but to my frustration, she didn't seem to know anything that might shed light on this bewildering change in events.

As we sat together while the other girls skipped rope, overjoyed to be free for the afternoon, I fingered the last marzipan in my pocket. I drew it out, handing it to Hilde. "Here."

"Oh." She accepted it as if I'd offered her a pearl. "Thank you, Maria."

"Marlene," I said, scouring the area for Mademoiselle. "My name is Marlene."

"It is? But I thought it was Maria . . . ? Marlene is such an odd name, but pretty, too." She shrugged, munching on the marzipan.

"You really haven't heard anything?" I asked again. "How can she have just left? She was Madame's replacement; it took weeks to hire her and she's only been here a few weeks."

Hilde paused, considering. "Perhaps it has something to do with the war."

"War?" I stared at her. "There is no war."

"Not yet." She took on the avid look of someone with important news, something her new friend didn't know. "But there've been rumors about the kaiser declaring war against—" She frowned. "Well, I'm not sure against whom, but my father's in the infantry and he wrote to my mother last week to tell us his regiment had been mobilized and war was imminent."

"Well, I've not heard anything about it," I declared, with more certainty than I felt. I wouldn't have. War could erupt in the very street outside our flat and unless the enemy came pounding at our door, Mutti would remain impervious.

I dreaded the thought that someone had seen us together and reported Mademoiselle to our *Schulleiterin*, the headmistress. Keeping a student after hours to correct deficiencies was acceptable, but to take that student out for coffee and an excursion to the flickers—that would be grounds for dismissal. Had I been the unwitting cause of her mysterious disappearance?

If so, I couldn't sit here. "*Tu etwas*," I said, and I bolted to my feet, grabbing my satchel.

Hilde gaped at me, marzipan crumbs on her chin. "Where are you going?"

"Out." I was starting across the courtyard when Hilde yanked me back by my satchel strap. "Marlene, you can't. The closing bell hasn't rung yet. The gates are locked."

"*Dumme Kühe*," I cursed. "Stupid cows. Is this a school or a prison?"

"Both," said Hilde, and I found myself smiling. Despite her ordinary appearance, she had a certain wit. "But the back gate is never locked. The fire marshal told them they must keep it open in case of emergency. Since everyone's out here . . ." She grinned.

I crept with her through the nearly empty building to the back gate, which let out onto a muddy path bordering abandoned pasturelands that not long ago had been Schöneberg's main attraction. Now tenements were rising where potatoes and lettuce had grown—cheap block edifices to house the population spilling over from Berlin. I recalled what Mademoiselle had told me about her aspirations. Had our experience last night prompted her to toss caution to the winds and leave for the city she'd dubbed "the fastest" in the world?

The path led to the side street where she'd told me she lived. But as we emerged onto uneven cobbles where stray dogs lolled and puny children squatted, playing with marbles, my heart sank. I hadn't seen her make her way to her actual building; I had no idea which of these decrepit tenement boardinghouses was hers.

"Well?" Hilde said. I had to admire her pluck. She hadn't hesitated a moment, guiding us to our escape without compunction, though she risked punishment as much as I did.

I blew out an exasperated breath. "She went this way, but . . ." My voice faded as a distant rumble reached us, the sound of marching feet and shouting. I turned in bewilderment to Hilde, who cried out, "It's begun!"

She raced down the side street toward the avenue, obliging me to follow. I cast a quick look over my shoulder, hoping the commotion would alert denizens in the buildings, but only the lazy dogs pricked up their ears. Laundry sagged outside windows that no one looked out from.

I came to a panting halt beside Hilde. Before us, pedestrians crowded on the sidewalks as a horde tromped down the middle of the street, waving banners and flags emblazoned with the kaiser's black eagle. Most of the demonstrators were youths, with rough hands and shirtsleeves rolled to their elbows, laborers and such from the nearby factories—common riff-raff, Mutti would sniff—chanting, "'Holy flame, glow! Glow and expire not. For the Fatherland we stand, valiant for one man. Gladly fighting for our empire!'"

"It's the '*Heil dir im Siegerkranz*,'" Hilde shouted in my ear. "See? We're at war!"

I couldn't believe it. As the demonstrators amassed, I saw the ladies with their parasols and little dogs on leashes, the gentlemen in their bowler hats, and the governesses with openmouthed children, applauding and lifting their fists in salute, as though this were some circus come to town.

"Are they insane?" I said, but no one was listening to me. The chanting had grown deafening, echoing through the avenue and into the cloud-ruffled sky, so that we almost didn't hear the faint ringing of the school bell.

Hilde gasped, "They're letting us out early. Hurry!"

She hauled me through the crowd, pushing and shoving until we reached the gates, which stood ajar, the girls clustered there to observe the parade with wide eyes, their oversize hair bows quivering as the teachers held them back.

Frau Becker spotted us. "Hilde, Maria," she barked. "Get inside this instant."

We crammed past the girls and earned a sharp pinch on our respective ears from the teachers. "How dare you slip out?" demanded Frau Becker. "What on earth were you thinking?"

Hilde slid her eyes at me. They thought we'd gotten out when the gates opened, so I quickly said, "We wanted to see what was happening. We didn't go far."

"You went entirely too far," retorted Frau Becker. "I shall inform the headmistress. The cheek of you, sneaking out when the world is about to explode."

"Explode?" All of a sudden, this alleged war became frighteningly real.

"Yes. His imperial majesty vows to avenge the archduke Ferdinand of Austria's assassination. Germany must defend her honor. But never you mind that; war or not, no girl can be allowed such insubordination."

She marched us directly to the headmistress's office. While Hilde and I endured a severe tongue-lashing followed by a week of extra study and no free time in the courtyard, just outside the gates, our entire nation plunged headlong into disaster.

V

M ust I?" My fingers were freezing; as I looked down at my feet at the basket of wool unraveled from old sweaters, which I must convert into mittens and scarves and caps, despair overwhelmed my permanently ravenous stomach.

"Would you have our brave men suffer frostbite or chilblains because you are tired?" said Mutti. "This is what we must do, our sacrifice for theirs. Cease your moping and finish that scarf. I must convey these to the front with the auxiliary nurses."

I resisted rolling my eyes at Liesel. She, too, sat sewing in the cavernous living room of the von Losch residence in Dessau, where we'd moved after the kaiser declared war.

To my relief, we'd barely interacted with the colonel before he had to depart for duty, but from the little that we had, I found him a prim, humorless man who invariably addressed Mutti as "Frau" and gave us a vague appraisal, as though we were extra suitcases she'd brought. We had taken care in those first weeks to avoid getting in his way, adhering to his rigid schedule for meals that required all of us to sit at the table and say as little as possible while he pontificated about Prussian honor and our need to defend it. Mutti, in turn, deferred to him as if she was still his servant, not the woman he intended to wed. To my surprise, when he left they still had not married. I wondered why Mutti had insisted on moving us here, even if I did not dare ask. How could Josephine Felsing reside with a man before the banns or church blessing? But then, she wasn't really residing with him, was she? He was gone, fighting for the empire, and to all outward appearances, she was his housekeeper, only she now oversaw his house in Dessau. Money, I thought, must be the reason, even if she'd die before she admitted it. We couldn't afford our flat without her employment, so we had to go wherever Herr von Losch ordained. I did not like it. I found Mutti's joyless subservience disturbing, as though I'd inadvertently caught her desperately mending her worn underclothes. I now began to understand what Liesel had said about a woman alone: Despite Mutti's extolling of our family name and the exacting propriety for it, we were not privileged at all, but rather, dependent on the whims of her employer.

And in truth, Mutti didn't have much to manage in Dessau. Besides a cantankerous Catholic cook, there was one anxious maid who dwelled in daily terror of Mutti's inspections and a lame coachman who, as far as I could tell, had nothing useful to do, as the stables were empty. All horses had been requisitioned for the war, and if the rumors were true, were now being slaughtered for the soup pot.

It was dismal and boring. I missed Schöneberg, even my school, for here we lived like prisoners, with mourning bands constricting our arms as we knitted, sewed, and assembled care packages, even as our own rations dwindled. Meat, milk, and flour had become impossible to obtain, so that our bread was mostly made with sawdust and entire menus revolved around turnips. My enrollment in Dessau's parochial academy got me out of the house every day, but between the obligatory studies, we performed much the same tasks as at home, supporting the war effort with our sweat and bleeding fingertips, along with weekly visits to city hall to sing patriotic choruses as the mayor read out names from the interminable lists of the fallen.

"When are Uncle Willi and Oma coming?" I ventured after another half hour passed and the clicking of knitting needles gnawed at my nerves. "Didn't you say they would visit soon?"

These days, my sole reprieve from the monotony was my relatives. Mutti's younger brother Max had died in combat, a tragedy that had us reciting prayers for days on end, although I'd barely known Max. More exciting was the fact that one of my paternal uncles had flown a daring zeppelin raid over London and earned a newspaper mention for it. Uncle Willi, however, had avoided the draft because he oversaw the Felsing business and the kaiser had requisitioned the clock-making factory as a munitions facility. To earn money, Willi had also rented out the top floor of the main store to a man who'd invented a revolutionary new optical device for film projection, which the kaiser commissioned to document the war. I looked forward to hearing about my uncle's ventures, eagerly awaiting his occasional visits with my grandmother, who resided with Willi at the Berlin family home. Regardless of the tribulations, they always brought a tangible sophistication when they came to see us, my uncle exuding the scent of his Russian cigarettes—a luxury he refused to part with—and Oma as pristine as ever in her sable and pearls. It never failed to strike me, as well, that had Mutti only asked for their help, we might have moved in with them in Berlin instead of a stranger's house.

"Travel is difficult now. You will stay with them when I depart for the front," replied Mutti, with a sharp glance at me that preempted my exclamation.

"We . . . we will stay with them in Berlin?" I asked, trying to subdue my excitement.

"Of course." Mutti's voice was terse. I might not have dared question, but she knew I saw far more than she wanted me to see. "I cannot leave you alone here, can I? Now," she said, lifting her voice to forestall my questions as to when we were leaving, "have you finished your work? No, I see you have not. Lena, this intolerable malaise reflects poorly on us all. There is a war going on. Now, *tu etwas.*"

I gritted my teeth and resumed my knitting. I couldn't wait for her to leave for the front, wherever that might be, if only so I'd be spared another reminder of the war. It had been going on for four years now, consuming everything in sight. But I knew little about it besides the fact that while thousands died, blown apart by artillery or gassed in trenches, Mutti believed that delivering boxes of mittens could somehow hasten its resolution. Mittens! As if the kaiser could offer them by the truckload to appease our foes.

My stomach rumbled. I was so exhausted and constantly hungry, I didn't know what to feel anymore. I realized I should be grief-stricken—it seemed a requisite—for the death toll was immense; the lists grew longer every day, so many young men like those I'd seen marching down Schöneberg's avenue perishing in terrible ways. To emphasize the gravity, Mutti had even embroidered and framed a needlework rendering of the poem by Freiligrath over our parlor mantel like a commandment:

> O love, while it's still yours to love!
> O love, while love you still may keep!
> The hour will come, the hour will come,
> When you shall stand by graves and weep.

She murmured it to herself as she went about her work, a constant litany like the prayers with rosary beads I'd seen the cook engage in whenever I sneaked into the kitchen to find something to eat. If I hadn't known better, I might have thought Mutti *enjoyed* the upheaval that had turned the world against us and brought Germany to its knees.

I should be as resolute as she was to see us triumph. I should take pride in our sacrifices and the dogged defense of our blighted honor. But all I could think about when I had the energy was Mademoiselle. I wondered where she had gone. Back home to France, I supposed. There could be no dream of becoming an actress now.

By nightfall, we had to stop. Lamp oil was scarce and we relied on stinking tallow to illuminate our paltry meal before we trudged to bed, our sole refuge from the long winter night.

Liesel slept like a stone. Her fortitude astonished me. For a seventeen-year-old girl who was too delicate to attend school, she could sit for hours without wincing, wielding her needle as if her life depended on it. She had made twice as many mittens and caps as I had, and not once had she complained.

I was too tired even to sleep. Shutting my eyes, I tried to recollect that magical evening when I'd sat beside Mademoiselle and beheld another tragedy unspooling before me. I desperately needed to conjure up the memory of her scent on my hands, to see her smile and hear her laughter, as she confided her aspiration.

Women with secrets must also be friends, oui?

But she had faded and become a memento—inanimate, sepia tinted. As lifeless as amber.

I had lost her.

All that remained was this endless drudgery and daily fear, and the fragile hope that somehow, someday, the war would finally come to an end and life would begin anew.

MUTTI DEPARTED FOR THE FRONT IN EARLY 1918, after urgent word arrived that Colonel von Losch had been wounded. As promised, she dispatched Liesel and me to Berlin.

At last, I was back in the city I loved, though I'd only experienced it through outings with Mutti. But Berlin was not lively; it was no longer the fastest city in the world. Everywhere I looked it was deflated and grim, the streets deserted save for old people and black-clad widows clutching tattered shawls, scavenging in the trash heaps or trapping stray cats.

Oma was insulated from the suffering. Uncle Willi still turned a decent profit with his munitions factory, paid by the kaiser himself, and the upscale Felsing residence with its chandeliers and velvet drapes was much the same as I remembered from my childhood, a pantheon to our familial industriousness.

"When did you become so beautiful?" my grandmother asked, peering through her spectacles at me. "You look like no one else in our family, *mein Lieber.*"

"I look like Mutti," I said. We were in her upstairs boudoir—she still used the word "boudoir," peppering her conversation with French phrases, though we were supposed to despise France and every other nation that wasn't our ally. "I have her hair and eyes—"

"Not her eyes." Oma's smile hollowed her face, her bracelets chattering on her bony wrists. "You don't have our eyes at all. Yours are more wide spaced and heavy lidded. No, much as I hate to say it, those are your father's eyes. And his forehead. He was handsome, your father. You probably don't remember him, but he was quite attractive in a robust manner. But a Dietrich—" She puffed out her sunken cheeks. "The name says it all. Skeleton key. He was like one, too, fitting every lock without opening a single door. He wasn't right for Josephine. We tried to tell her, but charity and advice are two things she's never been capable of accepting."

I avoided the mention of my father. He was indeed a shadow, an icon whom Mutti had set on a permanent pedestal. His photograph had hung prominently in our flat, edged in gilded rococo homage, but I'd never seen anything but a florid man I didn't know. I preferred instead to explore Oma's private room, with its clutter of perfume bottles, enameled gewgaws, and faux Fabergé eggs. A full-length looking glass occupied a corner, festooned with scarves and hats. Looking into a mirror wasn't something I'd done much of these days. Mutti had turned all the mirrors in Dessau to face the wall in honor of our dead.

Now, I beheld my reflection: thin, with my dress drooping like a misshapen sack on my diminished frame, but taller than I seemed to recall, and . . .

I inched closer.

Was I beautiful? I saw the face I'd always known, shaped by the deprivation of war: my cheeks drawn, my skin pale, and my lips chapped. I hadn't worn my hair loose during the day since the war began—another sign of respect which Mutti insisted on—and at night, I was often too weary to unwind it. Now, I reached up and loosened my braids, letting my hair fall, lank and in dire need of a wash, but with a more pronounced coppery tint than in my childhood.

"Do you really think I'm . . . ?" I met my grandmother's gaze in the glass. She had been beautiful once. Everyone said so. The portraits on the staircase landing attested to it. One of the most beautiful women in Berlin. The vestiges of her beauty lingered under her crepelike skin, in the glow of her plum-colored eyes and immaculate coiffure, now streaked with silver. When I was a child, Oma had been the most sublime being I knew, an apparition of elegance in her appliquéd coats and dresses from Paris; her feathered hats from Vienna; and her Italian gloves made to measure, fastened by tiny mother-of-pearl buttons—with everything saturated in her lilac *parfum*.

"You are," she said. "A beautiful young girl. Lift your skirt for me."

Though her request was odd, we were alone. Why not? She surveyed me with frank appraisal, her gaze roving behind her spectacles. "You have my legs." She chortled. "Or my legs when I was your age. Legs like ours can make fortunes, *Liebchen*."

"You never showed off your legs, Oma!"

"Not where anyone but my admirer could see," she replied. "I think it's time I showed you what you would look like if Josephine, bless her heart, wasn't so preoccupied with propriety and this tedious war."

Liesel was napping. From the moment we'd arrived at our grandmother's house, my sister had collapsed, betraying the fact that her fortitude had been for Mutti's sake. Surely, there could be no harm in a little fun?

"Go to my closet." She gestured to the carpeted area separating her dressing area from her bedroom, where racks of garments in silk and satin, velvet, wool, linen, and cloth of gold hung over bureaus crammed with Brussels lace undergarments—chemises, petticoats, corsets, and stockings. "Go on," she urged when I hesitated. "Choose something. You are right that you have our Felsing blood. You are almost the same height and weight as I was at sixteen."

"Not the same weight," I countered. "I've lost too much."

"Just enough." She sniffed. "You were getting rather fat, if I recall. All those cream cakes from the *confiserie*. This new diet of sawdust and turnips might be the cure for our overweight matrons. Look at me. Though I'm almost sixty-three, I've not gained an ounce."

"Not because you subsist on turnips." I laughed.

I selected an evening gown of gray silk chiffon draped over blue silk, with a fitted bodice, pleated cap sleeves, and a long skirt embroidered with beads. As I turned to her with the dress in hand, she sighed. "Ah. My Worth. He hand-fitted it for me at his Paris atelier. What a perfectionist. He oversaw every detail—and he charged for it, too. Try it on."

As I turned my back to her, she said irritably, "What is this prudishness? Are you in my home or Josephine's? There's nothing to be ashamed of. Your body is a gift from God, not something you must be ashamed of."

Having undressed before my sister all my life, I decided this was much the same. I unhooked my worn-out dress and let it slip to my ankles.

"What are you wearing?" Oma might require spectacles, but her horror was unfeigned. "What is that . . . *hideous* thing?"

I glanced down at my all-in-one knit underwear. "Drawers," I said.

She shuddered. "No, no. You cannot wear your first Worth over those ghastly bloomers. It'll ruin the line. Fetch a chemise and corset from the drawer, and stockings as well."

Once I managed to position the corset, I had to return to her on her settee and stand still while she laced me up. It was so tight, I could barely breathe.

"I'm not sure—"

"If you feel as if you might faint, it's perfect," she said. "Fetch the dress."

As I stepped past the mirror, I caught a glimpse of myself—svelte, my skin chalky under the sheer chemise, the satin corset with its rosebud motif pushing my breasts up until the nipples peeped out. My legs resembled pilasters sheathed in her silk stockings, tightened at midthigh by blue garters. The image was so arresting, so unlike anything I'd seen, that I paused.

"See?" said Oma. "There it is. Vanity, *mein Lieber*. You must be wary of it. It can seduce even its own reflection."

I hastened for the dress. She stood, wobbling. Her legs were weak from poor circulation, and from being encased in a corset all her life, I surmised. She hooked the fastenings, tucking the gown in at the sides and clucking,

"It's too large here and too loose there; you have long legs and a short waist, Marlene. Remember that when you go for a fitting." With her ringed hands on my bare shoulders and the cap sleeves slipping down my arms, she turned me to the mirror. "Voilà! A Felsing at last."

I couldn't believe it was me. I no longer saw a haggard girl but someone entirely different—enticing and mature. Elegant.

Dangerous.

My grandmother must have felt me recoil, for she patted my shoulder. "There's nothing to be afraid of. Beauty is fleeting. We must enjoy what we have before time steals it away. I told you, you were beautiful. Now you can see for yourself that indeed you are."

Tears pricked my eyes. "I . . . I don't know her."

"Yes, you do. She is you. With better accessories." She smiled, revealing stained teeth, for she was a proper lady who drank only tea. "When I die, I'll leave you my wardrobe. You can use it as you wish, refashion it to fit the times. I'll never wear any of it again. A dress outlives its occupant; it might lose its appeal eventually, but never as quickly as we do."

"Oma." I hugged her. "*Ich liebe dich.*" It came out, a spontaneous declaration of the heart, though I'd been taught that such emotional displays must be avoided.

"I love you, too." She kissed me and drew back. "You must attend supper tonight like this. We both shall, yes? We'll parade downstairs like queens, and won't Willi be delighted. He loves to see a lady well dressed; he's been complaining for months that since the war, every woman in Berlin looks like a hausfrau." She paused, with a malicious smile. "And your sister. Just imagine *her* reaction."

I could imagine it. And the temptation was too great.

That night, we appeared in our regalia, diamond combs from her jewelry coffer in our upswept hair, our lips rouged and feet shoved into low-heeled satin slippers that hurt like pincers, but I was determined to endure it, even if I had to adopt the mincing gait of a geisha.

Uncle Willi, dapper in an evening frock coat, with his mustache waxed to points and one of his endless black cigarettes between his fingers, cried out, "*Les dames sont arrivées.*"

Liesel's mouth hung open as I smiled, dipped my head, and said, "*Merci, monsieur.*" I asked him for a cigarette. He chuckled, lighting it for me. I didn't inhale; I didn't know how to, and the smoke tasted acrid, tickling my nostrils. Choking back a cough, I reveled in the effect of smoke trailing from my mouth as I drifted to where my sister sat, immobile, on the parlor sofa.

"What—what are you doing?" She spoke as if she feared I had lost my mind.

"It was Oma's idea. Why? Do you like it? Isn't it beautiful?" I twirled to show off the flowing train of my dress but the slippers cut into my toes, making me stumble.

"It . . . it is immoral." Liesel was trembling. "Mutti is at the front. Herr von Losch could be dying at this very moment, and you—you play dress-up like a stupid girl."

From her place by our uncle, Oma sighed. "Now, now. There's no need to be impolite, Liesel. We merely seek to liven up a dreary evening at home."

"Liven up?" Liesel rose angrily to her feet. "Dreary?" And then she burst into tears, fleeing the parlor and charging up the staircase. The slam of her bedroom door reverberated throughout the house.

"Well." Oma arched a plucked eyebrow.

I saw the forlorn expression on Uncle Willi's face. Unable to endure the pinch of the shoes another second, I removed them and limped to him. "What is wrong with her?"

He made a sad moue. "A telegram came when you were upstairs. Liesel answered the door, unfortunately, and read it first. I didn't want to spoil our evening yet, seeing as you're both so enchanting, but under the circumstances . . ."

"What? What circumstances?" I felt sick. Not only men were dying at the front; women were, too. Nurses and volunteers in the makeshift infirmaries, caught up in the savagery.

"It's not your Mutti," he quickly reassured me, and I sagged in relief. "But I fear her gallant colonel is indeed not long for this earth." He removed the crinkled paper from his vest. I couldn't take it with my shoes in hand, so Oma did, adjusting her spectacles to read it.

"It seems we are not the only stupid girls in this family," she said, lifting her eyes to me. "Josephine has married her colonel on the Russian front even as he received his last rites. My daughter went to war a widow and she will return as one—the Widow von Losch."

VI

Mutti brought with her the colonel's corpse for burial. She also claimed his death benefit, which allowed us to settle into a rented flat near the Felsing residence, from where she took up her housekeeping again. I found myself begrudgingly admiring her; Oma might have declared her stupid, but Mutti's arrangement with the late colonel had yielded its due. She had regained her independence and now we could live in Berlin.

The end of the war came in November 1918, sealed by a humiliating armistice and treaty hammered out in Paris by the allied powers. The kaiser was exiled and Germany sequestered under a blockade. Riots broke out, people taking to the streets to protest everything from food shortages to spiraling inflation and unemployment. There was no longer an emperor or an empire, and as the provisional government struggled to assert itself, Berlin descended into lawlessness. Uncle Willi lost his imperial patent and had to cajole bankers for loans to finance the business, as looters smashed store windows up and down Unter den Linden, grabbing goods before the police arrived to thrash them and drag them off to the overcrowded prisons.

After consulting with Oma, Mutti decided that Liesel and I must complete our education in the less chaotic environs of Weimar. As expected, neither my sister nor I was asked; most unexpectedly, however, when informed of our destination, Liesel refused.

"I want to stay here and complete my certification to be a schoolteacher," she informed them while I sat there, astonished. "The conservatory only offers training in the musical arts and I'm not a musician. The expense would be wasted."

She had a point. While I'd returned to public school and resumed my private violin lessons, paid for by Oma, Liesel had stayed at home, studying under a new governess, also furnished by Oma. This new governess had apparently instilled in her her life's ambition.

Mutti said, "A schoolteacher? But you are a Felsing. Surely, you can aspire to higher—"

Oma cut her off with an imperious lift of her hand. It never failed to send a thrill through me to watch my mother defer to her, much as we were expected to defer in turn.

"The child is sensible," said Oma. "With the situation as it is, a schoolteacher is a perfectly acceptable occupation. Lest you need reminding, Josephine, your daughters must find the means to support themselves. We can no longer stand on our pride. Being a Felsing means little anymore. And Marlene is the musical talent in our family. She will do us proud."

Despite Oma's confidence, I wanted to follow Liesel's example. I'd grown used to racing to the house after school for my violin classes, after which Oma invariably let me stay for supper. Despite the disorder in the streets, evenings at the Felsing residence were always lively. Food and luxuries might be scarce, but conversation was not. Uncle Willi had many friends, some of whom worked in the theater and brought gossip about backstage mishaps or criticisms of our country, where a slice of beef now cost more than a ticket to a play. The urgent need to discard the past and create the future, revitalizing our bereaved nation, was a favored topic. I sat wide eyed in the parlor as playwrights, actors, and artists congregated around me, flushed with cheap wine as they expounded on the idea that in the midst of disaster, art must flourish. I found it all incredibly exciting, even if most of what they discussed went over my head. Still, their vibrant enthusiasm permeated me; I sensed something marvelous brewing. It made me think that surely there was a place for me here in Berlin, where I could become part of their bold vision.

Oma now fixed her spectacled gaze on me. "You are the future. You and every other young person who survived this calamity. Germany depends on you for her survival."

She'd grown frail, unable to rise from her settee; I didn't want to disappoint her, even as I asked, "But can't we find a music academy here?" and Mutti snapped, "Nothing in Berlin can possibly compare to Weimar. The conservatory is renowned for its teaching skill."

AFTER WEEKS OF GRUELING PRACTICE, I traveled with Mutti to Weimar to audition for the scholarship. I had to play a Bach sonata selected by the committee; I was nervous, and while I knew the piece, I did not play as well as I hoped. The scholarship was denied. The committee expressed regret that they had many worthy applicants for few spots, but were willing to enroll me, if the tuition was forthcoming. I could start classes next year, upon my seventeenth birthday.

On our way back to Berlin, Mutti sighed. "How will we afford it?"

I swallowed. Though disappointed, somewhere within me, I was also relieved. I would not have to leave Berlin, though my last year of school approached, and becoming a musician was so ingrained in me, I couldn't think of an alternative.

Finally I said, "Maybe we shouldn't try to afford it, if I'm not good enough."

"Not good enough?" said Mutti. "Why ever would you say that? You've been playing the violin all your life; it is your God-given gift. They selected that sonata to challenge you; of course you made mistakes. But the conservatory did not say you lack talent, only that it doesn't have sufficient resources to finance every student. After the war, no one has sufficient resources. We must find another way."

I looked her in the eye. "If I have a God-given gift, wouldn't they have found a way?"

I thought she might chastise me. She regarded me as if expressing doubt were anathema, but then she said quietly, with a candor that went right through me, "We all doubt when we are young. Why take the difficult path when there are easier routes? But we must push past the doubt, because nothing worthwhile is achieved in this world unless we work hard for it." She met my stare. "You have no idea yet of what life can do. But with a talent to rely upon, you can survive almost anything. Don't make the mistake of throwing it away because you must make an effort. Do you want a life you choose or the one life chooses for you? Only you can decide."

Remembering how she'd been willing to surrender to what had no doubt been a loveless arrangement with her colonel, I realized, with some apprehension, what my mother was trying to say. She had unfulfilled aspirations of her own; a talented pianist herself, she had forsaken her gift to do the expected thing for a woman of her class: She married my father instead, thinking she'd be content as a wife and mother. Yet he had died prematurely, compelling her to do housekeeping out of necessity. She worked because she had no choice—or none that she could see—and she wanted more for me. All along, despite her coddling of Liesel, I was the one on whom she depended to justify her sacrifice. It was why she refused to admit defeat.

I remained quiet for the rest of the trip. But in the following days, I could not stop ruminating. Was being a musician the path I should choose? I played the violin because it was what Mutti wanted me to do. I loved it, yes, but did I love it enough to define my life? It frightened me that I did not know, that all of a sudden, I faced the end of my childhood and a looming decision about my future that I felt I could not make.

Shortly before Christmas, the decision was made for me.

Oma passed away in her sleep. I was grief stricken, though she'd been ill for some time and her death was expected. Her share in the family business went to Mutti—a significant investment, if Uncle Willi could revive the store's profits. Oma had also left a separate amount to cover my first year of tuition at Weimar. Following the funeral, as snow swirled over Berlin, Mutti announced that I must honor my grandmother's wishes.

"And you will excel," she assured me. "If you study hard, the conservatory will prepare you for a career. You will indeed do us proud, as Oma said."

I glanced at Uncle Willi. He gave me an odd, almost reluctant, smile. "Is this what you want, Lena?" he asked, even as Mutti pursed her lips, as though my opinion were of no account. "To become a concert violinist must be something you want more than anything else."

I was startled that my uncle had somehow sensed my uncertainty. Oma had indeed believed in me, and Mutti's belief was unassailable, but until this moment no one had asked me if I shared it. I forced back that surge of doubt which had assailed me after my audition, but could not evade it. If my mother had taught me anything, it was that a passionate conviction in one's self was required. And much as I wanted to say I had that conviction, if only for Mutti's sake, I wasn't sure that I did.

"I suppose I could try," I managed to say. "I'll never know otherwise."

Uncle Willi nodded. Before he could say anything else, Mutti declared, "Do not try. *Do*, Lena. Do and you will succeed." She motioned. "Now, come upstairs with me. We must look over Oma's things and see what you can take with you."

As promised, Oma had also bequeathed me her wardrobe. Mutti packed my suitcase with the least ostentatious outfits (carefully selected and altered by her) and accompanied me back to Weimar and a boardinghouse for girls studying at the conservatory, run by a redoubtable matron named Frau Arnoldi. The boardinghouse had a storied repute. In the eighteenth century, the platonic muse of Goethe, Germany's heroic writer and statesman, whose works had formed the basis of my literary education, once resided there. Advising me to be on my best behavior and not forget to wash behind my ears, Mutti handed me an envelope with enough money for my monthly expenses. Then, just as I drew back from kissing her cheek good-bye, she seized my arm and said, "No scandals. You will study hard and make friends, but do not cause me any shame. Remember who you are. A Felsing must be above reproach. Do you understand?"

I recoiled from the vehemence on her face. "Yes, Mutti," I whispered.

Her fingers tightened on my arm. "You are a very pretty girl. It will be tempting. But boys can ruin a reputation," she said. "And some things they do, you can never recover from."

"Yes," I said again, for she was starting to frighten me. "I promise."

She released me. With a narrow-eyed look, she nodded and departed for the station and her train back to Berlin.

For the first time in my life, I was suddenly on my own.

SCENE TWO
VIOLIN LESSONS
1919–1921

"I NEVER THINK ABOUT THE FUTURE."

I

"Marlene, do your harem-girl imitation. It's so hilarious!"

The girls sat in the bedroom I shared with my roommate, Bertha, all of us wearing our nightgowns and with our hair loose, the tinsel wrappings of our illicit feast scattered about. Smoke hovered in the air; several were smoking, a habit I'd started to pick up. Both cigarettes and sweets were verboten in the boardinghouse, but I'd organized a plan in which we set aside a certain amount of our weekly allowances, and once we had enough, I hiked into town to the local shops. Then I sneaked in the box of pastries, pouch of tobacco, and wrapping papers so we could indulge in my room after Frau Arnoldi retired.

I removed my nightgown—my silhouette worked better without it— and posed naked behind the sheet we'd slung on a clothesline in front of the lamp, arching my arms to imitate a dancer. Then I slowly gyrated, making the sound of drumbeats through my lips.

With their hands over their sticky mouths to muffle their laughter, the girls squealed.

My first year of studies in Weimar had been diligent; I had strived to excel, yet when my first grade report reached Mutti, citing that I'd failed to show the exceptional talent she'd believed I had, she promptly hired the best violin teacher in the conservatory for weekly after-hours lessons. My Thursday classes with Professor Reitz were an additional expense that I knew she could ill afford and I'd dedicated myself to my practice, hoping to advance. But not all was toil. I'd discovered in the boardinghouse something I'd never had: friends. Like me, most of the girls came from upstanding families who'd made sacrifices to place them in the conservatory; not one I'd met had a scholarship but all hoped to be musicians, or so they said. Already, in the first year, a few had given up, either from lack of dedication or boredom, returning home to marry the boy next door. My popularity had soared, however, when the girls saw my dresses, severely adjusted by Mutti but still made of fine fabrics that I innately knew how to mix and match. They begged to borrow items and I obliged; I'd shared clothes with Liesel all my life and was not possessive. Then one night, bored, with nothing to do except recite poetry or practice our instruments, I agreed to participate in their guessing game, which involved imitating diverse things. I improvised the harem (with my nightgown on) and the girls declared me a natural. I soon found they liked me for myself. It wasn't just because of my clothes or because I had a private instructor, though they envied these. They liked me because I liked them.

Bertha, my roommate and a plump girl who played the clarinet, clapped her hands. "More, more. Do Henny Porten."

We were obsessed with Henny Porten. She was Germany's premier picture actress, her flickers shown in the local kinos—the new cinema houses overtaking the country. With her perfect oval face, white complexion, and large dramatic eyes, she had a presence of seductive nobility, often playing doomed heroines who suffered for love. She inspired us to style our hair in rippling waves like hers, paint our lips in her signature red pout, and poise our hands at our breasts in her martyrlike suffering. We'd seen every picture of hers that reached Weimar, crowding the aisles on the weekends with our forbidden sweets in our laps and sighing in adoration as she pined, flailed, and pursued her faithless lovers on the screen.

Coiling the sheet into a turban and draping the edges over my breasts, I lifted a hand to my collarbone and stretched out my other arm, bleating,

"Why do you forsake me, Curt? Can't you see I am spellbound by the baron?"

"*Imprisoned Soul!*" cried out one of the girls, before Bertha, who knew all my tricks, could. I adjusted the sheet into a shroud and assumed a forlorn expression. "I must die for my honor."

"*Anna Bolena,*" said Bertha. She gave me a snide look. "That was too easy, Marlene. Do another—and make it less obvious this time."

As I twined the sheet about my waist, considering which of Porten's male lovers to evoke, I didn't hear the footsteps coming down the corridor until they were at the door.

"*Hausmutter!*" I hissed.

The girls scrambled in a panic, waving their hands frantically in the air to dispel the smoke. Then they raced to the armoire by the wall. In our haste to eat cake, we'd forgotten to push it against the door as we usually did.

"What in heaven is this abominable racket?" boomed Frau Arnoldi. She was so fat, she could usually be heard coming from a distance, only this time she must have made an effort to tiptoe up the stairs. The door cracked open just as the girls slid the armoire into place, blocking her entry. With only her eyes and her beak of a nose visible, she spat out, "Remove that furnishing at once. I can see you, Marlene Dietrich. I know what you are about. You are a disgrace to my house."

It was so absurd, I started to laugh, helplessly entangled in my sheet.

Bertha guffawed, too, until Frau Arnoldi cried, "And you, Bertha Schiller. You are as much to blame." She banged on the door. "Let me in this instant."

My laughter faded. The others looked horrified. Our housemother was notorious for searching our rooms while we were in class, confiscating our caches of sweets and cigarettes, and anything else she deemed indecent, but she had never actually caught us in the act.

With the sheet yanked to my chin, I retrieved my discarded nightgown. The girls hauled back the armoire to reveal Frau Arnoldi on the threshold, her multiple chins quivering and her large bosom heaving with indignation.

She raked her stare over me. "So. *This* is how you repay your mother's hard work and concern, the private teacher she has hired for you, all her hopes for your future—by parading about your room in front of everyone like—like . . ."

"Henny Porten," muttered Bertha. "She was doing imitations of Henny Porten for us." As soon as she spoke, she tried and failed to stifle her giggle.

Frau Arnoldi glared. "I'll not stand for it." She wagged her finger. "I shall write to both your mothers. Telephone them, if I must." She swerved from Bertha to me. "You think you're so clever, fräulein, so sly—but I know what I know. And now so shall Frau von Losch. I've held my tongue for too long."

The girls cowered. Bertha shot me a strange look. Ignoring Frau Arnoldi's gasp, I dropped the sheet and, as naked as the day I was born, slipped into my nightgown. As I buttoned it up, I said, "I have no idea what you mean."

"You don't?" Frau Arnoldi's tone turned malignant. From the moment I'd arrived, she had taken an inexplicable antipathy to me. I once heard her comment to another matron who came to visit, as I flew past them on my way to class, "That one. You should see her eyes. *Such* eyes. Salome herself could not be more brazen."

But Mutti footed my bill. I was a paying guest and a student at the conservatory. Whether she liked me or not was of no concern. Until now.

I forced myself to remain calm. In my experience, Frau Arnoldi was mostly bombast. She often flew into tirades if too much butter was served at breakfast—it was expensive, she never tired of chiding the maid, and Germany had a fat shortage—but she couldn't afford to scold too much. She relied on the income generated by her so-called house. Without us, her boarders, there would be no butter to waste or maid to serve it.

"If I've offended, you must allow me to make amends," I finally said, as the silence grew taut. "There's no reason to involve my mother in a simple misunderstanding—"

Frau Arnoldi snorted. "I daresay Frau Reitz would not call it that."

I went still. "Frau Reitz? I've never even met her."

"She might wish she could say the same about you and her husband." Frau Arnoldi suddenly looked very pleased with herself.

Her insinuation alarmed me. "What are you saying?" I demanded.

She laughed. "Don't play the virgin with me. All those high marks on your last report card! Do you think the entire faculty is stupid? Do you think this entire town is blind? I'm not the only one who's seen you leaving this house, dressed in chiffon with your hem hiked to *here*, and enough rouge to make Henny Porten herself blush. I've seen a hundred girls just like you, fräulein. And let me assure you, girls like you never come to any good."

If she'd struck a blow to my face, I couldn't have been more enraged. It was true that I dressed with flair, but only because I had better clothes. And the professor—was she insane? He was married, with children. And at least twenty years older than me. He gave me high marks because I worked hard. Never once had he—

That one. You should see her eyes. Such eyes!

Frau Arnoldi's smile cut across her mouth. "It seems you're not entirely without shame. That is as it should be. Men may do as they please when their wives look the other way, but when an unmarried girl does the same, it is another matter entirely."

I took a furious step toward her, even as Bertha hissed, "Marlene, no."

Meeting Frau Arnoldi's glare, I said slowly, with deliberate menace, "You must not worry my mother. She will think that you, *Hausmutter*, have been remiss or tell lies. She'll resort to compensation from the conservatory itself."

That did the trick. The last thing Frau Arnoldi wanted was the conservatory inquiring about her premises. She got a stipend from them for her boarders, in addition to our weekly rate.

Her jaw clenched. "Sweets," she said through her teeth. "You bring sweets into this house. And tobacco. And heaven knows what else. It is verboten."

"Then I won't do it again."

"No. You will not." Turning about, she barked at the others: "Out. Now." Throwing another glare at me over her shoulder as she herded the girls out, she left me with no doubt that financial concerns aside, she had set her eye on me and I was now on probation.

Bertha and I set the room to rights and sat facing each other on our twin beds. We should have laughed. Frau Arnoldi couldn't do any harm. Her purse strings didn't allow it. But it wasn't funny. I was so disturbed that I eventually said, "Is it true? Do they talk about me and the professor?"

Bertha sighed. "Of course they do. You're the only one who doesn't know."

"Know what?"

She went quiet, kneading her hands.

"What?" I persisted. "What don't I know?"

"How you are. How you look. How you move. There is *something* about you, Marlene. You are different."

"I am not," I declared, bristling at once. Different meant bad, as Mutti would have informed me. Different meant I was not being a well-bred girl from an upstanding family, and I did not want to be that. "How can you say that? I'm not different. I'm just like everyone else."

"That's only what you want to think." She tried to smile. "Some girls just have it, like a flame inside them. It's not your fault. You can't help it. You attract attention." She paused, her voice lowering. "Have you truly never . . . ?"

I didn't know what to reply. I recalled my passion for Mademoiselle. She, too, had told me I wasn't like other girls, and though I'd been too young at the time to understand, as I grew older I began to wonder if perhaps I might prefer women. I wasn't ignorant. Mutti had never instructed me on the facts of sex, but her warning had stayed with me, and living in the boardinghouse provided ample education. I'd heard stories of girls who'd been sent home in disgrace and knew some of the girls here were more than friends, their giggling and sharing of clothes turning into furtive explorations. It didn't bother me. But neither had it incited me to join them. Oh, I liked to dress up and sway my hips. I liked the way my body had bloomed and enjoyed admiring myself in the mirror, cupping my breasts and extending the length of my legs. I knew I was pretty. I could see it. But I avoided entanglements because I feared the repercussions.

"You do know how boys look at you?" Bertha pressed on. "You're almost nineteen, Lena. And most boys in the conservatory are desperate to take you out."

I was aware of how they looked at me. Male students in the conservatory weren't shy. I'd received my share of covert whistles and invitations to the dance hall. "Boys want to take out every girl," I replied. "They're always looking. I pay them no mind. I don't want . . . complications." My voice wavered. "Have you ever . . . done it?"

Bertha shook her head. "It's not easy for us. How can we protect ourselves? Some boys will use prophylactics if they can get them, but it's too risky. I am curious, though. Aren't you?"

Was I? I wasn't sure, or at least I hadn't met a boy I liked enough. Perhaps I was indeed attracted to women? I enjoyed coaxing pleasure from my body with my fingers while Bertha snored. But surely that wasn't unusual. The entire conversation made me wonder. Was there something wrong with me? Was this why I was different?

"I suppose I am curious," I said warily.

"Well. Frau Arnoldi thinks you're more than curious. She thinks you're sleeping with Professor Reitz. She thinks you're *loose*. And you have a way about you that doesn't help."

"Loose? I've never even had a boyfriend!"

Bertha gave me a look. "See? You flirt, you wear fancy clothes, but you're not running about with boys. You therefore must have a man instead."

"But it's not true. My mother pays Professor Reitz for private lessons. I'd never be so reckless. You must believe me. He's never made an improper gesture or remark to me."

"Oh, I believe you. I believe you don't notice. But if Frau Arnoldi said something, then something there must be. She said he gives you high marks. Are you improving so much? Maybe you should pay more attention the next time you go to see him."

"*If* there is a next time," I grumbled. "If Frau Arnoldi gets her way, I doubt it."

Bertha sighed. "There'll be a next time. How can there not be?"

II

I went to class every day and practiced every night. I avoided rambunctious gatherings at the house, sneaking cigarettes while leaning out my bedroom window. On the appointed Thursday of my private instruction, I dressed with such modesty that I thought I resembled a nun as I left the boardinghouse under Frau Arnoldi's baleful stare to make my way to the conservatory, where, after daily sessions, select classrooms were reserved for private use.

As I passed other students en route to their own lessons, I thought again of how ridiculous it was that anyone could think I'd take up with the very man my mother had hired to instruct me. Yet when I entered the room to find him waiting, a lean figure with tousled dark hair and ascetic features, whose most marked characteristic was his limpid gray eyes, my breath faltered. Now that I knew what had been said about us, I couldn't stop thinking about his hands—long and veined, his fingers as delicate as stems—as he watched me practice the Abel sonata he'd assigned, tapping the cadence on his trouser leg as he paced behind me, his head tilted to detect any errors.

"No." His voice, gravelly from smoking, halted me. "Your finger is on the wrong string. Again. And slower this time. You needn't rush through it."

I resumed playing, stumbling over the first chords. Catching myself, I regained my equilibrium, hearing the sonata in my head, so that my hand on the bow and my hand on the fingerboard worked in tandem.

He did not stop me again. When I finished, lowering the instrument to await his critique, he stood silent for a long moment before he said, "You have been coming here for how long?"

"Almost a year, except during the Christmas and Easter breaks."

"That long? Fräulein, much as it pains me, you are not improving."

I felt a sudden drop in my stomach. "But I practice every day."

"I know. And you are accomplished. You might eventually perform as part of an orchestra if you continue practicing. But as a soloist . . . I fear that's out of the question."

His eyes were fixed on me. I had to bite back a rush of tears. Of all the things I'd imagined might happen, this was not one of them. I had come to Weimar uncertain as to whether I could succeed, but then my desire to prove myself overcame my doubt. I wanted a life I chose, as Mutti said, and when I envisioned returning to Berlin without it, I couldn't bear it. She would never forgive me or let me forget I'd failed, after everything she had done to get me here.

"Can't you teach me to be better?" I said. "My mother wants me to be a musician, and—"

He interrupted me. "I know your Mutti has placed much hope in you. You don't want to disappoint, but it would be dishonest to give false assurance. Indeed, I shouldn't even be taking her money. No amount of instruction can create talent where there is none. You are a good violinist but not a superb one. You never will be."

To my horror, a single tear leaked out. Setting aside the violin and averting my face, I rummaged in my skirt pocket for a handkerchief. "Here," he said.

As I dabbed my eyes with his handkerchief, I detected a strong scent of tobacco, mingled with tweed and something indefinable, like musk. Was this what a man smelled like?

"But you—you gave me high marks," I said, my voice wavering. "You reported that I was improving. Why would you say that?"

"I . . . I thought—" He cut himself short. And then I saw it: that *look*, which Bertha had told me to watch for. His eyes lingered on me for a moment too long before he tore his gaze away, as if he'd been scalded. "You know why," he said, and he moved across the room from me, staking his meager distance.

Frau Arnoldi thinks you're sleeping with Professor Reitz. She thinks you're loose.

Anger flared in me. "I don't know why you would lie. If I cannot play the violin for a living, I cannot stay here. It's too expensive, a waste. I'll have to go back home to Berlin."

He did not turn to me, but his shoulders hunched about his neck, prepared for the blow. Just as I started to step toward him, he whispered, "I don't want to lose you. That is why I lied."

I went still. He gave an arid chuckle. "I am a fool. I think . . . I am in love with you."

Hearing these words slammed something shut inside me, and the blow of it knocked something else open. I didn't believe it, not entirely. He had falsified my grade report to keep me here; he was married, with children. Germany was poor. Even influential professors had to pay their bills. If he thought he was in love, he was a coward. I was his student, a girl half his age, who could cause his ruin. He must have heard the rumors about us. He'd tried to refute them by hiding his desire under fake praise, while pocketing my mother's money. It was a terrible, craven deceit, and suddenly I wanted to test his sincerity.

"You love me, so you lied," I said, extending his handkerchief. "How cruel."

He stepped backward again. "I know. You must hate me."

I should. I should hate him enough to go straight to the dean and report him. He was not honorable. But I didn't move, for now I saw the secret power I had over him—a power that had lurked all this time inside me. He had crushed my ability to fulfill my dream but I had invaded his. And in that instant, I decided to throw caution aside, toss it upon the wreckage of my aspirations. I did it out of frustration and out of spite; and to avenge myself, to ensure that everything was so thoroughly ravaged, he would never forget me. If I could never become a master violinist, if he stole that hope from me, I would take this from him.

I reached for his hand, shoving the handkerchief into it. "I don't hate you," I said, and I did not let go of his fingers. "I don't know why, but I don't."

He froze. "Do you . . . do you think you might care for me?"

I considered him. "Why don't you kiss me and find out?"

HE LOCKED THE CLASSROOM DOOR and flung himself at me, bruising my lips, his moans guttural as his hands, those veined hands with their tapered fingers, snaked under my dress until he found my hidden place and I let out a startled gasp. It was unlike anything I had felt before, those foreign fingertips dipping inside me, and while I wanted to remain un-moved, in control, I heard myself groan and my hips arched up against him. Animal ardor took over. I was doing exactly what people said I had done, and the savage realization of it was undeniable.

He laid me on the floor next to my violin case. He didn't remove his jacket, shirt, or tie; he was so flustered, he merely pushed down his pants and fiddled with something he had pulled from his pocket, a rubbery thing he slipped onto his engorged penis. He murmured, "I don't want to hurt you," and I replied, "You won't."

He thrust inside me. Fiery pain lanced my gut. It snagged my breath and it burned but I welcomed it. It was my punishment and reward; it was what I deserved. He bucked hard and his breath came fast. Then he suddenly shuddered, making me clench my teeth against my cry as he yanked out and grappled with his French letter, spilling seed on my thigh.

The moment afterward, he groaned. "*Gott mich retten,* you were a virgin."

"No." I cradled his face. "God has nothing to do with it. I wanted this."

He bit his lip, looking between us to my splayed thighs. "How can you know what you want? You're barely a woman." But he kissed my mouth softly, so I tasted his salt and smoke. "I didn't know," he murmured. "I thought you were . . . more experienced."

Had he done this before? I wanted to think not, but his surprise warned me that he probably had. I might be his first virgin but not his first seduction. Only, it felt as if I had ended up seducing him, which pleased me. I hadn't lacked sufficient talent in this respect.

Heaving himself off me, he stuffed his rumpled shirt into his trousers and fastened his belt. He kept his eyes averted, ashamed. I sat up, put myself in order. When I stood, a wave of nausea swayed me; I felt blood in my underpants. My groin ached. I'd be sore for days.

"It's unforgivable," he said. He fished a cigarette out of his jacket, lighting it with quivering hands, although smoking was not allowed inside the school. "I am unforgivable."

I regarded him pensively. I should be the one telling him this, yet apparently, he had enough guilt for both of us. And in truth, though painful, it hadn't been entirely unpleasant. With some time and a proper bed, I might even like it. He wasn't a raw boy making suggestive gestures; he wasn't going to boast of his conquest to his friends. He had to be discreet. He had a reputation to protect. What we had just done could destroy him, even more than me. The secrecy of it, the conspiracy that united us, appealed. I'd finally had something that I had seized of my own free will. And, more practically, I could stay in Weimar under his tutelage. I could perfect my violin playing and he would keep falsifying my marks. I wouldn't have to confess my failure to Mutti or return home to confront a future where I had no idea what to do.

"I wouldn't mind if we did it again," I told him as he reached down to hand me my violin case. He paused, startled, watching me take the case and move to the door. I could see by his expression that it was not what he'd anticipated. His voice had the ragged edge of someone who yearns for that which will do them harm. "I will resign, say I am ill, that I cannot teach anymore."

I paused, my hand on the doorknob. "Why?"

"Because it is what I must do," he cried. He looked desperate, as if he had only just realized the consequences of deflowering a girl on his classroom floor. I wanted to laugh at his contrition. How foolish he was. He could lie to me, to my mother, to his wife and the school at large, yet when he got what he wanted, he could only feel remorse. Like a child, I thought, who regrets breaking a cherished toy after he played with it too roughly.

"Don't resign because of me." I unlocked the door. "I'll never tell."

SO IT BEGAN.

His shame ran its course; overcome by desire, he resumed my private instruction. And at his home whenever his wife went away to visit relatives, he bedded me. He was tender; he had a musician's sensitivity, easily stoked. He played me as if strings vibrated beneath my flesh and taught me more than he ever could in the classroom. I learned I was not different. I was like every other girl. I had the same sensations and urges, the same hunger. And without realizing it, I began to see the fragility he carried inside him like an old wound.

One time, he took up my violin—which had cost my mother 2,500 marks, a fortune that reproached me every time I locked it in its case and took him inside me—and he proceeded to coax from it a sonata of such pathos, such exquisite perfection, that he brought me to tears.

"You are a maestro," I told him, clutching my hands to my chest.

He sighed. "No. I could have been. I loved this more than anything, but I gave it up—for marriage and respectability, for tenure and an income. I surrendered my soul."

He reminded me of poems by Goethe, of the melancholy we kept tethered because we were German and must not reveal weakness. With his thick dark hair tangled about his lined brow, silvery threads glinting in its depths, his mournful eyes and downcast mouth, which suckled me like a boy at his mother's teat—he was so beautiful, so anguished, I could not help but fall in love.

Or, what I thought must be love.

For he was right about one thing. I was still barely a woman.

III

Bertha suspected, and grilled me until I told her. The affair had emboldened me. I bobbed my hair, wore tighter sweaters, shortened my hems further, and rolled up my stockings. Forbidden sweets and cigarettes were no longer enough. I wanted to experience life beyond the boardinghouse and the conservatory, to explore Weimar itself, where under its stately veneer its boulevardier heart teemed with insouciance.

At my instigation, Bertha and I skipped classes and sneaked out with the boys to the beer gardens, the cafés, or local kinos. On sticky seats while the flickers played, I let the boys creep their hands down my dress to fondle my breasts—but no further. In my own way, I stayed faithful to Reitz, who knew how to avoid pregnancy. He used his French letters, made sure never to spill inside me, while the boys' hot pleas and clumsy gropes betrayed that they had less experience than I did. I learned the new American dances, kicking up my heels in grimy saloons to blaring saxophones. And while I danced, smoked, and guzzled schnapps, the world transformed. The old order crumbled as a revolutionary artistic movement dubbed the Bauhaus ripped down our pastel mask to construct a sleek minimalist facade. A new constitution gave birth to our Weimar Republic, providing all the necessary oratory and none of the stability.

Yet in the midst of the upheaval, I remained careful. One mistake and I could find myself in trouble. Bertha warned me repeatedly that I risked disaster, consorting with a married professor, but I assured her I was taking precautions and had no illusions. While Reitz never mentioned his wife, except to cite whether she was at home, her very presence was an obstacle I could not breach. He also had a son and a daughter, I discovered from the pictures on his mantel, his son close to me in age; he rarely mentioned them, either, but his silence was enough. I had no idea if his marriage was happy or if he still loved his wife, but I knew it was not happy or loving enough. And he made it clear without ever saying it that I must make no demands of him.

For a while, it suited me. As he couldn't see me every night, it left me plenty of time to do other things. I became enthralled by newfound friends rhapsodizing about the gaudy butterfly emerging from Berlin's war-torn carapace, the many theaters, cabarets, and vaudeville halls sprouting amid destitution. Children were dying in droves from typhoid and starvation. Maimed veterans had found no reparations from the government and took to begging or selling contraband goods. Women who survived the war, but whose husbands or sons had not, peddled what they had, or if they were nimble enough, auditioned to be chorus girls. Germany was chaotic, riddled with poverty and crime, but every boy I kissed and every girl I met wanted to go to Berlin—but not to extol Handel, Schiller, or Goethe. No, they longed to make abstract art, pen satires, parade down the streets and revel in freedom. It reminded me of Uncle Willi's friends in the parlor, their exuberance and belief that art could heal all ills. Berlin was where art was being made, a beacon of hope to chase away the drudgery.

In Berlin, everyone thought they could become someone else.

But I feared returning there.

REITZ NEVER SOCIALIZED WITH ME. We conducted our liaison like our lessons—in private, with no attempt to plan beyond the next time. Eventually, I grew impatient. I wanted more, but more of what? I was reaching the end of my third term at the conservatory. Much as I wanted to avoid the thought, I couldn't be a student forever. I had to start planning my future.

"Do you think I should move back to Berlin?" I asked him impulsively one night, smoking in bed after lovemaking. I'd begun smoking more with him, our ritual after sex, as he liked it and he could turn moody at times when we were done.

"Berlin?" He stood at the window, the tip of his cigarette glowing. "What do you expect to do there?" He sounded disinterested, as if I was making idle conversation, which only made me more impatient. Did he not care if I stayed or went? Perversity overcame me. After all these months, he still behaved as if we engaged in a transgression for which he could never atone.

"I don't know," I said with deliberate flippancy, to see if I could get a reaction out of him. "I'll never be a concert soloist, but I can still play music. There's so much opportunity. New musical halls and cabarets opening every day. I could do a violin duet or maybe sing." Stubbing out my cigarette, I ran my hand through my tousled hair. Affecting a throaty tone like the chanteuses used in our local dives, I crooned, " 'We are different from the others who love in morality, wandering through a thousand wonders . . .' " I paused, watching him turn to me with a slight smile. "I have a nice voice, don't you think? My friends tell me I sing very well."

"You do. A lovely voice. Do you know what that song is about?" When I shrugged, he said, "It's 'Das Lila Lied,' The Lavender Song. A homosexual anthem."

"Oh?" Of course I knew. I'd seen homosexuals in the cafés—lithe boys in skintight sailor pants and perky caps, sashaying with precision. I'd grown curious as they sidled past me, eyeing each other at the bar and sometimes disappearing into the alley behind the café, until I finally dragged Bertha outside with me, ignoring her protest.

We stood in the shadows, watching one boy lean against a wall while the other slipped to his knees before him. Right there, under peeling posters announcing Henny Porten's latest flicker and defiant slogans of sickles and fists, the kneeling boy took the other in his mouth. As he gulped, the standing boy slid his eyes at us. He winked. Bertha gasped, pulling from me to race back into the café. I stayed until they finished, the kneeling boy rubbing himself as his companion spilled. I found myself aroused by their random carnality; it made me think about the vagaries of desire in our new order, epitomized by boys who not only felt at liberty to do this but apparently enjoyed performing before an audience. It wasn't Mutti's Germany anymore. When decorum frayed, primal nature took hold.

"They have their own anthem?" I said. "That's original."

"Only you would say that. To everyone else, it's yet another sign of our descent into depravity." He reached for his robe. He'd already slipped into his underdrawers; he retreated into them as soon as we finished, a shapeless white sack that reached almost to his knees and always reminded me of Oma gasping, *What is that hideous thing?*

Recalling the boys in the side alley, I let the sheet slide down to expose my breasts. "Come here. Come suckle me, Daddy."

He liked being called Daddy in the midst of it; he liked calling me his *Liebling*, but not out of bed. His face shuttered. "It's late," he muttered. "Shouldn't you be getting back to the boardinghouse before Frau Arnoldi has something to say?"

I yawned. "She always has something to say. But my rent is paid every month, so she won't say much." I almost added that he got paid as well, though I knew what he implied. He never let me stay the night, lest the maid who came in the morning to clean might see me. The maid or the neighbors or a passing stranger: We could pull down the blinds to stain his bed, but we could not hide in daylight if I walked out his front door.

He tied his robe about his waist.

"So, what do you think?" I leaped out of bed, setting my hands on his bony shoulders. Again, my need to needle him took over. "You could come with me," I whispered in his ear. "You told me you gave up music and always regretted it. You can play again. We can move to Berlin, take new names, start a new—"

He stepped away. "That is enough." The granite in his tone brought me to a halt. "I never said I regretted it. I said I had surrendered to it."

I frowned. "Isn't it the same thing?"

"Perhaps it was. Not now. Berlin." He laughed. "To live among immigrants, Jews, and deviants. And at my age, with you of all people—it's preposterous."

He infuriated me. I snatched up my dress. As I shoved my feet into my shoes and prepared to march past him, he murmured, "Don't be angry. I didn't mean it would be preposterous to be with you, only—"

"Only what?" I glared at him. "Am I not sophisticated enough? Talented enough?"

"Oh, you are. You are not the girl I first met. But I have no interest in uprooting my existence to do—well, whatever it is you think you should do in Berlin."

It was the first time he'd spoken about where we stood, and as soon as he did, I realized how preposterous I truly was. I hadn't actually thought he would ever join me, but to hear him say it so flatly, as if I were a silly naive girl—it locked up something inside my heart.

"What you really mean is, you have no interest in leaving your wife," I said, and I saw his expression dim. Though he did not answer, he didn't have to. I had found his melancholy attractive. Not anymore. Suddenly, he disgusted me with his sad eyes and resignation.

"I'm not the first, am I?" I said abruptly.

He flinched. "Why do you say that?"

"Just a feeling. You were so mortified, so willing to resign your position. But now I think you weren't so guilty after all. It was well played." I smiled. "I think you missed your calling. You should have been an actor."

"Marlene, how could I resist? How could any man? Those eyes of yours, the way you don't seem to care who desires you . . . I was helpless."

"I don't think your wife would agree. Nor anyone on the faculty."

He moved quickly, grabbing me by my wrist. "Do not threaten me now. You are bored. There's an entire world out there, so why stay? I expected it. I knew this would happen. But you don't want me to abandon my home, my wife and children, to move with you to Berlin. If I said I loved you, would you believe me?"

"Not now," I replied. "But I would have liked to hear you say it anyway."

"Why? So you can torment me more than you already do, when I know—when *you* know—it cannot last? You are so young; you have no understanding of what love is."

I looked down at his hand. He removed it.

"You are wrong," I said. "I do understand. Perfectly."

Before he could speak, I walked out of his bedroom and out of his house.

I did not look back.

I wanted to cry. I thought it was what a girl should do. Henny Porten would have cried; she would have rent her breast and railed at her fate. But that was the flickers. This was real life.

I had slept with a married man, convinced myself that I loved him, but I'd confused love with something ephemeral, not meant to last. It hurt now but it would pass, because I really didn't want him. He had his wife and circumscribed life, where I would never fit. He'd grow old teaching violin and seducing less gifted students. I had always known he was weak. I had known and ignored it, because I'd longed for someone or something to call my own. But he had never been mine. How could I cry over a delusion?

And yet as I walked to the boardinghouse, I felt the tears smarting behind my eyes.

AFTER THE END OF MY AFFAIR WITH REITZ, I plunged into gaiety. I neglected all my classes, as the clamor in the streets seeped past the conservatory's gates and students marched down the halls, crying out for socialist equality. Weimar exploded with rebellion. Police shot tear gas at protestors as the price of everything rose to extremes. A loaf of bread now cost more than perfume, and newspapers blared headlines about how all over Germany workers raced with their savings heaped in wheelbarrows to purchase a single head of soggy lettuce. It was the death of a nation, and no one knew what would arise in its place.

I paid no heed. I danced, smoked, and let more boys rummage under my blouse, and do other things. I purchased my own prophylactics from the pharmacy, ladling out my marks before the pharmacist's outraged wife, and I used them whenever a boy could hold it in long enough, though most gushed onto my stomach. I slept around and I did not care. I tasted as many as I could, to rinse the sour dregs of Reitz from my tongue.

But I knew what was coming; Bertha warned me. One night after I staggered into our room to fling myself onto my bed with my underpants missing, she hissed, "Marlene, you're insane. You missed all your classes this month! Your instructors sent warnings that you'll be suspended. Frau Arnoldi is fit to be tied. She says you are a disgrace and she'll tell your mother."

"She should be tied," I slurred. "Tied and muzzled." I'd had too much beer. I didn't like to drink, because it always went to my head, but I drank anyway, as much as I could. It blurred the rough edges, made the boys seem less like farmhands as they rummaged up my skirt. And it made me more willing.

I passed out, missing my morning classes again. I slept till noon, until a sharp rapping at the door woke me. Before I could wipe the drool from my chin, the door shot open to reveal Mutti in her coat and hat, Frau Arnoldi gloating behind her.

"See?" said Frau Arnoldi. "Drunk and truant. It's a dishonor, Frau von Losch."

My mother's voice was impassive. "I do see," she said. She directed her next words at me like bullets: "Pack your belongings. You are coming home. Now."

SCENE THREE
SCREEN TEST
1922–1929

"I SIMPLY WASN'T AMBITIOUS,
NOR HAVE I EVER BEEN."

I

Mutti did not speak during the train ride home. I didn't, either, wondering if besides my delinquency, Frau Arnoldi had reported her suspicions about me and Professor Reitz. But once we reached Berlin, I discovered that even if she had, Mutti's decision to remove me from the conservatory had been spurred by more than my behavior.

Mutti was now working in various homes as a housekeeper, Liesel told me, to support my education and hers. My sister was finishing her credentials and seeking part-time employment in a local school. The behest left by Oma was gone. Inflation was such, it was all Uncle Willi could do to keep open the store on Unter den Linden. He was diversifying the merchandise to attract new clientele. Shortage of money, rather than lax morals, had ended my time at the conservatory, for my mother was proud and would never see me get behind on my rent.

Still, it wasn't long before she made her displeasure known.

"You will contribute to this household," she informed me after breakfast. "There is no place here for idle hands."

"Then I shall," I said sourly. "I'll clean the flat." After a week of her disapproving silence, and Liesel tiptoeing about as if the floor might crack open, they'd managed to make me feel as if I were a criminal. I had waited for Mutti to lash out, to heap her horror and disbelief on my head, but her icy silence had prevailed—until now.

"Indeed you will." She buttoned up her coat. "Clean, that is. I've found you a new music professor. He's agreed to teach you in exchange for house-keeping." She paused. "He's Austrian and over seventy, but renowned in his field. I trust you still remember how to wax a floor?"

"You—you want me to be his maid?" I was aghast. "But surely I can do something else."

Liesel, sitting beside me, shrank into her chair, her gaze fixed on her dish of lumpy porridge. She'd grown even more diffident, if possible, during the time I'd been away.

"Oh?" said Mutti. "What else do you think you can do?"

"Play my violin." My indignation erupted. "I've had three years of training at the conservatory! You sent me there to learn music," I added defiantly. "And so I did."

She sniffed. "I'm well aware of what you learned. I daresay, so is all of Weimar. I regret that I did not know sooner. Indeed, I should have listened to you and had you enrolled in a music academy here in Berlin, where I could keep a closer eye on you."

I clenched my teeth. I couldn't deny her accusation and I refused to try. I was tired of being treated as if I must do penance. Yes, I had done wrong and wasted her tuition. Yes, I had taken a lover, but the only person who'd ended up hurt by it was me. And that was over now; I was done with the conservatory. I had lost my head, and other things; but I had the training and some talent, and I would not be some old man's drudge.

"I'm twenty years old," I said. "There must be a hundred girls in Berlin who can wax the Austrian professor's floor. Let me talk to Uncle Willi. He must know of—"

"He has no openings at the store," Mutti said, "if that's what you're thinking. Indeed, he has enough on his plate without you going to him to beg for charity."

I had wondered why she and my sister remained in this rented flat when the family residence had plenty of room. But when I asked Liesel, she only said, "He has a guest"—a cryptic remark that piqued my curiosity. After my experiences in Weimar, I wondered if my uncle, with his stylish clothes, love of the theater, and perfect mustachios, might be homosexual. He had never married, though he was in his midfifties. I had never heard of a girlfriend or mistress, so I wanted to meet this mysterious guest of his. But Mutti refused to arrange a visit, prohibiting me from setting foot anywhere near the family house or the store.

"I don't want to work in the shop," I replied. "He knows people in the theater. Theaters need musicians for their orchestras and I could—"

"Out of the question. While you live here, under my roof, you will abide by my rules. Is that understood? No daughter of mine will work in a theater. It is not a profession; it's not even a respectable occupation. I'll not tolerate you making a spectacle of yourself. You will do as I say, when I say it. It is high time you understand how to behave in the proper way."

I wanted to reply that perhaps I should start looking for another living arrangement. I felt smothered; I might not miss the conservatory but I longed for the freedom of Weimar. How could she scold me like a child beholden to her mandates, when the rules she clung to had ceased to exist? Did she not see the demonstrations, the hunger and rage all around us, the bare larders in her own home that obliged her to work for a pittance? But I curbed my temper. Without money or any prospects, I'd end up on the streets, as Frau Arnoldi had assured me I would. No matter what, I had to prove myself. I wouldn't let my mother or anyone else make me feel useless. Reitz had taken my confidence in music from me, and now I had to get it back.

"Liesel." Mutti gestured to my sister. "Finish your porridge. You'll be late for class."

"Yes, Mutti," my sister mumbled.

Mutti returned her stare to me. "You will do the laundry today and practice your violin. Tomorrow, I'll take you to meet your professor." Without waiting for my response, she marched from the house. She'd be gone until nightfall, doing other people's laundry.

I growled. "*Gott in Himmel.* She's a dragon."

Liesel took up her dish. "What do you expect? You couldn't possibly think she'd ever condone what you've done. She was beside herself when she finally heard of those goings-on in Weimar. Whatever were you thinking? We were not raised like that. How could you be so . . . ?"

"So what?" I retorted. "What was I doing that is such a crime?"

"That professor," Liesel said, and I held my breath, expecting the worst, until she added, "Mutti sent him a payment for your private lessons and he returned it. He wrote that you were no longer studying with him, though you had promise. If you were no longer studying with him and not going to classes in the conservatory, Lena, what on earth *were* you doing?"

"Whatever I liked," I said angrily, though I was grateful that somehow my affair with Reitz had not reached my sister's ears. "I can still play the violin. I haven't forgotten how, if that's what concerns you."

Liesel lowered her eyes. "Mutti is right. I don't know who you are anymore."

She went into the kitchen. Moments later, I heard her slip on her coat and leave. She was working as a substitute teacher, filling in when someone on the faculty fell ill, retired, or dropped dead.

I looked around me at the peeling wallpaper, the mildew stains on the ceiling, the always impeccably clean but chipped and faded furnishings hauled from Schöneberg.

A wail coiled inside me.

No matter what, I had to escape.

II

Uncle Willi embraced me with joy when I entered the store. Times might be hard, but he looked fit and well, and he showed me all the items he'd added to the stock, augmenting our traditional watches and clocks with enamel frames and imitation Fabergé eggs, gilded perfume bottles like those I'd seen in Oma's room, and painted porcelain dishes. He'd dedicated an entire section on the mezzanine to jewelry—bracelets, pendants, earrings, brooches, and necklaces arrayed on blue velvet. I couldn't help but wonder why my mother, when she owned a share in the business, seemed barely to survive. But I did not ask. Instead, when I admired a cabochon emerald necklace, he removed it for me to try on before the mirror, sparking frozen green fire about my throat.

"My Jolie designed some of these pieces," he said. "Aren't they exquisite? And so popular. We're having some success with them. Women love them for the evening."

I fingered the stones. "Aren't they terribly expensive?" I had no idea what emeralds cost but I imagined they must be beyond the reach of everyone but the very rich, and how many people were very rich in Germany these days?

"Those are." He leaned to my ear. "Don't tell anyone," he whispered, "but with the exception of that piece and a few others, which are mostly for show, these others are fake. My Jolie is so clever. She says it's the current rage in Paris, using paste stones instead of real ones. No one can tell the difference; and in this economy, no one can afford to."

I would never have known. I had no eye for what was real or not, but it was the second time he'd mentioned his Jolie. "Liesel tells me you have a guest living with you? Is it Jolie?"

"Yes." He beamed. "She is my wife."

Before I could react to this momentous news, he went on, "You must meet her. Oh, she'll adore you. She reminds me so much of our dear Oma—so elegant and refined. She's done miracles to revive your tired old uncle and his business."

I had timed my visit to perfection. "I would very much like to meet her," I said, reluctantly unclasping the necklace to return it to him.

As he set it into the case, he sighed. "I'd have invited you over as soon as you came back from Weimar but Josephine wouldn't hear of it."

"Yes. I'm afraid she's very angry with me."

"Oh? She didn't mention it. She said you'd accomplished everything required of you at the conservatory and it was time for you to return." His voice softened. "I should have known."

I nodded, abruptly humiliated. I'd always liked my uncle, but I did not want to explain my sordid circumstances to him, though I sensed he'd understand.

As if he felt my discomfort, he smiled. "Don't worry, *Liebchen*. My sister is a good woman, but not a lenient one. And we've something in common, for she doesn't approve of my Jolie. She's so upset with me, she refuses to accept any money, though we're doing better now than we have since the war. I still deposit her share in her account, though," he said, winking. "I thought she must need it for your tuition and private classes."

I lowered my eyes lest he see how awful I felt. My mother had of course deprived herself to see to my needs. I mustn't let the knowledge deter me. She had done it because she wanted me to emerge from the conservatory as a soloist, take my place on the great stage. She still did, hence my housekeeping arrangement with the Austrian. Her disappoint-ment when she found out I lacked sufficent talent would only make her resent me more.

He took me to lunch at the Café Bauer, my first decent meal since re-turning to Berlin. Over pork chops and mint-garnished potatoes that must have cost a fortune, he told me he'd met Jolie at a reception for Prince Wil-helm, the kaiser's son, who'd stayed in Germany despite his father's exile, as sought after by society as he'd ever been. The prince had introduced Madame Jolie to Uncle Willi, who was immediately smitten.

"She was married at the time," he explained. "To some American in-ventor promoting a carnival attraction called the Devil's Wheel. She told me she didn't love him anymore and we decided there was no time like the present to start our life together. She's Polish. Very sensible. But she's trav-eled all over the world, and you'd never know it."

I refrained from asking whether it was unclear that she was well trav-eled or Polish, though I could see why Mutti disapproved. A foreigner and a divorcée, living in the family home as the new Felsing matron. Mutti must have felt Oma turn over in her tomb.

"She has an unusual name," I said, sopping up the sauce on my plate with my bread and not caring that this, too, would have turned someone over in their tomb.

"It's her pet name. Her name is Martha Helene. But everyone calls her Jolie."

"Everyone?"

He nodded, motioning to the waiter for the check. "We're holding soirees again at the house, like the old days. Jolie loves the theater as much as I do; she also adores being a hostess. And while things are hardly the same, people still need to be entertained. She's urged me to invest in a few productions—don't tell your mother—and I still have my renter upstairs. He's making quite a splash with his invention. After the war, the picture studios came calling, offering to patent his camera lenses for the kinos."

I sat upright. My eagerness must have shown on my face because after he paid the check, he gave me a sly look. "Shall I invite you to tea?"

"Oh, yes. Please."

"Good. As my Jolie would say, no time like the present."

SHE WAS INDEED SOMETHING.

A fine-boned woman with a piquant face, she wore chandelier earrings swinging from her earlobes, her hair was swathed in a turban, and her brows were plucked to fine arched lines. She also had the longest, reddest fingernails I'd ever seen. Her perfume enveloped me as she kissed both my cheeks in the French style; she smelled different from Oma, not like flowers, but as if she'd bathed in musky incense.

"Darling Marlene." A slight but detectable accent in her German betrayed her origins. Clearly, it wasn't her provenance that was mysterious, but I was bewildered as to whether her well-traveled person might deceive, for she seemed to me entirely exotic. Perhaps her sensibility? She was dressed at home in midafternoon as if she were expecting royalty.

"My Willi has told me so much about you. Sit here by me. I want to hear everything. I understand you're a violinist—a graduate, no less, of the esteemed conservatory. How sublime," she said. "You must be thrilled to be back in Berlin, with so much opportunity for musicians."

As I perched beside her on the sofa, now draped in patterned shawls, and she rang the bell for tea, I covertly surveyed the parlor. Her influence was everywhere. She'd replaced all the stiff lamp shades with fringed, tasseled adornments and removed the portrait of my great-grandfather Conrad Felsing, founder of the business, from above the fireplace. In its stead now hung an odd painting in muddy pigments of a square-faced, ugly harlequin.

"Do you like it?" she said. "The artist is Pablo Picasso. I bought that in Paris for a song. He's going to be very famous: a Catalan with an unsurpassed eye for color and form. And for women." She chuckled. "Quite an eye for the female figure, too."

The maid brought in the tea. With a lingering kiss on Jolie's lips and a peck on mine, Uncle Willi said he had to return to the store. He said to me, "Remember. Don't tell Josephine."

I nodded. If I ever breathed a word of this to my mother, she'd put *me* in my tomb.

Jolie waved out the maid and poured the tea herself, which was also unusual. Oma wouldn't have deigned to serve tea to the kaiser himself. "You haven't said a word," she said, offering a cup she'd heaped with sugar. "Do I disappoint?"

"No," I said. "Not at all, Frau Felsing—"

"Frau!" She trilled with laughter. "Please. Call me Madame. Or Jolie, if you prefer. Frau Felsing makes me sound ancient." She sipped her tea, her little finger crooked, displaying its lacquered nail. "I feared you might disapprove. Your mother certainly does. Oh, the way she stared at me when Willi introduced us." She rolled her eyes with such dramatic aplomb, she reminded me of Henny Porten. "If looks could kill, I'd be dead as we speak. You have a sister, too, I believe. Elisabeth? Your Mutti refuses to let her set foot inside this house."

I gulped my tea, scalding my tongue.

"Are you happy to be back?" she said.

I started. "Happy, Madame?"

"Why, yes." She gave a shrug. "Your mother isn't a happy woman, and when a woman is unhappy—well, she makes everyone else around her unhappy, too. It's our curse. Once Eve took a bite of the forbidden fruit, she gave us the power to affect the world—for good or for evil."

"Mutti isn't unhappy," I replied, surprised to hear myself defending the very woman whom I longed to escape. "But she's not very understanding, either."

"Alas. Those who condemn always live in fear. They deny their own hearts, for they would like to act as we do yet do not dare."

I was taken aback. She didn't seem like someone given to musings. She had hidden depths; I understood now why Uncle Willi was smitten. She wasn't German at all.

"So." Her smile revealed teeth yellowed by tea and slightly smudged with her red lipstick. "Tell me everything, my dear. I want us to be friends."

She was everything Mutti abhorred—a woman of the modern age, as loose with her mouth as her morals, having cast aside one husband to snag my uncle, and I told her everything. I couldn't hold it back. There was something so novel about her, her attentive candor easing the knot in my chest as I related my trials in Weimar, skirting the details of my affair with Professor Reitz, but not my realization that I'd never fulfill my mother's ambitions for me, and then of my return to find myself sold into servitude for lessons that couldn't provide any benefit. "I can play the violin well enough," I said. "I don't need more lessons."

She sat in contemplative silence before she said, "Perhaps this new professor is indeed as renowned as your mother claims and can help you play even better." She paused, gauging me. "But naturally, it makes no difference if you're disinclined. I see no reason why you shouldn't seek your own way. We do know theater managers who may hire you. But," she added, "the pay these days—I'm afraid it won't be enough for you to move anywhere. Everyone in the theater is as poor as a rat. The show must go on, as they say, but it goes on rather frugally in Berlin."

"It doesn't matter. I'll do anything."

"Except wax floors," she replied. She smiled again. "I don't blame you. You have the training, only . . ."

"Only what?" I leaned over to her. "What else do I need?"

She passed her gaze over me. "My dear, I do not wish to be insensitive."

I froze. Then, as understanding crept through me, I smoothed my rumpled wool skirt and muttered, "Mutti confiscated my clothes. She said I mustn't make a spectacle of myself."

"Instead she does it for you by dressing you like a widow." Jolie put her cup on its saucer. "You cannot possibly go on auditions like that. I've a few things I could lend you, a coat or two, at least. Your grandmother also left some dresses in the attic we might alter." She snapped her fingers. "No time like the present. *Allons-y!* Let's see what we can achieve."

III

It became my new secret.

I agreed to lessons with the Austrian professor, who proved as cantankerous as he was renowned, scrubbing his floors after practice because, as Jolie advised, I could refine my skill for auditions. But after three hours of practice and two hours of cleaning his cluttered flat, I went to my uncle's home, where Jolie had me try on the new dresses she'd had made for me.

Oma's discarded remnants were too outdated, she had pronounced. Impossible to alter styles that had gone out before the war. Instead, she inveigled Willi, who could deny her nothing, for money to have new attire made, though when I first beheld these lovely dresses with their drooping necklines and daringly high hems, I could barely fit into them.

"You're too fat," Jolie said. She did not fear insensitivity now. "Whatever your mother is feeding you, you must eat less. A Rubenesque figure is fine for the museum, but not for fashion. I had these made in your proper size. You'll have to diet until you can wear them."

Dejected but determined, prompted by her discreet use of pincers to pluck what she called my "jungle brow" and a discreet rinse on my hair to "highlight its fairness, as blondes are always popular," I set myself to a diet that nearly had me fainting as I plied the violin and the old professor banged his cane. "No, no," he declaimed, as intolerant as any Weimar relic. "Do you intend to play the violin or carve meat? You wield that bow like a cleaver. Softly, softly. It's an extension of your wrist, not a butchering utensil."

He honed my skill—not as much as I wanted, but it was better than before. Just as Jolie improved my appearance, while I deprived my body until the day came when I finally fit into my new clothes and Mutti grumbled over supper, "You look different. Have you been doing something to your hair?"

"I cut it shorter," I said, "for the violin. So it wouldn't . . . get into my eyes." I lowered my face as I spoke, lest she also decided to inspect my noticeably thinner cheeks and eyebrows. She didn't. She was too exhausted from work; she retired like a farmer's wife at sunset, leaving me and Liesel to wash the dishes and tidy up before bed.

My sister wasn't so myopic. "You've been visiting that woman, haven't you?" she said, so unexpectedly I almost dropped the plate I was drying. "Uncle Willi's guest. She's teaching you things. You pick at your food like a bird and your eyebrows are plucked. And you've not only cut your hair but also dyed it."

"Wife. She is Willi's wife." I squared my shoulders. "Are you going to tell on me?"

"No." She arranged the dishes in the cupboard; Mutti liked everything in order. "But she's bound to find out, Lena. And when she does . . ."

"I'll be gone. I'm applying for a job as a musician. As soon as I can, I'll get my own room."

She gave me a skeptical look. "On a musician's pay?"

She was right. Jolie had warned me. In fact, she'd offered to let me move into the house with her and Uncle Willi, but as much as I'd fallen prey to her influence, I couldn't go that far. If I left Mutti to move in with them, she'd disown me. It was enough that I contrived to deceive her. She'd be enraged if she found out I was going to auditions beyond the exclusive Kurfürstendamm Boulevard near the Behrenstrasse, where the trees strung with candelabra and the elegant facades of department stores gave way to a tawdry labyrinth of cheap theaters, kinos, and neon-lit cafés, as well as raucous cabarets, music halls, and other disreputable venues.

The auditions were excruciating. There were more unemployed musicians in Berlin than I'd supposed, my Weimar training and Uncle Willi's reference vanishing like smoke in the air as hundreds rallied to the job calls. Their desperation only made the theater managers haggle for the cheapest rate. Male musicians, regardless of their talent, always won. A woman in an orchestra was rare, unless one took into account the growing infamy of the Girl Kabarets, where women performed onstage, in the orchestra, and behind the scenes after the show. But just as I resisted moving into Uncle Willi's house, I resisted the lure of the cabaret because Mutti's rules, inculcated in me since childhood, were not so easily disregarded. A musician, yes. A performer in a band in an off-boulevard establishment—never.

After months of rejections that left me disconsolate, Uncle Willi intervened. He'd had lunch with the manager of a prospering chain of picture houses owned by the UFA—the Universum Film Aktiengesellschaft, a studio that had started by presenting short reels about the war and branched out into full productions, some of which featured my Weimar actress-idol, Henny Porten. The manager had complained of losing a violinist in one of his traveling orchestras that accompanied the films. The job, Uncle Willi assured me, was mine. UFA had no issue with hiring a woman, as I'd not be seen in the pit. But the pay was less than I'd heard theater managers offer, scarcely enough to put food in my mouth, much less get me out of Mutti's flat.

"I told you," Jolie sighed. "You can always move in here with us. We'd be delighted to have you. Wouldn't we, Willi dearest?"

My uncle didn't look delighted. Like me, he feared the wrath of the dragon, as I'd dubbed Mutti. "I'd have to consult with Josephine," he said. "It would be the proper thing to do. She holds a share in the business. I wouldn't want to cause her any more trouble."

"Of course," I said, before Jolie could protest. "There's no need. If I have the job, it's a start." I forced out a smile, though I felt wretched as I envisioned delivering the news to Mutti.

She didn't raise her voice. After I informed her that I'd accepted employment in a small orchestra accompanying the flickers, all she said was, "I see," before she left for her work.

Unnerved, thinking I should also have told her I was moving into the family residence, I saw Liesel glance at me. "You'd best start looking for that new room soon," she said.

I sighed. I should, indeed. Though how I'd manage it seemed as insurmountable as everything else.

THE JOB WAS TEDIOUS. We had a set repertoire for each film that screened overhead, the music as trivial as the pictures themselves. I had to wonder why I'd been so entranced by Henny Porten. Watching her pantomime her way through convoluted plots six days a week, I thought her a rather poor actress. But she was famous everywhere she went, while I labored in a pit with other musicians who ogled me at intermission. I'd learned my lesson in Weimar. Despite numerous invitations, I declined. I needed the work and the pay, as Mutti's pursed-lip response had turned out to be a percentage of my salary toward the rent, her punishment for what she deemed my willful rejection of a career as a concert soloist. The last thing I needed was a romantic mistake.

Even if I'd had the courage to tell her I was never going to earn acclaim for my violin, I lacked the time and energy. The job took us to various UFA picture houses in Berlin, Frankfurt, and Munich, where the scenery might change but the dismal hotel rooms and the repertoire remained the same. I learned every piece of music by heart and knew every film by rote; I could play my violin, watch the picture above, and hike up the edges of my skirt to get a draft of air on my sweltering stocking-clad legs without missing a note.

After four weeks in my employment, as I pulled on my coat one evening and prepared to trudge home with my violin in its now-battered case, the manager motioned me into his office. He slid an envelope across his desk. "Your final pay. I'm sorry, Fräulein Dietrich."

"You're dismissing me?" I was stunned. "But why? You told me I was doing very well."

"You were. However, some of the others have complained."

"Complained?" I knew at once which ones—all those whose invitations I'd refused. "Why should any of them complain? I've not missed an engagement. In fact, I should be the one complaining, as several of them fail to start with the picture or play the wrong score."

"The legs." He met my appalled stare. "They say you are too distracting. You pull up your skirt to show off your legs and confound them. It was a mistake to hire a woman."

Infuriated, I grabbed the envelope and stormed out, but by the time I was on the boulevard, I was nearly in tears. I'd been fired for my legs, when all I'd been trying to do was catch some relief before I roasted to death in that hellhole of a pit. Now I was unemployed, and when I thought of what Mutti would say, the triumph in her voice as she reminded me I should have kept to housekeeping and lessons until the *appropriate* opportunity presented itself—

I dashed into the nearest café. I never bought myself anything. I would at least enjoy a decent meal with my own earnings before I handed over whatever was left to Frau Dragon.

It was early evening, when anyone with anything to spend took to the streets. After ordering the most inexpensive meal on the fixed-price menu, balancing my violin case in one hand and beer mug in the other (yes, I would drink and let Mutti smell it on me), I searched the crowded interior for an empty seat. I spotted one in the corner, but the table was occupied by a dark-haired woman writing in a notebook, a coffee cup and overflowing ashtray at her side.

"Excuse me, Frau, is this seat free?" I asked.

She looked up. She was no Frau. Or at least, she appeared only a little older than me, with deep brown eyes and a tired mouth, her fingertips stained with ink.

"Yes." She removed her tapestry bag from the empty chair. "Join me."

I hadn't intended to join her. I merely required a place to eat my meal.

But as I sat and offered her a smile, she thrust out her ink-smeared hand. "Gerda Huber."

"Marlene. Marlene Dietrich." After a moment's hesitation, I shook her hand. Her palm was dry. But I liked her firm grasp. I'd only seen men greet each other with handshakes. Eyeing her, I saw she wore an old-fashioned shirtwaist with a frayed collar and a knotted black tie. She wasn't unattractive but looked as though she wanted to be, her black hair drawn in a severe bun, her dowdy air ensuring she'd go unnoticed.

"You look exhausted," she said. "Bad day?"

"The worst." And then I blurted out, "I just got sacked from my job."

She winced. "In this economy. For a woman, it's not easy to find work at all."

"That's why I was sacked." I paused as the waiter delivered my sauerkraut and overcooked sausage. I motioned down; as she looked, I lifted my skirt. "For being a woman. I played the violin in an orchestra for the UFA. The other musicians complained. Can you believe it?" I wasn't sure why I was telling her, only I needed to tell someone and I was unlikely to meet her again. "They claimed I showed off my legs to distract them." I gulped my beer. "Have they no sense? It's like an oven in those pits, and the manager insisted I must wear stockings at all times—with the price of stockings as they are."

"You aren't wearing stockings now," she remarked.

I paused. "Yes, well. My latest pair had a run in them. I took them off."

"Before or after you were fired?" She was smiling. She had uneven teeth, discolored from too many cigarettes and cheap coffee. "Not that it matters. Women are never respected in our world. We live in an age of rampant misogyny."

"*Mis*-what?"

"Misogyny. Prejudice against women." She flicked her finger at my plate. "You should eat. Cold sauerkraut isn't very appetizing."

Her words returned me to another time in another café, when I'd sat with the teacher whom I adored and she'd advised me to drink my coffee before it went cold. I gestured to the waiter, who returned with an impatient frown. "Another plate for my friend."

She started to refuse. I waved him off, saying, "It's my treat. This is my last paycheck for who knows how long, and as I must give whatever is left for rent, we might as well enjoy it."

She dipped her head. "*Danke*, Marlene."

Over our food, I told her about how I'd come to play the violin and she told me she was a journalist who wrote freelance articles for newspapers—"Stupid stories about stupid people," she said, grimacing. "Editors think all women can write about is Henny Porten's latest affair or the latest show on the Behrenstrasse with that ghastly Anita." She hooked her hands like claws at the sides of her face. "I'm Anita Berber. Do you like cocaine, darling? I *bathe* in it. *Willkommen* to my dance of horror, lust, and ecstasy."

I laughed aloud. It felt good. I hadn't laughed in weeks. I'd also seen posters of this Anita Berber, who posed like a crimson-mouthed vamp. "Is it true she performs in the nude?"

"Naked," corrected Gerda. "*Nude* denotes taste. She has none." She lit a cigarette, though she hadn't yet finished her meal, blowing out smoke as she pushed the package to me. I took one. Beer, cigarettes, sausage. Let Mutti have a fit.

"I want to write about serious issues that affect us now," Gerda said, glancing angrily about the café and its garrulous patrons. "About this terrifying economy, the political instability, and the emancipation of women— things people *should* be reading, not lurid tales of cocaine-addled sluts or the antics of some overrated actress."

"Porten is overrated," I agreed, cigarette in hand as I wolfed down the rest of her half-finished sausage. No reason to diet now. "I used to worship her. I saw all her films, memorized even her dialogue titles. When I was in Weimar, I could imitate her to perfection, but after this job—ugh. She's so unnatural. It's not life she portrays up there."

"No," said Gerda. "She imitates life. That's all anyone cares about: to escape and ignore the catastrophe we brought upon ourselves. Life is *too* real. Best to pretend it doesn't exist."

Now it was my turn to glance around. The war was still a raw wound. Everyone in Germany had lost someone to it. No one would welcome hearing it disparaged as a catastrophe we had brought upon ourselves, as that implied we could have avoided it.

"I've made you nervous," she said. "I have a big mouth. Too big, my editors tell me. Which is why they'll never let me write anything substantial. A woman who speaks the truth is also too real."

I was embarrassed that she'd seen right through me. "It's just that—my mother lost a brother and a husband in the war, and . . ." I faltered under her steady gaze. "I was taught to believe that an honorable German, a good German, must always support the cause."

"No matter what." She stubbed her cigarette out in the ashtray. "So was I. I lost two brothers to the war. After that, I decided it was time to think for myself. As Goethe wrote: 'None are more hopelessly enslaved than those who falsely believe they are free.'" She reached across the table, oblivious to her sleeve trailing over her plate. She grasped my hand. "I like you, Marlene. You have courage. Marx says men make their own history. Women can, too, if we're only given the chance. You strike me as someone who wants to make her own history."

I did? At this particular moment, I didn't feel like one. But all I replied was, "I like you, too," and I realized I did. Of all the places I might have gone, I'd come in here and met her. She'd made me forget for an hour or so that I'd lost my sole source of income and my dream of independence. But now I remembered and the weight of it fell upon me as I searched my pocket for the envelope, doling out the price of our meals.

"I must get home before it's too late."

"Must you? Or have I made you so uncomfortable that you feel you *must* leave?"

"I'm not uncomfortable." My denial was too quick. The truth was, although I liked her, she did perturb me. She was not feminine like Mademoiselle, refined like Oma, or glamorous like Jolie. She was unlike any woman I'd met—one who spoke her mind with a directness that was more like a man's.

Then she said softly, but with an undeniable challenge, "Why don't you come home with me instead?"

SHE LIVED IN A BOARDINGHOUSE in the Wilmersdorf district, one of those crumbling older buildings whose better days had come and gone with the empire, now reduced to cubbyholes for tenants. Her room wasn't much larger than the one I'd had in Weimar, though hers had a kitchenette. Stacks of books were heaped everywhere—volumes by Goethe, Marx, Zweig, and Mann, and writers I didn't recognize, American or English, it seemed, with names like Fitzgerald and James. She also had two tabby cats who meowed plaintively as we entered. I saw then that she'd not finished her sausage at the café because she was saving it for them, unclasping her bag and removing sections from a napkin to feed them in chipped dishes while I watched, thinking I'd greedily consumed her pets' dinner.

"Whatever I can afford," she said. "Parts of my meals and the cream off the milk that Trude gives me on Sundays. Poor dears. They don't look famished, do they? They should be skin and bones. But Trude adores them. She must give them extras. Do you like cats?"

"Yes." I squatted. "I've never had one, but aren't they considered good luck?"

"By the ancient Egyptians, perhaps." She unwound her scarf. "In Berlin, with the price of meat as it is, they're considered a staple."

I gasped, looking up at her. "Honestly? People eat . . . ?"

She chuckled. "So I'm told. I've never tried it myself. Coffee?" She went into the kitchenette; as I made kissing sounds, one of the cats meandered over to me and began to purr.

"He likes you. That's Oskar. Like Oscar Wilde. Handsome devil, isn't he?"

"Who's Trude?" I asked. The cat was so soft, its fur rippled like silk through my fingers.

"The landlady." Gerda emerged with a pot and two cups on a tray. "She's very nice. A bit daft, but one of the truly kindhearted souls I've met in this city. She runs this house. She only rents to women, mostly aspiring chorus girls or actresses. A few of her tenants study at the Max Reinhardt academy. Have you heard of it?"

I shook my head, picking up Oskar and settling with him in a lumpy chair.

"Neither had I, but Trude adores the theater." Gerda served the coffee, which smelled of chicory. "She wanted to be an actress herself, but in her day, it wasn't done. It still isn't. But most of us have to make a living somehow. Not many options besides the cabaret, modeling, or acting, and of course the oldest profession. Max Reinhardt's academy is considered the best; many of his graduates go on to perform in his repertory companies." She eyed me. "Better to try one's luck on the stage than on one's back. The competition these days is the same."

If she was trying to shock me, it didn't work. I'd seen plenty of prostitutes as I'd dashed to and from my auditions. Just beyond the Kurfürstendamm, the alleys seethed with them, men and women alike, beckoning from doorways or cruising the grimy cafés.

"Trude also reads tarot cards for money," Gerda went on. "She's quite good. She once foretold that a girl here would get a part, and the very next week, she did."

"She sounds interesting." As I reached for my cup, Oskar leaped from my lap, leaving fur all over my skirt. I smiled, brushing at it. "Mutti will be furious. Cat hair in the house."

"She sounds like a tyrant. How do you stand it?"

I sighed. "I didn't think it would be for much longer. I was saving whatever I could to rent my own place, but now . . ."

"Yes?" Her gaze was now fixed on me.

I hated to admit it. "I suppose I'll have to clean houses."

"Why don't you try acting?"

I laughed. "Acting? I have no talent whatsoever for the stage."

"You have those." She pointed at my legs. "Legs like yours—"

"Can make fortunes. That's what my Oma once told me."

"She was right." Greta lit a cigarette. "I've seen girls with far less than you do quite well for themselves. You should consider it."

I sipped my coffee; it was mostly chicory and as bitter as failure.

"You said you can imitate Henny Porten," she said. "Show me."

"Now?"

She nodded. "I'd like to see it, if you don't mind."

I assumed the pose, arching my arms above my head as I'd done so many times for my friends in Weimar. Affecting an anguished tone, I recited, "Why do you forsake me, Curt? Can't you see I am spellbound by the baron?"

She sat still, a pall of smoke drifting about her. I shrugged. "See? No talent whatsoever."

"But we proved our point. Porten is definitely overrated. With some dramatic training and voice lessons, I see no reason why you couldn't do better."

"Better than Porten? She's famous. I don't think I could ever be like her."

"You don't want to, remember? You want to be your own creation." She dragged on her cigarette before extending it across the table. As I smoked, coughing slightly from the harshness of it, she returned the tray to the kitchenette, her cats winding at her heels. I finished the cigarette and looked around for an ashtray; the room was filled with bric-a-brac, and I didn't see one anywhere until she said, "On the table. The pot."

Leaning over a chipped ceramic pot, I saw it contained an inch or two of filthy water, with sodden butts floating in it. "It helps with the smell," she said, coming back toward me.

I dropped the butt in. It didn't help; her entire room reeked of tobacco. I reached for my coat. During the walk here, I'd felt a chill in the air. Autumn approached, heralding another frigid winter. I had a long trek home, unless I could catch a tram at this hour. But I didn't want to leave. She made me feel safe, welcome. I thought we might be friends and she must have thought the same, for before I could thank her and say good night, she said quietly, "If things get bad at home, you could always stay here on the couch. Trude wouldn't mind and I could use extra help with the rent once you find work. It's not expensive. I travel now and then for assignments, so you'd have the room to yourself sometimes. But when I'm here, I'd enjoy the company."

I turned to her. Her eyes shone. "Company?" I said.

"Why, yes." Her words quickened. "I'll introduce you to the other tenants; the girls here know all the voice instructors and drama coaches. You could train for the theater, perhaps audition for the academy. I'll help you select roles. I have a lot of books with plays here."

Her voice held a slight tremor. In the room, with her one lamp casting more shadow than light, she looked different—prettier. Just a girl like me, like so many of us trying to survive. I remembered Mademoiselle, how I'd yearned to caress stray hairs from her cheek, and then Reitz, when I'd taken his hand and he clasped it. Would this be any different? I had always wondered about my affinity for women, and I felt an inexplicable kinship with Gerda, not like with a sibling, as Liesel and I were, but as I imagined true sisterhood might be.

"I could stay now," I offered, and she nodded.

"You could," she said. "Do you want to?"

I smiled. "I could try. I've never done this before. But I have thought of it." As I spoke, I tentatively reached out to caress her cheek. Her skin was dry. She didn't use any cream, not even the ubiquitous bargain lotions found in the drugstores, which always left a palpable film. My curiosity made me feel naive, exposed; I heard myself say haltingly, "Will you show me how?"

Her eyes dilated, like a cat's. "Tell me," she said thickly, "what you want to learn."

I let my hand linger on her face. "Everything."

Desire flamed up in her. I'd seen it before, on the afternoon I had seduced Reitz. But she was not like him; she did not hide her need in shame or deceit. It was on her face, young and brash; she burned as if she might melt. It excited me. It was conquest and surrender; we were women, equals, with nothing between us but our hesitation.

I abruptly kissed her. She tasted of stale tobacco; and when she returned my kiss, I felt her shudder. I liked the sensation, her vulnerability
wavering under her flesh like an elusive pool.

As she guided me to the tiny bedroom off the living area, I warmed to
her touch. She had done this before, perhaps not often, but often enough
that her kisses turned pliant, her hands sliding within my clothes, unfas-
tening, tugging, until I stood naked before her and she breathed, "*Mein Gott.*
You are beautiful. Like a goddess."

I could see that she meant it. She herself was small breasted, with heavy
thighs; her long skirt and shirtwaist had concealed a pear-shaped body that
made her self-conscious, another vulnerability that endeared her to me. She
wanted to be taken seriously as a journalist, to effect change in the world,
but like everyone else, she must yearn to be loved. I understood. I, too,
longed for it, and her sudden gasp as I knelt to clasp her was like being
in an elevator going down very fast. She strained against my mouth, moan-
ing aloud, and then we were tumbling onto the rumpled bed, tangled and
gasping as palms and tongues merged. I soaked into her; I wanted to please
her, and when I did, her cry shattered in my ear. Her breath was husky as
she whispered incredulously, "You've never done this before?"

"Never," I said, and then she rose over me, holding my arms over my
head as she lapped at my nipples, moving down slowly, teasing, until she
parted me and then, with a sly grin as she raised her gaze to my face, she
said, "If I do this, I might never let you go."

"Do it," I said. "Please . . ."

She sipped me as if I were a delicacy, peeling me like fruit, piece by
supple piece, until I was panting as she reached my searing core.

I thought I'd had a lover before. How wrong I had been.

I DRIFTED HOME THE NEXT DAY, a Saturday, feeling fragrant and
boneless as oleander petals, and packed my suitcase while Mutti sat stone-
faced at the table and Liesel gaped in disbelief.

"It's a respectable boardinghouse," I said. "For girls. Frau Trude runs it and insists on her tenants having proper employment. I'm sharing a room with a writer."

It was a lie of course. I no longer had a job, proper or otherwise, and when we'd happened on Trude as I left the boardinghouse and Gerda introduced me, I beheld a floozy of a woman in a faded housecoat, gray roots threading her dyed red hair. She was as sweet and absentminded as Gerda had described, smiling vaguely when told I was moving in. "Oh, how lovely. You've found a new friend, Gerda. I hope she likes cats. Welcome, dear."

Mutti didn't know any of this yet, but she had an unerring ear for falsehood. "Frau Trude?" She frowned. "You don't even know the proprietor's last name?"

"Handelmann," I said. "Or Herbert. I'm not sure. I only just met her, but she's very strict." I kept emphasizing the propriety of the situation, even though nothing I said would convince her and images of Gerda lifting a cigarette to my lips as we lay together, arms and legs entwined, flashed behind my eyes. Unmarried girls lived at home: That was the only propriety Mutti knew. Anything else was unacceptable. But I was about to turn twenty-one. She couldn't stop me, and even if she had tried, I would not have let her.

She did not try. She accepted my kiss good-bye and let Liesel see me to the door. Unexpectedly, my sister said, "I admire you, Marlene. You're doing what you want."

It was the nicest thing she'd ever said to me, and it eased my anxiety. Mutti would come around. She wouldn't be able to resist. She'd want to see this boardinghouse and roommate of mine for herself. Even if she no longer had me under her thumb, she must ensure that I didn't make a spectacle of myself. How she'd react when she discovered I wasn't playing the violin but was living with a lesbian and training to be an actress—I couldn't dwell on that now.

No time like the present.

I would live for the moment and deal with the future when it arrived.

IV

As ardent as she was in bed, outside of it Gerda could be as tyrannical as my mother. She had early access to the job advertisements and call sheets because of her newspaper contacts; every morning, she circled each potential prospect and forced me to wear out the soles of my shoes as I prowled smoke-filled theaters and music halls in search of a job.

No one would hire me without experience, but a few of the less distinguished revues expressed interest once they saw my legs, provided that I could give them evidence of my ability to carry a tune. I could do that; I had always liked to sing. Mutti had encouraged singing at home around the piano but not in public; she deemed it lower class unless one sang opera or hymns in church. But to me, singing was like the violin, only more personal and intimate; I could employ my voice as an instrument in ways I'd never been able to play my bow, and I had my training to inform me. I began practicing with songbooks bought at music shops, to learn the latest tunes, and Gerda saw to it that one of the boardinghouse tenants, a lively redhead named Camilla Horn, referred me to her voice instructor, Professor Daniels. Gerda also insisted that I must learn English, to assist in my pronunciation of popular American songs, and found a local woman named Elsie Grace who also taught actors. She was a frightful crone, with clotted eyeliner and a twisted back, who lived in a walk-up. But she was funny and very British; she made me repeat nursery rhymes, then regaled me over tea with stories of the sexual exploits of her youth.

"It's certainly an effective way to learn the language"—Gerda laughed when I showed her how well I could recite "The cunt jumped over the moon."

Gerda paid for my lessons, despite my protests. To reimburse her, I went to see Jolie and explained my circumstances. My uncle's wife proclaimed it a splendid notion for me to explore acting—she spoke as if I was taking up knitting—and loaned me a fox stole and a sum of cash, which I promised to repay. I covered the rent for the month and bought groceries, this time over Gerda's protests.

"We're in this together," I said. "I must do my share."

"Yes, but I may never get what I want, while you can," she replied. "You *can* be someone. I believe in you."

She did, more than I believed in myself. Herr Daniels was one of the finest teachers in Berlin; he'd trained opera singers before the war, until economic straits compelled him to take on other students. He had an unorthodox method for loosening the voice, having us prance about the room, squawking and flapping our arms before we performed scales and vocal intonations at the piano until our throats were raw.

"You have an interesting voice," he told me. "Not powerful—you'll never be a recording artist—but with a certain style. You must practice using a lower key. Don't force out those notes you can't reach. There's no need. Refine your register instead."

At night, I'd perform what I'd learned for Gerda, singing popular scandalous songs by Brecht until she growled and yanked me to her. "I can't stand it! You are devastating."

Perhaps to her, but I wasn't devastating to those I auditioned for. I heard "No. Next" so many times, I wondered at my own resolve. But Gerda refused to countenance misgivings.

"These things take time. Look." She brandished the newspaper. "The Rudolf Nelson revue is holding auditions. You must go. You can sing, and"—she lowered her eyes suggestively—"the advertisement says all applicants must have good legs."

"Well." I exhaled smoke. I smoked too much; it helped curb the hunger, as Gerda and our current budget had me on a strict regimen. "If it's legs they want, then legs I can give them."

I didn't expect to be hired. But I wore a short skirt just in case, with black stockings and a mangy wolf pelt I'd unearthed in a secondhand shop tossed around my shoulders. I performed a ditty that required kicks and twirls; I wasn't a very good dancer, but I gave it my best. Each applicant was assigned a number, as in a lottery. When the manager called out the winning ones, he said mine. I had a job.

Gerda and I celebrated with cheap champagne, forgoing our allotment of meat for the week. "You see?" she said, raising her glass. "I told you. You're on your way."

"It's only the chorus." I sipped the champagne, which had no fizz. "And the pay is appalling. Rudolf Nelson obviously doesn't think his girls need to eat."

"Still, it's work." She paused. "I have a new assignment. In Hannover, covering a labor dispute. I start next week."

"Oh, that's wonderful!" I had started to kiss her when she averted her face. "I'll be gone for a month," she said. "You'll have the room all to yourself."

"I'll miss you." Why was she being so strange? "If you're worried about the cats, I'll take good care of them, I promise." Oskar adored me; he slept at my side every night, while Fannie, the female, cleaved to Gerda, tolerating me but maintaining her distance. "I'll be busy with the revue. It's eleven shows a week, including matinees, but I'll telephone you whenever I can."

"Telephone?" She snorted. "Too expensive. And besides, that phone in Trude's parlor never works half the time, unless it's for Camilla. A carrier pigeon would be more reliable."

"You sound upset. Aren't you pleased about your assignment? A labor dispute sounds like the kind of event you've been wanting to cover."

"All those girls." Her voice was flat. "In the chorus. I'm certain you'll be busy indeed."

I went still. The sullenness on her face made me realize that possessiveness wasn't an exclusively feline trait. "You don't think I would . . . ? Gerda, that's ridiculous."

"Is it?" She set down her glass. "Don't you ever think about being with other girls? I know you've also been with men. Should I be concerned about them, as well?"

"I'm not thinking about other girls or men right now. I haven't decided if I prefer one or the other," I said, "or if I just like certain people. I'm with you. But I don't believe we have to own each other. You might meet a girl in Hannover; if you do, I wouldn't mind."

She gave me a troubled look. "You wouldn't?"

"No. And if I'm interested in someone else, I'll tell you."

"I hope so," she muttered. "I'm not jealous, just realistic."

She sounded jealous to me. Instinct urged me to reassure her. It was our first parting for any length of time and I'd discovered she did not feel secure. The journalist who declared utter contempt for the values of our society wasn't as contemptuous as she liked to think she was. And while we'd never said aloud that we were in love or discussed exclusivity, I could tell she was perturbed. But I had learned that desire can fade and trying to possess someone wasn't wise. Better to love freely while it lasted, without staking any claims.

"Do you not trust me?" I asked her. "Because I trust you. I'm happy."

"Are you?" She seemed so forlorn, so unlike her confident self, that I pulled her to me and whispered, "I am. Very happy. I'm not going anywhere."

"And I am happy with you," she murmured, nestling against me. "I just know this chorus job will lead to better things, you'll see."

It was typical of her, to flatter me and evade the uncomfortable, but as I embraced her, I felt a stab of doubt. She had not said she trusted me, and besides, she should be happy for herself. She, too, had dreams to fulfill. I didn't want her to make sacrifices for my sake; it reminded me of my mother, and of the resentment it carried. Gerda and I lived together yet we were also apart. I didn't know how to say this without hurting her, however, so I said nothing.

Still, I found myself wondering if I might actually be different after all.

NO SOONER DID GERDA DEPART FOR HANNOVER than Mutti arrived at my front door. She'd taken more time than I expected, and I was relieved I didn't have to deal with introducing her to my alleged roommate, particularly when her appraisal of my room consisted of an audible sniff.

"You have cats."

They were hiding under the bed, averse to strangers. But the room itself was immaculate; she'd trained me to cleanliness. I scrubbed the floors every week and cleaned out the box of dirt the cats used daily. I'd even polished the lackluster furnishings, packed away some of the clutter, and added potted plants. Mutti couldn't find cause for complaint—not that it ever stopped her. "It's also so small." She eyed me. "Where do you practice your violin?"

The violin remained in its case, where I'd left it on the night I first slept with Gerda, now propping up a pile of books by the sofa. Mutti hadn't seen it, so I stepped in front of it to hide the case from view. Even as I did, I wondered why I still felt the need to dissemble. She would find out everything soon enough. Lifting my chin, I said, "I'm not practicing at the moment."

"Oh?"

"I—I sprained my wrist." I cradled the alleged joint in question. "My instructor told me to take off a month to let it heal. But it still hurts."

"Not the instructor I found you. He told me he hasn't seen you in months."

"A new one." *Why* was I lying? I felt like a schoolgirl again, justifying my own insubordination. "Professor Oskar Daniels. He . . . he also teaches voice."

She stared at me, unblinking. It would take a few inquiries from her to discover that Professor Daniels's expertise didn't include violin lessons. "Voice? Whatever for?"

"To sing. I'm training to . . ." As I saw her face harden, I blurted out, "I'm going to be an actress. I have a job in the chorus of the Nelson revue. But I plan to audition for the Max Reinhardt academy as soon as I save enough for my dramatic lessons."

She might have chuckled, were she capable of it. "Such a waste. You have a God-given talent for the violin, yet you insist on pursuing absurdities."

"It may be an absurdity. But it's what I want."

Until that moment, I hadn't been certain it was. I needed to support myself. Unable to bear another round of auditions as a musician, I'd followed Gerda's advice. But it hadn't felt like *my* choice, just the path of least resistance—and that wasn't saying it was easy. Yet the supercilious disapproval now etching Mutti's forehead cemented it for me.

I would be an actress if it killed me, if only to prove her wrong.

"An actress," she said. "My daughter. Maria Magdalene Dietrich, child of a Felsing and a distinguished lieutenant who once served in the kaiser's grenadiers. On the stage."

"Papa was a Schöneberg policeman," I said.

Her gaze narrowed. "Would you insult the memory of your own father?"

"No. But I'll not pretend he was more than what he was. None of us are more than who we are, Mutti. Not even you. This is my life. If I succeed or fail, I must do it on my terms."

She drew herself erect, squaring her shoulders under her coat. "You'll only bring shame upon yourself and the family. You'll be a laughingstock, an embarrassment to us all."

"Not all. Uncle Willi supports me. So does his wife. They think it's a splendid idea. Even Liesel told me before I left home that she admires me. You're the only one who thinks making a living at anything besides cleaning floors is a disgrace."

"Do not mention that woman Jolie," she said. "Or your sister—I'll not abide it. Like you, Liesel has lost her mind. She carries on with some cabaret manager, Georg Wills, who's as oily as a salesman. She says they will marry. I'm beyond outrage that both my daughters have succumbed to the disorder and socialist fervor that destroys our nation's honor."

Liesel, with a cabaret man? I wanted to applaud. Who'd have thought she had it in her?

"I'm sorry, Mutti. But this is what I must do. If it doesn't work out, well—there's always the mop and broom to fall back on."

She clenched her jaw. "Not a mark. Don't come asking when you fall back, as you say, because I shall not give it. Not unless you apologize and return to your violin."

"I won't," I retorted. "I'd rather starve."

She stormed out, alerting everyone to her departure when she slammed the building's front door. Within seconds, both Camilla and Trude were at my threshold.

"Dear, dear," clucked Trude, as Camilla lit a cigarette and lounged against the door frame, her face already painted for our evening show. She, too, had been hired by the revue but for fewer performances, as she'd also been accepted at the Reinhardt academy as an ingénue. She'd been urging me to assume her vacant spot with her drama coach, but I still didn't have enough money to pay for the lessons.

"That must have been the Dragon," Camilla remarked. She had a flagrant nonchalance that I admired. Nothing ever troubled her too much; it was very "Berliner Luft."

"She cut me off," I fumed. "Not that she ever gave me anything to start with." Even as I spoke, I winced at my own lie. Mutti had given plenty, even if I was too upset to admit it. She'd instilled in me self-discipline and a work ethic; she had paid for my lessons in Weimar and provided, in her way, the strength I needed to pursue my life. But everything she gave me came at a price—her price. And I had found it too steep to pay.

"Zu schlecht," drawled Camilla, as Trude wrung her hands. "Too bad. I guess this means you must become an actress after all."

"Or perish in the attempt." Seizing my coat, I left Trude to fuss over the cats and departed with Camilla for the revue.

On the way there, as we stood on the crowded tram and Camilla held my compact while I applied lipstick, I told her about Mutti, of how antagonistic and demanding she was, embellishing my inability to ever please her. When I was done, more irate than when I'd started, she checked her own maquillage before she said, "Your sister's friend Georg Wills manages the Theater des Westens. It's an upscale vaudeville house. I've heard UFA executives go there in search of new faces." She slid her gaze at me. "You should get to know him. He might have important connections."

"So he can tell Liesel that I came begging and she can tell Mutti?" I said. "I don't think so. Besides, the UFA hired me as a violinist and fired me after a month. I'll not beg anyone for work, connections or not. I will do this on my own."

"Suit yourself." She dabbed a spot of rouge on her cheek. "But connections are how girls like us get ahead. The Nelson revue will give you nothing but sore ankles. Trust me. If you want to succeed, you'll have to beg someone. This is Berlin. We all must get on our knees."

The Rudolf Nelson revue did give me sore ankles. And sore feet and calves, and a sore jaw from smiling through performances clad in a spangled garment with more feathers than an ostrich (which we were responsible for replacing, never mind that the glue affixing them to our headdresses was so cheap, we bathed the stage in plumes), cavorting with nine other girls and often ignored by the audience, who drank, chattered, and suffocated us with cigarette smoke.

The revue traveled among three variety halls in Berlin, but every show was the same—garish and loud, designed to exalt our attributes, our talent or lack thereof incidental. Legs were the draw. Legs were what customers came to see and what we were paid to deliver.

I saved every mark I could. I ate as little as possible, offered to substitute for any of the girls who fell sick, sprained a toe, or quit. I also took odd modeling jobs, scouring the papers and applying to advertise stockings and other products, posing with a coy demeanor and visible garters. Some of the photographers offered to take extra pictures for my portfolio; in exchange, I let them see more than my legs. Within a few months, I had a decent collection of head shots and enough money to start drama lessons, with Gerda, back from Hannover but due to depart for another assignment in Munich, footing the bills at home.

Our relationship became strained. Camilla had taken to assisting me on occasion with my drama instruction, helping me improve my elocution and rhythmic movement for the academy's upcoming auditions. I had tried to explain that Camilla knew what the academy expected, seeing as she studied there, but Gerda replied that Camilla never gave away anything for free.

"True," I said. "She got a referral fee from Herr Daniels when I took her spot."

Gerda snarled, "I'm not talking about money."

It was futile to reassure her that all Camilla and I shared was mutual self-interest. I welcomed the extra tutelage, haphazard as it was, and Camilla in turn deigned to provide it because it would make her look good if I was accepted at the academy, as she could claim she'd referred me. Moreover, her interest in lovers was reserved solely for those who could forward her career, and I wasn't attracted to her. She reminded me of myself, with her too-wide nose and Slavic-boned face, though I was in awe of her flair for the apathetic, which had men and women chasing her all over town. The less she cared, the more they did: It was remarkable to see.

Gerda noticed my admiration. She saw how I perked up whenever Camilla dashed in for a quick cup of tea laced with gossip about her latest amour or drug-fueled escapade at the cabaret. She was forever arriving from or preparing to depart for a party or after-hours club; the telephone in Trude's parlor indeed rang more for her than anyone else. She danced at the revue, too, but it never interfered with her whirlwind social calendar. Once when we were at work on the same night and I complained about how few tips I got, compared with the other girls, she remarked, "What do you expect? You look like a schoolgirl. No customer wants to tip their daughter." I was so dismayed that I started emulating her style, draping ratty boas over sheer blouses and not wearing a bra or panties so my frocks would adhere to my curves. I even donned a monocle like an old general because Camilla assured me that it made me look "decadent."

"It makes you look like a transvestite," said Gerda. "You don't need to do whatever she says. Camilla isn't beautiful. You are."

But beauty wasn't enough. Beauty had me cramping and limping about like an invalid from dancing every night in the revue. "I have to get into the academy," I told Gerda. "It's my only chance. If I don't start acting soon, I might break a leg. And then," I added, "you'll have to shoot me like a lame mare and carve me up to feed Oskar and Fannie."

She selected exacting roles for me to rehearse. She was erudite, demanding that I learn parts from Shakespeare and Goethe. I wasn't convinced the roles suited me, but I painstakingly memorized every line and endured staccato corrections from my drama instructor, who informed me that I had a lisp and no presence to play Desdemona.

"You're very pretty," he said, "but you have no discernible talent."

I'd heard similar sentiments before; by now, I was immune to them. I might have no talent and might never acquire it, but this was the road I'd chosen and I was not going to stop until every theater in Berlin shut its door in my face.

Shortly before my twenty-second birthday, I auditioned for the Reinhardt academy. Not for Max Reinhardt himself, who lived in Austria and directed his Berlin establishments through intermediaries, but for a committee headed by his academy director, Herr Held. Gerda had chosen a speech from Goethe's *Faust*, the role of the virginal Gretchen. Camilla scoffed. "So antiquated. It's not Marlene at all," and Gerda exploded in a rare outburst—"What do *you* know about who she is?"—forcing me to make an uneasy peace between them.

On the appointed day, I took my position on the stage before the committee. Avoiding their inscrutable stares, I flung myself into my part. "Ah, look down. Thou rich in sorrow's crown. With the grace of thy face, upon the woe on which I drown." Dropping to my knees in grief, as I'd rehearsed innumerable times in my room with Gerda, I failed to realize the stage was made of wood in a cavernous auditorium until the sound of my knees striking the boards resounded. I faltered, fighting to stay in character as I cried, "And cruel smart, Thou needest—"

A seat cushion flew through the air, landing inches from me. Horror flooded my entire being when Herr Held drawled, "Thou also needest a pillow, we think."

The committee snickered. I choked out the next three lines and fled the auditorium.

Gerda waited in the reception area; she was leaving for Munich that night. I came to a halt before her, biting back my anguish. She lifted her gaze past me and whispered, "Marlene."

I looked over my shoulder. Herr Held stood in the auditorium doorway. "Fräulein Dietrich," he said. "That was absolutely the worst incarnation of Gretchen in *Faust* that this academy has ever had the dishonor to witness."

I wanted to die. It was over. Finished. Not only had I failed my audition, for which I'd scraped, toiled, and defied my own mother, but just as she'd warned, I'd made a fool of myself.

"But," Herr Held went on, "these show promise." He brandished two of the photographs I'd included with my curriculum, listing my revue experience, modeling jobs, voice and drama lessons. "Be here next week at seven A.M. You are accepted—on a strictly temporary basis."

He turned on his heel, disappearing back into the auditorium.

Pressing her lips together to keep from shouting in joy, Gerda clasped my hand. "See?"

"Yes," I replied, and for the first time I believed it. "*Now*, I have a chance."

V

Fräulein Dietrich, if you insist on arriving late, do refrain from coming at all. This isn't an after-hours cabaret where you can make an entrance whenever you please."

Herr Held's reprimand caused my fellow students in the academy to gloat as I flung my coat and bag onto the nearest chair, yanked off my cloche, and ran a hand through my short curls as I made my way to the stage. I hated being late, but the toll of nightly performances and matinees with the revue, coupled with the demands of class, had begun to exhaust me. I'd overslept again, waking with a jolt to the cats mewling for breakfast, as Gerda had returned to Hannover for another two-week assignment. I'd had no time to bathe, throwing on my clothes and applying lipstick before I fed the cats and flew out of the boardinghouse to catch the tram.

The girls onstage gave me malicious looks. Their barbed appraisal had stalked me for months, ever since I began my studies here. I ignored them, casting a quick smile at the young man playing the lead in the play. A rash of color spread across his face. I had no interest in him, but the girls did, and their thunderous expressions gave me satisfaction.

Then I remembered the script in my bag. I'd been memorizing lines during intermissions at the revue; as I started back to the chair, Held snapped, "Where are you going now?"

"My script—"

"Yes?" He stepped before me, trim in his sleeveless pullover, pleated trousers, and knotted cravat. "You need your script to recite twelve lines?" His keen brown eyes bored into me. "We open in two weeks, fräulein. I should hope you know the role by now."

"Yes," I said and nodded. "I do of course. But the blocking—"

He stabbed his finger toward the stage. "Take your mark. And, fräulein," he said as I hastened into position, "do not try my patience. Those fluttering lashes and saucy walk do not impress me. Save it for your revue. One more late arrival and you'll be dismissed. This is the Reinhardt Academy. You are not indispensable."

"Yes, Herr Held," I muttered, crumbling under his stare.

The play was Wedekind's controversial *Pandora's Box*, which had been banned in 1904 after its scandalous premiere in Nuremberg. I had the supporting role of the vivacious trollop Ludmilla—one of the play's best parts—and forgot my fatigue as rehearsal began, sauntering through my entrances and exits with my skirt hiked up and those hips that Herr Held disdained swaying until the girl playing Lulu, our besieged heroine, stomped her foot.

"Marlene is upstaging me. Again. She *always* ignores her marks and upstages me."

From his seat in the front row, where he sat in absolute silence until we finished the run-through and he began delivering crushing criticism, Held said in a bored tone, "If she does, it's because you let her. Rather than throw a tantrum, upstage her instead. You are the lead."

I preened. Then he turned to me. "Are you planning on picking up customers after the show? You sashayed through that second act like a streetwalker. Ludmilla might be a slut, but she's also a practiced seductress, while the only thing you're apt to seduce in your current performance is a drunk sailor. Do try to show some restraint."

And so it went, all afternoon, with the cast running through the play for hours, after which Held would re-direct, have us repeat every scene while ladling as much scorn as he could muster until everyone sagged in disillusionment under his poisonous contempt.

"Two weeks," he called out, as we slinked off the stage to collect our belongings. "We open in two weeks at the Kammerspiele Theater. Be grateful it holds less than two hundred seats. If you flop, at least you won't have a thousand audience members throwing potato skins at you."

While the others trailed out, he said, "Fräulein Dietrich, a moment, if you please."

I paused warily. We'd never spoken alone. He was not given to confidences, or at least not with the female students. I'd caught him covetously surveying our male lead, however, and thought he might impart some private instruction after hours. Now as he crossed his arms at his chest, I said, "I'll be good in the play. I'd never embarrass the academy by—"

He lifted an eyebrow, bringing my assurances to a halt. "You will be good," he said, as I crunched my hat in my hands. "You are perfect for the part. But you are not Ludmilla. Not yet." He paused. "*Sie müssen mehr ficken.*"

I gaped. "Excuse me?"

"Do you not speak German? I said, you need to fuck more." Reaching into his pocket, he extracted his silver cigarette case. Flicking his lighter, he lit one, exhaling smoke. "In order to be Ludmilla, you must know what she feels, what she's experienced, what she craves. For Ludmilla, sex is a weapon. The audience wants to despise her for it. You must make them pity her instead."

I couldn't speak. Was he *complimenting* me?

"If you do not," he went on, in the same matter-of-fact tone, "you will fail. You are meant to play seductresses—women of no virtue who must redeem themselves. I've seen your modeling advertisements and photographs, I've also seen you at the revue. I know of what I speak. You cannot play innocents or tragediennes, though, like every ingénue, you are desperate to do so. Every girl dreams of being Anna Karenina, but girls like you are not made for it."

He had seen me at the revue? I'd never spotted him there, but then how could I, with the cloud of smoke in the air and hundreds of faces that coalesced into one leering visage? And I never lingered. Unlike the others, who made a point of circulating among the patrons to earn drugs or money on the side, I left through the side door to go home, as much as the extra cash might appeal.

"You live with a woman," he said, startling me again. "I saw you with her after your audition. I have no problem with it, if that's what you prefer. But women do not fuck like men. Ludmilla is not a lesbian." He went quiet, staring at me.

I deposited my squashed hat and bag back on the chair. As I started to undo my coat, he laughed. "Don't insult me. You are not to my taste." As I felt embarrassment redden my cheeks, he added, "But you are to others'. Half the men in this academy, I should think, and certainly those louts who attend your revue. You don't lack for admirers. What you lack is incentive."

He was atrocious. Imagining what Mutti might have said had she overheard this exchange, I replied coldly, "Are you suggesting I should turn tricks like a whore?"

"You are a whore." He dropped his cigarette onto the wood floor, squashing it with his heel. "All of us who perform for a living are whores. We take the public's money to entertain them for a predetermined length of time. We pretend to be who they want us to be, to help them forget their sad lives and make ourselves feel loved. We fuck them for applause. When you think about it, it's not any different from what whores do."

A burst of laughter suddenly escaped me. "I suppose not, if you put it that way."

"There is no other way to put it." His smile was reptilian. "Consider this a private lesson in the realities of our profession. Fuck the audience and they will adore you. Lie to them and all you'll earn is their disdain. No one wants to know they're being lied to. The trick, as it were, is to make them believe you are sincere, even when you are not."

He turned away. Gathering my hat and bag, I hurried out of the rehearsal hall into the violet night. I knew I should be horrified.

I was not.

*   *   *

WHEN I REACHED THE BOARDINGHOUSE LATE, having missed the tram and the omnibus in succession, Trude came out from her parlor. "Where have you been? It's your night off from the revue, isn't it? Gerda told me. She's telephoned twice already."

"She has?" I resisted a roll of my eyes. She now called several times every week, from Munich or Hannover or wherever she happened to be, never mind that Trude's telephone line was so fraught with static, we could barely hear each other. "Did she leave a message?"

"She said she'd try back later. She wanted me to tell you when you got home to stay here and wait for her call." Trude gave me an anxious smile. "She worries about you."

"Yes." I forced out a smile. "She certainly does."

As I climbed the stairs to my room, anger curdled inside me. Gerda was being impossible. She'd become obsessed with the thought that I'd seek out Camilla, reiterating her reminder that success took time and I would reap the rewards if I was patient. I'd submitted to her adage to go to work, rehearsal, voice and drama classes, and return home. But I felt as if I had exchanged one mother for another, and I did not appreciate it. As Oskar now wound between my ankles and Fannie watched balefully from the bed, our cozy room felt intolerable, a cramped space echoing Herr Held's words back to me.

The trick, as it were, is to make them believe you are sincere, even when you are not.

I crumbled stale sausage into the cat dishes, cleaned out the litter box, and then stood smoking at the window, staring into the lamp-lit darkness, hearing the electric clatter of passing trams and the din of talk and table-ware from the restaurant at the corner.

The room grew still, submerged in gloom. The cats retreated under the bed, as if they sensed my brooding mood. "Enough," I whispered aloud. "I've had enough."

I had tried to do it Gerda's way. Instead of reward, I'd learned today that I needed something I hadn't thought I lacked. My bedding of Reitz and those clumsy boys in Weimar couldn't count; I couldn't possibly find inspiration in those dismal affairs.

But there was someone who could help me. Someone in this very boardinghouse, no matter that if she found out, Gerda would throw a fit.

Evading all thoughts of Gerda or her reaction, I went downstairs and knocked on Camilla's door. It might be late, but it was still early for her. If she had the night off from work like me, she'd be home, getting ready for her late-night jaunt.

After several minutes passed, during which I banged again and then started to turn away, the door cracked open. She stood on the threshold in her black negligee, which was so transparent I could discern her long, slim body outlined within it.

"Marlene. Have you locked yourself out of your room again?"

Despite her lack of apparel, her angular face was already made up, her lips like crimson slashes and her eyes heavy with shadow, predatory in their artificial perfection.

"No. I . . . I was wondering . . . ?" My voice came to a nervous halt. For a moment, I saw myself through her eyes—gauche, tired from rushing about, dejected and clearly at loose ends.

"Yes?" She set her hand high on her hip, displaying her lacquered red nails. Like Jolie, she cultivated long nails, though I always wondered how she maintained them while handling scripts and those dreadful costumes at the revue. My nails were blunt and splintered. Any attempt I made to grow them ended in disaster when I snagged them on a loose sequin or glued one to my headdress while affixing those endless missing plumes. "You were wondering . . . ?"

"If I might go out with you tonight," I said.

Her mouth widened slightly, revealing a hint of teeth. "What a surprise," she said, after a moment. "Didn't Gerda telephone today? She must be frantic. All these out-of-town assignments of hers seem to be turning permanent. However will she protect you from so far away?"

She could be vicious. Underneath that diffident exterior, her fangs were always bared.

"She did call," I replied. "But what does it matter? I have tonight to myself and . . ." This time, I deliberately let my voice fade. Explanations were superfluous, as Camilla well knew. Besides, I wasn't about to give her the satisfaction of admitting I'd reached an impasse. As she herself had told me, the time had come to get on my knees. I just refused to admit it aloud.

"So. It's like that now, is it?" She stepped back, letting me edge in past her. "Have a drink. Or a sniff, if you prefer. I've plenty of both."

It looked as if a cyclone had ripped through her room, garments strewn everywhere, along with dirty stockings, feather boas, and crushed hats in haphazard piles beside overflowing ashtrays, soiled plates, and playbills from the revue trampled on the floor like dead moths. My hands itched with the urge to tidy up. How could she abide living in this sty?

Doubt prickled me as I glanced at the compact mirror on her low table, its tarnished surface smeared with white dust. Gerda would be furious. She despised drugs, and cocaine coupled with alcohol was Camilla's pre-ferred mix. We'd both heard her stagger into the boardinghouse after her all-night debaucheries, raving like a lunatic, waking the entire house and obliging poor Trude to help her to bed. She invariably claimed amnesia when we saw her the next day, which may have been true, considering her consumption. I'd learned from witnessing her epic outbursts that such momentary pleasures had too many drawbacks.

She now leaned over the mirror to inhale the powder. Blinking watery eyes, holding her head back so her mascara wouldn't run, she drawled, "Were you thinking of going out with me dressed like that?"

I glanced down at my flower-patterned dress. "No. I was hoping you might help me. I . . . I need to research my new part. I'm playing a prostitute and . . ." I made myself shrug.

She eyed me, her irises dilated from the cocaine. "I can't say I have anything that will fit you, *Liebling*. You're so very robust these days."

Robust? I stared at her in disbelief. I'd been starving myself again to look more like Ludmilla. But then I remembered the cream cakes I bought on the sly, hoarding them under my coat and gorging on them in my room.

And Trude kept bringing me slices of home-baked chocolate cake along with milk for the cats, insisting I must eat to keep up my strength.

"Nothing?" I motioned at the heaps surrounding us. "In all this?"

She shrugged. "Feel free to look. If you find something you like, try it on." Rising from the chaise, she wandered through the curtain of colored beads separating her living quarters from her equally disordered bedroom. "I'll just be a moment."

As she peeled off her negligee, giving me an eyeful of her taut form, on which not an ounce of extra flesh showed, I turned away to dig through the piles. I found a green silk blouse and a skirt with a high slit. Feeling her gaze through the beads as she slipped into one of her shapeless black gossamer frocks that nevertheless always fit her like a second skin, I undid my dress and slipped on the blouse and skirt. I couldn't fasten the second button on the skirt at my waist (how could it possibly fit anyone larger than a child?) but then remembered a fox fur stole Jolie had loaned me for my auditions. I could drape the stole over my shoulders, pin the dangling tails with a brooch at my waist to hide the gap from the button and—

A sharp laugh preceded Camilla, the fringed hem of her dress swinging about her silk-stockinged legs. "Now, isn't that quaint? You can be my chaperone tonight at Das Silhouette."

Through my teeth I said, "Must you be such a bitch?"

She paused. "What did you say?"

"I said I wanted your help. If all you can do is ridicule me, I'll go."

Her indifferent mask faltered. "I'm sorry. It's only when you said you wanted to go out with me, I assumed . . ." Her self-deprecatory smile was rare but genuine. "You've refused all my invitations before. I know Gerda doesn't approve of my decadent ways."

"I'm here, aren't I?" I said, and the only button on the skirt I'd managed to fasten popped loose. Camilla glanced down as I tried to hold the skirt in place, even as it unspooled and collapsed to my ankles. I stood there in my stockings and garters, nothing else on underneath.

"Well. I see you've at least taken my advice to not wear those ghastly underthings that Gerda thinks can preserve your chastity," said Camilla.

All of a sudden, I laughed. I couldn't help it. I felt ludicrous, a plump younger sister playing dress-up in my sophisticated sibling's wardrobe.

"Take that off," she said, and as I removed the blouse, she surveyed the piles. She seemed to know exactly what she was looking for, though I could find no order in it. "Here," she cried, and she plunged behind the chaise, withdrawing something black and rumpled and—

"A waistcoat?" I was hoping for something more alluring, like what Oma had dressed me in—a corsetlike garment that would both enhance and contain my offensive fat.

"Not just a waistcoat. I've the jacket with tails, too, and trousers to match. It's formal wear, darling. A tuxedo. Very posh. All the fine gentlemen are wearing it."

"You want me to dress like a *man*?"

One of her pencil-thin eyebrows arched. "Do you have a better idea? Garters and stockings may be feminine, but without a skirt or underpants, you're bound to catch cold."

"No." I shook my head, even as she walked around me, sizing me up. "I'll go upstairs, I must have something in my closet—"

"You have nothing." Her fingers were icy as she fastened the waistcoat at my back. "I've seen what you own, and while it's decent enough for desperate ingénues, if you want to make an impression, nothing you have will do." She paused, her lips at my ear. "You do want to make an impression tonight, yes?"

"Yes," I whispered, but I thought she'd make a fool of me as she unearthed a white shirt with faux-pearl studs, the coat with tails, and trousers with the suspenders still attached. I didn't want to ask whose it was. Not hers, I assumed, if she thought it would fit me. And I smelled a trace of cologne on the cloth, an unfamiliar masculine scent.

As I buttoned the trousers, which were too long, and tightened the suspenders to the right length, she assessed me. It was then that I saw something sharpen in her eyes, like the glimpse of a serrated blade. "You need a bow tie and hat." As she moved back into her bedroom to search for the items, I followed at her heels. She must have a mirror somewhere.

As I moved, I found I liked the way the trousers hung loose on me, a liberating comfort that erased any concerns of unwittingly exposing myself. I was shorter than Camilla but didn't feel like it now, as she scavenged in the piles by her bed. I looked around and spotted a half-length mirror on her closet door.

I came to a standstill.

It was nothing like when I'd seen myself reflected in Oma's undergarments. This was entirely different. Almost perverse. Standing in the glass was a shockingly androgynous figure, the shirt flattening my chest under the waistcoat, which slimmed my midsection and contained the extra width of the high trouser waist (whomever it belonged to, he was bigger than me), the curve of my hips and thighs filling out the pleats, while the cut of the tailored jacket with its tails broadened my shoulders. Reaching up, I pushed my curls from my face. I saw what Camilla must have glimpsed—my features round, flushed with youth, but with the bones of my adulthood beginning to surface, like the nascent angles of an unfinished statue.

Vanity, mein Lieber . . . *It can seduce even its own reflection.*

Camilla materialized at my side. Tying the white bow tie about my throat, she said, "Keep your hair back," and she set a black satin beret on my head. "Ravishing," she breathed. "I'm not sure I want you to accompany me now. You'll be too much competition."

"Do you really think so?" I turned to her. "You think it suits me?" I knew it did, as unbelievable as it seemed, but I needed to hear it from someone else.

"Don't beg for flattery. Sit on the bed. Let me paint you." After fetching her cosmetics, I watched in silence in the glass as she applied a touch of rouge and far too much lipstick, dark liner around my eyes, and sparkling green shadow on my eyelids.

"There. Perfect." She glanced at my feet. "Except for the shoes."

"Upstairs," I said. "Gerda . . . she has a pair of wingtips."

Camilla grimaced. "Of course she does." She waved her hand. "Go. And bring money," she called out as I raced to the door. "Das Silhouette charges by the person for a private booth."

In my room, I slipped on Gerda's wingtips after stuffing balled nylons inside, as her feet were larger than mine. Then I pinned up the trouser cuffs before I retrieved the marks I kept in a sock, tips flung at me by patrons at the revue, which I'd been saving for emergencies. As guilt stole over me, for Herr Held's advice hardly qualified as an emergency, I shoved the money into my pocket. At the last minute, I grabbed my monocle and inserted it over my left eye.

If I was going to risk everything tonight, I might as well make it worthwhile.

VI

Das Silhouette on the Nollendorfplatz was infamous for catering to the most devout degenerates in Berlin. Gerda detested it, though she'd never set foot inside the place. But we'd heard all about it from Camilla, who delighted in describing its flamboyant ambience—the frenetic American jazz that had become the rage, the open use of opium and other substances, and its serpentine vacuum tube system coiled about the walls, satisfying patrons' appetite for everything from illicit packets of cocaine to clandestine invitations not safe to convey via telephones in the booths. Sight unseen, Gerda had deemed the cabaret one of the worst—a seedy watering hole for riffraff, where acts of sordid disrepute were offered on an hourly basis.

A burly doorman detained the queue before the neon-lit entryway, signaling imperiously and seemingly at random at whomever he deigned fit to enter. He obviously knew Camilla, for no sooner had we pushed our way before him than he gave a wolfish grin and with a lewd look over me said, "And who is this delectable pussy?"

"A friend," said Camilla. "Don't be a brute. She's a virgin."

He guffawed. "Not for long," he said and waved us through the leather curtains into the coat-check area. Camilla flung her fur stole and umbrella at the pretty girl behind the counter, who had coiled braids with a big bow and wore a school dirndl that reminded me of my uniform from Schöne-berg. Then I stared as she gathered up the stole and gave Camilla her claim ticket. Not a pretty girl at all, but a very pretty boy.

He winked at me, fluttering pearlescent lashes. "Anything to check, *Liebchen?*"

"No." My lipstick felt caked on my mouth. "Nothing. *Danke.*"

"Have fun," he said, and he turned to hang Camilla's stole, revealing that his prim dirndl was so short, it sat above his naked buttocks.

"Did you see his lashes?" I whispered to Camilla as we descended a steep staircase plastered with posters. "They were beaded! Do you know how long that takes?"

"Hours and hours," she replied, fishing out her cigarette case from her little bag and fitting a cigarette into a black filter. "The ladies live only for the night. If they're not beautiful by sundown, they don't come out at all."

Ladies who were boys. It was a new world, one I struggled to assimilate as we entered the cabaret, where the air throbbed with a pungent, narcotic sweetness. Overhead, mirrored balls revolved like gigantic eyeballs, captur-ing and fracturing the smoke-infused light.

My heart quickened. Here I was at last, in Ludmilla's arena. But I was thinking less of my character than of the stories that had fascinated me in Weimar, of the rending apart of the old to let in the new. Only, in this case, the new was outrageous, an overturning of expectations—a fantasti-cal playland where nothing was as it appeared. I realized I had craved this all along—a world without rules, where I could become anything.

The cabaret was crowded to capacity, people crammed at the bar or clustered at the black-and-white tables before a stage festooned in cheap Christmas tinsel, where a squat man with a fake bosom and an askew red wig moaned naughty lyrics made famous by the Café Megalomania star, Rosa Valetti. I knew Valetti's songs; her recordings were extremely popular and lascivious, extolling the subtleties of female pleasure over the impatient thrust of a man.

Camilla led me past the tables, smiling here and there at those who called out her name. As we threaded our way through, I caught sight of a debonair man in a white dinner jacket watching us, sitting alone at a table a short distance away. I thought Camilla saw him, too; she shot a sharp glance in his direction and then pointedly looked away, quickening her pace.

"Come," she said tersely. "My friends must be here somewhere."

In my tuxedo, I felt both invisible and glaringly obvious. I tried to add a swagger to my step as the crowd thickened but found myself jostling past a group of simpering boys in skimpy peignoirs, with tattered stockings and ruffled little-girl panties. One of them smiled at me and inched up his negligee, exposing a prominent erection. It was shocking—and hilarious, especially as he saw me stare, so he reached into his panties to extract a dildo, which he put to his mouth and licked like a child with a lollypop. I couldn't help but laugh, both at his lascivious outlandishness and at the thought of what Mutti would say, her horror that her great nation of Sunday social calls and Handel could harbor such decadence. Still, despite my enthrallment, I began to regret not confiding in Camilla the true purpose for our outing. Das Silhouette appeared to be a homosexual club, where I was as unlikely to find a willing man as I was likely to—

I came to a halt. We'd reached the private booth area, where spangled curtains on sagging rods acted as makeshift walls, either closed to outsiders or draped open to reveal built-in upholstered seating arranged around tables cluttered with glasses and bottles, along with spindly telephones. Here sat an impressive array of manhood in tight-fitted jackets and silk vests, pant-sheathed legs crossed as they gesticulated to one another with cuff-linked wrists. I assumed they, too, must be homosexual, until I looked more closely and realized that not everyone was male. There were women, too, in men's apparel, some in tuxedos like mine. And when one of these women, her cheeks darkened with greasepaint to mimic a beard, met my eyes in brazen solicitation, I understood.

Camilla had dressed me like this on purpose. She thought I was a lesbian, wanting to go out on the town to be unfaithful to Gerda. She hadn't misread my intent entirely.

The woman crooked her finger at me. "I just adore a gentleman with a monocle," she purred. "So regal." Her drag companions chuckled, patting an empty space in the booth, indicating that I should join them. I turned to see Camilla drifting toward another booth.

"Don't be shy." The woman stood. She wore a dark suit and a white cravat, her hair slicked from her brow, so black it looked inky blue. "Come here. Don't you want to know if I'll let you take me from behind, Herr Monocle?"

In that moment, I did want to know, and before I could step away, she stepped before me—lithe as a knife, her hands flowing down the ribbed lapels of my tuxedo to pause, taunting, upon my breasts under the shirt.

"You're new here, aren't you?" Her breath smelled of smoke and mint. "I haven't seen you before. Such charm . . . and such tits. You must have a drink with us."

Her fingertips seemed to dissolve my clothes. I wanted to have a drink with her, and more. She intrigued me. The entire situation intrigued me. Women dressed like men, and men like women, acting out their fantasies. I found it deeply erotic. Audacious.

"I can't," I managed to say. "My friend . . . she's waiting for me."

"Friend?" The woman glanced to the booth where Camilla had disappeared. "You can't possibly be friends with her. That cunt isn't friends with anyone who can't get her a part."

"She is my friend." I smiled. "Some other time, perhaps?"

The woman sighed. "Don't wait long, *mein* Herr. And be careful of your so-called friend," she added. "She's poison."

I moved on to the booth, feeling the woman's gaze like a brand in my back. I heard Camilla's rough laughter; she had found her coterie, and half-turned to me as she regaled a heavyset woman in a frock several sizes too small, a skeletal brunette who might have been lovely had she gained twenty pounds, and a husky dyed-blond youth in a sailor cap and leather vest laced over his bare chest. A mirror with lines of cocaine and a tiny spoon sat on the table.

The boy whispered to Camilla. Her laughter faded as she looked up at me. "Back so soon? I thought you'd found some amusement back there."

I heard the bite in her tone. "Not yet."

Camilla said to the others, "This is Marlene. It's her first night here and—"

The boy clapped his hands. "A virgin. Hello, Marlene. I'm Hans. And I'm most definitely *not* a virgin, not since . . . well, I can't remember since when."

They didn't mean it in the literal sense. I was a virgin to this place, to their underground lair. "Neither am I," I replied, with a smile. "Or not for long, I've been told."

As Hans wriggled closer to Camilla to make room in the booth, she interjected, "Unfortunately, virgin or not, Marlene does have a rather impossible impediment: a lover."

"Only one?" piped up Hans as I sat beside him under Camilla's glare. Her entire demeanor had altered. I could see she was displeased but I had no idea why. Did she expect me to accept the first invitation that came my way? Was that her plan, to ensure that I found what she thought I'd come for without disrupting her night?

"Camilla misunderstands," I said. "I have no lover tonight. I do as I please. And I haven't decided who or what might please me."

I saw with a thrill that the others responded to my words, the heavy-set woman quivering, pressing her thigh against mine while the brunette nodded in cruel appreciation and Hans crowed, "Camilla, wherever have you been hiding her? She's marvelous."

Camilla's eyes narrowed. "She certainly is. Even in borrowed clothes." She paused. "But all dressed up with nothing to do. No lover, no booze, no cocaine—such a shame."

Just as I thought I might have to sniff some of the odious powder or order a cocktail, the stage show ended and a four-piece band—men in corsets and top hats—struck up a tune. The occupants of the booths around us rushed to the floor, fully lubricated and ready to gyrate. The heavyset woman whispered to me, "Shall we Charleston?" and as Camilla smirked and I hesitated, I caught sight of a tall figure in a white jacket walking toward us. I recognized him at once. It was the same man I'd seen watching us earlier, whom Camilla had pretended to ignore.

"Ooh." Hans shuddered. "Here comes my Austrian meat."

Camilla said dryly, "Rudi is Czechoslovakian. And he likes to dive, not suckle."

"Perhaps the Czechoslovakian hasn't tried it yet." Hans reclined, unlacing his vest to expose his rouged nipples as the man reached us. "Have you, Rudi? Suckled, that is?"

Rudi gave him a languid smile. He had square teeth in handsome Prussian features, a thin aquiline nose, and a defined chin. Up close, I saw he was well shaped, though not muscular like Hans. Rather, he had a sleek appearance, a man who liked to be groomed, his dark blond hair plastered with brilliantine, save for a tawny lock that tumbled onto his forehead. Splashes of red and blue light from the stage turned his crisp jacket opalescent, enhancing the bronze in his skin. As he inclined his head with old-fashioned courteousness, Camilla said indifferently, as if she'd failed to notice him before, "Back from Prague, I see. How was it? Hot, I imagine. You're tan. Did you shoot outdoors?"

As Hans giggled at the double entendre, I detected a jarring note in Camilla, almost indecipherable. Resentment? Was he the reason she had wanted me to make myself scarce?

"We did shoot some exteriors outside. I forgot to wear a hat." Rudi's voice was low, confident. As his smile deepened, I realized he wasn't like the others here—he was elegant and without artifice, fully cognizant of his appeal. A homosexual, no doubt. A man like him must be. Or maybe not. Camilla seemed to think to the contrary, and if anyone would know, she would.

He turned to me. "Who might you be?"

"Marlene Dietrich." I gazed at him through my monocle, thinking perhaps here at last was what I needed. Then Camilla said, "She's a student at the academy. Perhaps you can promise her a test? I'm still waiting for mine of course, but maybe she'll have better luck."

Definitely resentment. She wasn't joking when she said I might be too much competition.

Rudi looked bemused. "Are you an actress, Marlene?"

"I hope to be." I saw no reason to lie.

"Have you done any film work?" As he spoke, he glanced at the mirror on the table, over which the skeletal brunette was noisily inhaling cocaine from the spoon.

"A little." This time, I did lie. He had mentioned shooting exteriors; he worked in the business. All of a sudden, ambition surged in me. If he was so important that Camilla had to pretend to avoid him at first, he must be very important. She never invested time or emotion in anyone who couldn't provide opportunity.

"Really? In what?" he asked, and I wasn't sure if he was genuinely curious or merely making conversation. "I've never seen you before."

"This and that. Nothing important." I sensed Camilla start to bristle, clearly wanting to draw his attention back to her. "It's very nice to meet you, Herr . . . ?"

"Sieber. Rudolph Sieber. Rudi, to my friends. Likewise, Marlene Dietrich."

Hans said, "Oh, no. Watch out, Camilla. This virgin has claws."

I was lighting a cigarette when I realized Herr Sieber was still looking at me. I raised my eyes again. "Yes?"

"Would you care to dance?"

Hans guffawed. "Bull's-eye."

Camilla's face turned stony. Draping her arm around the brunette's shoulders, she said, "Yes. Go on, Marlene. Dance with him. You'll be the only two dancing with the opposite sex, though in your getup, who will know? How droll."

Rudi escorted me to the floor, where the Charleston had given way to a slow dance, with couples swaying against each other, kissing and fondling.

This was what I wanted, why I was here. Yet as he set his hand at my waist, I wondered if he'd responded to me or sought to goad Camilla. She'd said he preferred to dive, a euphemism that was obvious, but after what I'd seen, one could never know until proven.

He held me at a discreet distance as we danced, increasing my suspicion. Hans was beautiful. Any man here would want him. Perhaps Herr Sieber did not appreciate blatancy?

"So, you work in the picture industry," I finally said.

"And you are an actress who has done nothing important," he replied. Up close, I saw he had a slight cleft in his well-defined chin. "Do you want to act in film or only on the stage? The Reinhardt academy is quite prestigious, but they train actors for the theater, not the camera."

"I've worked before a camera; I model for magazines. And my sister's fiancé," I added impulsively, though I'd not seen Liesel in months, let alone met her boyfriend, "is Georg Wills, who manages the Theater des Westens. He says he can hire me after I finish my training."

Hearing my own rush of praise for myself, as if I were verbalizing my résumé, secretly appalled me. Why did I care about impressing this stranger? But I couldn't deny that I did. His air of sophistication, the slight pressure of his hand at my waist, and his almost disinterested smile made me feel as I had with my French schoolteacher, eager to show how skilled I was.

I want to sleep with him, I thought, and the realization opened in me like a warm bloom.

"Well, then," he said. "You have options. In Berlin these days, options are everything." He skillfully guided us away from a drunk couple. The floor was jammed. I was sweating in my tuxedo, my shirt drenched under my tails. I suddenly felt as if my inexperience was so evident, he could read it on me like a price tag—a girl playing dress-up in a naughty club.

"Do you like men?" he suddenly asked.

I started. "Why do you ask?"

He considered this. "Because I think I might want to see you again."

"Then I do. *If* you want to see me again."

His laughter was soft. "I think I must. You're extraordinary. I agree with Camilla. You should come to the studio for a test, if that doesn't present one option too many."

I went still, stunned. The dance ended. A gong sounded and another act took to the stage—boys in lace nighties, with nectarine lips and blond wigs, dragging fringed stools with protruding dildos that they proceeded to straddle. The crowd hooted; Rudi took me aside, observing the antics with a sardonic expression. Unsure as to what to say or do, I fumbled for my cigarettes in my trousers. When I extracted one, I found him with his lighter ready. As I was leaning to it, hearing the crackle of tobacco and feeling the sting in my lungs, he said, "I'm serious about the offer. I work for Joe May. Do you know who he is?"

I almost choked on my cigarette. "I do," I said. "He makes pictures."

Rudi chuckled. "He's one of the best in Germany. Your fellow students at the academy, they queue for hours to get a part, any part, in one of our pictures. So, can you come to the Tempelhof tomorrow after five? We run our tests then."

I had a sudden lump in my throat. "I can."

A hint of a smile crept across his mouth. "If you can, don't tell Camilla. She'll rake my eyes out. She's been begging me for a test, but she'll never be a picture actress. She's too overt. You, on the other hand . . ." He let his gaze pass over me. "I suggest you wear something else. As enchanting as your current apparel is, Joe prefers pretty girls who dress like pretty girls." He gave me a short bow. "*Gute Nacht*, Marlene Dietrich."

He turned and strode away as if he'd said nothing of import, as if he hadn't just upended my entire existence. A test at the Tempelhof Studio with Joe May! It was unbelievable. Had he not left me standing there, I would never have believed it. I'd have thought he was saying whatever he thought I wanted to hear to lure me into bed. Ironic, as I'd have gone to bed with him anyway, without the offer.

My evening had not gone as planned. But I wasn't disappointed in the least. I had come here to find a man and I had found one—and he could change my future.

The question was: How would I tell Gerda?

VII

The question was superfluous. Of course I wouldn't tell her until I was certain. A promise in a cabaret meant nothing, I thought the next day when I woke with a terrible headache, for I had stayed at Das Silhouette until closing, no longer caring if I met anyone else of interest, ignoring Camilla's glower as I danced with Hans and flirted with the transvestites. By the end of the night, I'd made several new friends, who insisted I must come back to the club. Camilla was so furious that she left me alone to call a taxi for myself, which depleted my emergency marks.

After I brewed coffee to get rid of my hangover and saw to the cats, I called up the revue manager to tell him I was ill. He delivered a blistering threat that if I did not show up, ill or not, he'd sack me, though I'd not missed a single performance since he hired me, while other girls dropped out like flies.

"Fine," I shouted into the telephone. "Fire me. I don't care." I slammed the receiver onto the hook, turning to find Trude with another of her anxious looks.

"Gerda won't like it," she said. "Skipping out on your job for a test."

In my excitement, I'd confided in her. I now regretted it. "Gerda isn't here. She has her own job. If she doesn't like it, she can sack me, too."

The studio was located in the Weissensee suburb. I had to take three trams and walk several blocks to reach it, arriving disheveled and lamenting my choice of attire—a white slip dress and new stockings that sagged at my knees, so that I had to keep yanking up my garters. But I gave the receptionist a bright smile and my name; a few minutes later, Rudi came out.

"I thought you might not come," he said, cupping my elbow.

"Really?" I said, and I allowed him to lead me into labyrinthine corridors abutting shooting stages and cramped offices. "You'll be fine," he assured me. "Just be yourself. You look lovely. Don't be nervous. It's only an interview and a test."

Easy for him to say, I thought. I was trembling as he took me into an office with posters tacked to the walls, all featuring pictures produced by May. A rotund, heavy-featured man wearing glasses and a scowl stood before a paper-heaped desk. He gave me one look before he barked at Rudi, "You kept me waiting for this?"

"Joe." Rudi's tone was soothing, as if he'd known the director for a long time. He drew him aside. While they murmured, I tried to hide my nerves by affecting a bored stance, a hand on my hip as I looked about in disinterest at the impressive display, though I was far from unimpressed. The posters and photos on the walls attested to May's repute; he had produced and directed a series of highly successful crime pictures, known as noirs, as well as exotic adventures like *The Indian Tomb*, whose epic lengths were screened in two parts at the kinos. I had played my violin for one of his pictures while working for the UFA: *The Mistress of the World*, starring his wife, Mia May. It was one of my favorites, about a woman's revenge and the lost treasure of Sheba.

Rudi returned to me and whispered, "Do whatever he asks."

What Herr May asked was for me to turn left, turn right, and back again. To lift my chin and look at him, then look away so he could check my profile. He asked me to smile, to pout, to feign anger, joy, and sorrow. He issued his directives with as much terseness as Herr Held at the academy, albeit without the sarcasm, before he made a clicking sound with his teeth and announced to Rudi, "She's nice looking. But too fat under the chin and she has an upturned tip on her nose. It spoils her profile."

"We can shoot her from the front. And she can diet." Rudi set his palm under my jaw and pressed upward. "She's got the right look. We only need to rid her of this excess."

Herr May looked unconvinced. "Yes, her face is unusual. Nice, as I said, but too wide. She'll look enormous on camera."

"We don't know that yet," countered Rudi. "We need to test her first."

"And no experience," added May. "The leads are already cast; we have professionals in every role. I have no time to prepare a novice. We're already running late on this picture."

"Which is why we need a fresh face for the part. She's not a novice. She's studying at the Reinhardt academy and has done some modeling. She knows enough to learn on her own."

They were talking as if I wasn't standing there, listening to them judge me as if I were a cow at the fair. I might have made a scathing remark of my own had Rudi's hand not been clamped below my jaw, keeping my mouth shut.

May made another sucking sound between his teeth. "Fine. Test her. But if I don't like it, I don't want to see her again." He turned to his desk; as Rudi steered me out the door, May said without looking up, "Eva told me she hasn't seen you since we returned from Prague. You're her husband, Rudi. Stop roistering about Berlin looking for new faces and make time for her."

Husband? As soon as we exited the office, I yanked away from him. "You're married," I said. I wasn't sure why it bothered me, but it did—quite a lot, it seemed.

"Engaged," he explained, as if that made a difference. "Eva is Joe's daughter. Come. The light is perfect now; we'll test you outside. We have a great cameraman, Stefan Lorant. He'll know exactly how to shoot you."

I found myself seething as he led me outside. He was engaged. He might as well be married. Like Reitz. Which meant complications. I had to make myself focus, remind myself that it didn't matter. I wasn't here to sleep with him. I was here to further my career.

We reached a field bordering the studio, where a man with a camera on a tripod waited. Rudi squeezed my elbow again. "Break a leg," he said, the traditional good luck phrase of theater people, before, to my dismay, he retreated back into the studio.

For over an hour, I followed Lorant's instructions as he filmed me standing by a white prop fence, sitting on the fence, falling off the fence, crawling under the fence, posing behind the fence, until I knew I must look a mess, the September balminess turning my dress translucent, my taut curls loosened into tendrils, and carefully applied makeup streaked. After Lorant was done, he showed me out. I wanted to ask him if I'd photographed well but by that point I didn't care.

And by the time I returned home to the hungry cats and rushed about preparing the materials for my morning class, followed by rehearsals all afternoon and the evening revue, if I still had a job, I cared even less.

I never expected to see Rudi Sieber again.

WEEKS WENT BY.

The play opened to a limited run. As soon as it closed, we began rehearsing Shakespeare's *The Taming of the Shrew*. Herr Held believed no actor was worthy until he could play the Bard; more important, money was scarce at the academy, like everywhere else, and repertory performances of classics made a profit. As students, we were expected to earn our share and give back to the vaunted academy, which was paving our way to a profession.

I finally surrendered to the inevitable and quit the revue; the manager did not sack me as threatened, but I couldn't devote myself to acting while dancing into an early grave. To supplement my income, I continued to go out on calls, accepting modeling jobs. It wasn't enough to pay for more than food and the roof over my head, but I managed. Gerda wired money, too. She was still in Hannover and kept telephoning with promises to return soon, though I'd begun to think that as Camilla had claimed, her jobs away were becoming permanent. It was as though she didn't want to return, I found myself thinking. As if she was pushing me to do the very thing she most feared, which was to betray her and leave.

Then one evening as I left the Deutsches Theater after another draining rehearsal with Held, who hissed that I had clearly failed to take his advice, I found Rudi waiting beside a two-seater blue automobile—a rarity in Berlin. I strode past him as if I didn't know who he was.

He ran after me, taking me by the arm. I glared. "Let go."

"What is the matter?" He appeared bewildered. "Why are you upset?"

"Upset?" I said. "Why would I be upset? You made me look like an idiot at your 'only an interview and a test.' You had that cameraman photograph me like a milkmaid. And," I added, "you left me to see myself out."

"Marlene, I had to. I couldn't influence any decision. Joe is very particular; he doesn't like me meddling with casting. I was already pushing my luck by bringing you in for a test."

"I see. Well, if you don't mind, I have a chorus to perform." I didn't, but I'd started to turn about anyway when he touched my arm again.

"You got the part."

I froze. Not wanting to believe what I'd just heard, I met his eyes. He was smiling. In the ebbing summer light, he looked so young, not like the glossy stranger of the cabaret, but who he was—a twenty-something man with more charm than anyone should be allowed.

"I—I got the part?" I said.

"Yes." He was grinning now, showing off his perfect teeth. "The test was horrible, but it showed Joe what I saw from the start. You have potential. You shine on film. I couldn't take my eyes off you."

"There wasn't anyone else to see. And if the test was so horrible, how can I have shone?"

"You don't understand yet what the camera can do. You try too hard and film exaggerates. But it knows how to capture you. All you have to learn is how to let it." He softened his voice. "It's a small part. The picture is called *Tragedy of Love* and you'll play Lucie, the judge's mistress. Two scenes, but it's a perfect introduction. And you must wear your monocle. I told Joe about how you looked in it with your tuxedo, and he agrees . . ."

A dull roar in my ears drowned out his voice. I had a part in a picture— a Joe May production, no less. If he'd said I'd been chosen for the lead, I couldn't have been more elated or grateful. Or terrified.

"I can't," I heard myself whisper. "I can't do it. I don't know how. You just told me," I went on, in a panic. "I don't know anything about the camera. I'll make a mess of it. It's Joe May. I'll never get another role again—"

"Hush." He pulled me to him, as protective as a father, though the heat coming off his body was not paternal in the slightest. "Of course you can do it. I'll be there. It's just acting, Marlene. Instead of an audience, there's a camera. It's what you want to do."

"Do I?" I murmured, and he lifted my chin. "Yes," he said. "You were born for this. You may not know it yet but you were. Trust me."

Like Gerda before him, he had seen something in me that I failed to see in myself. I allowed him to take me to his automobile. When we pulled up at the curb by the boardinghouse, he got out and opened the side door for me.

"Do you want to come up?" I asked. I wanted to return the immense gift he'd given me, the renewed hope for a future. I knew how. I'd felt the stir in his pants as he held me. I recognized desire when it was directed at me. It didn't matter if he was engaged or married. He had earned it. Besides, I wanted to; it was what I had wanted from the moment I met him. Only now, I wanted more. I wanted to feel loved, if only for one night.

"Maybe later." He averted his eyes. As I made an uncertain move toward the boardinghouse, glancing at him, motionless by his car, he said quietly, "I want you, Marlene. Very much. But not like this. Not out of gratitude or lust; I want you to want me as much as I want you. And you cannot. You have . . . other obligations."

"So do you. A fiancée. I may live with someone but I'm not engaged."

"True." He held my gaze. "But engagements can be broken. Can you say the same?"

He'd obviously spoken with Camilla, who told him everything he needed to know about my arrangement with Gerda.

"I'm not who you think I am." I turned to the door, inserting my key in the lock. "And yes," I said over my shoulder, "I can say the same. You just need to give me a good enough reason."

VIII

Filming on *Tragedy of Love* was delayed until the start of 1923. Despite his success, even Joe May had difficulty scraping together financing, but I received my script and studied my role obsessively, even as I performed in several more plays with the academy, including *Timotheus in Flagranti*, where I had three revolving roles. The play flopped after nine performances, but to my delight, Held offered me the begrudging compliment that I'd acquitted myself "better than most."

But my inquiries of fellow students who'd had minor roles in pictures forewarned me that working on a film set wasn't like the stage; nothing was painstakingly rehearsed. Scenes were often shot out of sequence, the script adjusted at a moment's notice; and while multiple takes could erase mistakes, stamina and knowledge of one's best angles were required. A primitive art, some declared it, not a civilized way to perfect one's technique.

None of which eased my anxiety, which escalated to such a point that I went to see Uncle Willi, imploring him to use his contacts to find me a role in any film starting now. I needed the experience, I said, citing my role in May's picture. He made a few calls and secured me a part in *Little Napoleon*, a historical farce directed by Ernst Lubitsch about the imperial brother's amorous exploits. I was cast as the chambermaid—a silly role, requiring giggling and conniving as I assisted my lady in evading the hero's advances. But I was before a camera and strived to learn enough about lighting and how to stay in character while a crew hovered nearby. Weeks later, I attended a screening of the rough cut and was dismayed; I looked like a fat potato with frizzy hair.

I put myself on a strict regimen. No cakes or meat or bread, I was subsisting on water and tiny slices of cheese. By the time production began on *Tragedy*, I had lost several pounds, confirmed by my frequent probing of that now-diminished mound under my chin.

I had to be perfect.

The leading actors in *Tragedy* were household names. Germans had not yet seen the Hollywood stars being minted like fresh coins across the ocean, except for Charles Chaplin, who, like the rest of the world, we worshipped. But the extreme devaluation of the mark made distribution of American pictures impossible, prompting us to grow our own crop of celebrities. On *Tragedy*, I worked with one of our most renowned male stars, Emil Jannings, famous for his rough-hewn looks and brooding persona. He played a brutal Parisian wrestler who murders his mistress's lover in a fit of jealousy and is brought to stand trial. My role as Lucie, the judge's vivacious mistress, was one of callous self-interest. The first of my two scenes was shot in close-up as I made a telephone call to my lover, cajoling him to let me attend the trial that would decide the wrestler's fate.

The day of my scene, I was so nervous that the monocle I wore along with my feathered bed gown kept falling out. Joe May grew terse, finally demanding I leave the damn thing alone. As I sat with the phone receiver in my hand, trembling and near tears, Emil Jannings came to me with a tube of spirit glue and muttered gruffly, "Glue it on."

"Thank you," I whispered, applying a bit of glue about the monocle's edges. As I inserted it back on under May's impatient regard, Jannings told me, "You're so lovely, Marlene. Too lovely for this bit of foolishness that May seems to think will be a masterpiece."

His kindness did wonders for my performance. Rudi was there, too, watching from the sidelines. Taking a deep breath, I did my entire scene in a single take, conjuring up the memory of my youthful self in Weimar with Reitz. I knew how I should look, how to use my eyes and expression to beguile an older lover, even over the telephone. After the take, the crew went silent, waiting as they always did for May's approval or denunciation.

He grunted. "Not bad. Let's do it again."

In my next scene, I sat among the packed tiers at the trial. Although the judge had not relented even given her persuasion, Lucie schemes her way in, and at the last moment, I opted to employ opera glasses rather than the slippery monocle. I hid the glasses until shooting began, then whipped them out to avidly watch like a bird of prey as the wrestler was found guilty and sentenced to die. I had no lines but made the most of my moment, imbuing Lucie with the zeal of a Roman empress on her balcony as lions devoured Christians in the arena.

After four days of shooting my scenes, May signaled to me. I expected a reprimand; opera glasses were not in my wardrobe. Rudi had loved the idea, but he, too, looked apprehensive while May scanned me up and down as he had at my initial test before he said, "The lorgnette was a good touch. But next time, Fräulein Dietrich, consult with your director *before* you make any wardrobe changes. You're not famous yet."

"Not famous yet," I exclaimed that night as Rudi drove me home. We were tipsy, having gone out to celebrate; the shoot would continue for another month, but my part was done and I was so excited, I'd thrown aside my customary guard around liquor and had four cocktails.

Outside the boardinghouse, Rudi took my hand. "He meant it, Marlene. He means that you will be famous sooner than you think."

I was bursting with elation, adrenaline coursing with more force in my veins than my intake of booze. Leaning impulsively to him, I pressed my lips to his. He did not respond, sitting as if paralyzed, until I trailed my hand to his groin. Before I could touch him, his fingers coiled about my wrist. "No," he whispered.

"No?" I drew back. "Why not?"

My suspicion about his sexuality hadn't left me. While he'd admitted he wanted me, he had made no move toward consummating it, and he liked to frequent the Nollendorfplatz, where Das Silhouette and clubs like it thrived. He had me wear my tuxedo, which I'd kept, smiling as unsuspecting women made advances and he pretended to be a stranger nursing a drink at the bar before he suddenly materialized at my side to inquire, "Darling, anything here you like more than me?" I knew that some men liked to dive and suckle, but when I asked if he was one, he laughed. "No. But I enjoy watching others want you."

Now he gave that same laugh. "I told you. I don't want our first time to be like this."

"Like what? Surely, there's no reason to—" I paused. "Do you love her? Is that it?"

He swallowed. "I thought I did. Now, I'm not so sure."

Gathering my bag and coat, I flung open the car door. "Then tell me when you are sure. But don't take too long. I'm tired of waiting."

"Marlene."

I glanced back at him. His eyes were beseeching. "Must you torment me?"

"You torment yourself. Go get married, Rudi. You obviously need it. I do not."

I didn't look at him again as I let myself into the boardinghouse. From the parlor, Trude's gramophone emitted scratchy music; my joy plummeted as the amalgam of old carpet, dust, mold, and stale cat piss overcame me. Gerda was still not home and I was back where I started—still an ingénue at the academy, still an unknown like thousands all around me, still struggling and still broke, though less so once I got paid for my picture work. I needed another job. I couldn't subsist on hope.

My entire being sagged. I didn't yet recognize my dejection as that inevitable fall from the heights of make-believe, the first pangs of withdrawal from the narcotic of the camera. Unlocking the room door, remembering I had nothing to feed the cats, I failed to notice I was not alone until the lamp switched on in the living area and Gerda said, "Where have you been?"

I stood in a daze, my coat half off my shoulders. "Been?" I repeated thickly. The effects of my overindulgence hit me like a tumbling wall. I felt sick.

"Yes. I asked, where have you been?" She stubbed out her cigarette in an overflowing ashtray. The air was dense with smoke. I wanted to tell her to open a window, the stink was awful, but I tasted vomit in my throat and had to swallow.

"I . . . I was at work."

"So I understand. Trude says you got a part in a Joe May picture." Her voice was flat. "Congratulations. I also understand you've met a new friend."

I blinked, let my coat slide down into a puddle at my feet.

"Was that him? In that fancy automobile outside? Did he drop you off after your day at work?" Gerda rose, taking a step toward me. "Don't look surprised. Trude told me a nice gentleman has been picking you up and bringing you home every night. She says he's very handsome and charming."

"He is." Anger overcame my intoxication. "But no matter what you think, Trude has never met him. He hasn't set foot inside this house."

"Oh, I doubt that."

"Doubt whatever you like." I stepped over my coat, moving to the kitchenette. My mouth was parched; I needed water.

When I had drunk my fill, settling my queasiness, I turned back around to find her in the middle of the living room, the small bedroom area visible behind her. Her suitcase lay open on the bed, belongings scattered about it. The bureau drawers were ajar, my own undergarments and stockings dangling over the edges, evidently picked through.

I had to smile. "Were you searching for a pair of his socks left behind?"

"Don't you dare mock me," she said.

My smile faded. "I'm not. I'm mocking your absurd jealousy."

"You haven't slept with him? He escorts you to and from the studio every day, brings you home every night—but he hasn't laid a finger on you?"

"Not yet." I returned her stare. "But not from lack of an invitation." I meant to disarm her, maybe even hurt her a little. I wasn't prepared for this;

I hadn't expected to find her here. She hadn't told me when she was return-ing, and between my classes, rehearsals, and the picture—I hadn't thought to ask. Or rather, I had avoided asking when she called. I had avoided it because this was the last thing I wanted to deal with.

The color drained from her face. "Are you in love with him?"

I stood quiet. She seemed to collapse into herself. "I thought so. So much for being honest with each other." She went into the bedroom, to her suitcase. Staggering forward, I said hastily, "I didn't know what to say. Nothing has happened . . ."

"You said you'd tell me the truth, remember? You said that if you ever were interested in someone else, you would let me know." Her tone was not accusatory but her words stung me with their reproach. She folded one of her skirts, stacking it in her valise. She must have been here for hours already, sorting through her garments. "I suppose this is how you have."

"It's not like that," I whispered. I felt horrible. I had known she must be told, but I'd wanted to do it in my own way, after she came back and we had time together.

She stared at me. "How is it like? You don't love him, is that it? Does he love you?"

"He . . . he says he does." He hadn't really said it, but it was how it felt. It was the only explanation I had for his reticence. "But he's engaged."

"Naturally." She chortled. "I'd expect nothing less from a charming, handsome gentleman." She paused. "But you still haven't answered my question."

She held my gaze. I had to look away. "I think . . . I might love him, too." I finally said it, for she wanted the truth and it was the only explana-tion I had for my own persistence.

"Congratulations." She began packing again, her movements method-ical, though she'd never been neat, often leaving for her assignments with an unraveled hem or sleeve poking out of her suitcase. "I'm not surprised."

"Gerda." I moved, reaching out to touch her. "Nothing has been de-cided. We haven't done anything. Don't be angry. I didn't mean for it to happen, it just did."

She flinched. "Don't." Her voice wavered. "Don't make this any harder than it has to be. I came back to tell you that I've accepted a full-time position in Munich. My editor likes my work; he thinks I can have a writing career there. I'm leaving Berlin."

"You're leaving?" I was stunned. "Just like that? What if I hadn't come home tonight?"

"I would have left you a note, asking you to join me when your picture was done. But that's never going to happen, is it? You can't. You think you're in love."

I felt a knot unravel inside me; it felt uncomfortably like relief. "He's not the problem," I said quietly. "We are. You and I . . . we want different things."

"Perhaps."

I gazed at her. "What am I going to do?"

She frowned. "You'll stay here of course. Trude would love to keep the room rented and she's very fond of you. You have plenty of work now and—"

"I had a part in a picture. Two scenes."

"There'll be more." She retrieved her stockings from a drawer. "You have Herr Charming to see to it." She wasn't being sarcastic. She seemed to honestly believe that I'd found a replacement for her, someone better equipped to fulfill my needs. But this hurt less than the fact that she'd think me so indifferent, so uncaring of what she meant to me.

"I . . . I do love you," I whispered. "I did not lie about that."

"Come now." She patted down the items in the suitcase. "I asked for the truth, Marlene." Then she went still before she said, "I wish it were true. But it isn't. And I, too, must get ahead. I can't find work in Berlin; now, I have the chance to do something meaningful with my life."

I could only look at her, dumbfounded. I'd expected anything except those words to come out of her mouth. I had underestimated her. I had thought she'd cleaved to me in order to achieve something she was incapable of, but I was wrong. She was much stronger than I believed.

"How can you say that?" I whispered. "I do love you, very much."

She smiled. "In your own way, you probably do. But it's not the kind of love I feel for you. No," she said, cutting me off, "don't make excuses. It's not necessary. I don't blame you. You are who you are; you never pretended to be anyone else. It was my mistake, thinking I could make you mine. But I want you to be happy and have all your dreams come true. You will always be very special to me."

Tears filled my eyes. "I can't believe this. I can't believe you're leaving me."

"Leaving you?" A hearty laugh escaped her. "No one leaves you. I'm simply moving to another city. You can't be left, Marlene, because you can't be forgotten." She softened her tone. "No tears. You'll ruin our good-bye."

"What about Oskar and Fannie?" I asked belatedly, thinking I'd not seen the cats and they must be hiding under the bed because of the commotion.

"Trude fetched them earlier. They adore her and she needs the company. That old cat of hers is on its last legs. She'll spoil them rotten."

"But I can care for them," I protested. "I've been doing it all this time."

"Have you? You forgot to feed them today. They were starving and their water dish was dry when I arrived. Better to let Trude do it. You're too busy for pets."

I sat down, disconsolate, watching her finish her packing. "I'll send for my books later," she said, stepping past me to put her suitcase by the sofa. "I'll stay out here tonight. I've an early train to catch tomorrow. Do you want me to wake you before I go?"

I nodded. I was about to ask her to sleep with me, one last time, but I understood how cruel that would be. "Yes," I said weakly. "I want to accompany you to the station."

But when I woke the next morning with a dull headache, the sofa was empty.

Gerda and her suitcase were gone. On the living room table, she'd left a paper with her new address in Munich, but I already knew, as she did, that I'd never visit.

IX

Gerda's departure devastated me. I had known from the moment Rudi entered my life that she and I would have to separate, as she'd never understand it, not with a man; but the reality of it wasn't easy for me to accept. She had been my friend and lover, as well as my supporter, the first to believe in me. I missed her as I never had when she'd gone away on assignments, because this time I knew she was never coming back.

I stayed in the room. Trude was indeed fond of me—so much so that she let me slide on the rent, paying her in haphazard installments whenever I could. I took more modeling and substitute chorus jobs, though my schedule at the academy was demanding, with one play after another, some running for as many as forty-nine performances each. Earning a steady income proved so impossible, I began to resent the academy, where, as students, we were expected to perform for a pittance from the box office, while otherwise supporting ourselves as best we could. In a fit of desperation, I pawned my violin for less than half its worth. I hadn't touched it in months, indeed had forgotten about it until I had to pack up Gerda's books to send to Munich. I considered visiting Uncle Willie and Jolie to ask for another loan, but I couldn't do it. It would only make me feel even more like a failure. Abandoning my violin in the pawnshop increased my sense of loss. I felt adrift, no longer sure if I would ever amount to anything.

Then one of my fellow academy actors, William Dieterle, who was establishing himself as a leading man onstage, decided to launch himself as a director and cast me in a supporting role. Pulling together a small budget, we shot his picture outdoors—a Russian fable titled *Man by the Roadside*, inspired by Tolstoy's short story about an impoverished villager who aids a stranger and is rewarded with good fortune. The dark-haired, rugged Dieterle played the mysterious stranger; I was the peasant girl who falls in love with him, complete with flaxen braids and a dirndl. It was my first experience on location, under natural light, with all the inconveniences these entailed. But the picture was well received; it picked up UFA distribution and had a decent premiere, gaining me critical notice as a "fresh-faced newcomer." I cut out this one line to paste into a scrapbook, along with the review I'd earned on my "delightful comedic turn" in Joe May's ponderous *Tragedy of Love*, which had been released shortly before, all three lugubrious reels of it.

Germany was floundering. Poverty and crime plagued Berlin. Going out at night meant risking one's life, with thievery, rape, and murder becoming so commonplace, often over a fake gold-plated watch or paste pearls, that Rudi began to insist on accompanying me everywhere.

He did not move in with me, however. We did not become lovers. I had plenty of other opportunities—Dieterle, for one, had held me closer than his script called for—but every time I left rehearsal or a performance, there was Rudi by the curbside, either with his car or on foot, dapper in his suit and bowler hat, a cigarette between his fingers as he took me to dinner, to the cabaret, or whichever sordid vaudeville house had temporarily hired me that week. And as I twirled onstage in costumes that left little to the imagination, warbling woeful tunes of the need to live and love now, for tomorrow was a ghost—a prevalent Berlin sentiment—all I had to do was peer through the fog of smoke to find him at a table, a drink in hand and a smile on his lips.

"I hate it," I grumbled as he drove me home. "I've done endless plays and three pictures to date, and nothing is happening. Joe May was mistaken. I'm definitely not going to be famous."

"Patience." He patted my knee. "These things don't happen overnight."

He sounded like Gerda, like my mother. I shot a barbed look at his hand. This time, however, he did not remove it, his fingertips sending shivers up my thighs as he parked the car.

"I'm broke." I lit a cigarette to distract myself from his touch. "Patience isn't going to buy me food. Or pay the rent. I owe Trude two months. By next week, it will be three."

He reached into his vest, extracting a bill clip. "How much do you need?"

I exhaled angrily. "I'm not your child, Rudi. If you're going to pay me, then at least let me do something to earn it."

"You will." He lifted his eyes. He had beautiful eyes, a hint of amber mellowing their chocolate hue; his eyes were always smiling, even when he was not. "I know you will."

In no mood for an argument, I stuffed the cash into my purse. As I leaned over to peck his cheek, wondering why I persisted in this bizarre courtship that had more of the dead empire in it than the urgency of today, he yanked me to him. I hadn't a moment to realize what he was doing before I felt his kiss flooding me, his mouth moist with gin from the drinks he'd had at the cabaret, his hands roving, cupping my breasts under my blouse until I gasped.

His mouth curved against mine; he breathed, "Marry me."

"What?" I pulled back.

"Marry me," he repeated. He was grinning now, and as my gaze dropped to the thrusting tent in his pants, I had to laugh. "You're drunk."

"I am. I also broke off my engagement with Eva May."

"You—you what?"

"You said you needed a good enough reason, although your obligation ended before mine. I thought it was time to give you one. What do you say? Marry me. Be my wife."

I gaped at him. "You're not only drunk. You're mad."

"Mad with love for you!" He grasped my hands. "Say yes. Say yes and I promise you, I'll make you famous. I'll make you the most famous woman in the world."

I should have paid heed to his enticement, but I was too overwhelmed. I knew by now that Rudi Sieber was considered quite the catch. Most of the girls at the academy were so envious of my relationship with him they could barely utter a civil word to me, and Camilla had ceased speaking to me at all—proof that he was both coveted and pursued. I'd begun to think he kept me dangling for his amusement. I couldn't believe a man like him, with his looks and cachet, had been celibate and pining, while I toiled at rehearsals and onstage.

"I . . . I need to think about it," I said.

"Why? What is there to think about? Don't you love me?"

I gave him an appraising look. "I might. But I prefer to see the menu before I order."

His expression shifted. Somberly, as if he were accompanying me to a funeral, he followed me upstairs to my room. It was dark, the glow of distant streetlamps filtering through the lacy curtains I'd hung at the windows. As I moved to the lamp, he said, "No. Leave it this way. I want to see you bathed in the night."

It was such an absurd sentiment, I almost scoffed. But I couldn't. My heart hammered in my chest, my mouth gone dry as he crossed the room and slowly undid my blouse. I wore a slip underneath; I'd noticed how he frowned if I went out without a bra, and as his fingers slid under the straps, I said, "You do realize I'm not a virgin?"

He raised his hand to my cheek. "Pretend you are. For tonight."

Inwardly, I shrugged, but I soon discovered I didn't have to feign. As he tugged off my skirt and sank before me, teasing my slip up above my midriff, I began to pant. His tongue flicked out, licking me. A groan escaped me. He licked again, more strongly. Shudders coursed through me. I groped for the edge of the sofa as he burrowed his mouth into my sex. God in heaven, it was divine. Gerda had done this to me, but not often. Rudi did not falter; he was eager and skilled, reducing my body to that pulsation between my thighs, his hands spread-eagling me, collapsing me onto the cushions, hiking my legs onto his shoulders as he nibbled and sucked until I cried out.

"Ssh," he said, coming up from between my legs to kiss my mouth. "You'll wake Trude."

He tasted of me. It was intoxicating, the wet of me on his lips. I didn't feel him pull off his clothes, only that suddenly he was naked, smooth yet firm to the touch—a supple body, not overly developed, but beautiful and slightly bronzed. And then I felt his hard length parting me and he whispered, "Don't move."

My hips were rising of their own accord. He held himself back, the tip of his penis at my entrance, just enough to make me want to explode. "Now," I said. "Do it now."

He smiled. It was enough. Even as the waves of my climax crested, drowning out my very breath, he slid inside me to the root. He barely thrust. He moved gently in and out, while I heard my own whimpers, my pleas for him to go faster, deeper, until he, too, could endure no more and bucked hard, crying out his release.

He fell upon me, gasping for air. After a long moment, as my heart subsided and I floated upon a cloud of waning pleasure, he said, "Does the lady wish to order now?"

"Yes." My voice was hoarse. "I want to dine here every night."

"And so we will." He kissed me. "Every night until we die, Frau Sieber."

HE WAS THE ONE TO SUGGEST that I move back in with my mother. At first, I was outraged. I had no wish to return to that dragon's lair. I'd not spoken to her since our confrontation; I'd vowed to only see her again when I could prove how wrong she had been. I had imagined the scene in my head countless times, sauntering into her flat dripping in fur and fame, flinging marks like confetti. I had never told him this, only that she and I did not get along because she disapproved of my decision to be an actress.

"But now you'll marry me," he said. "I want it to be proper. I want to fetch you for walks in the Tiergarten on Saturdays and have tea with your mother on Sunday afternoon. I want to meet your uncle and buy your engagement ring at his store. I want everyone to know we are serious."

"Engagement ring?" I looked askance at him. "With what money? And why can't we be serious living here? I see no reason to—"

We were in bed, after a rousing night of cabaret outings, dining, and lovemaking. I had the day off. I wanted to luxuriate, cook a meal, and do some much-needed cleaning, not find myself coiled in knots over Mutti.

"We can't afford both." He drew on his cigarette. "Joe May fired me."

I bolted upright in bed. "You never told me that."

"I'm telling you now." He sighed. "He didn't take my leaving his daughter well. He told me I was a cad who had broken Eva's heart."

"But we've been out every night this week," I exclaimed. "We've been going to restaurants, to the nightclubs—" I couldn't fathom his lackadaisical attitude. "I don't have a job. I haven't applied anywhere yet because I have rehearsals coming up next week for a new play at the academy. How on earth are we going to exist?"

"I have enough savings to get by for a while. I'm also going to apply for a position with the UFA; I know people there. Just think, Marlene. By the time we get married, I could be working for the most powerful studio in Germany. There'll be plenty of work for both of us."

"If they hire you. You don't work for the UFA now. My rent is due. I can't keep making excuses to Trude. That loan you gave me paid off what I owed, but not next month."

He nodded. "Like I said."

I wanted to shriek. This room was all I had, my one freedom. I was loath to give it up. I'd started to pull back the sheet to get out of bed when he said, "It'll only be for a short time, to give us respectability. You still want this, don't you? You still want to be my wife?"

At that moment, I wasn't sure that I did. His sudden need for propriety perturbed me. I had never cared much about the right way to do things, and hadn't expected him to care, either. Why had I said yes? The notion of having someone I could belong to was a lure I'd always both fought against and gravitated to. I did not like the idea of being owned, but in turn I wanted to feel safe. With everything around me seeming to fall apart, marriage to Rudi beckoned like an island. Together we could accomplish so much more than apart; he could help me advance my career, at least in theory, and I'd have him with me, a man to love and care for, a family of my own. But for how long? Could we truly be content or would the daily obligations, the chore of it, and the passage of time that inevitably dampened passion end up stifling us both?

"Marlene?" Alarm crept into his voice. "If you're having second thoughts, you must tell me. I love you. I want to marry you more than anything, but not out of obligation."

I regarded him, his eyes troubled as he met my gaze. He must love me to break his engagement and lose his job. And if I failed as an actress, as I'd failed as a musician, what would I do? At least with him, I'd have a husband. I would never again teeter on the edge of a precipice, because he would be there. And surely, I loved him, too. I had never felt like this. If he wanted us to marry, it was only because that was what people in love did.

"Is it really that important to you?" I said softly.

"Yes. Of course it is. I want a wife and children. Don't you?"

"I suppose. But I also want a husband who earns a living. Mutti will want it, too."

"I'll provide everything you need. It's going to work out. Move in with your mother, go to the academy, and keep doing plays until we wed. By then, I'll have an offer from the UFA and can recommend you for parts. The important thing is that you keep gaining experience. Forget those music halls and chorus revues; they aren't worth the effort."

"I'll have to forget my voice lessons, too," I said glumly.

"You don't need voice lessons." He wrapped his arms around me, bringing me beside him. "You sing like an angel." He started kissing me. "My beautiful wife, my angel," he said, and I closed my eyes, surrendering to him.

Marriage still felt like a whim to me, almost a gamble. I might regret it. But I had never run away from risk.

*   *   *

MUTTI DIDN'T SAY A WORD when I showed up at her door with my suitcase and bundle of books under my arm, having bid good-bye to Trude, who kept telling me I could stay as long as I liked. When I told her I was leaving to get married, her sorrow turned to delight and an unexpected, "*Gott sei Dank*. This is no life for such a lovely girl like you. You should be a wife and have babies—and with such a nice young man, too."

She practically shoved me out the door. The room would be rented again within the week; like me, there were other lovely girls in Berlin and Trude ran a decent establishment.

I installed myself in my old bedroom. I had it to myself, as Liesel lived with her cabaret manager, also engaged to be wed. My sister came to visit soon after, a diamond ring on her finger, color in her cheeks, and undeniable satisfaction exuding from every pore.

"Imagine the coincidence," she said as we sat in the parlor, sipping tea. "Both of us engaged at the same time. What are the odds?"

"Not in your favor," remarked Mutti. "Your future husbands are in the entertainment business, which is run by Jews. Forget kitchen, children, and church. Jews make the money from those who work for them. You'll both have to earn your keep."

"Georg doesn't work for Jews. He's a theater manager," said Liesel. "He earns a very good salary. He's assured me I only need to keep teaching if I want to. And Lena's fiancé—what's his name again?" she said, looking at me.

"Rudi Sieber," I replied through my teeth, wondering why I had let myself agree to live again under Mutti's thumb and Liesel's insufferable superiority. She kept flashing that ring on her finger at me like a weapon.

"Sieber?" She pouted. "That's not a German name. Is he Jewish?"

I glared at her. "Czechoslovakian. And he's a Catholic."

"Oh." She shrugged. "In any event, I'm sure he also earns a salary, even if he does work for Jews." She didn't take her eyes from me, as if her surety required my confirmation.

"He worked for the producer Joe May," I said, as I wasn't about to let her get away with exalting her fiancé over mine. "He's between jobs at the moment, but has applied for an executive position at the UFA, which, as far as I know, is not run by Jews. He's very experienced. Every studio in Berlin wants him. He's already had several offers," I lied.

Mutti made a skeptical sound. Liesel smirked. "Well, I hope he accepts one of those offers soon," she said, and the rest of our visit was tense, my silence turning her into a chatterbox, going on and on about her fiancé's excellent position until she abruptly said to me, "If your Herr Sieber doesn't take an offer, you must let me introduce him to my Georg. I'm certain he can find something. You, too, Lena. Georg knows everyone at the UFA. He can refer you to their casting department, if you like."

"I would not like," I said, biting back the retort that I'd rather sell myself on the street than go begging to Liesel and her Georg.

When Rudi came to fetch me for one of our Saturday outings in the Tiergarten, I exploded. "I can't abide it another second. Mutti doesn't say what she thinks, but she shows it: 'Lena, is that your towel on the bathroom floor?' 'Lena, must you leave lipstick on your pillowcase? There is no laundry service in this house.' 'Lena, do you recognize this? It's a broom.' Lena, Lena, Lena. I'm so sick of hearing her say my name, I could scream."

He chuckled at my uncanny imitation of my mother, and instead of another afternoon of beer, he mollified me by taking me to the Felsing store, where we met Uncle Willi and he purchased a gorgeous diamond ring for me, at a family discount—but, Willi assured us, a real diamond, nonetheless. Afterward, Willi invited us to the house, where Jolie, delighted to see me after so much time and clearly impressed by Rudi, served us strudel and coffee while Rudi charmed her with conversation and looked about at our family heirlooms with obvious interest.

"He's very handsome," Jolie said after she admired my ring and Willi took Rudi off into the library to smoke a cigar. "And so intelligent. However did you meet him, darling?"

"At a cabaret." I was so disgusted by having to pretend with my mother and my sister, I didn't care to mince my words. "I was wearing a tuxedo. He thought I was a lesbian."

Jolie's eyes widened. "Is he . . . ?"

I laughed. "No. But at first, I thought he might be."

She gave me an odd look. "Are you quite sure? These days, one never knows."

Her words took me aback. I suddenly had the disturbing thought that she'd discovered something about my uncle. I had wondered about him before, and he, too, seemed rather taken with Rudi. Jolie was also not herself; she looked tired, though impeccably turned out in her turban and jewelry, but with a strange wariness in her gaze. She'd been flirtatious with Rudi, fluttering about him, refilling his cup and plate before he'd finished what he had. I wanted to ask her what was wrong, but Willi strode back into the room with Rudi at that moment, both stinking of cigar, his hand on Rudi's shoulder as he declared, "You're very lucky, Lena. I think he's going to be a fine husband."

As we returned to Mutti's flat, I glanced at Rudi. "Did you like them?"

He squeezed my hand. "Delightful. I had no idea your family was so distinguished. The store and the house: You come from very good blood. Your uncle Willi made me promise I'd take excellent care of you."

Before I could probe further, he went on, "Even more reason for us to be respectable. I see now why your mother is so difficult to impress. Old families are like that."

And he set out to do just that, on Sundays bringing Mutti fresh-cut roses that I had no idea how he could afford after the price of my ring, and tins of Lyons tea biscuits, the kind she loved, never mind that only the expensive emporiums sold them and he still didn't have a job.

"Do you intend to squander on her every mark you've saved?" I grumbled. "She won't approve. I could marry the kaiser himself and she'd find some fault in it. Even Liesel's Herr Wills isn't up to her standards. He runs a playhouse, she says. What kind of honest man makes a living hiring mimes and actors?"

"I'm not running a playhouse," replied Rudi. "Give me time."

He had a way about him, an even-tempered approach that could set my nerves on edge even as his attentiveness wormed its way into Mutti's exacting heart, until one evening as I prepared to go with him to my performance at the academy, I heard her laughing—actually laughing—in the parlor and emerged to find her with a rare smile on her face.

"Your Rudi is most amusing," she said. "He tells me he's accepted a job at the UFA but they made him do a screen test first, though he's not an actor. He had to jump around a fence for hours. Can you imagine it? A grown man leaping about like a sheepherder."

I turned to him. "They did?" I said suspiciously, for it sounded to me as if he had cited my very experience at the Tempelhof Studio.

"It was a joke," he said after we bid Mutti good night, promising to have me back after curtain call. "She isn't so terrible. She has a certain wit, when she cares to."

"And the job? Was that a joke, too?"

He smiled. "I have a second interview tomorrow. Don't worry."

I didn't appreciate the way he now expected me to accept whatever he said at face value, but I had to concede that he'd gone above and beyond his duty to please my mother. And he was right about the job: The UFA hired him as a production assistant, a lower position than the one he'd held with Joe May, but much better paid. I pounced on his first paycheck, demanding he rent us a room somewhere. He found an apartment on the top floor of a building at 54 Kaiserallee, not far from Mutti. I had hoped to move farther away, only he again cajoled me into doing the right thing. "If we must live together before the wedding, Josephine must be able to visit us whenever she likes. We want her blessing. Once she gives it, she cannot find fault later."

"That's what you think," I retorted, but one of my neighbors turned out to be a lively brunette named Amelie Riefenstahl, or Leni, as she called herself. She was my age, twenty-two—a painter, poet, and interpretive dancer who'd traveled around Europe in an extravaganza produced by none other than my academy founder, Max Reinhardt. We became friends. An ambitious girl about town, when she invited me to go out with her and I showed up in my tuxedo, she promptly donned black trousers and a white dinner jacket, which suited her slim physique and dancer's legs.

"I'm going to be a film star," she told me as we dined at the Café Bauer and other expensive establishments where she managed to never pay for anything, always knowing someone there, usually a married man, who kept a tab for her. "Cabarets and music halls aren't for me. I love painting but selling art is such a bore, and most artists I know are as poor as Russians. I want money and fame. Where better than in the movies?"

She was another Camilla—intent on her success, no matter the cost. But I found her company agreeable, for unlike Camilla's, her avid pursuit of opportunity included me. While I found her poetry insipid and her paintings incomprehensible, and had no idea if she even knew how to act (she never mentioned any credentials aside from the extravaganza with Reinhardt), she generously referred me to casting calls where she didn't fit the stated requirements.

We made a sensation together: me in my monocle and bow tie, and she in her suit, our hair slicked back and lips bloodred as we stormed about Berlin, raising eyebrows and other things among delighted film executives, who hastened to offer us drinks and invitations to dine and dance.

I was certain not a few of these invitations ended with Leni in their bed; like Camilla, she had no compunction about sealing the deal with her body. "It's what they expect. Really, Marlene. Look around you. There are hundreds of girls, all competing for the same parts. Believe me, *they* won't think twice about opening their legs for a contract."

She was right. Most girls didn't. And I certainly had my share of offers. Rudi often worked late at the studio or went out afterward to do his own schmoozing; he expressed no concern over my gallivanting with Leni. He said it would do me good to be seen and meet people who could advance my career, so I took him at his word. But I resisted the smarmy advances and creeping hands under the table, if not out of any moral obligation. Rudi and I were engaged but I didn't know if he was faithful to me, though I assumed he was.

One night as I prepared to go out with Leni and he arrived home early from work, I asked him. From the startled expression on his face, I saw I had caught him by surprise.

"I haven't slept with anyone else since we met," he said, "if that's what you're asking."

"Not once?" I applied lipstick in the mirror, already dressed for the evening. "I wouldn't mind. It doesn't concern me." I was baiting him, trying to penetrate his unflappable reserve. Jolie's words to me had sunk in; he was not homosexual, but he must desire other women. In a part of me, I hoped that he was unfaithful; a flaw in his perfect facade would be welcome.

"I haven't." He came up behind me, trailing his finger across my nape. "Have you? Perhaps with Leni or . . . some other man?" His voice quavered.

"Would it disturb you if I had?"

He averted his eyes. "It shouldn't," he said. "Considering the business we're in."

"I see," I said. I had the feeling that my sleeping with women would disturb him less. He had enjoyed showing me off, watching women make overtures that he could intercept. Perhaps he deemed liaisons with my own gender as harmless or even erotic, but not a threat. But another man was different. With another man, he'd have to compete. He wasn't so perfect, after all, to my relief. He had a human frailty.

I shook my head. "I haven't." I refrained from adding, "Yet." The truth was, I hadn't met anyone since him who appealed to me in that way. Leni had tried. She'd attempted to seduce me but I gently rebuffed her. She wasn't really inclined, but merely did it to establish her modernity. To her, sex and power were the same thing. Taking her as a lover would spoil our friendship.

He met my eyes in the glass. "I suppose we'll have to trust each other."

I smiled. "Yes, trust is all that matters."

He did not say more, but I understood he'd tolerate an occasional infidelity if he must, as long as it didn't interfere with our relationship. It suited me, too. I was not looking for complications. And even if I'd had the inclination, I didn't have the time, not with my demanding roster of plays at the academy and preparations for my wedding.

Liesel had to marry first of course, determined to beat me to the altar after she saw the size of my ring. Georg Wills made sure she also had the necessary trappings—a lavish gown and carriage ride along the Friedrichstrasse to the Winter Garden, where their reception was held in a pavilion, with the tiered cake and orchestra.

In contrast, our finances obliged Rudi and me to conduct a subdued affair. On May 17, 1923, in the town hall of Berlin-Friedenau, we wed in a civil ceremony, with Mutti and Liesel as my witnesses and the actor Rudolf Forster as Rudi's best man. Uncle Willi gave me away; I wore a white dress with a crown of myrtle, traditional symbol of virginity. Rudi found it highly amusing and had me wear the crown to bed that night. Our exertions pulverized it; for days afterward, I was picking out crushed fragments of leaves from the sheets.

The following month, I left the Reinhardt academy after Rudi got me an audition for the producers Meinhardt and Bernauer, who operated a chain of successful theaters. Their repertoire wasn't refined, consisting of popular fare, but offered more varied roles—and a salary to go along with them. As Mutti had foretold, Rudi wasn't earning enough to fully support us, but I wanted to keep working anyway.

I appeared in six new plays and had a small part in a circus melodrama picture, *The Leap Into Life*, before I discovered I was pregnant.

X

My pregnancy was unplanned, but I'd also not made a fuss when Rudi stopped using prophylactics. He wanted a family; in my own way, so did I. Mutti was overjoyed at the news. She became a different person, as if my apparent willingness to settle into a life she approved of had made up for my former rebellious ways.

I had no trouble, save for the usual malaise and morning sickness, but I had to stop working as I entered my fifth month. Audiences didn't want to see a woman with a belly playing comedies by Molière. And to my surprise, I was content to spend time at home, without a schedule and with a nearby bathroom, with Rudi supplying cheeses, strudel, and anything else my ravenous appetite might crave, while Mutti visited every day to attend to my comfort. Though we were not affectionate, she took such good care of me that our discomfort with each other lessened; she kept telling me a grandchild was something she had always longed for.

But the moment my birth pangs began on December 17, 1924, ten days before my twenty-third birthday, the idyll ended. It took me eight hours to deliver my baby and I suffered an internal rupture, followed by an infection, with the fever and accompanying weakness leaving me disoriented. The doctor advised Rudi and me that another pregnancy might kill me.

Perhaps this accounted for my initially tepid reaction to my newborn daughter, whom we baptized with my name, Maria, but affectionately dubbed Heidede. She was healthy, already sprouting tufts of silky auburn hair, but she felt like a stranger as I held her, a foreign intruder with her wails and burping. Only when she nursed (my milk miraculously did not sour) did I surrender to rhapsody, her toothless maw clamped to my engorged nipple.

Mutti imparted endless advice, from how to avoid diaper rash to the best way to ensure an early weaning. I heard it all through a stupefied fog; as time wore on, more than devotion bound me to my child. I also sought to escape the fact that in becoming a mother, I'd forsaken more than I intended. A newborn needed constant care, and my subsequent illness had taken its toll. I refused to look at myself in a mirror or ponder the inescapable reality that while I'd been away, life had moved on without me, including my contract with Meinhardt and Bernauer.

Rudi broke the news. With the mark having soared to the unimaginable inflation rate of 2.5 million to one U.S. dollar, and with Germany facing the collapse of an already decimated economy, America had come to our rescue, implementing a plan to restore the mark to its prewar rate. In the wake of this surge in credit, Meinhardt and Bernauer had sold their theater chain to a Viennese producer. Given my absence, my contract had been voided under the new ownership.

"But there's no need to worry," Rudi assured me as I sat with Heidede at my teat, dismayed to hear I was unemployed, my figure in need of urgent attention if I ever hoped to work again. Girls who disappeared for less time than me disappeared forever, and I had put on almost ten extra kilos. "I've spoken with my boss at the UFA," he went on. "He says once you recover and the baby can be entrusted to another's care, he'll offer you a test. This new economic plan has everyone racing new pictures into production. You'll find plenty of work."

I still worried. However, I committed to nursing Heidede for eight months. Following a much-needed summer holiday by the North Sea with the baby, Liesel, and her husband, Georg Wills, who was indeed, as Mutti had declared, as oily as a salesman, remarking that my legs needed toning if I planned to show them again in a chorus. His remark so enraged me that I gave my daughter to my mother in the mornings so I could plunge into an excruciating regimen with a Swedish trainer referred by Leni. I spent three hours at the gymnasium every day on my back, pedaling an imaginary bicycle to tone my thighs and rid my stomach of stubborn excess fat. I sweated like a Trojan and was as devoted to my cause, reaping the rewards when my UFA screen test yielded me the role of the coquette Micheline in a film adaptation of *Manon Lescaut*.

The part offered more screen time than anything I'd done before, though Mutti asked sourly how I planned to contend with work and a baby. Then Rudi was fired. He offered no logical reason for it, answering my urgent questions with a diffident "I think my boss wanted to hire his nephew in my place." I thought I'd get fired, too, before shooting even started, but I was reassured that the part was still mine. Rudi suggested that while I went to work, he could stay home with Heidede. For all her dedication, Mutti was middle-aged and caring for an infant sapped her stamina. She also had her housekeeping, for like everyone else, she needed to pay the bills.

I was taken aback by Rudi's suggestion, after all his declarations about propriety and respectability. Though everything in Berlin was upside down, with people doing whatever they must to survive, the arrangement was hardly orthodox. A husband caring for a baby was not the norm, regardless of how terrible one's finances might be.

"Are you certain?" I said. "It'll seem very unusual."

"You have this picture," he replied. "I don't. Your mother is tired and Heidede needs one of us here. It might seem unusual, but it's all we can do for now. After you finish shooting, you stay home and I'll start looking for another job."

If he was fine with it, I wasn't going to complain. I was starting to feel smothered, much as I loved my daughter, bored with diapers and snatching naps whenever I could. I was exhausted; I needed to get back to work to save my own sanity. I had to have more in my life.

Mutti was not pleased. "Men don't know the first thing about rearing a baby," she said when I informed her. "Let him go out and earn a living. He's the man, not you. Men are supposed to support their families. You'll make him feel like a failure. I thought this nonsense of becoming an actress was over. You have a child. Do you want her to grow up without a mother?"

I sighed. We had come full circle. "We need money. We need it for our child. She can't live on pride alone. We still need to eat and pay our rent."

Mutti pursed her lips. Despite Rudi's assurances that he'd be fine, she scaled back her own work to help him in the mornings. I would have to make up the difference in her pay.

My role of Micheline in a picture bankrolled by the UFA and directed by the renowned Arthur Robison, with Lya de Putti, Berlin's reigning queen, in the lead, was certain to garner notice. I felt rusty, uncertain after more than a year away from acting. My first day at the Babelsberg Studio did not go well. I missed my mark several times and fumbled my lines, requiring retakes for which Robison lambasted me.

"You have one week to prepare," he threatened. "One week off to learn your lines and get this part right. If you don't return ready to work, don't return at all."

To distract me, Leni arranged a night out to the kinos, bringing along a new Chinese-American actress-acquaintance of hers, Anna May Wong, who'd recently arrived in Berlin and caused a sensation. Slithering to our seats in our gamine apparel, me in a tweed suit of Rudi's that I'd altered and paired with a bowler hat, Leni in trousers with suspenders over a vest, and Anna May in a slinky kimonolike garment that revealed plenty of thigh, we had the other patrons eyeing us in lustful admiration or intolerant condemnation.

But everything around me faded as the film began. *The Joyless Street*, directed by G. W. Pabst, starred a new revelation—the Swedish actress Greta Garbo. In a doleful plot about murder and greed in postwar Vienna, Garbo played a devoted daughter whose decision to take in a lodger leads to romance with an American lieutenant. Critics either eulogized or panned the picture, but all were unanimous in praise of Garbo. On the stage, she couldn't have gotten away with such enigmatic complexity, but the camera revered her, enhancing her poise, the translucence of her skin, and the flame in her pale eyes. Without doing much of anything, she conveyed a passion far more persuasive than mere dramatics; she had me, and everyone else, swooning in our seats.

I left the kinos in a daze, barely hearing Anna May as she told Leni, "She's already left for Hollywood. Louis B. Mayer attended the premiere of this film with the sole purpose of getting her under contract. He's announced that MGM will make her a worldwide sensation."

Anna May turned to me. "Marlene, did you hear? One picture. Garbo has become famous with one role. And you look a little like her, doesn't she, Leni? Those same hooded eyes and that beautiful white skin. Lighten your hair and you could be her sister."

I didn't think I looked anything like that sphinx who had just devastated me with her beauty. Neither did Leni, who said tersely, "I suppose there is a slight resemblance."

Anna May's eyes gleamed. "I've heard that our new star prefers violets, too."

"Violets?" I'd never heard the term before. In delight, Anna May explained it to me. "French gourmands and certain women covet the petals as a delicacy. Do you understand?"

I went still, feeling Leni's stare as Anna May used her fingernail to wipe a clot of lipstick from the corner of my mouth. "All the girls know it. Fräulein Garbo prefers to dive."

With a smile, I hooked my arms between theirs and refrained from commenting on this lurid tidbit. But the next day, I invited Anna May to lunch, plying her with questions about Garbo's technique as well as Anna May's own experiences in Hollywood—she'd made twenty-three films there, playing secondary roles, before coming to Berlin to increase her visibility—until she took my hand and said, "Marlene, you can't possibly be so blind. You walk around like you own the world yet fail to see what's in front of you. Leni sees it, though. She's so envious of you, she can barely stand it."

"Envious? Of me?" I started to laugh. "Don't be absurd. Leni knows everyone."

Anna May tightened her fingers on mine. "She may know everyone but she'll never amount to anything unless she gets it on her back. You can act and sing; you trained at the Reinhardt academy. She is obsessed with you. She wants to *be* you."

I sobered at once, recalling my broken friendship with Camilla. We'd not spoken again since Rudi, though I had once run into her at a nightclub. She was having some success lately in pictures herself, and she turned her back to me, refusing to even acknowledge my presence.

"Everyone thinks Garbo is a great actress," Anna May said, "but she's not. She simply knows that what she implies but doesn't reveal gets our attention. That is her gift. You have it, too. You just need to perfect it."

After lunch, I invited her to bed. My return to the world had woken me to everything I had missed; I found her sensual, attentive, and she returned my interest. She didn't expect more; like me, she wasn't looking for any permanency. "I'm not sure how long I'll stay in Berlin," she said. "But while I'm here, you're always welcome, Marlene."

Our afternoon of sex and advice changed me. On my way home, I submerged my guilt over being unfaithful to Rudi by pondering my career. Was I trying too much to prove myself? Perhaps I didn't need to. Perhaps all I needed to do was cultivate a magnificent indifference like Garbo. If she had become a star, why shouldn't I do the same?

I decided not to play Micheline as a flirt, but rather as a world-weary schemer. Rudi wasn't convinced; he felt it was too understated, but during the shoot, I put my theory to the test. I raised my eyes slowly, at half-mast, as if just awakened from slumber, cultivating an insouciant yawn as a foil to Manon's hysterics.

My director liked my performance. So did the critics who noticed, calling me "an arresting presence"—which brought offers to appear in a stage production of *Duel on the Lido*, portraying an amoral demimondaine, and as a Parisian playgirl on the make in Alexander Korda's film satire *A Modern Du Barry*.

Leni bared her teeth. "Are you sure you're not putting out, darling? Because you seem to be working far more than a girl who doesn't put out should."

I shrugged. I liked that she didn't know. If I had her guessing, I could make others do the same, including the public who saw me on-screen and on the stage.

My career was finally on the rise. At home, Rudi and I had to face it. He couldn't look for another permanent job until our child was older. He could take occasional work when I was available, but one of us had to be with Heidede.

He finally revealed what must have been gnawing at him all along, abetted no doubt by Mutti. "You don't want to stop working, do you? Our life together is not enough for you."

We sat at the table, having finished our dinner. I still tried to cook for him every night, as busy as I was, either on the set or the stage or racing between casting calls.

I lit a cigarette. "No," I admitted, "it's not. I want our life. But I want a career, too."

"And what about me? Am I supposed to give up my career? Imagine how it looks: I am your husband. I should be providing for you and our daughter."

"Does it matter who provides, as long as one of us does? I have work now. Rudi, you know that if I don't take opportunities when they come, there won't be any more."

"In other words, your career is more important," he retorted, but he didn't sound convincing, as though he were mouthing words he believed were the right ones to say.

"I'm telling you what I want," I replied. "Now, tell me what you want."

"I don't know what I want." He tossed his napkin on the table. "Right now, I want to take a walk." He threw on his coat and left. After washing up, I spent time with Heidede until I heard his key in the door. He came into our bedroom, where we'd set up her bassinet. "Very well," he said. "But if you don't succeed, promise me you'll give it up. I know you want this, and I want you to have it, but I won't be made a fool."

"I promise," I told him.

Thus, it was established. Following work and suppers at home to save my marks, evenings were taken up imbibing cocktails, attending the latest hit play or revue, followed by the cabarets. I tried to be seen wherever I could make an impact and make contacts, finagling my way even into the exclusive El Dorado nightclub to see Josephine Baker stage an impromptu act from her box-office-shattering *La Revue Nègre*, frolicking on tabletops in her strings of pearls and nothing else. Sleek as a panther and as gutsy as an empress, she inspired me, particularly when she sauntered among the gaping patrons singing her signature "I've Found a New Baby."

I kept up my socializing with Leni and Anna May, and Leni must have sensed the intimacy between Anna and me, for she began to openly vie for attention, emulating whatever outrageous outfit I happened to wear, until I found myself purloining one-of-a-kind items from wardrobe departments to disconcert her, such as a shaggy wolf pelt I paired with a lacy blouse, baggy sailor pants, and military boots. Leni promptly went and found herself a mottled tiger skin that she donned as a cape.

"She's absurd," laughed Anna May as we sprawled on her bed in her little flat close to the Kochstrasse, where we met once or twice a week. "Did you see her last night? She kept dragging that poor tiger skin around like she was on safari. If you ever show up naked with a feathered fan à la Baker, there will be Leni in all her glory behind you."

I lit a cigarette, inhaling first before putting it to her lips. "Speaking of La Baker, what do you think about starting our own act? We'd have fun and earn some money while we're at it."

She slid her eyes at me. "An act? Such as . . . ?"

"How about singing? We can call ourselves Sisters About Town, find bookings on the Nollendorfplatz. Not in the nice cabarets of course," I said. "They'll never take us—but the others. I'm sure we can do as well as the drag pansies or dildo queens."

"Especially if we pin violet sachets to our cooches," said Anna May. "But Leni can't carry a note to save her life. She'll be furious if we exclude her."

"Who says we'll exclude her? If she can't sing, she can introduce us and tell dirty jokes."

Anna May inched her fingers down to my navel. "Not so blind anymore. You're learning. To oust a rival, make her wilt in your shadow."

Leni glowered but refused to be left out. I imposed a strict rule: no drugs or drinking. Anna May could control herself, but Leni had a penchant for too much of everything, particularly when in a certain mood. I chose songs by Brecht and had us wear matching tuxedos, only mine was in white broadcloth. At Das Silhouette, the White Rose, Always Faithful, and other cabarets, we booked our act whenever we weren't working elsewhere, Leni warming up the crowd with a risqué comedic routine before Anna May and I took to the spotlight, her sultry voice accompanying me as I sang before an enraptured audience of rouged boys, gaudy transvestites, and besotted lesbians, smoking my lyrics as I did my copious cigarettes.

The transvestites adored me. I was besieged for advice on everything from makeup—"Marlene, is this shade of lipstick too garish?"—to accessories: "And these lamé wrist cuffs? Are they too divine or does it look like I lost the matching gloves?" In turn, I learned tricks from them, observing how they exaggerated femininity by cocking a hand higher on the hip to minimize the size of their hands or walked with the pelvis thrust forward to appear more curvaceous and distract the eye from their ropy calves.

My cabaret performances also gave me access to influential people, slumming it on the town. Theater producers often went to the cabarets to find new ideas; decadence was in, and where better to breathe it than the place where it had been born? Like Anna May and Leni, sometimes I took these influential people to bed, though my liaisons were fleeting, and were always designed to ensure that when passion faded, goodwill remained.

Margo Lion, wife of the homosexual producer-writer Marcellus Schiffer and a violet devotee who wore black lipstick and had an alabaster pallor, accosted me after my act; she and her husband wanted to cast me in their new musical revue at the Komödie Theater, *It's in the Air*, a satirical play about a department store, which mirrored the social upheaval in Germany. I had several numbers, including a song titled "Sisters," which Margo and

I performed together, two women buying underwear for each other while their boyfriends were away.

"'Perhaps it sounds pathetic,'" we sang as we pored over panties, bras, and garters, "'but we find it magnetic. Though our palms and pants get wettest, it is nothing but a fetish.'"

The song's sapphic tone was blatant and such a hit, audiences demanded encores. My other number involved singing about the joys of kleptomania while dressed in a provocative green gown with a slit up my hip, a drooping fedora, and black gloves with fake diamond bracelets on each wrist. Growling the lyrics "'We steal as birds do, despite that we are rich, for sexual licks,'" I stood motionless onstage, then took a slow, deliberate walk across the stage, casting detached glances at the audience as if they were objects I might purloin. In a rush, they shot to their feet and bombarded me with applause.

It was my first standing ovation.

Much like a magnet, it seemed indifference did indeed draw an opposing reaction.

RUDI MUST HAVE KNOWN I WAS UNFAITHFUL. I came home every night, but often so late he was already asleep. In the mornings as I dashed about, gulping coffee and selecting outfits for the day, he didn't ask where I had been and I did not volunteer it. I reasoned that as long as I didn't rub his face in it, there was nothing to say. As he had pointed out, it was the business. And we'd settled into a routine. I went to work while he stayed home with our child and his new occupation: raising pigeons on our rooftop and selling them as delicacies to local restaurants. He did all the cleaning and cooking now; he took Heidede to the park and the bakery for cakes and chocolate. She was happy and plump. He seemed content. But we no longer had much of a sex life. And while he sometimes took a temporary assignment as a production assistant or script manager, I could see his heart was not in it. He did not want a job that took him away from home, constantly fretting over Heidede, though his assignments only lasted a few weeks and we left her with Mutti, who adored her and instilled the same practical upbringing that my sister and I had.

I couldn't begrudge him. I was earning money and our daughter needed a parent; I missed her, too, when I had to work, but I was too restless for constant motherhood. I wanted the very best for her, but I wanted the same for myself, even if Mutti groused, "It's not how things were done in my day. Men worked while their wives stayed at home. You have it upside down."

From 1926 to 1928, I made nine pictures and did numerous plays, with some roles bigger than others, some dramatic or comedic. Then I had the good fortune to win a part in the film *The Café Electric*. It was shot in a studio in Vienna, a beautiful city with magnificent scenery. My leading man was Willi Forst, Austria's top male star, who proved as seductive off the set as on it. He relished flaunting himself in café society with pretty women. I was amenable, for it earned me extra press. The picture was a lurid yarn in which I played a dance-hall girl who falls for Forst's pickpocket. But my legs and wardrobe were given ample screen time, and our canny director had Forst and I perform at night in a revival of America's hit play *Broadway*, thus gaining double attention. Our affair (designed more for the press than an actuality, though we did sleep together a few times) became an item, reported in all the scandal sheets.

I did not expect Rudi to notice. Until he arrived unannounced at the studio.

"Enough," he said, barging into my tiny dressing room as I prepared for my next scene. He had a newspaper rolled in his hand, which he flung at my feet. "Look at the entertainment section. Pictures of you and Willi Forst all over the place! It's gone on long enough. Will you make me a cuckold before everyone we know?"

Ignoring the newspaper, I took a cold look at him, disheveled in his rumpled suit, as if he'd raced from the train station without pausing to comb his hair. "Where is Heidede?"

"With your mother of course. Unlike you, I care about her safety."

Fury singed my voice. "Are you accusing me of being a bad wife or a bad mother? Because," I warned, "I'll admit to the one charge, but God help you if you dare make the other."

"Which one?" He stared at me. "Which do you prefer? They're both true."

I bunched my fists. "You have a nerve. I've tolerated your inability to keep a job and raise Heidede while I pay our bills. But I will not stand for this."

"You only tolerate it because it suits you. You tolerate it because it's what you want. You love being the center of attention, even if it means breaking our marriage vows in public."

"If I broke my vows, it's only because you're a pathetic excuse for a husband," I lashed out, and then, trembling, realizing it was the first time I'd insulted him, I turned to my dressing table for a cigarette. "You're being ridiculous," I said. "Go back to Berlin. I'll be home soon enough."

"No. I will not let you make a fool of me."

He stood before me with a ham-fisted defiance that was oddly reassuring. He'd not lost his pride, at least. Yet I was struck in that moment that much as I appreciated the gesture, it came far too late. I no longer cared. "You always did think too much about appearances," I said. "I'm still your wife. Willi Forst is not going to change that."

"I should hope not. He's also married, like you. Or have you forgotten?"

"Careful, Rudi. I don't respond well to threats."

He snorted. "You respond well enough when it's in your best interest."

"Yes, and if you continue to badger me, it'll be in my best interest to stay in Vienna longer than I intended."

I saw despair overcome him then. His eyes, which had lost their smile, brimmed with tears. I was repulsed. If he started to cry, I thought I would leave him, though the very notion was anathema to me. We had a child. We had a comfortable life. I saw no reason to end our marriage, which had thus far been agreeable, over something that meant nothing.

"Rudi," I said. "Everyone is unfaithful, more or less. It's not as if I'm in love with him."

He sank onto a stool, his face in his hands. "But you're not in love with me."

I went still. I couldn't lie. There was no point. He knew the truth. I wasn't in love with him. Looking back, I probably had never been. I'd been in love with the idea of him, with his charm and nonchalance, with the illusion of security he seemed to present, not with the man he had turned out to be. I was stronger than him. I hadn't known how much so until now.

A knock came at the door, followed by the production assistant's nervous request, "Fräulein, you're expected on the set." My dressing room walls were nylon thin; no doubt everyone within earshot had overheard us shouting.

"Look at me." When he did, I said, "We are husband and wife. We have a beautiful daughter. What more do you want? To return to work? Do it. We'll hire a maid, arrange our schedules so one of us can stay home when the other is working. We can do both—"

His bitter laughter cut me off. "You don't see it. You think it's just a matter of hiring someone or rearranging our schedules. But it's more than that. I never expected you to . . ."

"What? Just say it. What did you never expect?"

"This," he whispered. "All of it. I thought you'd pursue acting for a time, but you'd eventually grow tired of it and come home. I thought it would pass. I thought you'd give up this obsession with becoming as famous as possible."

"You thought I'd give up?" I stared at him. "You were the one who told me you wanted to make me the most famous woman in the world."

He sighed. "I meant it at the time. I thought it was what you needed to hear. If I hadn't promised, you wouldn't have married me."

I curbed my anger, stamping my cigarette out in the ashtray. "Well. I believed you. I can't stop now. And I must go to work. We can talk more when I return home." As I started to move past him, he abruptly thrust out his hand, detaining me. "I've met someone," he said.

"Oh?" Though I pretended to be amused, a pit opened in my stomach.

"Her name is Tamara. She's Russian. A dancer. She worked as an extra on my last job and she likes me. I like her. But we must sneak around because of Heidede and your mother. I didn't want to cause you humiliation, but if you're not willing to do the same for me . . ."

A lump rose in my throat. I hadn't anticipated this. For a second, I wanted to hit him. He'd come all this way to accuse me of adultery, to force a confession that in reality hid another motivation. All those nights when I'd tiptoed home with my shoes in my hands, determined to never let him sleep alone, he'd been betraying me. But I held back because I understood how hypocritical it would be to berate him for something I had done and would no doubt continue to do. It was inevitable; I had no one to blame but myself. He loved me. I could have prevented this if I only submitted, as so many women did, shoving him out the door to go work instead. Perhaps he had needed it more than he ever let on, for me to be like my mother and hand him his marching orders—the ever-efficient hausfrau, reminding her husband of his proper place.

"And if I told you to not give it another thought?" I said at length.

"Then I won't. But I'm warning you, Marlene, it could be the end of us. I'm not like you. I can't give myself to whoever catches my fancy and then walk away."

"I suppose we'll have to risk it. As I said, everyone is unfaithful, more or less."

His expression underwent a bewildered change. "That's it? It's over between us?"

"That depends." I softened my voice. "I'm not like other women, Rudi. Perhaps it's not very feminine of me, but I'm not." I reached down to brush his unshaven cheek with my fingers. "I'm not in love with you but I will always love you. Compromise isn't part of who I am."

He shuddered. "Do you want a divorce?"

"Not unless you do. I'm content to stay as we are. I'll try to be more discreet," I said, with a slight smile, "but I can't promise it. If you'd rather we lived apart, it can be arranged. And if you decide in time that you want to marry someone else—well, we can discuss it then."

He nodded, though he seemed irresolute. "Yes. I think it's best if we lived apart."

"Very well. I've this picture to finish, then the play. We can arrange it afterward. Now, please go home. Heidede must miss you terribly."

I left him sitting there. I thought I'd feel pain, sorrow that what had begun with such hope had turned out to be another disappointment. I wanted to feel it. It was the end of my marriage, even if we never divorced. The line had been breached; we could never again recapture that heedless moment when we'd believed we had our entire lives together as one.

Instead, as when Gerda left me, I only felt an unsettling sense of liberation. I didn't have to pretend anymore, treading a fine balance between my career and my marriage. The less that bound me, the more I had to give, to my work and to myself. I was free to pursue whatever and whomever I pleased, even if I had to do it alone.

Or that is what I told myself.

XI

In early 1929, after having extended my stay in Austria to give Rudi time to adjust to our new circumstances, I ended my affair with Willi Forst and returned to Berlin. I'd acquired a new skill. While waiting on set for lights to be adjusted or a camera change, an extra had taught me how to play the musical saw. I found it amusing, coaxing a bow across a toothless narrow plank of flexible steel held between my thighs, while it emitted mournful vibrations. I hadn't picked up another violin, but the saw might prove useful; it kept my wrists nimble if nothing else, and upon my arrival home, I regaled Rudi with a few Gypsy tunes I had learned.

"See?" I said. "I didn't just make a scandal. I can play a new instrument."

"I'm sure Willi Forst would agree," he replied archly. "But at least it's not his organ."

I laughed. I was determined to ease the bitterness between us. As he appeared to be enamored of his Russian dancer, there was no reason for me to look the other way. I insisted on arranging a time to meet her, alone. It was the civilized thing to do. Moreover, she would have contact with our daughter and no doubt my mother, too. I had to get a sense of her character.

Tamara Matul was pretty, poised, and very thin, with a long face, red-gold hair, and hazel eyes. She was in dire need of a decent meal. I soon learned she hadn't had much luck forging a career in Berlin. By now, we had Russian ballerinas by the dozens, all fleeing the Marxist bloodbath. I admired her candor as she related her trials—she confessed she didn't have the talent to compete with Bolshoi-trained rivals—and admired even more her respect for me.

Over coffee and strudel, she told me she had no wish to usurp my place, and in a touching gesture, handed me a small package wrapped in tissue. When I opened it, I found an exquisite icon, the kind Russians revered, lacquered and beautifully detailed, fit to grace a church.

"Oh, no," I said, trying to give it back to her. "This must be worth something. You should pawn it. Have you seen the price of shoes these days? Eight hundred thousand marks for a pair of simple black heels." I laughed to offset the moment; I'd glanced at her feet when she first sat down and she was wearing soiled ballet flats. On the street in winter.

She smiled wanly. "It's my gift to you." She paused. "Have you seen the secondhand bazaars these days? Every Russian in Berlin is pawning their belongings. You could buy a dozen icons like this one—and for less than your simple black heels."

I liked her. Destitution aside, she had class. "Then I will treasure it. And you mustn't worry. Rudi and I have agreed to separate."

"Not because of me?" she said in alarm.

I flicked my wrist, calling over the waiter. "More strudel," I said, and then I leaned to her and pressed her little hand with its blunt cracked nails and visible chilblains from whatever garret she'd been holed up in. "Because of me." I winked, bringing a flush to her pale cheeks.

She promptly moved in with Rudi, while I rented an apartment nearby so I could easily visit Heidede. Mutti expressed predictable dismay, haranguing me for throwing over a good man for "frivolities," as she deemed my career. But Liesel had suffered a recent miscarriage and she was more concerned with nursing my sister back to health than with wagging her head over my deplorable modern ways.

I took some time off to devote to Heidede, who at first didn't understand why I was no longer living at home. I couldn't explain the reason to a child, so instead I tried to distract her with trips to the ice cream parlor and to the zoo, to buy new clothes and visit Uncle Willi and Jolie. She was now a sturdy four-year-old, lacking for nothing save my frequent presence, and guilt over my separation from her father made me overcompensate, lavishing her with kisses until she pushed me away with a headstrong pout.

"How can you be my Mutti?" she demanded. "No one has two Muttis"—reminding me of how much time she now spent with my mother, which didn't please me. I resolved to be a better parent, but my pursuit of new opportunities subsumed my dedication, as my Vienna frolic with Willi Forst and all its attendant publicity had suddenly made my name recognizable.

Though I still had the ring on my finger, I was free to come and go. I danced at the nightclubs and had a few brief affairs; I might have enjoyed it more had I not found Berlin changed. The hedonism had adopted a darker edge. Drugs were everywhere, with new cabarets opening in bewildering succession, all catering to lethal predilections. Boulevard vamps like the famed Anita succumbed to overdoses only to be replaced within days by others of their ilk. Even at industry parties, cocaine was heaped in glass bowls on tables and opium smoke choked the air; it seemed almost everyone I knew was addicted to something. I'd never been comfortable with excessive drinking or drug taking. It clouded the senses, turned people into strangers; I avoided the fervor, and accepted a part in the picture melodrama, *The Woman One Longs For,* playing a femme fatale who ensnares a married man, replete with numerous headpieces and slinky lingerie. The picture was a success, snapped up for American distribution after a critic for international *Variety* praised me as "a rare Garbo-like beauty." It was the first time my name had been linked with MGM's queen and the comparison spurred me on in my quest for fame.

Yet even as I sought out parts that could broaden my appeal, something menacing began to taint my city—a political movement calling itself the National Socialist German Workers' Party, commonly referred to as Brownshirts or Nazis. It was headed by an Austrian zealot, Adolf

Hitler, who'd served time in prison in 1923 for inciting a failed coup in Munich.

Few took him seriously—in fact, most scoffed at his diatribes—but his party had gained momentum, winning twelve parliamentary seats in the recent elections. His followers wore distinctive swastika-emblazoned armbands, marching down the boulevards and handing out crude pamphlets on corners, extolling a rabid nationalistic agenda that I found contemptible.

While out with Leni one day to audition at the Berliner Theater, we came across a group of these rubicund Nazi youths. They stopped us; one thrust his ideology into my hand as his circle of brown-shirted cronies contemplated us with infuriating presumption.

"We must stop the Marxist Jews from destroying Germany," the youth declared. "They've succeeded in Russia. Now, they threaten our fatherland. Read *Mein Kampf.* Save our nation by voting for Hitler as chancellor."

I glanced at the pamphlet: *When I am chancellor, I promise to provide* Lebensraum *for our people. We must annihilate the Jewish Marxist conspiracy that has stolen our dignity. Vote for me, Adolf Hitler, and I'll restore Germany to its rightful glory.*

Confident little Austrian, wasn't he? I thought. The illustration on the pamphlet, a caricature of a Jew with a hooked nose and a prayer shawl, herding schoolchildren into a synagogue over which hung a banner of the Communist sickle, turned my stomach.

I tossed it aside. "Don't you have anything better to do than harass citizens?" I snarled and strode past them, ignoring their catcalls of *"Jüdischen Hure!"*

Leni hurried after me. "Why did you do that?" she said, nervously glancing over her shoulder at the shouting youths. "They didn't insult us."

"No?" I gave her a disgusted look. "Isn't being called a Jewish whore insulting enough for you?"

"They didn't insult us at first, not until you threw their paper away."

I paused, eyeing her. I'd heard plenty of remarks against Jews; anti-Semitism was rife, running like a virulent sewer through Germany. Mutti had never been fond of them and often complained about some Jewish seamstress down the street who always overcharged her. Yet Jews patron-ized our Felsing store and ran luxurious emporiums themselves; Berlin had a large Jewish presence, particularly in the arts. Meinhardt and Bauer, who'd hired me for their theater, and Max Reinhardt, founder of the acad-emy, were Jews. I'd also worked with Jewish directors, stagehands, costume people, and actors. I had found them no different from anyone else.

"Do you agree with them?" I asked, though I was certain that she did. Leni was always keen on anything that reeked of popularity, forever chas-ing the latest fad. It wouldn't surprise me if she supported these ugly Nazis. Next week, it would be something else.

"Many people think Hitler is right," she replied. "We lost the war because of the Jews. They forced us to surrender because they are in league with the Marxists, preying on us to—"

I laughed, cutting her off. This, I knew something about. I hadn't lived with Gerda without absorbing some of her socialist inclinations. "Have you ever read history, Leni? Jews have fled Russia for centuries because of the pogroms. Do you think they'd support their own exile or slaughter? The Marxists are no more friends to them than the czars were."

Leni shrugged, revealing, as I'd suspected, that she'd not read any his-tory. "And why do you care about what Hitler says, anyway?" I went on. "He's not even German."

She squared her shoulders. "I heard him speak at a rally once. He's an excellent orator. He cares deeply about Germany. He says the Jews hoard so much wealth because they are an inferior race, and a hundred of them cannot equal one purebred Aryan."

"Does he? Then he's a purebred idiot."

"Marlene, I don't think that's fair. His party is—"

I interrupted her again. "Every time we attend a casting call or audi-tion, as we are today, someone looking to hire us will be Jewish. Can you tell?" I turned my hands into claws about my face, as Gerda had done for me in the café at our first meeting. "Do they have pointy ears and snouts like that ridiculous pamphlet? Do they hand us scripts of Bolshevik pro-paganda?"

She pouted. "That's not the point."

"I think it is entirely the point. Your excellent orator is the one making all the noise."

I began walking briskly toward the theater. She hastened to follow me. "I had no idea you cared so much about Jews," she said, with an undertone of resentment.

"I don't," I retorted. "I don't care much about politics, either. But I don't like being told what to think. And neither should you."

I paid no mind to the incident after that. Unlike Leni, I was hired for the new play at the Berliner. Called *Two Bow Ties*, it was a lavish musical modeled on hit American shows like *Broadway*, which I'd performed in Vienna and had thus won me the part. Cast as Mabel, a jazz-crazed American heiress, I sang in English and German, wore a cross-dressing tweed suit, sultry evening gowns, and enough fake jewels to make me shimmer as far as those seated in the back row. The libretto was scintillating, written by Georg Kaiser, a successful Expressionist playwright, and the production values oversized, with fifty chorus girls and revolving sets that included a luxury ocean liner. It proved to be the hottest ticket in Berlin, selling out weeks in advance, but my salary was only one thousand marks. I was in no position to quibble.

I was also unaware that the play was about to change my life.

SCENE FOUR
THE BLUE ANGEL
1930

"AND IF THEIR WINGS BURN,
I KNOW I AM NOT TO BLAME."

I

Fräulein, can you try to appear less *bovine*? You're not modeling cheap underwear."

The director's drawl was as caustic as his demeanor, though I couldn't accuse him of being ordinary. On the contrary, I found him bizarre, which was saying something in Berlin.

He stood no taller than five feet five, a few inches shorter than me—and in those riding boots with thick soles that I suspected contained lifts. He was finely made, however, from what I could see, though costumed in a poison green velvet frock coat; jodhpurs, which added girth to his thighs; white gloves; and a fringed scarf. On his head an aviator's cap sat like an afterthought. In one hand, he clutched an officer's wand—an affectation that gave him an aristocratic air that had gone out with the empire. He slashed about with this wand, jabbing it toward where I stood, regarding him with feigned boredom.

He did not bore me. Not in the slightest. He could insult me to his heart's content, for I knew how important he was, how elevating his attention could be, regardless of his eccentricity.

Everyone knew Josef von Sternberg.

At first, I hadn't believed it. When his card was delivered backstage after my evening performance at the Berliner, summoning me to the UFA's Babelsberg Studio, I ignored it. I was tired from six nightly performances and matinees, and in no humor for jokes. But then Rosa Valetti, the cabaret-star-turned-actress, whose pugnacious mug and raspy voice had charmed our audiences, came into our shared dressing room to scold me.

"Von Sternberg is here from Hollywood. He can make a career. Look at Emil Jannings: His role in von Sternberg's *The Last Command* won him America's first Academy Award for a male actor. Jannings is the lead in this new picture of his—our first UFA talkie, based on Mann's novel *Professor Unrat*. I've been cast in a supporting role. If he wants to test you for a part, *any* part, Marlene, you must go. Everyone is desperate to work with him."

Rudi echoed the sentiment. Now ensconced in domesticity with Tamara, he'd regained his interest in my work. "Von Sternberg is indeed renowned. His *Underworld* and *The Docks of New York* are heralded for their unique way of using light and shadow. And you've worked with Jannings before, in *Tragedy of Love*. Maybe he put in a good word for you."

"Jannings?" I made a rude sound. "He went to Hollywood to be a star. Why would he remember me at all, much less recommend me? We made one picture years ago."

"Well, clearly you impressed someone," countered Rudi. "But I've heard von Sternberg has no respect for actors. Rumor has it, he thinks actors should only do as they're told."

"Then he sounds like every director," I replied, but I was intrigued enough to cancel my morning off and make the trek across the city to the studio. I had no doubt that he only sought extras or supporting players. But my thousand marks had been spent on my expenses, as well as on Rudi, Tamara, and Heidede. A few days of work on a picture, no matter how insignificant the part, would supplement my income. Adding von Sternberg to my résumé couldn't hurt, either.

He wasn't friendly when we were introduced, no more than any other director. He seemed indifferent, and had only one other person with him in his office, a fidgety man holding a single sheet of paper. There was no camera, no lights or makeup people. It was an audition, not a screen test, and I felt deceived when his assistant handed me the page and von Sternberg said, "Read."

"Which lines?" I asked him.

"Any," he replied, peeling off his gloves to insert a cigarette into a long white holder that might have come from my props in *Two Bow Ties*. I noticed his hands—delicate, with slim fingers, as delicate as a child's. Then I looked up and found his gaze fixed on me.

I looked down at the page. "Lola-Lola?" I didn't remember much about Mann's novel but had no recollection of anyone by that name. There was a waterfront tart named Rosa, whose capricious sexuality brings about the ruin of Professor Unrat, the novel's titular character. Was this Lola-Lola an invented colleague of Rosa's for von Sternberg's adaptation?

"Any," he repeated, but there was only dialogue for Lola-Lola. I'd uttered one line—"So you didn't come to see me?"—when he interrupted, "Again. This time in English."

I translated the lines into my stilted English, which I could sing well enough, but rarely used in conversation. He cut me off with a flip of his wand. "Now, walk."

The office wasn't large. Trudging back and forth before him, plucking up my hem to expose my garters—this Lola-Lola character must be saucy, not unlike the heiress in my play, which he must have seen and which had prompted him to call for me—I was rewarded with a severe "Enough," followed by his bovine comment.

I now stood regarding him, anticipating his dismissal. While I was willing to tolerate his deprecation because of who he was, for the life of me I had no idea why he'd asked to see me. Judging by his behavior, I assumed that whatever reason he'd had, I had not impressed him.

His assistant leaned to him, murmuring.

"No, no," he said impatiently, the only emotion he seemed to express. "I already told you, I'll not have Jannings dictate to me. Lucie Mannheim isn't right. She's too polished. I want to hear this one sing."

That gave me pause. Lucie Mannheim was a popular film actress; she wouldn't be considered for just any part. Was I being auditioned for a major supporting role?

He shifted his gaze back to me. "Fräulein? Can you?"

I pressed my hands against my thighs. I hadn't thought the call would amount to anything, so I hadn't prepared. I didn't have any music with me.

"Do you have a particular song in mind?" I asked, and he flung his wand upward, retorting, "Any song will do. I asked if you can sing. You do know how, I presume? You sing often enough in both languages in that dreadful concoction at the Berliner."

I was starting to dislike him. "Yes. I can sing."

He greeted my insolent answer with leaden silence before he barked at his assistant, without taking his eyes from me, "Get the accompanist. And do something with her hair and wardrobe."

Before I could react to these imperious dictates, the assistant whisked me away into a nearby cubicle, where a disgruntled woman applied a curling iron to my hair, frizzing it into curls and leaving a scorched stink in the air. Then she gestured at me, saying, "Off," and as I removed my dress, she brought over a gauzy black frock. It was too large. As I tugged at the excess fabric, she clucked her tongue, and with a few safety pins, adjusted the frock to my body, bypassing the side buttons and pricking my skin through my slip.

"There. That ought to do, as long as you don't move around too much," and she pointed me out to the waiting assistant, who led me back through the office, down a passageway and into a windowless room with a piano and felt cloth tacked to the walls to muffle sound.

Von Sternberg was fiddling with a strange contraption that resembled a wood box on stilts. Despite myself, I edged toward him. "What is that?"

He stared at me as if he'd forgotten I existed. "What does it look like?" he said, but he lifted the curtain over the cabinetlike structure's opening to reveal a camera ensconced inside. "It reduces ambient noise. It's required for sound," he said, pointing to a large microphone hanging overhead. "Not that you care."

"I care," I said, bristling at his tone. "Herr von Sternberg, I may not have made a picture with sound, but I've been on film sets before. You must know that. You asked to test me and—"

"Yes, yes. I know all about your immense experience. But I wonder, have you ever actually watched yourself in one of your so-called pictures?"

Was he insulting me again? "I am told that I can act," I said. "Directors do hire me."

"They might hire you, but your acting talent remains to be seen." He motioned me to the piano, where an accompanist sat on the bench, looking as harried as everyone else I'd met. This von Sternberg was a tyrant, I thought, as I took my stance and the accompanist checked the score. I waited. And waited. Von Sternberg was fussing with the camera crank while signaling to his assistant to reposition the microphone. I smoked three cigarettes in a row, exhaling clouds of smoke, until he said, "Now."

With a frustrated sigh, I turned to the accompanist. "What am I singing?"

At this point, I truly couldn't have cared less. It was a setup, one I was bound to fail. Who would test an actress for a major supporting role without allowing her to know beforehand what she was supposed to do?

"'The Cream in my Coffee,'" blared von Sternberg from his contraption, where he had his head and arms submerged but clearly remained attuned to whatever was being said, despite the reduction in his ambient noise. "In English, if you please."

Irate at his demeanor, not to mention I barely knew the lyrics unrehearsed, I set my fourth unfiltered cigarette on the piano lid, picked stray tobacco from my tongue, and launched into an impertinent rendition of the American tune, or at least as much as I could remember of it.

"'You're the cream in my coffee. You're the salt in my stew. You will always be my necessity. I am lost without you . . .'"

I canted my head and batted my eyes, affecting a mocking falsetto, as far from a waterfront tart's husky range as I could manage. I wouldn't win the part and I didn't want it; it would be a torment to work for him, but when the accompanist stumbled over the keys, it angered me. I glared at him, puffing on my cigarette and flicking ash in his direction before I ordered him to start over. I might not win the role but I'd not be made a total fool. He began playing again. Yet as I warmed up to the ridiculous performance I created, fluting my hands about my chin like Henny Porten just to see how von Sternberg might react, the accompanist inexplicably began playing off key again. I heard von Sternberg chuckle from within his box, to no one in particular, "She sounds worse than I thought. Like a schoolgirl ringing a cowbell."

I'd had enough.

Slamming my hand on the piano lid—"Are you doing that *on purpose?*" I hissed at the accompanist. "Don't you know the right key? Is that music before you or a newspaper?"

He glanced nervously at von Sternberg, who offered no comment, his head and shoulders inside that box.

"Forget that stupid American song," I said. "Play something German instead."

The accompanist returned his gaze to me. "German?" he said, as if it were unheard of.

" 'Wer Wird Denn Weinen,' " I told him, and when he began playing, I stepped past him, climbing onto the bench and clanging my heel on a key with a discordant twang that I hoped von Sternberg captured on his microphone. Perching on the piano, I hiked the spangled frock high above my knees to expose my legs, cocked a hand on my hip like the transvestites at Das Silhouette, and gave the song everything I had. Von Sternberg thought I sounded like a schoolgirl? I'd show him what I could do. I'd give him a performance from the very pits of the Nollendorfplatz. I pitched my voice low, hoarse now from too many cigarettes, ripping the forlorn lyrics about life and love from my lips like shards.

When I was done, and raking my fingers through my damp hair—I'd started to sweat under the lights—I looked up to see von Sternberg emerge from his box.

He stood perfectly still.

In that moment, I thought that while he was rude and conceited, he wasn't unattractive. With his prepossessing nose and close-set pale eyes, his drooping inverted mustache over full lips and mop of silver-threaded dark hair swept to one side of his forehead, he was actually quite masculine, despite his stunted stature. Paternal, even, especially in that instant as his countenance seemed to soften, as if he'd just heard a recital by his favorite niece.

"Fetch Jannings," he told his assistant.

"But he—he's not here," quavered the fidgety man. "He's not due on set until—"

"He's arrived in Berlin by now, hasn't he? Fetch him."

I was left waiting for hours, changing back into my frock and chain-smoking in the office as both the assistant and von Sternberg vanished. I was about to leave myself, thinking they'd forgotten about me, when they reappeared, this time with Emil Jannings in tow.

I'd not seen Jannings since 1923 when we'd filmed my second picture together. He had left for Hollywood soon after, and it had evidently agreed with him. He'd gained weight and was now portly and dignified, sporting a goatee that accentuated his sneer. After von Sternberg had me sing again—now I sounded like I was spitting gravel, my throat chafed—Jannings shrugged, as if he'd never heard or seen me before.

"We should test Lucie," he said. "No one knows this one's name. She brings nothing of substance to the marquee. Who knows how she'll come across?"

I was about to remind him that *he* certainly knew my name. American laurels notwithstanding, both of us had started out doing casting calls and he had worked with me before.

Von Sternberg preempted me. "I don't want an insipid lady with perfect diction. I want raw. Uninhibited. I told the accompanist to flub her song. Another would have started crying or become flustered. She got angry. *That* is what I want. You cannot buy what she has. She is Lola-Lola."

I half-rose from my stool, so enraged I barely heeded the announcement that I'd just won the part. He'd instructed the accompanist to deliberately flub the song? Was he insane?

"Herr von Sternberg, begging your pardon," said Jannings, drawing himself to full pompous height, "but I am the lead in this picture and you—"

"I am the director!" Von Sternberg thumped his chest in a gesture worthy of Jannings himself in his most torrid role. "This is *my* picture. *My* script. *My* decision. Paramount loaned me to the UFA to make it. You are no one to me. Don't dare contradict me or go running to the producers, for I will resign and then we'll see how well any of you come across. Must I remind you of how your recent foray into sound went? You sounded like an elephant with a head cold. Try me and I'll find ten other actors in a minute to take your place."

Silence fell. I might have gloated at seeing Jannings tumbled from his lofty perch, until with a sidelong glance at me, Jannings groused, "I rather think she is too raw. She'll steal the entire picture with those legs. You will rue the day."

"Not if everyone does their job." Von Sternberg jabbed his finger at me. "Fräulein Dietrich, I wish to cast you as my female lead—the cabaret singer, Lola-Lola, who brings Professor Rath here to perdition." He didn't wait for me to respond, as if my acceptance was a given, turning again to his assistant. "She needs the most recent version of the script. Fräulein, come with me."

I followed him out, sidling past Jannings, who offered me a grimace. "Congratulations, Marlene," he muttered. "Welcome to purgatory."

So, he *did* remember me. I allowed myself a pert nod before von Sternberg brayed from the corridor, "Today. I'm a very busy man."

On the soundstage, where I stood dazed by the sudden turn of events, unsure about how I should feel but aware that if I took the part I'd be handing myself over to a despot, von Sternberg commandeered a ladder and scaled it. He turned on an overhead bank of lights, blinding me.

"Stand still," he said when I lifted a hand to block the glare.

He turned the other lights away, repositioning one to slash its light directly upon me.

"A mirror," he yelled to no one in particular, clambering back down the ladder. Someone hurried over with a compact; he lifted the lid, shedding powder, and held it to my face. "See that little butterfly-shaped shadow under your nose? It should always be there. Your nose has an upturned tip that mars your profile. No one should shoot you without this shadow; it means the key light is at the perfect height."

I peered at my reflection, turning my face to either side. I did see the shadow, and the effect was astonishing. That single light narrowed my features, hollowing out my cheekbones and sculpting my eyelids, reducing the problematic width of my nose.

"*Mein Gott,*" I whispered. I looked up at him.

"You can have your nose corrected later," he said. "For now, the key light will suffice." His smile revealed nicotine-stained teeth. "And your films, Marlene," he said, using my name for the first time, rolling it in his mouth like hard candy, "do you no justice. I've seen them and they are terrible. You are terrible in them. But I can change that. If you listen to me, if you do exactly as you are told, I will make you famous."

I found myself nodding, mesmerized by his lighting and his bewildering, contradictory confidence in me. Only moments before, I'd been ready to toss the part in his face. Now I wanted only for him to turn that magic light upon me so I could bask in the hypnotic visage I hadn't known I possessed.

"This picture is very important," he said. "The UFA has invested a significant sum to have me shoot it in German and English. American pictures are starting to swamp the European market. The UFA must compete; they hired me to do it. Do you understand?" he asked, and I caught my first glimpse of the cruel humor under his gruff facade, an impish grin lighting his face. "Jannings can call himself the lead all he wants, and in the novel, he is. *Professor Unrat* is the book's title. But my picture is called *The Blue Angel* and Lola-Lola is my star."

Again, I nodded, speechless.

"You must lose five kilos before we start next month," he said, as his assistant rushed to his side with the script. "And roughen your German. Your accent is too refined. I expect you to forget your Berliner air. Lola-Lola is not a good girl; she's not well bred or sophisticated. She's a whore who makes her living off men. She doesn't sip champagne or discuss art at parties. You must talk like her. Know her lines. But above all else, be her. Inside and out. Live and breathe her. Everything you feel and do until we wrap must give her substance; nothing can interfere. Can you do it? Or should I schedule a test for that insufferable Lucie Mannheim?"

"No. I . . . I can do it." I took the script he handed me, reduced to abject flesh. I couldn't comprehend it. I had no explanation, when I'd never let anyone dominate me before, but I was prepared to submit to him. Utterly. I believed everything he said. I recognized the moment for what it was: the chance I had waited for, to become what I'd always dreamed of being.

He nodded. "That will be all. I'll send for you next week to be fitted for your costumes; they'll be too small, but you say you can do this, so that extra weight must come off. Good afternoon, fräulein. I must now go convince the UFA idiots that you're my only choice. And stop Jannings before he tells them you are not." He gave me a stern look. "I believe we can prove them wrong. But whatever we do, do not ever disappoint me."

ON THE TRAM RIDE HOME, I read the script. I read it again in my apartment before I rushed over to Rudi's flat, interrupting his evening with Tamara, Mutti having taken Heidede out to the zoological gardens.

"Read this," I said, taut with excitement. "Read it and tell me if this isn't the most magnificent part I've ever been offered."

Before he could, Tamara took the pages and after a silent query, to which I nodded, retreated to the sofa. When she was finished, she said, "It's unlike anything else I've read."

I sagged on my chair, smoke from my cigarettes drifting about us. "You really think so? It's not too crude?" Trepidation overcame me. "She's a whore. It might be too much for me."

Tamara smiled, emptying my overflowing ashtray and serving me a cup of tea, while Rudi perused the script. When Tamara started to cut a slice of strudel for me, I held up my hand. "No. I have to lose five kilos."

"Five?" She looked taken aback. "In how long?"

"A month. Less, if I can manage it." I sipped the tea, glancing at Rudi, his brow furrowed as he turned the pages. Tamara sat opposite me as we waited for his verdict.

"It's the role of a lifetime," he said. "But you are right: It's also a risk. She's not nice. She's practically immoral. Rath's obsession with her kills him in the end. I don't know, Marlene."

"Don't know?" I edged forward on my seat. "But it's his obsession, not hers. He comes to see her at this cabaret, the Blue Angel, and is besotted with her. She never pretends to be anything other than what she is. He gives up his life for her."

"And she gives nothing in return. He leaves his school, his students; he wrecks himself for her. He ends up degraded, working in her act as a buffoon until she throws him over for another man and he dies of grief. I think audiences and the censors might object. It's too . . ."

"Real?" I said.

He chuckled. "Among other things."

"Then it's perfect," I declared. "Real is what I want, what I've been looking for. It's as if Lola-Lola was waiting for me. There are musical numbers, too. Did you see? Songs I'll perform in the cabaret. I don't know which ones yet, but von Sternberg made some notes in the margins, mentioning Friedrich Hollaender. He's one of our best composers."

"He is. And you certainly can sing and perform. But in English?"

"I'll learn. I'll take up lessons again." I looked eagerly at Tamara for reassurance; she nodded. "I can do this. I know I can. And the way he lit me. He has the eye of a painter. Wide distribution, he said. He's here from Paramount. What if they distribute the picture in America? It could change everything for us."

"It could." Rudi still appeared hesitant, which puzzled me. As though she sensed our need for privacy, Tamara gathered up the cups and plates to retreat into the kitchen.

"What is it?" I sat beside him.

He tried to smile. "I'm just surprised. The lead in a von Sternberg picture, the first UFA-produced talkie, opposite Emil Jannings—it's incredible."

Detecting the undertone in his voice, I set my hand on his. "If you miss working, I'll ask him to hire you. He must need professionals and you know your way around a UFA set."

"No." His smile faded. "I've accepted a job with Terra Productions for three pictures as a script assistant. Tamara is here now, to look after Heidede," he added, dampening my enthusiasm. "It's not much paywise, but I must start doing something besides selling pigeons."

"You do. You raise our daughter so I can work." My euphoria over my newfound fortune allowed me to be benevolent. I never could begrudge him for long.

"I meant later. When you are gone."

"Gone? I haven't started shooting yet."

"No, but it will happen. I always knew it would." He leaned over to me, kissing me. "Von Sternberg is no fool," he murmured against my lips. "He only sees what I saw from the start."

I kissed him back.

It was the nicest thing he'd ever said to me.

II

I went on a strict regimen. I exercised so much and ate so little, I almost fainted over my sparse meals of lean chicken and steamed carrots, without any bread, butter, or potatoes. I took up lessons again in English, too, determined to perfect it. When I returned to the studio for my fittings, I felt svelte and eager, until the efficient but harried costume matron, Resi, whom von Sternberg had obviously been nagging, along with everyone else he hired, presented the outfits for Lola-Lola.

I stared at them in dismay. "Beads and sequins? Feathered headpieces? But she's a waterfront tart. That's what he told me. This will make her look like an heiress."

"Herr von Sternberg oversaw these costumes himself. He was very specific," said Resi, with a sniff. "She may be a tart but she's a glamorous one. Now, please. I have the entire cast to fit today. If you would undress and try on—"

"No," I said. "Where is he?"

"No?" She regarded me as if she'd never heard the word before.

"I want to see him." I met her offended stare. "None of this is right. Had I known, I could have just as easily used my costumes from the Berliner. Lola-Lola can't afford these gewgaws. She has to dress like—like . . ."

My voice faded into uncomfortable silence. I hadn't considered what she might wear, assuming von Sternberg and his wardrobe experts had.

"Yes?" Resi gave me the condescending look of an older professional, whose sole interest was to keep her job and had no patience for upstart actresses with opinions. "Please do enlighten me, Fräulein Dietrich. Seeing as you have met Herr von Sternberg, I'm sure you'll wish to state your preferences to me first, before you inform our director."

"I don't know," I retorted, stung by her supercilious tone. "But none of this is right."

"Then by all means, you must wait for Herr von Sternberg. He's at the UFA offices this morning for a meeting but is due back here by the afternoon. Shall I fetch you a stool?"

She spoke as if she relished the upcoming confrontation between me and von Sternberg over my costumes, which made me realize I should indeed have my preferences ready. Not just my preferences, I decided, taking up my handbag and coat, but the very garments themselves.

I had an idea of where to look.

Returning to the city, I went to see Rudi. He was on the rooftop, tending to his caged pigeons, a leather apron tied about his person to protect his suit. I had to smile. No one else but Rudi would feed birds while wearing a jacket, shirt, and onyx cuff links.

"Marlene." He gave me a disconcerted look. "Back so soon? How did the fitting go? It must have gone well, if it only took—" He checked his wristwatch. "Less than an hour."

"Is my theater trunk still in your closet?" I asked.

He nodded. "With everything from your various places of employment that you forgot to return. Do you want help? After this, I was going to take Heidede to the park but if you need me?"

"I can manage." I turned around and paused, glancing over my shoulder. "They stink, you know. Your pigeons. It smells like a barnyard up here."

"Yes, well. They're food." He waved me off. "Go. I can see you're desperate."

I scowled. "If you'd only seen what von Sternberg wants me to wear—" I shuddered.

He returned to his birds while I marched downstairs to yank my trunk from the closet, filled to the brim with things I'd stolen from my theater and movie engagements over the years to replenish my personal wardrobe.

Heidede was delighted to join in my scavenging, squealing as I tossed out furs and shawls and flimsy dresses, capes and satin shoes and posh hats, even my opera glasses from *Tragedy of Love*. It was all marvelous, perfect for nights in Berlin, though I'd grown more attached to my masculine attire, preferring trousers with smart jackets to these items that required coordination and care, and were never warm enough for our unpredictable rain or gusty winds.

But once I had everything strewn over the bed and floor, my daughter rolling around in it like a scone in flour, Tamara chuckling at the mess, I sighed. "None of this works, either," I said, looking up at my husband's mistress. "It's too stylish. Lola-Lola isn't a fashion plate. She's—"

"Yes, we know what she is," said Tamara quickly, widening her eyes at Heidede, who sat up to watch us with a five-year-old's avid interest.

"What is she, Mutti?" asked my daughter, and I melted to hear her use that word with me.

"A naughty girl," I growled, "like you." And I swooped upon her, grabbing her about her chubby waist and smacking her with kisses, tickling her ribs until she shrieked.

When Rudi appeared, his apron gone and looking as if he'd just gone out for a cognac, he gave me an amused smile. "Not what you were looking for?"

"In the least. I need tawdry. Used. Tatty. I need—" I suddenly knew. "I need you to take me tonight to the Nollendorfplatz."

"You do?" He was startled. "Why?"

"Because I need your car. It's for Lola-Lola. I must find her clothes. At Das Silhouette."

THE "GIRLS" WERE THRILLED to see me again. I hadn't been back in a while, not since my incident with Leni over the Nazis and winning my role in *Two Bow Ties* (our friendship had cooled considerably after that, Leni claiming I'd stolen the part by showing too much leg). With Anna May's departure shortly thereafter to shoot a picture in London, it put an end to our Sisters About Town act. But transvestites marked time differently. They were loyal even during absence, provided that one was loyal in return. When I told them what I needed, they hauled me backstage to show off their wares.

"What about these lamé wrist cuffs?" one asked, pulling them out from a drawer. "You told me they made no sense without the matching gloves, but maybe for her?"

"Perfect." I stuffed them into the large tapestry bag I'd brought. I had left Rudi at the bar, where he was clearly enjoying our old ambience. "And that kimono. Whose is it?"

"Mine, *Liebchen*. And I'm very fond of it," said Yvette Sans-Souci, a regular performer at the club with the voice of a baritone and the smoothest legs I'd ever seen on a man. He must wax them every day, I thought, as I made pleading eyes at him.

He harrumphed. "Fine. But I want it back." He retrieved the kimono from its peg. "I mean it. I know how you are. 'Yvette, darling, can I borrow this? Can you lend me that?' And I never see any of it again. You took those beige gloves from me, remember, that time you were here with your friends and yours had a nasty stain. Where are those gloves now, I wonder?"

"I promise." I bent over a trunk crammed with the rattiest items imaginable, things no one but them could wear and make seductive. "Oh." I extracted a pair of oversize ruffled knickers. "I remember these. When I first came here, centuries ago," I said, winking at Yvette, "boys were running around in these under pink peignoirs. Very fetching."

The girls gave each other snide looks. "The dildo queens," said Yvette. "Sluts."

"Lola-Lola would wear them." I stuffed the knickers into my valise. "She's a slut."

"Naturally," said Yvette. "All of von Sternberg's ladies are sluts. He hates women."

I paused. "He does?"

"Oh, yes. Haven't you seen his pictures? He *loathes* them. Must be because he's so short. Little cock and all that."

"I'd fuck him," piped up Yvette's sidekick, a very thin and nervous redhead who was probably addicted to everything. "For a role in his picture, I'd do him and his entire cast."

Yvette slid his heavily mascaraed eyes at me. "Have you?"

I wagged my finger. "Wouldn't you like to know? Now, is there anything else here you think I can use? Not shoes. I have plenty of those, and your feet are too big."

"*Liebchen*, you'll strip us as naked as urchins," drawled Yvette. "What more do you want? She's a cabaret girl. She makes do with what she has. Though," he said, contemplating me, "you might think of giving her a little of you, as well."

"Like what?" I said eagerly, and Yvette's red lips widened in a knowing smile. "I'm sure you'll think of something. You always did know how to please the customer."

THE NEXT DAY, Rudi took me to the studio in his car. After von Sternberg gave him a tour of the set, his congenial air masking his fury that I'd walked out on the fitting, he couldn't resist raking his gaze over me and remarking, "I hear our costumes were not to your liking."

"I thought they were lovely but hardly . . ." My confidence in my haul from Das Silhouette evaporated. He was watching me like a raptor, as if to convey that he had no idea who I thought I was, but he was considering gutting me for dinner.

Rudi said, "You realize, Herr von Sternberg, that Marlene has often selected her own costumes. She has an infallible instinct for character and has been working very hard to create your Lola-Lola. Perhaps if you can give her a moment to show you? I find that with Marlene, it's easier to see than to listen."

Von Sternberg frowned at my husband, who stood a foot taller and was impeccable in his gray flannel suit. I remembered what Yvette had said, *He hates women,* and wondered if he might hate some men, as well. Rudi was everything he was not, at least physically.

"Very well," he conceded, though he couldn't curb the bite in his tone.

Shouldering my bag, I went behind a stack of crates containing props for the set, divesting myself of my trousers and coat to pull on the ruffled knickers, a sleeveless tunic top, tattered stockings, and low-heeled white shoes that I'd dunked in wine and then scraped with sandpaper to make them appear weathered. At the last moment, I grabbed my silk top hat. A touch of me, Yvette had suggested. What better than something from my cabaret look?

When I emerged, sauntering as the girls did, pelvis thrust forward in bawdy invitation, I glanced at Rudi's reassuring smile and then I waited.

Von Sternberg looked as if he'd turned to stone. Then he said, "I see."

I set my hand on my hip. "She's poor. She can't buy new things, so I thought—"

"Yes." An indecipherable expression came over him. He turned his back to me. "You are right," he told Rudi. "She has an infallible instinct. It's why I hired her. Will you join me for lunch, Herr Sieber? I think it's time we became better acquainted."

They left me standing there, in Lola-Lola's clothes.

Von Sternberg might never admit defeat, but I had still won.

III

She is every man's forbidden fantasy. Blue silk top hat, sleeveless black dress slashed open to reveal schoolgirl knickers, a sequin-edged gold kerchief corralling her throat and thigh-high stockings molded to her thighs, held by suspenders to a garter belt, though she is so ripe, so unfettered, her audience waits breathlessly for one of those suspenders to snap. With her hands at her hips, she strides across the crowded stage, unique among her bedraggled companions—overpainted women in flouncy dresses, smoking cigarettes—before she gestures to one on a nearby barrel, who glares at her, indignant, but vacates her seat.

Lola-Lola assumes her perch, a stuffed seagull bobbing on a wire at her side. As she raises one leg and curls her arm about her knee, she leans back to croon in her smoke-and-dagger voice, " 'Falling in love again. Never wanted to. What's a girl to do? I can't help it . . .' "

And as she sings, she gazes to the balcony hung with life preservers, where Professor Rath sits, the unwitting guest of honor, pudgy hands clasped before him as if in prayer, flanked by the masthead of a bare-breasted siren as the siren on the gaudy stage below smiles with covert knowledge, as if she can feel his growing erection, beckoning with her eyes, promising—

"Sow!" bellowed von Sternberg. "Pull up your panties. I can see your gash."

On his balcony, Jannings guffawed. "I can see it, too. From all the way up here."

I hastily closed my thighs, almost tumbling off the barrel. With a beseeching look at von Sternberg as he emerged from behind the box camera, I said, "It's the underwear. It stretches out. This is our hundredth take and—"

"A hundred and one now," he interrupted. "Again. And try to remember this time that our censors won't appreciate seeing your pubic hair, much as you like to show it."

I avoided looking past the snickering crew to where Leni and her new director-friend Arnold Fanck stood. He had "discovered" her and turned her into an Alpine heroine in his grandiose landscape films. She had insisted on coming to see me on the set and now watched with sharp eyes, reveling in my humiliation. She'd wanted the part of course. She telephoned me as soon as she heard the news, though we'd not spoken in months. According to her, she and every other actress in Berlin had campaigned for it.

"Lucie Mannheim took ill," she told me. "She had to go away for a cure. Von Sternberg promised her the role, so she introduced him to Höllaender. But he only hired the composer. Everyone is wondering what you did to earn it, if someone as famous as Lucie could not."

"Nothing," I said. "I didn't even know what he was testing me for."

"Marlene, please. You must have done *something*. After all, he is a Jew."

I hung up on her. But she finagled an invitation to the set anyway, wielding her director's cachet; everyone who was anyone in Berlin came. They were agog. Already the UFA churned out advance publicity, their concern over the disastrous stock-market crash in America, known as Black Tuesday, hurling the studio executives into panic. Von Sternberg was on a tight schedule and a tighter budget, on loan with penalty fees in his contract, payable by the UFA for every day he went past the wrap date. When the UFA rats, as he'd dubbed them, arrived to tell him he must hasten things along, his roar was so loud that those of us waiting on the set could hear him.

"I'll not be thwarted by such petty concerns. This film must be shot sequentially, in German and then in English. I must be left alone to fulfill my vision!"

The rats obliged. They had no choice. They'd invested $360,000— the highest budget for any picture made in Germany. Of that amount, my pay was 20,000 marks, a mere tenth of Jannings's salary, but for me the money was the least of it. I knew von Sternberg had much more in mind for me, that his rage and copious insults only fueled his artistry.

I had discovered fury was his most defining characteristic. He had so much of it pent up inside him, the legacy of a troubled past that he had shared with me and Rudi over dinners at the flat, often joining us after the long days of shooting like a lost soul seeking shelter. Fury at his father, who'd beaten and neglected him; fury at the deprivations of his childhood in Austria, where a lack of proper nutrition had stunted his growth; fury at all the menial jobs and apprenticeships he'd taken in America in his youth, working under directors he deemed unfit to sweep cuttings off the floor. But most of all, fury with himself, for craving more than he had.

I understood. To me, he was a genius. I made it my mission to provide him with solace, to anticipate whatever he might need, from the goulash we could eat between takes for lunch to a fresh pencil to gouge the script, which he was endlessly revising; from cups of steaming coffee to keep him on his feet to his inevitable invitation to take me to bed.

I knew it was coming. Whenever he dined with us at the flat, where I happily cooked his favorite meal of pork chops and sauerkraut, I could feel his stare following me, so intent on my every move that even Rudi pulled me aside to whisper, "He's in love with you, Marlene."

"Nonsense." I peered over Rudi's shoulder to where von Sternberg sat on the sofa, chatting with Tamara while Heidede, fascinated by him, played with his discarded gloves and officer's wand. "He's lonely. He's married but his wife went back to America and he's alone, shooting an important picture and fighting constantly with the UFA. He's under tremendous pressure. Besides, you know how infatuations develop during shoots and how they always end when the camera stops."

"That may be part of it," said Rudi. "But the other part, the darker part, goes much deeper. Be careful. He's haunted by his obsessions. I like him very much. He's unlike any filmmaker we've ever known. But I also think he must be quite mad."

"Some might say the same of you with your pigeons," I replied, smiling.

But that very night, when I accompanied von Sternberg to the Stadtbahn—he preferred the overhead railway for traveling to and from his hotel, saying it gave him the privilege of seeing ordinary people doing ordinary things—he suddenly gripped my hand.

"I must have you. I can't wait any longer."

I might have laughed at his clichéd declaration, so out of character from the dictator in the studio, but he held my fingers with such force, he was hurting me.

"Come now." I pried my hand away. "We work together. It's not wise to risk our professional relationship for—"

"When have you ever cared about that? I know everything," he hissed. "I know you never give a shit about professional relationships if you like someone. Or is it me?" His face turned thunderous. "Am I not good enough for you? Too squat and foul for my fine Berlin lady who must rehearse her lines every night in the mirror so she can sound like a whore?"

His unwitting echo of the way Yvette had described him gave me pause. In autumn's evening light, which always turned Berlin the cool hue of steel, I didn't see the master I coddled on the set or suffered in silence as he shouted like a maniac. I saw a strange little man bedeviled by inadequacies—haunted, as Rudi had said, by his obsessions.

"One time," I told him. "I won't be your lover. Just once."

"Once is all I desire," he said.

He was a fierce lover, so conscious of his frail appearance with his pallid hirsute chest and bowed thighs that he attacked me like an acrobat. As he lavished his fascination upon me, I could feel the anguish in his poet's hands, in the scratch of his mustache between my splayed thighs, and the stubby penis he thrust into me like vengeance.

"You are my muse," he whispered afterward, "my Circe. You will not betray me. You will never disappoint. You are everything to me."

He did not hate women, I realized. He worshipped at our altar like a penitent.

Josef von Sternberg might seek to mold me to his image, but I soon learned how much I could shape him with mine.

AS SHOOTING PROGRESSED, Emil Jannings began to openly detest me. In only three months, from November 4, 1929, to January 30, 1930, the time it took to complete *The Blue Angel,* he became my avowed foe. Unlike me, he dreaded the microphone. In America, his career had faltered with the advent of sound. Insecure about his delivery, which tended to the ponderous, he trembled every time von Sternberg berated him for speaking his lines "like Hitler in the bathtub." And although he had top billing as the puritanical professor brought to his knees by Lola-Lola, Jannings could see that he, too, was being brought to his knees—by me.

Von Sternberg insisted on long takes in chronological order, frequently stopping to adjust the lights, test an angle, or fidget with my costume— anything to bring out the best in my performance. It didn't help that whenever I took to the stage for my cabaret numbers, he demanded absolute silence, watching me as Rath watches Lola, fixated on what he might discover, though there's nothing in her to find. She only appears mysterious because everything she is, she gives away. She exists for the moment. She is feral desire—fleet and cruel, a furtive yank in the back room and the hard exchange of cash. She doesn't need to be understood. And after Rath in his despair tries to strangle her only to have her laugh in his face, he trudges back to his abandoned schoolroom to cower, while she straddles a chair in her top hat, alone on the stage, defiant in her autonomy as she sings that she must fall in love again because she can't help it.

When we shot the scene where Rath assaults Lola, Jannings said under his breath, "I'm going to kill her," and squeezed my throat so tightly, he cut off my air. He left bruises that required special makeup, as we had to repeat the scene in English. I forgave him, having seen the desperation in his eyes. It was the best performance he'd ever given; like his character, he, too, felt helpless against my triumph.

At home, however, I fell apart. "Von Sternberg is a monster," I cried. "He'd see me dead to suit his vision. He torments Jannings on purpose, goading him to make our scenes come alive."

"I did warn you," said Rudi, as Tamara set compresses on my brow and plied me with tea and cake, for I'd lost more than five kilos, starving myself to fit von Sternberg's ideal. "He has no respect for actors. He's notorious for it. In America, he directed Paramount's star William Powell, and after the picture wrapped, Powell demanded a clause in his contract that specifically stated he would never work with von Sternberg again."

I thought this William Powell was a fool. For much as I detested being treated like chattel, hounded and yelled at, made to repeat take after take until I wanted to scream, I also felt what Jannings did—that elusive magic brewed by von Sternberg, a debauched mirage that would enrapture audiences, if not our wary censors.

I trusted him entirely. He could make me a star.

IV

The offer arrived shortly before the shoot ended. I sat in my dressing room—actually, my dressing closet, for it was tiny—when von Sternberg arrived at the door.

"Paramount wants to sign you to a two-picture deal," he sneered. "The rats have spies on my set. They cabled Hollywood to say you are sensational, a rival to Garbo." He eyed me. "I suppose you'll accept. It must be trumpets in your ears, the idea that you can depose her."

"Since when has Garbo been my rival?" I asked, refusing to take his bait, even if I wanted to shout in joy. "But of course I'll accept—if you will be my director."

He grunted, pretending indifference when he felt anything but. "I can ask. I have to return to that miserable town in any event and have nothing new lined up. Why not?"

Paramount's agent in Berlin drew up my contract. The UFA made a ruckus. I was under contract to them; to release me, they insisted Paramount must pay for an early termination clause. Von Sternberg didn't stay for the negotiations. He was running late, over budget and out of time. He left for America before the final cut. Jannings was horrified. I was not.

His magic was spent, imprinted on canisters of celluloid. Our director had exhausted himself.

He was already bored with *The Blue Angel*.

As the editing team wrangled the reels into a release version for the censors, I packed my bag and vacated the set. That world, which had been my entire existence, where I'd given birth to the woman who would define me, stood empty now, the echoes of tyranny dissipated.

I had less than a month before the premiere and my date to set sail for Hollywood.

WHITE GOWN. WHITE MINK. Platinum skin and hair. An emerald bracelet and matching necklace, like the one I'd admired years before, gifts from Uncle Willi to celebrate my success.

The emeralds were paste of course, but it didn't matter. I took to the curtain call like a newly minted goddess, bestowed with a bouquet of roses as the audience went wild, their applause and jubilant cries bathing me in justification. Did anyone notice the spray of violets pinned at my cleavage like a taunting corsage? If they did, no one mentioned it. Nobody cared.

The Blue Angel was a hit.

We had defied the censors—already kowtowing to moral rectitude imposed by the Nazi backlash against decadence—but the nervous UFA executives overlaid a Beethoven score on von Sternberg's monstrous silent take of Rath's demise, though nothing in the picture was remotely classical. He'd be enraged when he learned of it, but it was a minor setback in what otherwise promised to be a massive success.

My name was suddenly everywhere. Before I'd even left the Gloria-Palast theater on the Kurfürstendamm, boulevard of my earliest aspirations and defeats, the UFA was begging me to stay and re-sign my contract with them, at whatever price I requested.

"And miss meeting Garbo?" I said as the press blinded me with flashing bulbs and fans eager for autographs crammed the cordons separating them from my waiting car.

I was taken to Uncle Willi's house, where a celebratory party had been arranged. Rudi wasn't there. His new job had taken him to Munich for a picture. He sent a telegram to congratulate me, and Tamara came in his stead, lovely in a pink satin gown, with Heidede at her side, grumpy and sleepy, a huge bow affixed to her curls (Mutti's doing) that I yanked off at once, the sight of it reminding me of my school years in Schöneberg.

"I'll only be gone six months," I told my daughter, cupping her chin. "I know you'll miss me, but I'll be back before you know it, my precious girl."

"I won't miss you," she retorted. "Mutti says you're going away to please a gnome with delusions of grandeur." As I stood there, astonished to hear such words come out of her six-year-old mouth, she turned away to bury her face in Tamara's skirt.

"She's tired," said Tamara. "I had a casting call today, so Josephine took her to housekeep and . . ." She sighed. "I'm sorry. It won't happen again."

I was distressed by Heidede spouting my mother's venom, and suddenly doubt overshadowed my elation over the premiere and the offer from Hollywood. Was I doing the right thing, leaving my child and family behind for a country that wasn't mine?

"Perhaps I should stay," I said. "The UFA wants to retain me. I could work here."

Tamara shook her head. "You must go. How can you not? Hollywood is where you belong. Von Sternberg is there; he'll take care of you."

I wasn't so confident. He'd take care of my career, but my well-being? Suddenly, his departure before the picture's release seemed to me an omen.

"It's just last-minute nerves," said Tamara. "You'll be fine once you're on the ship. And you mustn't worry. I'm here. I'll care for Heidede as if she were my own. You know how much Rudi and I love her."

"Yes." I smiled weakly. I did know, and while reassuring, it did not give me confidence. My child was growing up without me, just as Mutti had said she would. I leaned over to kiss Heidede, who refused to say good-bye. Once I saw them to the car I'd hired to take them home, exhaustion washed over me. I was in no mood to celebrate.

My trunks crammed with new outfits bought by the studio for my arrival were already loaded on my ship. At midnight, I was scheduled to take the last train to the dock at Bremerhaven for the five-day crossing. Thinking I'd slip upstairs to change and wipe off my makeup, I'd barely crossed the parlor when Jolie besieged me, giddy on champagne, her eyes glittering as she said, "I knew it. I told Willi from the moment I met you, she'll astonish us all."

All of a sudden, I remembered. "I owe you a debt. And a fox stole." Reaching into my beaded handbag, I extracted a fistful of marks. From counting out coins for tram fare, I was now walking around with more money than I knew what to do with. "Here. Whatever extra is left, have Uncle Willi save it for Heidede."

Her gaze fixated for a second on the cash in my hand. "You don't have to."

"No, no. I always honor my debts. Sooner or later." I softened my voice, seeing how downcast she looked. "Thank you for everything. I would never have made it this far without your encouragement. Please, take good care of my uncle Willi."

She bit her lip. I glanced behind us to where Willi was laughing with his theater friends, many of whom remembered my youth and how I'd been enthralled by their artistic conversations. As always, Willi was dressed to perfection, his mustachios waxed to points.

"It's not going so well between us," Jolie said, bringing my gaze back to her. "Willi . . ." Her voice lowered. "Marlene, he's—"

"Yes," I said. "I know. But he loves you, and that is something in this world."

Jolie sighed. "I suppose. You go," she said vehemently, wrapping her arms about me and holding me close. "Be everything you were meant to be. Never give up, Marlene. We have this one life and we must live it to the fullest. Now, you are the one who inspires me."

I drew back. That fatigue I'd first noticed in her before Rudi and I wed had wilted her. She looked almost defeated. My uncle was a homosexual; she would not stay with him. It saddened me, both for her and for Willi.

He could not declare himself and I doubted he ever would. He was a Felsing. The humiliation, for him, would be too great. He would lose this marvelous, eccentric woman out of dishonesty, making me glad that Rudi and I had not clung to our failing marriage but had behaved as adults and settled on an arrangement so we could stay together. Unhappiness was a terrible price to pay for conformity.

I kissed Jolie again and went upstairs to prepare for my departure. I thought I would never see her again, and it saddened me that in saying good-bye to her, I was saying good-bye to my youth in Berlin.

DESPITE THE ROUGH MARCH WEATHER that tossed the ship about like a toy, I found pleasant company onboard—Larry and Bianca Brooks, young owners of a theatrical costume company returning to New York after a long vacation abroad.

Still desperate to persuade me, though I was halfway across the ocean, the UFA cabled me at considerable expense with notices coming in from the nationwide release of *The Blue Angel*. In need of diversion, I invited Bianca to my cabin to read my reviews.

" 'She sings and performs common without being common. Altogether extraordinary,' says the *Berliner Börsen-Courier*," I quoted, setting my burgeoning scrapbook on Bianca's lap. "And look here: The *Licht-Bild-Bühne* calls me 'fascinating, with her narcotic face and exciting voice.' " I laughed. "From nobody to somebody. Such a difference does one part make."

I thought she'd appreciate it, as her husband was in the business and during our meals together in the dining hall, they'd plied me with questions when I told them Paramount had signed me. Now seated at her side on my stateroom couch, I watched her sift through the pages until she came upon some forgotten illustrations I'd purchased in Berlin years before, erotic sketches of women I'd intended to give to Gerda but hadn't. I froze, anticipating her reaction. When she did not say a word, staring at them as if mesmerized, I said, "Exquisite, aren't they? He's a very talented artist, but for the life of me, I can't remember his name."

I heard her draw in a quivering breath. "I fear you've made a mistake, Miss Dietrich."

"Oh?" Intrigued, I reached to my side table for a cigarette.

She came abruptly to her feet. "Yes. A mistake. I'm not inclined that way."

I leaned back. "Which way would that be?" I blew out smoke, amused by her discomposure. "Surely you know that in Europe, we make love with whomever we like."

"In Europe, perhaps. But not in America," she said, and she fled from my cabin.

I sighed. Would I find America as tedious as she made it seem?

REPORTERS ALERTED BY THE STUDIO, which had its financial head-quarters in New York, mobbed my arrival as though I was a celebrity. It was my first demonstration of the studio's power, summoning herds of journalists to the dock to report on someone they'd never heard of.

I posed for them in my sable coat on my stack of trunks, answering a battery of inane questions. "How do you like America so far, Miss Dietrich?" they shouted.

"How would I know?" I replied. "I've only been here ten minutes."

I was then taken by private car to my hotel. I had a few days to rest and intended to roam this astonishing high-rise city, albeit accompanied by the anxious studio-assigned publicist.

Prohibition was in effect, but there were speakeasies with plenty of hooch, I found out, when a Paramount East Coast executive took me out for a night on the town. I had no idea what a speakeasy was until I realized it literally meant that: hidden places with bars that could be upturned and converted into dance floors, where one didn't raise one's voice lest it alerted the police. I found it absurd, forbidding people to do something they'd do anyway, and once I recovered from my overindulgence, I decided to sit for new head shots. The ardent executive's compliments had fortified me more than the liquor; I wanted to present my best angles when I reached California. My profile, especially. I was still sensitive about my nose and uncertain about submitting to surgery. I wanted them to see that I knew my way around a camera.

As I sat for the most expensive fashion photographer New York had to offer, ringing up a significant fee that I forwarded to the studio, my publicist must have been busy in return, for two days later a cable arrived from von Sternberg that bristled like the hairs on his forearms:

> *NO ONE CAN TAKE YOUR PORTRAIT WITHOUT MY CONSENT. DESTROY ALL NEGATIVES. COME TO CALIFORNIA. AT ONCE.*

"Oh, my," I said, turning to the studio escort, who looked pale. "Did I make a mistake?" My voice dripped with sarcasm, mimicking Bianca Brooks's dismay in my cabin.

"It is the protocol," he said. "You can only be photographed under studio regulations."

"A pity." I took up the folder of stunning black-and-white glossies of me in my *Blue Angel* tuxedo, gazing languorously at the camera. "But if the studio insists."

I signed each photograph in bright green ink, *Love, Daddy Marlene,* and had the hotel reception dispatch them to the UFA in Germany, for all the magazines and newspapers who had reviewed me. My American contract might bind me to studio regulations, but it said nothing about promoting myself in my own country.

Of course I knew some of these magazines—which promptly reproduced my picture on the covers, splashed with the headline "*Vati* Marlene"— would make their way to Los Angeles.

I wasn't a star here yet. Reminding Paramount that Berlin waited for me with open arms couldn't hurt.

V

California was as hot as an oven, with a vast blue bowl of a sky, and spiked with palm fronds and traffic fumes. Automobiles had become so commonplace in America, they'd eradicated the quaint horse and carriage that was still seen, albeit less and less, in Berlin. Here, everyone who could afford a motorcar took to the roadways dissecting the city like blackened arteries, without a decent metro in sight. Perched on its hillside pedestal, the block-letter Hollywood sign could be seen from almost everywhere in the city, the genesis of this sprawling town, its deity and scourge, luring thousands to try their luck before or behind the camera.

I found it fascinating, so unlike the decaying grandeur of Europe. But I reminded myself not to form any attachment. I was here for two pictures. After that, who knew?

Von Sternberg picked me up at the train station. This time, there was no fanfare. Looking tanned and rested, he took me in a chauffeured Rolls-Royce to the furnished apartment on Horn Avenue that the studio had rented for me, a short drive from the gilded gates of Paramount Studios on Marathon. Another car followed with my luggage.

I'd only just removed my shoes and coat, sinking wearily onto a sofa draped with a leopard skin that made me think of Leni, when von Sternberg said, "You've a full day tomorrow. Makeup and lighting tests, followed by a photo session. I'll supervise everything; we've assigned you the best makeup specialist in the studio, Dottie Ponedel. After that, we'll shoot a publicity reel, *Introducing Marlene Dietrich,* for the sales reps."

I gazed at him through tired eyes. "Bring me a cigarette, please." When he did, lighting it for me, I inhaled deeply. "Why was there no one at the station to greet me?"

"I was there. Am I so unimportant?"

"I meant no reporters." Melancholy overcame me. I wondered what Rudi and Tamara were doing right now (probably sleeping, given the time change), and Heidede—did she miss me? I missed her. I missed Berlin, the rustling lindens on the Kaiserallee and the winged chariot above the Brandenburg Gate, the crowds lining up outside the cabarets on the Kurfürstendamm, and the smell of sawdust, perfume, and sweat mingling in the air as the show began.

Von Sternberg scowled. "No one was there because your stunt in New York was not appreciated. The corporate offices heard all about your boozed-up evening with their smarmy honcho. And then sitting for that photographer. They burned up the wires, telephoning Schulberg himself, our production head, to ask why you were so intent on derailing their plans for you."

I sat upright, wincing at the crick in my neck from the three-day train ride. "That wasn't my intention. It was just a night out and some extra photographs. For fun."

"You are not on holiday. You're a new personality for Paramount and they're banking on our collaboration. You have a contract. They've bought the American distribution rights for *The Blue Angel,* but they won't release it until we make a successful picture for them first. Your salary is five hundred dollars a week—quite the sum for an actress who has done nothing yet to earn it. You belong to the studio now. You must do exactly as they say. That is their system."

I gave him a cool look. "Their system? Or yours?"

"I *am* them. Schulberg is my boss. He approved my offer to import a new star who can give MGM and Garbo a run for their money. Paramount owns two thousand screens in America, as well as bicoastal studios and an interest in the Columbia Broadcasting System. They have the best talent in the business: W. C. Fields, the Marx Brothers, Claudette Colbert, Clara Bow, and Fredric March. Everyone works together from preproduction to premiere; it's how these studios excel, through a unity of vision. This isn't one of those seedy cabarets or low-budget studios you're used to in Berlin. Defy Paramount and your career will be over before it's begun."

I drew on my cigarette. Paramount had approved *his* offer. He'd been the rat on his own set. I should be flattered, seeing that he'd gone to such trouble to get me here. But I didn't thank him, waiting until he looked ready to explode before I said, "Then I should get my beauty sleep, yes?"

He glowered. "My apartment is down the hall. Do not go outside. The entire point is to veil you in mystery. I don't want to hear another word about how much you miss your family. You should never have told those New York reporters that you're 'happily married.' There are no happily married women of mystery." He scoured me with his eyes. "And you must lose some weight. Your ass is enormous. Did you eat that entire ship on your crossing?"

He marched out, to my relief. Melting into the sofa with its leopard pelt, I shut my eyes.

In my entire life, I'd never been so homesick.

"IF WE PLUCK YOUR BROWS HERE, at the outer corners," said Dottie Ponedel as I watched in the bulb-lined mirror, "and here to heighten the arch, then pencil them in, it will enlarge your eyes." She smiled as she expertly pricked with her tweezers. "See? Much better. You have marvelous eyes, with such deep lids. Ideal for all sorts of effects: smoky shadows, bright paint, long eyelashes. Here we call them bedroom eyes, Miss Dietrich."

"And my nose?" I asked, inspecting her handiwork. "Is it too . . . ?"

"Too wide? I can see why you'd worry. The camera does tend to exaggerate our slightest imperfection. But I have a simple solution." Taking a thin tube from her tray of cosmetics, she drew a nearly imperceptible silver line down the bridge of my nose.

I laughed. "Now I look like a clown."

"Not under the right lighting. And Jo is our best. No one knows how to light a face like him." She winked at me. I was impressed with her technique and the fact that she was on a first-name basis with my director, though I would soon learn that in Hollywood, everyone was on a first-name basis until they were not. "It's the reason we put up with him. He might be a bear when he's not behind the camera, but when he is, he's a magician."

"That's what I think," I said, peering at myself. I did look different, my cheeks more sunken—not eating much helped—and the artificial penciled brows she'd created angling higher on my forehead to give me a sultry, if slightly artificial, look.

"You're very lucky," she went on, painting my lips with matte crimson, over which she applied a sheer layer that gleamed like nail polish. "He's been extolling you to everyone. You're quite the find, he assures us." She stepped back, admiring my reflection. "I must say, I agree. That face will put Garbo to shame."

"Is the studio really so intent on making me into her rival?" I managed to ask, though my mouth felt stiff from the layers of lipstick.

She dabbed clear gel on my mouth to moisten it. She didn't answer my question, but I assumed the studio must be, for once I was transferred to the hairstylist, he whipped my curls into a froth of lacquered waves like Garbo's. "We should bleach it," he said, a prim well-dressed man I suspected would have enjoyed Das Silhouette. "It has too much red in it. It will look too dark on film. And I think these curls should be marcelled. But there's no time today. Next week, we'll schedule you for a coloring and heat treatment, if your director approves."

If my director approves . . .

Von Sternberg certainly had full charge of me.

Hours of photography later, during which I posed in a variety of sumptuous gowns that astonished me with their glamour, I was weak with hunger. Breakfast under von Sternberg's eye had consisted of coffee and a lone grapefruit.

He took me to the commissary, the studio cafeteria, where the actors and crew ate while shooting on the adjacent soundstages and back lots. It wasn't crowded, lunchtime having come and gone. I was disappointed. I'd hoped to catch a glimpse of some of Paramount's much-vaunted talent and suspected von Sternberg had engineered it so I would not.

Over a tasteless hamburger served on a tray he told me that I was scheduled to make my first public appearance at an upcoming studio party. "Schulberg's assistant, David O. Selznick—who's rising in the ranks—is engaged to Louis B. Mayer's daughter Irene. Paramount is hosting the reception at the Beverly Wilshire. Schulberg wants to introduce you there."

"Isn't Garbo at MGM?" I said, excited by the thought that I might meet her.

"She is." He gave me one of his impatient looks. "But she won't be there. It's a silly party and she's a star," he added pointedly, "but many other important people in the industry will be there, including the actor they're proposing to play the male lead in our next picture."

"Oh." I perked up. We hadn't discussed actual work yet. "Is there a script?"

"Not yet." He waved his hand. "It's based on a novel about a Parisian prostitute who finds redemption after falling in love with a Foreign Legionnaire. I'm rewriting the script now."

"*Amy Jolly?*" I said, and his eyebrow cocked. "You've read it?" he asked.

"Years ago when I was in Weimar." I hesitated. "It's not very good."

"That's why I'm rewriting it. Schulberg didn't like *The Blue Angel*. He wants a simpler role for your debut for the studio. And your English," he said, "needs improvement, too."

"He didn't like *Blue Angel*? How odd. It's a hit in Germany. Have you seen our notices? They say—"

"I know what they say. It doesn't matter. They have codes here, like our censors, only theirs are self-imposed. Pictures must meet certain criteria before release, so they'll edit *The Blue Angel* to fit their criteria. And our Parisian whore will be a chanteuse with a murky past."

He shrugged, to my bewilderment. In Berlin, he'd wrestled to the death with the UFA to do as he wanted, yet here he would accept whatever he was told?

"Like I said," he went on, "it will work once we get the script in shape. I want to pare down your dialogue to as few lines as possible. Your accent is too noticeable, so you'll be taking English lessons with a coach hired by the studio."

"A Parisian chanteuse with a murky past." I pushed aside my tray with its inedible hamburger. "No script. My English needs improvement. They don't like how I look or I don't look enough like Garbo. They have self-imposed codes. Sounds like a lot of trouble."

"It is." He bit into his hamburger, dripping bright yellow mustard onto his tray.

"Do I even get a say?" I said. I was starting to regret having come all the way across the ocean; the way he described it, working in Hollywood sounded like slavery.

His voice hardened. "A say in what? You're under contract. The studio chooses your parts. And I'm perfectly capable of guiding them toward the best roles for you."

Tension sparked between us. It didn't perturb me; I knew how he blustered and it didn't scare me, but there were people coming into the cafeteria now, extras dressed in togas, on a coffee break from a set. A few glanced in our direction. We were speaking German, so they probably wouldn't understand a word, but I'd rather not cause a scene so soon after my arrival.

"Yes, of course you can," I said, lighting a cigarette. "But another chanteuse? It doesn't sound simpler to me. It sounds like the same part, designed to not offend."

He went still. "And?"

"And I'd like some input. I'm the one who has to play this chanteuse, after all."

He scowled. "I'll bring you my script tonight. But I warn you, it's not finished."

"*Danke.*" I smiled. I could see he was irritated by more than my insistence on reading the script and thought it must be the pressure to make me into a star in a picture ordained by the studio. In Berlin, he'd been the master, despite budget and time constraints. Here, it appeared he had meddlesome overlords to please.

"Tell me about the actor for the male lead," I said, hoping to ease that glower off his face.

His glower only deepened. "Not my choice. I wanted John Gilbert, but he's under contract to MGM and they refuse to release him." He paused, with a sudden malicious grin. "Probably because they, too, have heard of our success in Germany and know you'll soon eclipse their cash cow, Garbo."

"The actor's name?" I prompted. I was getting tired of hearing about this fake rivalry with an actress I'd never met. Garbo was certainly the star to emulate, if I must copy someone. But I hoped to make my own mark, not toil in the shadow of another woman.

"His name is Gary Cooper," von Sternberg said with evident distaste. "It doesn't get any more American than that, does it? That toad Selznick is Cooper's friend and has been lobbying Schulberg for the part. Selznick thinks Cooper can be a leading man, though he's done nothing thus far to prove it."

"Oh. I've never heard of him."

"Who has? He's had some success of late, they tell me, as the shy-hero type. In some picture called *Beau Sabreur*, he played a Legionnaire, which is why Selznick is pushing him on me. And he was a cowboy in one of their Westerns. Awful pictures, those Westerns, but audiences here seem to love them. Anyway, Selznick is determined to get Cooper the part and I'm just as determined to stop him."

I had a feeling he wasn't telling me everything. "But if we must use him, he has talent?"

"As much as any actor needs. I'm only concerned with *your* talent." He stood abruptly. "We're late for your publicity reel. Stop smoking so much. I need you in your best voice."

Late that night, after I'd arrived in a state of utter fatigue at my apartment, von Sternberg came by to drop off the script.

I glanced at the title page. *"Morocco.* I like it."

"Don't like it too much. As I told you, we're still revising it. Titles can change. So can everything else." He didn't linger, making me wonder if he was nursing his offense that I'd asked for input or because of this male lead he was resolved to thwart.

Whichever the case, I found myself curious to meet my proposed costar.

VI

I detested the gown von Sternberg had the studio deliver to me at the last minute for the party—a blue organza frock with enough ruffles to cover me from neck to toe. He was clever, I had to give him that. Anyone at the party who'd seen *The Blue Angel*, and no doubt most of the executives had, would find me unrecognizable. But once I tried the dress on, it flowed beautifully, cut on the bias, giving me that enigmatic quality everyone kept harping about. It also didn't fit. Though I'd been on a daily exercise regimen and strict diet, so that I'd reached the lowest weight of my adult life— one hundred and thirty pounds, according to the American scale—von Sternberg had sent the gown made in his ideal size for me, and I couldn't pull the zipper all the way up the back.

"Impossible," I said to my studio dresser, who'd come to help me and was trying to yank the zipper up without ripping the seam. "The first breath I take, I'll burst out of it."

I waved her aside. She was one of those ginger-haired American girls with a name like Nancy or Susan; I never remembered it, though she'd been at my beck and call during the endless photo shoots. "What is he thinking? Is every actress in the studio a size zero?"

Nancy or Susan said nervously, "They're sending a car for you in twenty minutes, Miss Dietrich. Maybe if we use a foundation garment—"

"A foundation garment? Absolutely not. I'll wear something else," I replied, and I searched my closet, hung with items brought from Berlin.

I'd already caused a minor scandal when I appeared for one of my photo sessions in a jacket and trousers, which here they called "slacks." No one had advised me on what to wear and when I walked into the studio, the publicity man assigned to me was dismayed.

"Women don't wear slacks," he informed me. "They're unattractive."

"You're wearing them," I pointed out.

"Yes," he said, "but I'm a *man*."

"And I'm a woman who wore them in Berlin. Do you want to take my picture or not?"

He did but he grumbled to the photographer that Schulberg would have their heads, leaving me in no doubt that he'd have the photographs cropped so my slacks wouldn't show. He had me return the next day, too, where I found myself greeted by an assortment of gowns from the wardrobe department and Nancy or Susan to watch over me for the remainder of my session.

Now, I hummed to myself as I sorted through my hangers. "This should do nicely," I said, and I turned to Nancy or Susan with my chosen apparel in hand.

Her eyes went wide. "Oh, no," she said.

"Oh, yes." I smiled.

THE BEVERLY WILSHIRE HOTEL was a pink stucco villa surrounded by rampant greenery. Like everything else I'd seen thus far in Los Angeles— and I had not seen much—it was ostentatious without any defining features: a lavish showroom, where those who came through its doors were more important than their surroundings.

As soon as I entered the lobby, von Sternberg rushed forth to detain me. In his black tuxedo paired with a cravat, riding boots, and a silver-handled cane, he looked demented.

"What are you wearing?" he gasped.

I might have asked him the same. "A sailing outfit. Do you like it?" I twirled once for him in my white beret, navy blue blazer with an insignia crest, and wide-belled trousers.

"I do not like it. You will return to the apartment this instant and change into the dress I sent you. Now, before anyone sees you."

"The dress you sent me doesn't fit. It's either this or my tuxedo, and I assume the tuxedo might be too much for the occasion. I wouldn't want to be mistaken for the groom."

He went so white, he looked as if he might spew. But he had no time, for a page in hotel livery came to tell him that Mr. Schulberg was waiting for us at the ballroom entrance.

Von Sternberg gripped my arm. "He's going to announce you. But I think he'll send you home instead, and then—" he said, tightening his hand as he led me forward, "you can apologize to him."

I regretted my decision. I'd thought it would be a lark, setting Hollywood tongues to wagging as I had in Berlin, but I hadn't met Paramount's chief production executive yet, while he'd certainly already heard of my defiant slacks at my photo session.

"Do you want to work in this town or not?" von Sternberg hissed in my ear. "Because thus far all you seem to be doing is ensuring you will not."

He let go of me as a dapper man who was younger than I'd expected, only in his midthirties, with curly dark hair and a noxious cigar in his hand, came to greet me. With a courteous bow that reminded me of Rudi when we first met, he kissed my hand.

"*Verzaubert, Sie zu treffen,* Fräulein Dietrich," he said in perfect German. He paused, with a small smile. "Charming outfit. Are we going yachting later?"

"If you have the boat," I said, keeping the quaver from my voice.

"I do. Two, in fact." He extended his arm. As I stepped beside him, I heard someone ring a champagne flute with a fork, calling for attention.

The room went silent. In his sonorous voice, Schulberg proclaimed,

"Ladies and gentlemen, I present Paramount's new star, Miss Marlene Dietrich."

"*Now*," said von Sternberg. Pressing his hand into the small of my back, he pushed me forward in tandem with Schulberg, who escorted me inside.

I couldn't see anyone. They all blended into one staring visage as I sauntered into the room with Schulberg, him nodding to those he passed, me with a smile etched on my lips. I was certain that I looked ridiculous, promenading in my sailor's attire before more famous people than me, but I did my best to stay poised, remembering that mystery begets interest. No one else here was dressed like me. If nothing else, there'd be plenty of talk.

Schulberg introduced me to his assistant, David O. Selznick, a coarse-looking man with wire-rimmed spectacles, and his pretty bride, Irene Mayer, who gushed, "Oh, Miss Dietrich. Such style. I *adore* your blazer. Wherever did you find it?"

"Berlin," I told her, and I congratulated them on their engagement, feeling Selznick's beady gaze assess me as if he were tallying my net worth. I was grateful when von Sternberg materialized at my side. I looked around, wondering if I could smoke and then recalling I'd left my handbag in the limousine because it didn't match my outfit.

"Do you have a cigarette?" I started to ask him under my breath, but he ignored me, already engaged in discussion with Schulberg and Selznick.

I heard Schulberg say, "Now, Jo. Be realistic. We've discussed all this. You must start shooting in July. The soundstage is booked through September. Yes, we know," he said, interrupting my director. "I realize the script still needs work and you prefer to shoot in sequence, but we've given you enough latitude. And yes," he added, "we do insist on Cooper for the part. Just make the best of it, okay?"

At the mention of my costar, I stepped toward them. Von Sternberg said, "Excuse me, please," and with a sharp look at me, he said, "Go. Mingle. Meet people. It's why you are here."

It felt as if he'd thrown ice water over me. Smiling at the executives, I excused myself and moved away, as lost as anyone could be in a crowd of foreign strangers.

I began to recognize the stars: petite Claudette Colbert in a silver sequin gown that looked sprayed on, laughing with a matinee idol. And an inebriated Groucho Marx with his hand on a starlet's rump, though that didn't stop him from giving me a wink. And a giggling woman with an outdated flapper haircut and ruby lips who must be Clara Bow, next to a breathtaking sinewy blonde in a bright yellow dress. I hoped to catch a glimpse of Garbo, but as von Sternberg had said, she wasn't here. Given her status, she must eschew these social events, having no incentive to display herself.

Nevertheless, those I did see were enough—as beautiful as icons, polished to a surreal perfection that made me feel as though I were in the midst of idealized replicas who only proved that Marlene from Berlin didn't belong here at all.

My stomach rumbled as I meandered to linen-draped tables by the walls, weighted down with trays of hors d'oeuvres and chilled bottles of Dom Pérignon, despite Prohibition. I'd been perpetually hungry since arriving in America. After checking to make sure von Sternberg was still arguing with Schulberg—he was—I hurried to the tables to fill up on canapés.

I was biting into a delicious salmon pâté when a deep voice drawled, "I understand we're going to work together."

I turned around. And froze.

He was a god. There was no other way to describe him. And tall—so tall I had to crane my neck to meet his hazel eyes, which seemed golden in the chandelier glow. He had a lean, beautiful face. A lock of light brown hair streaked by the sun tumbled over his forehead. He couldn't have been more than thirty, a year or so older than me. In a cream-colored evening jacket, black bow tie, and trousers, he had an impressive figure, his lanky limbs imbued with a confidence that was indeed pure American.

I must have been staring, for he chuckled, and with his fingertip removed a smudge of pâté from my mouth. Anna May had done that to me in Berlin, on the night we went to see Garbo's picture. A frisson of pleasure tingled in my groin.

"That good, huh?" he said. "Guess the studio doesn't feed you much."

"You—you must be Gary Cooper." My air of mystery deserted me. This was a star if ever I'd seen one. But I could also see why von Sternberg had denigrated him. He was just the kind of man—handsome, poised, and athletic—my director would detest.

"Guilty as charged. And I know who you are." His gaze roved over me with admiring insolence. "But if I'd had any doubt, that getup disproves it. I heard you like to wear slacks."

"You did?"

"Yes. All of Hollywood and most of America, I should think, has heard by now." His smile made fetching crinkles around his eyes. "Your publicity photos. You've been keeping the studio busy, plastering your mug shot in *Photoplay* and every other fan rag. 'The Woman Even Women Can Adore.' It's a lot to live up to. I hope you're ready."

I laughed. "Schulberg released those photographs."

"He did. He thinks you're sensational. I think he's right."

Drawing myself to my full height (I did not reach his shoulders) I said, "Would you happen to have a cigarette, Mr. Cooper?"

He took out a gold-plated case from his jacket. As I leaned over his lighter, I caught a hint of his smell. Or rather, I noticed the distinct absence of cologne. He smelled like a man—of hair tonic and tobacco, and something faint, almost indecipherable, but salty, I thought, like the sea.

Like sex.

I lifted my eyes to his telling smile.

He'd recently, perhaps only an hour or so ago, had sex. And hadn't showered afterward.

"I've worked with our director before," he said, a sardonic lilt in his voice, as though he could tell what I was thinking. "In *Children of Divorce* with Clara Bow. I was fired because the rushes were awful, but they replaced the director with von Sternberg and he reshot my scenes. He made me look good, helped save my career. I owe him."

Heat stirred in me like a fire. It had been months since I'd—

I made myself stop, using my cigarette as a deterrent, inhaling smoke while he stood there, as attentive as a gentleman but not gentlemanly at all.

He was thinking the same thing I was, and I darted another look to where I'd left von Sternberg. He was no longer there.

"I'm looking forward to working together," I managed to say, turning back to Gary. "Von Sternberg has told me how much he enjoyed making that picture with you."

"Oh, I doubt that." His smile widened. "He wanted Gilbert for the part. But he's stuck with me, thanks to Selznick."

"Well." I coiled my voice. "I'm glad we are stuck—with you."

His eyes gleamed. "I also heard your English wasn't very good. Sounds good enough to me." Leaning to me, he whispered, "How would you like to ditch this party and go out for—"

He didn't have the chance to finish. From seemingly out of nowhere, a woman in a white sleeveless dress slithered to his side. Her glossy black hair was parted, drawn in an intricate bun at her nape to show off a face made for the camera, highlighted by her surly cat-green eyes.

"Gary, *mi amor*," she said, hooking her arm in his. "Where have you been? I've looked everywhere for you." She had a Spanish accent. An actress, no doubt, but I had no idea who.

"I was talking to Miss Dietrich here," he said quietly. "She's working with me in my next picture. Remember I mentioned her?"

"No." The woman stared at me. "I don't remember. Who is she?"

"Marlene," I said. "I'm new to Paramount and—"

"*Sí*," she interrupted. "I remember now. You are a Kraut."

Gary looked down at his feet as she tightened her arm about his. "I'm Lupe Vélez," she said. "From Mexico. I work for RKO."

She wasn't trying to instill camaraderie, that much I understood. She must be his lover, the one he'd recently had sex with. Feeling threatened, she was claiming her property.

"Strange, no?" she said, looking me over. "You dress like man."

"Yes. It's all the rage in Krautland," I replied.

She frowned, unsure if I was mocking her. Then she gave a fake laugh. "You make fun. But everyone talk," she said, her voice taking on a venomous edge.

"Better to be talked about than ignored." I forced out a smile. "It was lovely to meet you," I said, though it wasn't. I did not like her and she didn't like me, with that unerring instinct women have for a rival. Only I wasn't her rival. Not yet.

"Come, Gary." She reverted to little-girl plaintiveness. "Claudette ask for you. You so strange, always disappearing. Come, *mi cielo*. Say good-bye to Miss Marlene."

He lifted his gaze, holding mine for a moment. "See you on the set."

I nodded, watching her tug him to where Claudette Colbert sat surrounded by her friends. It was a deliberate snub. I'd been introduced to the room by Schulberg. Everyone knew who I was. But Lupe Vélez had seen Gary flirting with me and orchestrated an insult, excluding me from the inner circle, left to stand by the appetizers like an aspiring nobody.

How tedious. I ate another canapé, and then made my way to the ballroom entrance. Von Sternberg had vanished. Going into the lobby, I called for my car and directed the driver to my apartment.

Nancy or Susan was still there, waiting for me. "It's not so bad," she said, waving the script nervously, as I'd caught her lounging on my sofa, reading. "You've a wonderful part as Amy Jolly. At the end, she forsakes everything to follow her lover. It's very romantic."

"Yes." I shed my cap and shoes as I drifted to my bedroom. "I think it's going to be very romantic, too. Please lock the door on your way out."

VII

Shooting on *Morocco* began in late July, later than scheduled because of the script. In the end, we never saw a complete version. Instead, von Sternberg distributed daily pages for each scheduled scene; as promised, he reduced my dialogue to a minimum, although I'd spent weeks with the studio-assigned coach to refine my English. I still had an accent—it would never leave me—but my character was French, so I didn't see why everyone was so concerned.

But my lack of words enhanced the mood. As Amy Jolly, the chanteuse who flees from her past to Morocco, I played that enigmatic woman the studio wanted. And unlike Lola-Lola, love is Amy's salvation, as she becomes enraptured by Gary's careless legionnaire.

I had two songs, including the seductive "What Am I Bid for My Apples?" which I sang in a black romper cut high to reveal my legs, and a raven-tipped boa. My favorite scene was when Amy first enters the café-cabaret in her black tails. The costume was my idea, approved by the studio. My publicity photos had indeed caused a sensation. Every magazine in America printed them, and having heard of my penchant for tuxedos in Germany, Schulberg exploited it.

But the lesbian kiss was not in the studio plans.

Smoking a cigarette as Amy strolls among her audience, I decided to have her pause by a pretty woman with an oleander in her hair. On impulse, Amy kisses the woman on her lips—then tosses the flower at the legionnaire. Like von Sternberg, Gary was taken by surprise by my gesture but stayed in character, placing the oleander behind his ear. He was a professional; he knew every line and mark, even as von Sternberg unleashed immediate vitriol toward him that soured the shoot from the start. When I expressed concern later that my sapphic kiss might make Gary's character look weak, von Sternberg scoffed.

"He's a pretty soldier boy," he declared, loud enough for Gary to overhear. "She's the one pulling the strings. She is the star. Everyone else is here to make her shine."

During our much-delayed lunch break, Gary muttered to me, "Didn't I tell you? He's never going to forget that the studio forced me on him. He'll ruin every scene I'm in."

I didn't think he could. I saw how von Sternberg glared when he viewed the rushes. Gary was so handsome and assured that nothing could detract from him. He, too, was a star on the rise—and von Sternberg knew it. Their hostility simmered like the desert beyond the movie's garrison setting. In our scenes together, von Sternberg insisted Gary remain seated, exalting my presence while diminishing his. When Gary finally lost his temper, shouting that he wasn't going to be made to look like "a goddamn pansy" and storming off the set, von Sternberg said snidely before the crew, "What does he know? He's an actor. Chosen for his physique, not his brain."

I had thought *Morocco* was going to be romantic.

Instead, it turned into a nightmare.

ONE NIGHT, AFTER ANOTHER FOURTEEN-HOUR DAY, every bone in my body aching as I prepared for bed, a banging came at my apartment door. I opened it to find Gary swaying there, so drunk he could barely stand. As he lurched inside, he gazed with bleary eyes at me, still gorgeous in his dishevelment but, I feared, about to topple over and hit that handsome face on the floor.

"You see? He does hate me," he said. "That fucking dwarf—he thinks I'm not important. But I am the male lead! Without me, who will his precious star fall in love with? Him?" He let out an ugly laugh. "I bet he doesn't have enough dick to get it up."

"You are drunk," I said coldly. "It's the only reason I'm not throwing you out. But if you insult him again, I will. Now, please go home."

"I can't." He dropped onto the sofa. "My wife hates me, too. So does that bitch Lupe. Always nagging at me. Nag, nag, nag." He belched. "Why do women think they own us?"

I wondered what I should do. Sending him away in this state was out of the question. I could call a taxi, but if he was recognized, the press would hurt his image, not to mention our picture. And it was too late to telephone the studio, while von Sternberg, who was down the hall, would fly into a rage if he found Gary here.

"I'm sorry you have problems at home," I said at length, as his chin bobbed. "But I'm a woman and I don't think I own anyone. I have no interest in collars, unless you're a dog."

"You're not a woman," he said. "You're . . . something else."

He passed out. As I took off his shoes and managed to heave him onto the sofa, overwhelmed by the stench of whiskey, he started to snore. At least he hadn't thrown up. I'd deal with him in the morning. Thank God, the shoot was almost over. Gary with a hangover, directed by von Sternberg—I dreaded the thought.

IT WASN'T YET DAWN when I suddenly woke from sleep. Groggy, momentarily confused, I started to grope for my alarm clock, thinking I'd missed my call and was running late. I had to be at the studio for makeup at five every morning before shooting.

Then I saw him in the doorway. He did not move or say a word, but the look in his eyes was unmistakable—and remarkably sober.

He closed the bedroom door. Taking hold of the bedcovers, he yanked them aside. He looked down at me. I slept in the nude. My heart started to pound as he unbuttoned his shirt, flung it to the floor, and unbuckled his belt. He had a smooth, muscular chest; I found myself wondering if the studio made him wax it. Then his shorts came off. I stared.

"Like it?" he said.

"Impressive," I replied. "Like New York."

He took hold of his large shaft. "If you want it, you can have it. But not if you're screwing that dwarf. I don't mess around with another man's woman, though he deserves it."

"I'm not." I slid back on the mattress. I, too, was as camera ready as he was.

"God," he breathed. "I want you so badly. All day long on that goddamn set, all I can think of is what I'd like to do to you."

"Then why wait? No time like the present."

He missed my Berlin allusion. But he came. Before he even entered me. He did not roll off me. Instead he waited, kissing me slowly, trailing his tongue down my body until he was dipping into my wetness and I was arching my spine. Then he slid his newly hardened length into me, inch by magnificent inch, making me gasp.

"Does it hurt?" he whispered. "My wife used to complain I was too big. Lupe loves it, though. She likes to sit on it."

"I . . . I think I should, too," I said, as it might be easier to manage.

Grasping me in his arms, he hiked me on top of him. His erection thrust like a skyscraper. I had never felt anything like it, and though it still hurt a little, by the time I started rocking, I forgot the sting, the burn of it. It became one with my pleasure, my climax imploding from within. I saw sands and white scarves; I felt the scorching heat of the desert, and then I felt him, shaking, withdrawing from me before he came again.

Plunging downward, I took him in my mouth. He cried out.

He was pure American, as robust as the plains of his native Montana. But he tasted like the sea.

WITHIN WEEKS, EVERYONE ON THE SET KNEW. We couldn't have hidden it if we tried. Our scenes crackled with electricity, every look between us charged with the aftereffects of our nights together. Gary stopped letting von Sternberg get under his skin. He had no room, not when I was there instead, so that when we passed each other on our way to our dressing rooms, he'd waggle his hand and quote his dialogue suggestively, "What am I doing with my fingers? Nothing. Yet."

Von Sternberg went as dark as a thundercloud, reducing his directions to as few words as he could muster: "Move to the left. Turn to the light. Hold. Cut."

And that was with me. With Gary, he ceased speaking at all. Through his silence, he made it clear he didn't care how his male lead performed, confirming that he considered *Morocco* to be my picture. He was making it only for me.

"I don't give a crap," Gary said as I rested on his chest while he smoked lazily, as nonchalant after sex as he was ardent during it. "He can't hurt me. Selznick told me, forget about that asshole. He'll make you famous despite himself. It's a terrific part. I'm not the nice guy in this one. I'm the heel who walks away. The girl chases after me." He ruffled my hair. "Betcha it won't be like that in real life, huh? You don't seem like the type to chase after anyone."

"Why should I?" I took his cigarette from his mouth and inhaled. "We're both married. And your Mexican spitfire does quite enough chasing after you for the three of us."

"Do you love him?" he suddenly asked. "Your husband, I mean?"

I paused, smoke drifting from my mouth. "Yes," I said quietly. "I do. There are many kinds of love. We have a daughter. I miss them both. I miss Germany."

"Never been." He folded his arms behind his head, stretching out his long limbs. "I hear it's not so nice now. Lots of unrest. That war knocked you Krauts down pretty hard."

"It did." All of a sudden, I wanted to be alone. "Are you staying tonight?"

"Nope." He uncoiled from under me, padding to the chair littered with his clothes. "Got to get up early. We've that final scene to shoot. Then I have to see Lupe." He grimaced. "Talk about driving a man crazy. She's got a screw loose or something."

I didn't comment, though I agreed. From what he'd told me, Lupe Vélez had a nasty habit of following him around—she wasn't stupid—shoving her fist into his crotch and threatening to cut off his *huevos*. I had no idea how he put up with it, trapped between a marriage he no longer wanted and a jealous mistress who might castrate him at any moment.

"She thinks I'll leave my wife," he said, pulling on his jacket. "But she's wrong. I'll file for divorce as soon as the studio says I can, but not to marry her. She needs a mental ward, not a husband." He pushed his fingers through his hair without glancing at my dressing table mirror. His lack of vanity never ceased to amaze me. He wasn't like any actor I'd known. Once he was away from the camera, he couldn't have cared less about his appearance.

"Will you?" he said. "Someday, maybe?"

"Will I what?" I reclined against the headboard.

"Divorce. You say you love him, but, baby—a woman in love doesn't fuck like you do."

"Is that so?" I chucked his chin as he kissed me. "Go home to your wife. And get a gun. Lupe might actually try to cut off those big balls of yours and, I must admit, I'd miss them."

Laughing, he strode out.

It wouldn't last. I knew it already. I enjoyed his company but we had nothing in common save for mutual lust. But until the picture wrapped or he started to bore me, I was content.

Even if von Sternberg was not.

*   *   *

IN THE FINAL SCENE, when the trumpet calls her legionnaire to duty, Amy sees her name carved by him on a tabletop. Unable to resist, she joins his departing caravan, her white skirt and blouse billowing in the sirocco as she kicks off her shoes and vanishes into blistering sands.

It was my idea to shuck the shoes. The studio was stifling, wind machines blowing acres of sand hauled from a nearby beach; as I stood with my hand shielding my brow while the caravan snaked over the ridge, I thought Amy would want to hurry. She'd want to join her man as soon as possible. The moment I kicked off my shoes, von Sternberg erupted from behind the camera. "Cut!" he said, and he marched up to me with his megaphone in hand. "What are you doing?"

"Taking off her shoes. It's the desert at high noon. She can't walk in heels."

"She can." His spit needled my face. "She'll burn her feet. Put them back on."

"No. They stay where they are. Make it the last shot. A symbol of her past."

"A symbol! Are you directing this picture now?" But he trudged away to consider and the shoes remained where I'd left them, on the sand in the final shot.

By the time we wrapped, no one ever wanted to see a grain of sand again. The preview was held in a dusty suburb called Pomona. I'd never heard of previews, but we did our duty by dressing up and attending. The theater was half empty. No one applauded at the end, though the film was sublime and far less simple than I'd supposed.

I thought we had a flop. The studio had aimed for a tamer version of Lola-Lola, but the undercurrent of perverse longing, my chemistry with Gary, and the cross-dressing lesbian kiss would be too strong for America's white-bread taste. It wasn't as overt as *The Blue Angel,* but no one could mistake it for anything else but what it was—a tale of masochistic surrender.

Paramount must have feared the same. They held an extravagant premiere at Grauman's Chinese Theater, the first ever by the studio in that legendary Asian-themed palace, with all the industry's influential columnists in attendance. I was stunned by the crowds, the photographers, and the cheering fans—a panoply of glamour fixated on me as I walked down the carpet in hip-clinging black chiffon and a silver fox stole.

To our surprise, *Morocco* was a hit. Critics hailed me as "a seductive rival to Garbo," which thrilled the studio. When I got the call from Schulberg himself that the picture had broken box-office records, he offered an immediate contract renewal, doubling my salary along with the stipulation that von Sternberg would continue to direct me. He also offered a spacious Mediterranean-style villa, paid for by the studio, in Beverly Hills.

I had just become Paramount's new female star.

My next picture, *Dishonored*, was rushed into production. Kept busy from dawn to dusk with fittings for costumes by the studio's premier couturier, Travis Banton, and publicity shoots, I was permitted studio-organized evenings at the Cocoanut Grove or Club New Yorker, escorted by several of their upcoming male stars, although I found enough spare time to continue my dalliances with Gary.

I had everything I'd worked for so long to achieve. I was famous, regaled wherever I went. I earned more than enough money to support my family; even my manufactured duel with Garbo, stoked incessantly by the studio press, ceased to bother me, for I'd accomplished as much as she had in the same span of time. I might not be deemed worthy of coveted dramatic roles yet, but those would come. I'd hone my skills and master my craft. No actress would know more than me about filmmaking. I would be an asset, a tool, von Sternberg's willing marionette. I had only just begun to explore my potential.

Yet instead of reveling in it, all I wanted was to see Berlin again.

SCENE FIVE
GODDESS OF DESIRE
1931–1935

"THEY SAY VON STERNBERG IS RUINING
ME. I SAY, LET HIM RUIN ME."

I

Dishonored was about a widowed Viennese streetwalker recruited to spy during the war. She falls for a Russian agent and is betrayed, then shot to death by a firing squad. With a complete script, Schulberg mandated that we finish the shoot in under two months, so he could capitalize on my success and keep audiences begging for more.

He was wrong. Perhaps because it was rushed, my second picture did not fare as well as *Morocco*. After being inundated with initial publicity about me, the new face at Paramount, audiences had flocked to see my first film; now, they weren't so curious anymore. Nevertheless, a few perceptive critics lauded my performance and Schulberg affirmed his trust in my collaboration with my director, stating that no picture was doing very well at the moment.

Von Sternberg chose to be insulted. "All they care about in this town is profit," he said, tossing our notices aside. "It's a better picture than *Morocco*, and you're better in it, but as they don't understand it, who cares? America did not suffer as we did during the war."

He was restless, tired and fed up with the studio oversight. He needed a rest. We both did. We'd been working nonstop for over two years, shooting three pictures in a row. My new contract wasn't due to start until the spring. With *Dishonored* finished and Christmas upon us, I took advantage of the lull, hiring staff to prepare my new house while I departed for *Morocco*'s London premiere, followed by a long-awaited reunion in Berlin with my family.

RUDI, TAMARA, AND HEIDEDE GREETED ME as I disembarked. I rushed to embrace them while photographers yelled out my name. My family looked well; Heidede would soon turn eight, and I was astonished by how much she'd grown, her long legs, messy curls, and defiant expression reminding me of myself at her age.

"Did you miss me?" I asked her as the studio-assigned chauffeur evaded the clamoring reporters and drove us via side streets to the flat. "I missed you so much." I held her close until she wriggled away, looking askance at me, as though she wasn't sure who I was.

"Children forget," Tamara reassured me that evening, after Heidede was put to bed and we sat at the table. Tamara had made a gloriously fattening supper of roast pork loin, potatoes, rye bread with butter, and sauerkraut. I hadn't eaten so well since I'd left. "But she'll come around. You have changed. She doesn't recognize you."

"I haven't changed that much." I took a swig of my beer and deliberately let out a burp.

"Evidently not." Rudi grinned. He seemed content. He was working full time now, employed by the UFA and Paramount as an associate producer, in charge of the American studio's distribution in Germany. I got him the job, lobbying Schulberg to hire him; the studio had agreed, no doubt because keeping Rudi busy would preempt his appearance on my doorstep in Beverly Hills with our daughter. Paramount was still trying to hide my marriage, offsetting my unwitting remarks in New York with a barrage of fabricated gossip in Louella Parsons's newspaper column about the idol du jour spotted on Miss Dietrich's arm at the Cocoanut Grove.

"I'm still Lena," I said. "Dietrich is an illusion. Lighting and makeup."

"She's more than that." Tamara touched Rudi's shoulder before she

started to clear the table. "You're so slim and stylish. And that fur coat—
it's lynx, isn't it? Must cost a fortune."

"Take it." As her eyes went wide, I said, "Whatever you like in my luggage, you can have. It's just clothing. The studio can buy me more."

"Oh, thank you, Marlene." Tamara floated out with a smile on her
face.

I gazed at Rudi. He said, "You've just made her very happy. Everything
here is so expensive, she can't afford brand-new clothes."

"Well, she makes you happy. She loves and cares for Heidede. It's the
least I can do."

"You do more than enough by sending us money. You don't have to
give away your wardrobe. Tamara adores you, no matter what."

Smiling, I lit a cigarette. He might look well, but I detected a reserve
in him, as though he was holding something back. "Everything okay in the
new job? Are they treating you well?"

"Okay? That's very American. Yes, it's fine. I'm the secret Mr. Dietrich."

I winced. "It wasn't my decision. I announced when I first arrived that
I was married and had a child. The studio was upset. Apparently, women
of mystery must remain unattached."

"It's not that." He met my eyes. "Marlene, have you been reading the
newspapers?"

"Yes, whenever I can. They send me clippings of my notices and—"

"Not about you," he said. "About Germany. Don't you know what's
happening here?"

I recalled what Gary had said, *I hear it's not so nice now. Lots of unrest. The war
knocked you Krauts down pretty hard,* and guiltily shook my head. "Not really."

"Well, things are worse." He reached for my cigarettes. I was taken
aback to see his hand tremble as he struck the match. He wasn't just holding something back; he seemed frightened in a way I'd never seen before.
"Unemployment and inflation are at record highs. In September, Hitler
gained forty-five percent of the vote. His party is now the second-most
powerful party. He uses the wireless to give speeches written by his propa-

ganda minister, Josef Goebbels, who wrote a novel that no publisher will touch because it's so anti-Semitic. Goebbels has refined Hitler's message that Jewish financiers plot our downfall. Many people believe it."

I had a sudden memory of that day when Leni and I were stopped by Hitler's acolytes and felt once again the same surge of revulsion. "Surely, not everyone is so stupid. The wealthy, the financiers and literati—no intelligent person would ever believe such nonsense."

"The steel tycoon Thyssen made a major donation to the party. So did the industrialist Quandt. Even the American Henry Ford supports them. They think only Hitler can save us." Rudi sighed. "Many of our best talent are starting to leave. William Dieterle, whom you worked with, has gone to America to direct pictures. So are others. Among those who do read the newspapers or listen to the speeches, there is fear. We think Hitler will win the chancellorship in the next Reichstag. It's what he's been campaigning toward and he won't stop until he gets it."

I clenched my hands. "What are you saying? Do you want to leave, too?"

"No. At least, not yet. But Heidede—we want you to take her with you. Tamara and I have spoken about it, Marlene. We don't want to send her away; we know you love her dearly, but with this business about hiding our marriage because of the studio . . ."

"Forget the studio." I leaned to him. "What do *you* want?"

"She's in school now," he said. "The Nazis have support among teachers, who tell the children that Jews are our enemies. I don't want her exposed to their propaganda."

It horrified me to hear this, but his request also took me aback. "You want me to take our daughter away from everyone she knows, from you, Tami, and my mother? Rudi, she is German. She was born here, like you and me. I may work in America, but it's not our country."

"I know. But I don't think Germany will be our country for much longer."

"You can't possibly be serious," I said.

"I am," he replied somberly, "as everyone who has heard Hitler should be."

I made no immediate decision. I wasn't due to leave until April, so I focused on celebrating Heidede's birthday on December 12 and my own, my thirtieth, two weeks later, amid the Christmas and New Year's festivities, which my family celebrated with us.

I found Mutti careworn yet as stalwart as ever, and as unimpressed by my success. "Such drivel," she said. "That desert picture. And must you always show your legs and arms? You're not exactly slender. Is it the new style there, to have fat women parade about half naked?"

I sighed. "Mutti, I'm not fat. And I'm under contract. I do what the studio tells me."

She eyed me. "Or what that Austrian Jew tells you. I'm not saying being fat is bad. I'm saying you should be more discreet. Playing prostitutes and showgirls is not an honorable way to make a career."

At least, she admitted I had a career. I knew it was useless to argue, as her opinions were engraved in stone. I gave her money, told her to stop housekeeping (she wouldn't), and saw Liesel, who was happy in her marriage but forlorn over her inability to bear a child. During a sad afternoon with Uncle Willi, whose business had suffered from the downturn, I learned that Jolie had indeed left him—for an aviator, of all people. My uncle was disconsolate. I gave him hugs and advice, and money, as well. I longed to ask him about his homosexuality but didn't want to force a confession or a barrage of denial; with Jolie gone, there seemed to be no point, and it was, after all, his secret to keep, even if it had cost him his marriage.

Then I went to visit my old haunts: the cabarets in the Nollendorfplatz, the Reinhardt academy, the Nelson revue, and other places where I'd performed. I was eagerly welcomed, invited to drink and dine, but my fame proved unavoidable. One night at Das Silhouette, where I'd hoped to arrive incognito, dressed in a man's overcoat and fedora, I was identified within seconds. A mob erupted, tearing at my clothes; I had to be ferried out the back door. And when I attended Friedrich Hollaender's new show, the audience refused to let it start until I took to the stage and sang. Eventually, I had no choice but to agree to the UFA's repeated behest to go into their studio and record some of my stage and film songs in German for a limited-release disc.

I wanted to feel flattered. Germany had not forgotten me. But for the first time, I realized I might never be able to return and live in my own country. I was too exposed here, without the muscle of an American studio to protect me. Becoming famous had been my ambition, but the reality of it didn't fulfill me as much as I'd imagined. I was beginning to discover that fame could gnaw away pieces of my life that I might never recover.

And Berlin was no longer the same. The Nazis had plastered their swastika on buildings and marched down the boulevards just as they had in the past, only now in ever-increasing numbers. Just the sight of their brown shirts and the tromping of their boots made me sick. And as I heard the people cheering them on, crying *Heil Hitler!*, Rudi's warning rang in my ears. That taint I'd sensed years ago had started to spread like a cancer.

Still, while the climate was tense, how could Hitler amount to more than a passing phase? He hadn't contended with our character. We were too practical. His aggressive stance would unmask him as a petty tyrant, grinding his grievances on everyone's back.

Nevertheless, the Jews bore the brunt of it. Their districts had been vandalized; I saw shocking evidence of hatred in the grand emporiums of the Wertheim chain on Leipziger Platz and the Kaufhaus des Westens on Wittenbergplatz, the display windows smashed, the facades spray-painted with insults like *Judenschwein!* In defiance, I took Heidede and Tamara with me to shop there, allowing myself to be photographed and purchasing as much as I could. But these venerable stores, some of Berlin's most refined, were now half empty, the shelves depleted of goods and the sales staff clearly on edge.

Then von Sternberg telephoned me. *Morocco* had been the most successful picture of the year in the midst of the Depression, earning four Academy Award nominations, including one for him as director and me as best actress. Before I could absorb this incredible news, he went on to say that on the heels of *Morocco*'s success, the studio had released *The Blue*

Angel. It, too, made a significant profit, cementing my image as an erotic temptress.

"*Dishonored* may not have paid off," von Sternberg said, "but even Garbo has been forced to take notice. A journalist asked her what she thought of you and do you know what that Swede bitch replied? 'Marlene Dietrich? Who is she?'" He rattled on, not allowing me a moment to get a word in. "I've a new picture for you, about a fallen woman on a Chinese train. *Grand Hotel* on wheels. I need you back as soon as possible. Schulberg is enthused; he's hiring the Brit Clive Brook as your love interest."

"But the studio told me I had until April," I exclaimed. "I only just got here."

"You're scheduled for fittings on the first. Be here. And don't get fat." He hung up.

I knew that as soon as I returned, I'd be relegated to the studio, shooting all day and often long into the night. How would Heidede fare in an American school for children of celebrities, transported to and from home in a hired car, and only if Paramount let her stay with me?

The answer to my dilemma came unexpectedly. After returning from another shopping expedition with Tamara and Heidede, we entered the apartment with our purchases to find my past waiting for me. I came to a halt, dumping hatboxes at my feet.

"It—it can't be," I said.

Rudi chuckled. "She called me at the studio. I have no idea how she found me."

"I'm a journalist, remember?" said Gerda. "Or I was. Now, I'm unemployed."

I embraced her, so overwhelmed that I started to cry.

"Oh, no," she whispered. "None of that. I won't have it."

Over coffee, she told me she'd been let go from her job in Munich. "That would be the genteel term to use. Actually, I was fired. My editor went on vacation, so I wrote an opinion piece on Hitler." She grimaced. "They're bullies, criminals, and thugs. The assistant editor agreed with me, so we ran the piece in the Sunday edition. When our editor came back, he was enraged. Turns out he wasn't on vacation at all; he was attending one of their rallies! He sacked both of us without a reference. He said if he has his way, we'd never work in Germany again."

"Oh, Gerda." I took her hands in mine. She looked the same, in her dowdy skirt and old-fashioned shirtwaist, but thinner, her cheeks hollowed and her eyes dull. And when Tamara set a plate of cakes on the table, she devoured them like a fugitive. "What are you going to do?"

"I don't know. Get out as soon as I can." She gave me one of her mordant looks. "It's what we must do these days before Hitler eats us all alive." Her mirth faded. "Only I don't have any money." She forced out a smile. "But enough about me. Tell me about you. I saw *The Blue Angel*. Marlene, you were wonderful! Remember how I used to make you recite Shakespeare? Who would have thought you'd end up straddling a barrel in your underwear instead?"

I laughed but didn't let go of her hand. "Gerda, you must let me help you."

Her hand trembled in mine, even as she said, "No. I didn't come here for charity. I wanted to see you, and well—I had nothing else to do."

"I'm serious. You helped me so much. Just tell me where you want to go. I insist."

She averted her eyes. Gerda hated tears, but she was perilously close to them. "I don't know. Paris, maybe? They must need female journalists there with no sense of fashion." She lifted her gaze. She was crying. "I have no idea. I don't know where I belong anymore."

I hugged her, letting her weep on my shoulder. Heidede wandered in and stopped, staring at us. As I looked over Gerda's shoulder at her, I suddenly knew what to do.

II

I boarded the ship for America with my sullen daughter, who berated me for taking her away from Rudi, her grandmother, and Tamara. Perversely, she clung to Gerda, whom I'd hired to be her official governess. To my surprise, Gerda had a knack for calming my daughter's tantrums; and once again, as with Tamara, I had to endure my child transferring her affection to a woman who wasn't me.

It couldn't be helped. I needed someone I could trust in America to look after my child, and once Gerda accepted my offer, I'd telephoned von Sternberg with my decision. There was a long silence during which I held my breath before he said, "Schulberg won't like it, but what can he do? He can't separate you from your child indefinitely."

"Tell him I'll do my best to keep her out of the press," I said, suddenly anxious that I might put my contract at risk. "She has a governess, so she can be educated at home. Perhaps after this picture, we can do one where I play a mother, to prepare the public. I've just turned thirty. I can't play cabaret girls forever."

"We'll see," he said.

My ocean crossing was uneasy because I was uncertain if he agreed or thought me irresponsible and reckless. By the time we reached New York,

I braced for the onslaught, dressed to the teeth in my new European fashions, hoping to distract the reporters. I had Gerda and Heidede disembark first and take a private car to the Hotel Ambassador. I appeared an hour later, followed by my mounds of luggage. The press flashed their cameras in my face, besieging me with questions about my trip, but to my relief, no one asked about my husband or my child.

"Don't think they've forgotten," chided von Sternberg when we arrived in Beverly Hills. "You may have dangled couture bait to confuse them, but someone will spot the child coming and going from here, and that will be that."

"Then I'll tell the truth. Germany isn't where she should be right now."

"The truth is hardly the point. A loving mother, anxious for her child, can always be turned into good publicity, but the husband she left behind? Not so easy."

He was astute. Within days, the *Los Angeles Times* printed on its front page a photograph of Heidede and me shopping in Berlin—leaked by Paramount's associate and rival, the UFA, who wanted me back and must have thought adverse publicity would spoil my carefully crafted American image.

Paramount sprang into action, spinning, as von Sternberg had assured me, hay into gold. A series of studio shots supervised by my director were taken, with Heidede and me in matching velvet outfits. This visible evidence of our reunion proved irresistible to the gossip mill, with Louella Parsons herself coming to my defense. But my secret was out. Marlene Dietrich had a husband, too, the studio had to declare, lest anyone thought my child illegitimate. He worked in Berlin under Paramount's auspices, but the studio hoped to secure him a job soon in America.

In the meantime, Heidede was tutored by Gerda, who also assumed the role of my private secretary. I went back to work.

ENVELOPED IN A SHEATH OF BLACK and a veiled cap, egret plumage sprouting about her throat and a skullcap of raven curved enticingly around her left cheek, Shanghai Lily has a chance encounter with a British officer and former flame upon the serpentine train traveling through war-torn China. "It took more than one man to change my name to Shanghai Lily," she purrs, but he is the man for her, and her surrender to the sadistic Communist rebel leader in order to save him brings her full circle, back into her officer's arms.

Clive Brook played my flame. Already established in his own right, all jawline and British stoicism, he had no issues with von Sternberg's authoritarian style or mandate that I be front and center. He understood my name had top billing and was confident enough to take it in stride. I didn't find him nearly as engaging as Gary, but who was? He could recite his lines and knew when to step aside—and that, said von Sternberg, was all we required of him.

To my delight, *Shanghai Express* reunited me with Anna May Wong. She'd returned to Los Angeles and von Sternberg cast her as Lily's companion-in-sin, Hui Fei. Being with Anna again was a joy; we laughed together off camera at the ridiculous script and gossiped in my dressing room, where she told me that our other sister about town, Leni Riefenstahl, was still acting in Fanck's Alpine epics and had taken to hobnobbing with influential Nazis.

"After she lost *The Blue Angel* to you, she decided she wanted to be a director and make her own films," said Anna, with a sarcastic roll of her eyes. "She's become very friendly with Goebbels. Probably sleeping with him, too. Leni always did know how to work a trick."

I grimaced. "She'll regret it. I was in Berlin. What they're doing there is awful."

"Yes, I heard you made quite the splash, taking your daughter out to shop in Jewish stores." Anna smiled at me impishly. "Did you indulge in violets while you were there?"

I lit a cigarette. "How could I? The press followed me everywhere."

She slid her long-nailed hand over my thigh. "They like violets in Hollywood, too, though here we call them sewing circles. I could show you. It's more common than you think. Louise Brooks and Garbo herself are known to partake. Unlike men who suckle, everyone turns a blind eye to us, provided we're not too outré."

"That's the second time you've mentioned Garbo," I said. "How can you be so sure? No one ever sees her. As far as I know, she never leaves her house except to go to the studio."

"I know because she has a lover. Did you think that noli me tangere air of hers is just for the press? She does indeed want to be left alone. To do as she pleases."

I considered. My affair with Gary had waned. He'd called me to suggest a rendezvous, but I heard Lupe ranting in the background and decided her lunacy wasn't something I wanted to risk, not with Heidede living with me. And with Gerda back in my life, albeit in a platonic way, I missed the intimacy of women. I never felt as though I had to be an ideal with my gender; it was easier, less fraught with expectation.

The call came at the door. "Ten minutes, Miss Dietrich."

Stubbing out my cigarette, I said, "Why not? I could use some divertissement."

Anna purred, "When our circle sees you, you'll be more than entertained, *Liebchen*."

IN WHITE TIE, my hair slicked from my brow and monocle in place, I danced the tango with Anna May before the ladies in a back-alley club. As we pivoted in our ballet of seduction, the women's lips parted as they leaned to whisper to one another in their seats.

"Is she . . . ?" I imagined one of them saying.

"She must be," another replied. "I hear before she was famous, she did it often in Berlin."

Thrusting my hips against Anna May, I kissed her ruby mouth.

The company of the sewing circle was delectable.

III

*S*hanghai *Express* premiered in February 1932. It was a huge success, earning more than any of my previous pictures and staving off bankruptcy for Paramount. It was also nominated for five Academy Awards, but not for me. I didn't win for *Morocco*, either, nor did von Sternberg, who remarked, "We're still Krauts, no matter that we pay the studio's bills."

And the studio knew it. Determined to avert the lackluster receipts of *Dishonored*, Paramount had wallpapered the country with posters for *Shanghai Express*, promising a return to the Dietrich of incongruous glamour. My languid drawl and fluttering eyes—during the preview, I cringed at my own performance—as well as my lavish wardrobe became a national conversation, with moviegoers quoting my lines. No one questioned how Shanghai Lily could possibly fit all of her luggage, along with Hui Fei and her gramophone, into a cramped train compartment. Nobody cared. The picture was classic escapism, crafted by von Sternberg in lavish detail—a fantastical China, where the locomotive spouted steam like a dragon as its unlikely passengers are tossed into an unlikely cauldron of passion and intrigue.

In Germany, the Nazis picketed the film. Under an agreement with Paramount, the UFA was screening my pictures, but *Dishonored* had touched a nerve with its indictment of the war. Hitler's propaganda lackey, Goebbels, detested it so much that he called for a party ban on me, declaring me unpatriotic for playing degenerates—and non-German ones, at that.

"'If she cares so much for her nation,'" Gerda read aloud from Nazi press releases, forwarded by Rudi, "'why does Marlene Dietrich refuse to live here? Why does she take American dollars when so many Germans are suffering? She is not one of us. If she were, she'd support Hitler and our cause.'" Gerda snorted. "Not only does he write appallingly, but he makes no sense. American dollars over worthless marks? What is there to question? You must be doing something right if they dislike you so much."

I tried to laugh, but I didn't find it funny. Lighting a cigarette, I paced to my drawing room window. My fully furnished Beverly Hills mansion was as sumptuous as I could want, a pantheon to my elite status, with eucalyptus and bougainvillea rioting at the gates and twelve spacious rooms. I found it cold and uninviting, like a set waiting for the crew to arrive. Outside in the garden by the aviary which von Sternberg had bought for me to celebrate our success, Heidede was feeding the captive birds with my maid, scattering seed into the cages, just like her father with his rooftop pigeons, I thought.

Without looking over my shoulder to where Gerda busied herself at the desk, I said, "Rudi telephoned me at the studio yesterday. The UFA is collaborating with the Nazis and has pulled *Shanghai Express* from their screens. The executives offered him a higher position, but he thinks the suggestion came from Goebbels, to make Rudi, and me, indebted to the party."

Gerda paused in her rustling of papers. "What is he going to do?"

"I told him he should leave. He said he'll consider it as long as he can stay in Europe." I turned to her. "I'm requesting a transfer for him. Schulberg owes me, with all the money I'm making for the studio, and Paramount has an affiliate office in Paris. Schulberg said he'd look into it. He also said Rudi should come here for a visit, that it's time for us to be photographed together as a family. But not Tamara. The studio won't give her a visa." I blew out smoke in exasperation. "Hypocrites."

"Well, if Rudi transfers to Paris, he and Tamara will be safe enough there." Gerda met my eyes. "You look worried. Did he tell you anything else?"

I grimaced. "Only the usual. Hitler shrieking over the wireless and gaining more popularity every day." Unease went through me. "Rudi believes he'll win the next Reichstag. He lost this last election, but that fool Hindenburg is now making concessions to the party. Rudi says many think that if Hitler wins, he'll start another war."

Gerda went quiet. She'd shown only gratitude for my assistance, setting aside her journalistic career to assume charge of my correspondence and Heidede's education, handling the overwhelming volume of fan mail forwarded by the studio and preparing signed, glossy publicity shots of me for admirers in far-flung towns I'd never heard of. But I knew she remained attuned to events abroad. Our circle of expatriates was growing, and while I had no time to socialize, she did. She went out several evenings a week to meet with fellow journalists who'd washed up in California, all penniless and bedraggled.

At length, she said, "I think he will, too. He wants power, legally or otherwise."

"You think he'll go to war?" It was becoming my most pressing fear, that this little Austrian with his ridiculous mustache would pull Germany into conflict.

She lifted her shoulders. "Many of those I've spoken to think the same as Rudi. They say the signs are all there, that he's whipping up patriotic fervor to prepare the country for it."

"Dear God. I can't imagine it. Not after the last one."

"Neither can I. Maybe he won't win the election," she said, but she didn't sound convinced as she returned to her agenda. "Shall I make the arrangements for Rudi's visit?"

"Yes." I turned back to the window. Heidede was clapping her hands, making the parrots caw. "I'll telephone him next week; I should know about the Paris transfer by then."

RUDI ARRIVED WITH TWO STEAMER TRUNKS filled with teddy bears and books in German for Heidede. He was dapper and smiling, as if he hadn't spent the last twelve days traveling, and I was so happy to see him that I insisted on taking time off. Von Sternberg was not pleased. He was impatient for us to start working on a new script, telling me that Schulberg was willing to consider a maternal role for me, if, after the studio writers had failed to deliver anything worthwhile, we prepared a suitable treatment. I delayed von Sternberg with the excuse that I had to spend some time with Rudi and Heidede, which prompted him to join us as we toured sites around the city and took a trip to Monterey. Because of his brooding presence, I did not query Rudi about the situation in Germany, as the mere mention of Hitler could make von Sternberg rabid. But I did let Rudi know he had the job in Paris, and Gerda would handle, via studio intermediaries, moving Tamara to an apartment there and terminating the lease on the Kaiserallee flat.

I took comfort in my renewed domesticity. I liked having my family about me, and cooking for them gave me a sense of purpose, the one activity where I could brew the ingredients and create the result, rather than be something others brewed in my name. Besides, Rudi wasn't used to American cuisine, if there even was such a thing, so I inaugurated my cavernous kitchen by making him roast beef, goulash, potato pancakes, cheese blintzes, and scrambled eggs with slices of the Bavarian sausage that he'd brought stashed in his trunk.

Von Sternberg often joined us. He had no other place to go since his recent divorce, his wife having left him and suing him for alimony he couldn't afford to pay. He watched me sardonically as I served the table in my apron, my brow beaded with steam from the pot.

"Ah. The devoted hausfrau," he mocked. He'd been drinking too much, already halfway through his bottle of bootleg vodka. "You'll do anything to get a picture made, won't you?"

"Josef, please," I said. Heidede was watching him curiously. She liked him. She enjoyed his oddities, as he came by frequently to sleep in a spare bedroom and sometimes dragged out an easel and canvas to the garden to paint. Unlike his films, his paintings swirled with color, vivid skies and clusters of birds of paradise or lemony acacia. She had one of his paintings in her room. I always wondered how such a monochrome mind on camera could produce such joyous riots on canvas.

"Cooking soothes me," I went on. "And we have nothing to shoot. But I've started drafting a story about a mother who loses her child. I'll show it to you when it's finished."

"She'll show it to me!" He turned a spiteful smile on Rudi. My husband had been congenial, accepting of von Sternberg shadowing our every move, though it was clear that my director, embittered over his divorce, was envious that despite the odds, Rudi and I were still married. "She's rejected a dozen ideas since *Shanghai Express,* insisting she must play a nice girl this time, and now she has a story. Schulberg is not impressed. He refuses to consider it."

"What?" I stared at him. "You told me he was considering it. As long as we gave him something in writing that he could show to New York."

"Did I?" Von Sternberg poured himself another glass. As he shifted the bottle to Rudi, my husband declined with a polite shake of his head. "I must have been mistaken. You're not Kate Hepburn. You should stick to what you do best."

"What I do is being banned, and not only by Goebbels. The Hays Office here is starting to complain, too. They say my image is 'incompatible with American values.'" I quoted the direct source. The Hays Office was a hideous American censorship organization that Hollywood had endorsed and in so doing had created its own monster, with increasingly tight regulations as to what could or could not be seen on the screen that threatened us all.

Von Sternberg made a farting sound, making Heidede giggle. "Those Hays idiots are so full of gas, they wouldn't know an incompatible value if it blew out their bottoms. Controversy is good. It sells tickets." He paused, lighting a cigarette, though we hadn't started eating. "Regardless of what the Hays Office says, the studio won't hear of you donning an apron and serving goulash like you do here. That is not the Dietrich they hired."

I turned to Rudi. "What do you think? You read some of those treatments the studio sent. Did you find anything remotely interesting in them?"

Conscious of von Sternberg—as amiable as they were on the surface, theirs was always a détente, as my director did not tolerate interference—my husband said, "I thought they were consistent. It's what the public expects. You've made a lucrative career playing a certain type of woman and—"

I cut him off. "Must you agree with everything to avoid confrontation? I support you, don't I? I found you a job in Paris. A certain type of woman is not who I am."

Rudi went cold. "I never asked for your help."

"You certainly take it," I retorted. Pushing back my chair, heedless of Heidede's astonishment, I marched out into the garden, pulling my cigarettes from my apron pocket.

I heard footsteps behind me. Without turning around, I said, "Leave me alone."

Von Sternberg chuckled. "This is the woman I prefer." He came to stand beside me, abruptly placid. "Does it matter so much to you, this silly idea of playing a mother?"

"Yes. It should matter to you, too. I'm not going to have a career much longer if I keep doing the same part. Much as *you* may lament it, I am not a whore."

He tugged at his mustache. "You earn four thousand dollars a week. Others would suck Schulberg off for half your salary."

"Let them." I flicked my cigarette away. "As I said, I'm not a whore."

"Is this about losing that Academy Award for *Morocco*?" he asked sardonically. "I lost, too. We both did. It's no reason to change what we do."

"Don't be ridiculous. I don't care about some foolish award." I wanted to sound indifferent but a suspicious undertone had crept into my voice. "Maybe you don't think we're capable of making a picture that strays from our formula. You seem as unmoved as me by Paramount's suggestions, only you never expressed an opinion until tonight."

"My opinion is that I should go back to Germany," he said, startling me. "I'm bored with this town, tired of Schulberg and the entire carousel."

"Germany?" I was appalled. "But our friends are leaving in droves. Why would you consider going back there, with that hog Hitler breathing down our necks?"

"Hitler isn't the hog yet. He might never be. He's a brute, but like the Hays Office, I think, he's also much ado about nothing." He met my eyes.

"You could come with me. I know how much you miss it. It's your country, after all, and Rudi is there—"

"Rudi is going to live in Paris. He accepted Schulberg's offer as soon as I told him. Josef, they've banned our pictures. You're a Jew. They hate us. I thought you hated them."

He shrugged. "I do. But I know how these things work. It's all in the details. Goebbels is only making such a stink because he knows how much you could boost morale. The UFA wants you; they'd sign you in a second. And yes, I am a Jew, but I'm also the director who made you famous. Tell me you're not tempted. We'd have so much freedom there. We could write our own contract. You want better parts? In Germany, you can have them. Any part you like."

I regarded him in horrified amazement. I remembered Rudi, what he'd said that night in Berlin: *He's unlike any filmmaker we've ever known. But I also think he must be quite mad.*

"Better roles playing a Nazi fräulein?" I said. "Never."

Yet deep within, I felt myself hesitate. He had roused an unnerving doubt, stoking my anxiety that the longer I stayed in Hollywood, accepting roles that cast me in a certain light, the more captive I would become. I'd heard plenty of stories of stars who'd overstayed their welcome and found themselves relegated to bit parts or no parts at all. Not working didn't frighten me. Becoming obsolete did. I wanted to stay or go on my own terms.

Von Sternberg sensed it. He knew me too well. "Never, because you're too proud?" he asked. "Or never because you can't refuse Paramount's salary?"

"You know money doesn't mean a thing to me. I take what they give and I spend it."

"Perhaps. But fame means something." He lowered his voice, but not his scathing insight. "You're not a devoted wife or mother. You might be one day, but right now you're too busy being Dietrich. I saw that passion in you when we met. You represent the Zeitgeist: the spirit of our age. And you can't leave it behind. No matter what, you want all of it."

"Didn't you just tell me I could have the same in Germany?" I retorted, resisting the horrid truth in his words, which made me feel callous and soiled.

"Yes, but here you're overpaid for it. The UFA cannot match your salary. So. Money does mean something, after all."

"Damn you. You are supposed to be my friend."

"Your friend? I am not your friend. I am your mentor. Your creator. Your slave." His face hardened. Without warning, he pulled me to him. "How do you think it makes me feel knowing that everything you are, everything you give, is because of me? Do you think it's been easy for me, letting you take over my existence and knowing you'll never fuck me like Gary Cooper? Do you think I *enjoy* it, being made a cuckold, like that worm you call a husband? Or don't you think about me at all?"

His eyes had turned to slits, his breath rank from tobacco and drink. Looking down at his fingers pinching my arm, I said, "Let me go," and when he did, furious now, understanding, perhaps for the first time, that I didn't think about him that way, I never had and never would, he snarled, "You'd step over Heidede's dead body for a part."

I whipped out my hand, cracking him across the face. "Never say that again. *Never.*"

He suddenly laughed—a harsh, scornful caw. "Devoted mother and wife, indeed. *This* is who you are. *This* is the woman the studio pays for and the public demands. Dietrich the strong, the capable, the ruthless. The sultry trollop with a heart of stone."

"Go." I was trembling. "Get out of my house."

He smiled. "Am I to be exiled?" Swiftly, before I could stop him, he seized my chin and kissed me, his mustache scraping my lips. "I'll get you your role," he whispered. "I'll sell it to Schulberg if I have to suck him off myself. You'll have your chance to play the mother, but don't say I didn't warn you. Because you'll have no one to blame but yourself."

He left. As I heard his automobile roar out of the driveway and I realized he was drunk and could have an accident, I stood frozen, more aware of the danger he posed to me than the danger he might be to himself.

He had seen inside me, to that dark place where corruption had started to take root.

For he was right. I did want it. All of it. No matter what.

IV

As soon as I saw Rudi onto the train back to New York and his ship for Paris, I was summoned to the studio. Von Sternberg had submitted a sketchy treatment for our next picture.

"Helen Faraday," said Schulberg as we sat in his white-paneled office, his permanent cigar smoldering in the ashtray on his desk, turning the air acrid. "A foreign ex-chanteuse married to an American chemist, with a son, who must return to the stage when her husband is diagnosed with radium poisoning and needs money to go abroad for a cure." He looked up from the paper he held. "That's it. One paragraph. Is this really your idea?"

I wore my tweed suit, a tie, and a beret, with almost no makeup. I'd dressed like a man on purpose, to meet him as an equal. I understood now how ludicrous it was. Clothes were not going to sway a studio executive with absolute control over my career.

"It is, but he'll flesh it out more," I said, reaching into my pocket for my cigarettes. I'd been taken unawares but wouldn't let him see it. "There'll be songs. Costumes and the rest."

His brow furrowed. "Marlene, this concerns me. *He* concerns me. He mentioned a UFA offer, told me you're both unhappy. I hope I don't need to remind you that you're under contract to us. Negotiations with another studio are cause for immediate suspension."

I paused, my lighter at my cigarette. Von Sternberg had wielded the UFA as ammunition, to push the studio into yielding to us. I had to admire his gall.

"You did say you'd consider a role like this for me next. You had the studio photograph me with my daughter and husband to show the public I have a family. It's not such a risk. Is it?"

He gave a troubled sigh. "Not in theory. Adoptions are up nationwide since we announced you have a daughter. Everyone wants a little girl of their own now, with the matching outfit of course. You've done the improbable: a woman of mystery, a sophisticated lady, and now a devoted mother."

"Then what is there to object to? Not even Garbo has managed to play a mother, a singer, and a sophisticated lady at the same time."

He narrowed his gaze. "She hasn't, but if she wanted to, MGM would still need more than a paragraph to sell it to corporate."

"I'll get more. Jo has it all figured out in his head. You know how he is."

"Unfortunately, we both do." Schulberg hesitated, his fingertips tapping the paper. "But I trust you. Nevertheless," he said as I rose to my feet to shake his hand, "I need a script. Or something that at least reads like one."

I went straight to von Sternberg's studio bungalow. In his habitual manner of disdaining what he no longer deemed relevant, he behaved as if he'd forgotten about our confrontation, handing me a sheaf of paper. "Here it is. *Blonde Venus*. It's your story idea; you'll sing and suffer your way into America's heart as a heroic woman who'll do anything for her family."

"I am going to read it," I warned. "If I don't like it, neither will Schulberg."

"Whatever you don't like, we'll change. Go. Take it to him. I want to start as soon as possible. I've had enough of sitting around. We're here to make pictures, so let's make one."

The script wasn't complete, but it contained enough to assuage Schulberg. My character becomes an overnight sensation, providing me with the picture's signature number. Courted by a millionaire sophisticate, Helen falls into an affair. When her husband returns from his cure abroad, he threatens to take their son because of her adultery and she flees with the boy across Depression-riddled America until she has to surrender her child. Then she disappears only to reemerge in Paris, where she's found fame at the Moulin Rouge—another opportunity for me to flaunt my white tie. After her sophisticate sees her there, he takes her back to New York to visit her son. Her husband forgives her. She sacrifices fame and fortune for domestic bliss.

I was determined to show I could do more than spout witticisms or display my legs. The studio cast a contract player named Cary Grant as the sophisticate, his wavy black hair and matinee chin marking him as a star on the rise. He was charming, but I felt no attraction to him, which troubled me until Anna May told me that Mr. Grant was a man who suckled, sharing a home with the actor Randolph Scott. Von Sternberg filled the film with lingering shots of trains and squalid shantytowns, shot in his visionary black and white.

It all made me squirm in my seat when I attended the studio preview.

To my dismay, when the camera wasn't peering up my nostrils, I kept my face averted as if I feared someone might throw stones at me. I almost laughed aloud, my performance was so wooden, my scenes with Cary Grant sodden and unconvincing. Only in my three songs did I come alive, especially in "Hot Voodoo," where Helen emerges from a sweltering gorilla disguise clad in a bugle-beaded short dress and donning a blond Afro wig, throws aside her destitution to embody the very persona I'd sought to escape. I'd seen none of this in the rushes; I thought I was playing a completely different character. Von Sternberg had assured me of as much. Instead, when the lights flickered on in the screening room, Schulberg met my gaze and shook his head.

"It won't work," he said, as his invited executives—the head of publicity and sales, the other menials whose only job at the studio was to please him—hurried out.

I stood, looking around for von Sternberg before I remembered that he never attended these screenings, considering them a demeaning pandering to the studio might. "He must still be editing it," I said. "It's obviously not finished yet."

"I sincerely hope not," said Schulberg. "It'll never make it through the Hays Office codes as it is. She sleeps with another man while her husband is away. She abducts her own child and sells—well, we both know what she sells to support them."

"Yes, but she has no other choice." Despite my effort to stay calm, my voice rose defensively. "She's protecting her child. She can't sing for their food."

"I wish she would. I wish she'd do anything but what I've seen." He sighed. "Have you forgotten the Lindberghs, whose baby was recently kidnapped and found dead? How can I submit a picture to the Hays Office that features an abduction, the very thing that's become a national tragedy?"

I hadn't forgotten. Or rather, I hadn't paid attention, so preoccupied with the work that I'd failed to mark the coincidence. But von Sternberg must have. Belatedly, I realized my mentor, creator, and slave had fulfilled his promise. He'd given me what I wanted, and, as he'd warned, I had no one to blame but myself.

"I'll speak to him," I said. "We'll reshoot anything that needs it, I promise."

"Don't promise. Do it," replied Schulberg. "He went over budget again with that 'Hot Voodoo' number. Two chorus girls weren't enough. I'll let him fix it—*if* he does it right this time. Otherwise, I'm pulling it. And if I do, I'll assign your next picture myself. Without von Sternberg."

I reached for my cashmere coat, adjusting my hat when his secretary arrived. She whispered to him. I watched his face change, his disappointment over the picture turning into something more serious. He looked up at me. My stomach plummeted.

"We've had a call from your assistant, Miss Huber. There's a car ready to take you home at once. Pack your bags; we're booking you into a hotel. Forget the picture and von Sternberg for now. Someone has threatened your daughter."

*   *   *

I ARRIVED AT MY HOUSE in a panic to find police milling outside. One came toward me, a notepad in hand. He started to say, "Miss Dietrich. Not to worry. Your daughter is fine—" But I pushed him aside and ran shouting into the house, "Gerda! Heidede!"

They were in the drawing room, with more policemen surrounding them. Heidede looked terrified. As I swept her into my arms, I met Gerda's stunned stare and then looked past her to the ransacked desk, papers strewn everywhere as a detective sorted through them, sheet by sheet.

"What—what happened?" I was gripping Heidede so tightly that she whimpered.

Gerda murmured, "Not in front of her," and I reluctantly called for one of our maids to take Heidede up to her room. "Pack her suitcase," I ordered, and I heard my daughter ask as she was led out, "What's wrong? Where are we going?"

I yanked out my cigarettes, lit one with a trembling hand as the detectives finished their work and the one with the notepad, whom I'd shoved aside, showed me a note, enclosed in cellophane. The envelope had no reply address, the note written in crude block letters:

> YOU MARLENE DIETRICH. IF YOU WANT TO SAVE MARIA WAIT FOR INFORMATION. PAY $10,000 OR BE SORRY. DON'T CALL POLICE.

"It says to not notify the police." I whirled to Gerda. "Why did you call them?"

Before she could respond, the detective said, "She did the right thing. Since the Lindbergh case, we've had a rash of these copycat threats. Nothing to worry about."

"Nothing to worry about? They threatened to take my child!"

"No," he said, to my aghast disbelief. "They're saying they'll contact you for money. I suggest installing bars on the windows, changing the locks, and hiring a full-time security detail, Miss Dietrich. The studio can provide it. We'll trace the note through the postal service but these people know how to cover their tracks. They'll send one or two more notes to see if you cave in, and when you don't, they'll stop. They want easy money, not a federal charge of kidnapping."

"They can send whatever they want. After this, we are *not* staying here."

He jutted out his lower lip. "Suit yourself. But we'll assign extra patrols to the area. Your house will be closely watched. I assure you, your daughter is safe."

"Tell that to the Lindberghs," I retorted, and with an uncomfortable nod, he reviewed the remaining papers, sifting through my fan mail, and then departed with his men, carrying a box full of letters from strangers who wanted my photograph.

All of a sudden, Gerda and I were alone, though the maids were still here, tiptoeing about the house, and the studio chauffeur, an ex-prizefighter named Briggs, waited outside with the car.

"You shouldn't have called them," I said to her.

"I did what I thought best." Her voice was subdued. I could see she'd suffered a terrible fright; she was colorless, her eyes like bruises. "It's been all over the newspapers and the wireless, that horrible kidnapping of the aviator's baby. When I opened the envelope and saw the note—what was I supposed to do? I telephoned you at the studio, but whoever answered at the switchboard said you were in a screening with Schulberg and couldn't be disturbed."

"You should have insisted. Did you tell whoever answered that we'd received a threat?"

Gerda's mouth thinned. "I didn't. I thought of the press; you know how some people at the studio sell gossip to reporters. I called Schulberg's office instead, but I had to try several times before his secretary picked up. By then, I'd decided to alert the police. I take care of Heidede every day and she was in no danger. She was here with me the entire time."

"Some care." I heard myself and knew I was being hysterical. The police had arrived. Heidede was unharmed—scared, but not hurt. But I felt myself unraveling, fragments of my composure breaking apart inside me. "You let her play alone in the garden, feeding those nasty parrots. She's constantly running around. Thank God we don't have a pool. She could drown before anyone would notice. I pay you to look after her, and now I have to worry about her safety on top of everything else."

"Marlene." Her firm tone of voice wrenched my gaze back to her. "I take my responsibilities very seriously. This is not my fault."

"I don't care whose fault it is," I shot back at her. "She's my child."

Gerda regarded me in tense silence for a moment. "I'm sorry about all this. I'd rather die than let anything happen to Heidede, but you have to admit—"

"What? What do I have to admit? Are you implying this is *my* fault? Did I send that note here for extra publicity?"

It was an absurd thing to say, and she confirmed it. "I would never think that. But the very fact that you think I might means everything. You are not the person I thought you were."

"*Gott in Himmel.* Are you accusing me of something? If so, just come out with it."

"Heidede," she said, and the way she spoke my daughter's name, the squaring of her shoulders under her button-up blouse with that antiquated collar she still favored, made me clench my fists. "She's growing up without a mother. Without a father. She eats too much. She's miserable. She doesn't like it here. She never has. Have you noticed? Have you ever asked her? When Rudi left, she cried for days. She begged him to take her with him. Did you know?"

"No," I spat out. "But if I had, it wouldn't matter. She belongs with me. And it's none of your business. I hired you so it would be nobody's business but mine."

"I see." She reached into her skirt pocket and removed her house key, setting it on the desk. "I'm resigning, Marlene. I love you. But this is not my place. It's not my country or the job I was trained to do. I won't be your servant."

"When did I ever expect you to be my servant?"

"You do. But you can't see it. Me, Rudi, von Sternberg, the studio, even Heidede—in your mind, we exist only to please you. Nothing is more important than your success. When you're happy, we're happy. When you are not . . ." She sighed. "You're extraordinary. But all this business of being Dietrich is destroying you."

I flung out my arms. "Without this, there would be nothing to destroy. No Dietrich. No money. And no servitude for you to resign from." And then, as I realized what I had admitted, the enormity of it, she replied, "You think that. You may even believe it. But none of this is real. Don't forget it. One day, you may need your friends more than you know."

As she stepped past me, moving to the staircase down which Heidede was coming with the maid and her suitcase, I wanted to stop her. I wanted to implore her forgiveness for being so selfish, so blind, that I'd not seen how much she'd given up for me, her career and her ambition to write, and Germany, our country, which neither of us recognized anymore. Instead, I said to her retreating figure, "I'll leave your final pay on the desk," and I let her go. I let her walk out of my life.

In that moment, she was a sacrifice I was willing to make.

FROM THE BEVERLY HILLS HOTEL, in a top-floor suite with a guard at the door, I phoned Rudi in Paris, sobbing. He said I must send Heidede to him at once. But Paramount and the police investigated the threat and it turned out to be a scam. The culprits were never found. Still, reporters caught wind of it, exaggerating the drama until I had to declare in an unauthorized telephone interview with *Photoplay* that while no harm had been done, besides the tremendous fear we'd endured, I couldn't stay in America and was considering returning to Europe.

The studio was furious. I'd spoken out without permission, intimating they hadn't protected me, though they'd provided every security measure possible—a bodyguard for me and Heidede, a private car, a German shepherd watchdog, and enough grills on the windows to keep out Houdini.

I was under contract, with a picture that required urgent attention. Von Sternberg was nowhere to be found; he'd disappeared before that abysmal screening. The studio suspended him, hired another director, and demanded I return to the set at once. Demonstrating that he wasn't entirely without scruples, von Sternberg resurfaced in New York to issue a statement. He refused to reshoot the picture, citing creative license. Schulberg sued him for breach of contract. Sequestered with Heidede in my prison of a home in Beverly Hills, as she cried incessantly for Gerda or Rudi, for anyone but me, I would not leave her alone for a second.

The studio suspended me, too.

Blonde Venus was a disaster. I wasn't surprised when von Sternberg eventually called me, apologetic. "I honestly thought we'd made a splendid picture. But if we don't do as they say, we'll never work in Hollywood again." He paused. I did not say a word. "Schulberg is willing to rescind both our suspensions if we agree to reshoot the offending scenes."

I didn't have to ask why he had relented. He needed the money. He had court-appointed alimony payments. I could hold out, not for very long, but longer than he could.

"Which scenes?" I finally said, not caring if the picture was consigned to a bonfire. Gerda's departure had taken time to sink in, but when it did, I wept bitter tears. She was right. I had let my success change me. I'd been so mired in my own preoccupations, I'd lost her friendship and alienated my child. I was beginning to question my willingness to be a star.

"What else?" he said. "Helen's prostitution. Hiding her boy under the bed so she can meet a john. Oh, and a new ending, where she runs a bath for her son. In an evening gown."

"Of course." I sighed. "I'll meet with Travis Banton. When are you arriving?"

By the time he appeared on the set, Helen had a new black satin dress, backless and clinging to me like wet skin. Despite the uproar and excoriation by critics, *Blonde Venus* proved popular with audiences. The Lindbergh tragedy gave it timeliness, as did its depiction of a mother forced

V

It was 1933, the year of my thirty-second birthday.

Hitler had won the chancellorship in Germany, ousting the cabinet, and abolishing the Weimar Republic. More friends fled, joining our ranks of exiles in the United States. My former director from *Little Napoleon*, Ernst Lubitsch, had been one of the first to leave and established himself in Hollywood. He suggested an adaptation of the classic Sudermann novel, *The Song of Songs*; the author was German, as was the setting. Not only would my role be unique—a devout girl in turn-of-the-century Berlin, who poses for a statue of the faithful lover in the Song of Solomon—but our collaboration would demonstrate solidarity with our nation, and our shared odium for Hitler, for Sudermann had been Jewish.

Schulberg liked the idea, but did not endorse Lubitsch as my director, hiring instead the Russian, Rouben Mamoulian, fresh off a popular screen adaptation of *Dr. Jekyll and Mr. Hyde*.

"A former stagehand," I complained to von Sternberg as he prepared to leave for his own directorial assignment. Since the kidnapping threat and Gerda's departure, he'd been attentive, staying in my spare bedroom to keep us company at night. Though I had more staff than I knew what to do with, given my chauffeur, the maids, the bodyguard, and the dog, I no longer felt safe. I wanted to change residences, which the studio would not allow. "What can he possibly know about Germany or Sudermann?"

"Mamoulian was a theater director in Russia; he's been working here since the talkies." Von Sternberg serenely folded his clothes into his bag, which only made me angrier. My resolve to be less attached to the foibles of fame had crumbled with the moment of truth upon me. He had built my career; I considered it *our* career. How could he now so blithely disregard it?

"That doesn't make him an expert," I said.

"Marlene. This stagehand, as you call him, was first hired to coach actors with their dialogue. He'll make sure your English pronunciation is perfect. And he's had some success."

"So have we. Don't you care anymore?"

"Of course I care. I'm not abandoning you. It's just for one picture. And, my beloved, you chose it; it'll be a good one, even without me, and especially without Lubitsch. Mamoulian has a refined visual style. And you'll sing only one song, in period dress." He chuckled. "No legs."

Everything he said made sense, but I still didn't like how easily he could say it. "I don't see why, if you have such an understanding of the material, you can't direct it yourself."

"How soon we forget." He kissed my cheek, unfazed. "Telephone me whenever you like. This film they've ordered me to do shoots nearby, at some dreary location called Mono Lake."

"Why bother?" I retorted. "Mamoulian might be teaching me how not to lisp."

I wasn't about to let von Sternberg's absence derail me, and set out to show my new director that my years of experience had provided me with a master class in technique. By now, I could test my key light by licking my finger and holding it up to gauge the heat, and I viewed the daily rushes to see if the telltale butterfly shadow was under my nose. Every day before shooting, I lowered the boom mike and said into it, "Oh, Jo. Why have you forsaken me?" which made the crew laugh and turned my director apoplectic. I also had a full-length mirror installed off camera, so I could gauge my angles, and insisted on modeling personally for the nude statue of Lily in the picture so it would look like me, all of which amused von Sternberg to no end.

"Banton may cover you in muttonchop sleeves and bustles," he said over the phone when he called me, "but you've made sure Dietrich remains on full display. More so, I believe, than ever before."

He made me laugh in spite of myself, and to my relief, the shoot took only ten weeks. After the premiere, which prompted another thundering Nazi condemnation of me for daring to make a movie featuring a nude statue and based on a Jewish novel, the wrap party was held in an ocean-front home in Santa Monica.

Here, I met Mercedes de Acosta.

SHE WAS A BIRD OF A WOMAN, with bright dark eyes, a spare frame, and a long neck enhanced by ropes of painted beads. She styled her lush black hair simply, coiled at her nape, and wore a flowing antique dress that gave her the look of a cameo. There was nothing overtly seductive about her at first sight, but her languid air, belying the intelligence in her gaze, attracted me as I sipped champagne and chatted with my fellow cast members. I could feel her watching me from across the room, poised by balcony doors and an impressive view of the Pacific surf beyond.

She did not approach me. I wandered about as though I hadn't noticed her, until I was beside her and she said in a soft voice with a hint of New York, "I hear the picture is beautiful, Miss Dietrich, and you are beautiful in it. But I imagine it must have been difficult, working with another director after all this time."

It wasn't a question. With a sidelong glance at her, I said, "It's never easy to become someone else, no matter who happens to be behind the camera."

"Ah, yes. The dilemma of acting. Where does the fantasy end and reality begin?"

I found her interesting. She was a writer, she told me, hired by the studios, but unlike others I'd met in Hollywood, she seemed unimpressed by celebrity—and by me.

"I don't believe I've had the pleasure?" I extended my hand. I wore a black-and-silver man's suit over a tuxedo shirt and a bow tie, a velvet cloche on my head and my fingernails and lips painted red.

She took my hand lightly, as if it were a petal. "Mercedes. And I'd like to see if pleasure is what I can offer you."

I did not look around, although we were steps away from Paramount's crème de la crème, including Schulberg, who appeared harried. If *The Song of Songs* tanked, he would sink with it. With the economic crisis eating into studio profits and his resolve to separate me from von Sternberg for this picture, he couldn't afford a misstep.

I smiled at her. "Perhaps it can be arranged."

"Perhaps." She let go of my hand. My fingertips tingled. "Look me up, Miss Dietrich. I'm in the sewing circle directory."

A few days later, I had lunch with Anna May. She cackled when I told her. "She is Garbo's lover. They've been off and on for several years, but Garbo is away at the moment in Sweden. How cunning of you to steal from her, on-screen and off."

"I had no idea," I said. "Mercedes didn't mention her."

"She wouldn't. You're not exactly Garbo's favorite person." Anna May lowered her voice. "I hear our MGM queen had Mamoulian give her a private screening of your new picture. She liked it so much, she lobbied her studio to hire him for her next project."

"Did she?" I wished her the best of luck, as I had found him detestable. "Mercedes said I could find her in the directory. Is there such a thing?"

Anna May burst out laughing again. "Mercedes de Acosta *is* the directory."

The very next day, I had my chauffeur drive me to the oceanfront house. In the daylight, it wasn't so fancy, low and huddled into the cliff, but expensive enough, I assumed, located in a prime area of real estate. I'd heard Cary Grant and his lover shared a beach cottage nearby.

Before I rang the bell, Mercedes opened the door. Her hair hung loose, a cascade of midnight melting over the sloped shoulders of her Japanese robe.

"Marlene," she said. "What took you so long?"

✻   ✻   ✻

I FELL IN LOVE FOR THE SECOND TIME.

I sent lavish bouquets of roses and violets; when she sighed and said her house was starting to look like a flower shop, I sent Lalique knickknacks. I cooked German pot roast and organized her writing studio, which was a chaos of papers. I alphabetized her library, filled with books on every subject, from art to architecture, music, painting, fiction, biographies, poetry, and bound screenplays. I did her laundry and folded her sheets. I might have cleaned her floors, too—parquet got so dirty in beach houses, with all that sand and those bare feet—but she chided me, saying, "I have a maid. If you must get on your knees to please me, do it here. On my bed."

She fascinated me, with her magpie conversation and darting caresses, her small fingers sliding inside me. I found her intoxicating; I'd never met anyone who knew so much about so many topics yet never managed to bore me with her erudition, nor anyone whose tongue could probe me like a hummingbird seeking nectar.

It was she who opened my eyes to the darkness descending upon Germany. She held private salons for exiles, many homosexual immigrants who'd fled Hitler's stranglehold.

"They're burning books," Ernst Lubitsch said. Though he'd not gotten the chance to direct me, he became a friend, and like many exiles, kept a yearning eye on the fatherland. "By the Mann brothers, Marx, Freud, Einstein, and others. They've arrested thousands and abolished free speech. Hitler authorized a censorship office, the Lichtspielgesetz, which specifies regulations for creative works that conform to Aryan ideology. Soon they'll be burning whatever doesn't fit their requirements—and anyone who creates it."

"Hitler used to paint postcards for a living," I said. His very name made me see red. "He hates artists because he failed as one. He's an ugly, envious man."

Yet that ugly envious man was erasing the Berlin I loved, that fabulous playground of decadent joy. I wondered about the girls at Das Silhouette, Yvette and the other transvestites who'd helped me to dress Lola-Lola.

Were they being arrested, too? Had the Nazis barged in and burned all the cabarets to the ground?

"He's not a failure now," said Mercedes. "His manifesto *Mein Kampf* is selling by the millions, both there and abroad. I can only assume no one's bothered to read it. He's very clear about his intent in his book. Germany has no idea of what's coming if he stays in power."

Ernst Lubitsch nodded gravely. "It's true, Marlene. Important people are being assassinated even after having left the country. The philosopher Lessing was shot at his home in Czechoslovakia by a Nazi hit squad. They're rounding up dissidents, sending them to a work camp in Dachau. Anyone with resources is trying to get out now, before passports are revoked."

"Then he's insane!" I exploded. I was incensed as I looked around the circle, at their haunted, disoriented expressions. "How can we let this happen? How can Europe stand by and watch?"

"They believe Hitler is good for Germany." Mercedes clasped my shoulder where I reclined on a cushion by her chaise; I felt her squeeze me in warning. She knew how talk of the Nazis roused me to fury, but her gesture confused me, as her salons were always open to discussion.

"Yes," added Lubitsch. "France and Britain have implemented policies of appeasement; no one is doing anything to help the Jews." He said to me, "Better warn von Sternberg; rumor is, he's been making overtures to the UFA again. He's the last person they want to see."

After they left, I asked Mercedes why she had stopped me. "I must hear everything, no matter how awful. My husband is in Paris now, but my mother, my sister, and my uncle are still in Berlin. If they're at risk, I need to know."

"Are they dissidents?" she asked. "Jews? Marxists? No? Then they're not at risk. I suggest you say as little as possible. Listen, but don't state an opinion."

"Why? I've made no secret of my loathing for Hitler. And that propaganda minister of his, Goebbels, the failed novelist with the limp—he's been campaigning against me."

"Let him. You must remain circumspect. You're worried for your family?

Well, not everyone who comes here can be trusted. Goebbels is known for sending spies disguised as refugees to get a sense of the mood abroad. The Nazis are doing more than attacking Jews and dissidents; they're passing new laws to restrict women's rights as well. They praise Kindersegen, mothers blessed with children, as national heroines; they want German women at home, cooking, cleaning, and bearing babies for the Reich. You are Germany's most famous movie star, but you wear men's clothing, you live away from the fatherland and your husband, and you show off your body. If you start denouncing the Reich, imagine how they'll react."

I didn't want to imagine it, but as soon as I returned home, I placed an international call to Uncle Willi—Mutti had not installed a telephone in her flat—and he reassured me, sleepy because of the time difference, that everything was fine.

"Josephine is still cleaning houses. The situation isn't as dire as you think. Yes, we have a new chancellor"—he chuckled dryly—"but how is that any different from the last twenty years? These regimes rise and fall like hemlines."

"You will let me know if it gets any worse?" I said. "You won't wait?"

"Of course. But where would we go, Lena, at our age? Your mother wouldn't hear of it. You know how she is. This is her home. She continues to behave as though the Nazis are an inconvenience one must put up with, like poor manners from a guest at the dinner table."

I had to smile. It would take more than a few book burnings to rattle Mutti.

Ringing off with promises to call back soon, I then telephoned von Sternberg in New York, where he'd gone to see his ex-wife again, forever trying to cajole her into returning to him or at least reducing her alimony demands. Before I could deliver my warning, he said, "I'm not going. Perhaps to Europe at some later date, but not Germany. I've heard all about it; I've no wish to end up cleaning latrines in a camp. I'm headed to the South Seas to shoot a hurricane. I'll call you when I get back. Oh, congratulations on the picture. I hear it's going to be a great success. Didn't I tell you? The Russian knows how to film a beautiful woman."

I didn't ask why on earth *he* was filming tropical storms. It seemed fitting, for him.

But he was wrong about my picture. *The Song of Songs* opened to excellent reviews but its tepid box office sealed Schulberg's fate. He lost his job, moving to Columbia Pictures. To my delight, Lubitsch was made production chief in his stead—which explained von Sternberg's dislike of him. A fellow émigré and competitor in the directorial chair, he couldn't abide Lubitsch's rise to power, though Lubitsch did not share his antipathy. When he invited me to his office, he said that given the poor receipts for *The Song of Songs*, he was open to my suggestion as to how we should move forward with my career.

"I've been instructed to renew your contract for two more pictures, with an increase in salary. Paramount still believes in you, Marlene. You are our biggest female star."

"Then renew von Sternberg's contract, too," I said at once. "He's the reason *The Song of Songs* failed. Had he been the director, he would have seen its flaws."

"I already tried." Lubitsch rubbed a sore spot on his nose from his wire-frame spectacles. "He won't take my calls. I suspect he's still trying to woo the UFA, but as I told you before, he won't find any work there, and no studio here will give him the license that we do."

I felt vindicated. As argumentative and combative as von Sternberg could be, we belonged together. I missed working with him and was certain that he missed me. I barraged his address in New York with calls and telegrams. He took his time to reply; when he did, he said he'd return to Hollywood as soon as he could, but he had other obligations to attend to first.

"What obligations?" I grumbled to Mercedes. "His wife doesn't want him and Lubitsch does. Now he has other obligations? I don't understand it. The man is impossible."

"Why don't you take a holiday?" She stifled a yawn. "You have some free time now after working so much. Paris is lovely this time of year, and your daughter must miss her father."

I understood her meaning. With Gerda gone, I'd hired two bodyguards to watch over Heidede while I was at the studio and my daughter attended a private school run by the studio for celebrity children. She was doing well, her English getting better than mine, but with my schedule, we only shared occasional evenings together. I fussed over her, bringing her with me on the weekends to visit Mercedes, to walk on the beach and collect seashells, but Heidede found Mercedes "creepy"—an Americanism I had to look up—and Mercedes didn't like having a curious child underfoot. My lover was growing impatient with my domestic obligations.

"What?" I reached for my cigarettes. "Is Garbo getting jealous?"

Reclining on the bed like a sylph, she sighed. "Marlene. Why ask?"

Indeed. I went home nursing a tiny wound in my heart that appalled me. The very next day, I booked passage for Heidede and me to Paris.

VI

I fell in love for the third time.

Paris enamored me with her incandescence, her sweeping boulevards and cobblestone labyrinths, her spiky cathedrals and noisy cafés, her chestnut Tuileries and the open-legged thrust of her Eiffel Tower. She was glamorous and bawdy, sophisticated and vulgar. She straddled the Seine like a cabaret girl and paraded down the Champs-Élysées like a goddess. She laughed and smoked and drank red wine; she ignored the foibles of celebrity and celebrated everyday joys.

Most of all, she gave me privacy. I did not fear kidnapping threats here, and I dispensed with my security to take Heidede to the parks and open-air markets, where, when I was recognized, the interest rarely translated into a stammering request for my autograph. Parisians understood that even famous actresses still use the bidet.

I could have stayed forever.

In Paris, I found a lover who cared as much and as little as I did.

RUDI WAS CONTENT. He and Tamara had a cozy apartment not far from his Paramount job, though the international economic malaise meant he didn't have too much work. No one worked too much in Paris anyway, unless you were Coco Chanel, whose atelier I visited for a fitting. She was an intense, simianlike woman, devoted to her craft, chattering nonstop about everything as she adjusted my jersey dress. She showed me newspapers with photographs of my arrival at the Gare Saint-Lazare splashed across the front pages, dressed in my beret, oversize sunglasses, pearl gray man's suit, and chocolate mohair polo coat.

"Public transvestitism is a crime in Paris," she jeered. "You risk arrest by the police. Not that I mind. That mohair coat is sublime. But here, we like women who *dress* like women."

"What about the men?" I said, and she laughed, her profusion of enamel bracelets jangling. "I don't bother with men," she said. "And I prefer it if they don't bother me."

All lies of course. Her reputation for lovers exceeded mine. Besides, what she really was saying was that she liked women who dressed in *her* clothes. I ordered a dozen outfits from her, including several evening gowns, but continued to wear my suits and ties to the Hungarian restaurant on the Rue de Surène where I liked to dine, daring the police to lay a finger on me. They put me under surveillance—it became a game for me, eluding them as they dogged my steps—but I wasn't arrested. And wherever I went, I made headlines. It might be a crime to cross-dress in Paris, but the French newspapers adored it and couldn't get enough of me.

I decided to use the attention to shed light on the plight of refugees after Rudi arranged a visit with Kurt Weill, who wanted to meet me. Famed composer of *The Threepenny Opera*, whose ballad "Mack the Knife" had convulsed Berlin, Weill had been forced to escape the Nazis. He and his wife were now holed up in an apartment on the Left Bank, waiting for a visa to go to New York. A tremulous, nearsighted man with huge round glasses that made him look like a starving owl, he clasped my hand, bemoaning the decimation of our culture. I was deeply moved by his circumstances, and outraged that one of our finest talents had to flee Berlin like a thief. I promised to put in a good word for him with my contacts in Hollywood and he in turn implored me to record German songs as a tribute.

"You must be our voice," he said, "before everything is lost."

I thought it a splendid idea. I hired him to write two songs for me, but they were as gloomy as his mood, and I couldn't sing them. I did, however, record "Allein" by the Jewish composers, Wachsmann and Colpet—a haunting anthem to the dying Weltschmerz of Berlin, our melancholic homage to a world-weary existence. I did it on purpose, to highlight the Nazis' denial of Jewish contributions. The recording, issued by Polydor, was an immediate hit.

"Let Goebbels ban it." I laughed with Rudi, and we went on to Vienna, where Mutti joined us. I'd sent train fare for her and Liesel, but she arrived alone, her hair newly styled for the occasion. She was smiling and conciliatory, affectionate with Heidede, but she refused to talk about the Nazis. When I asked her if she and everyone else in the family were okay, she sniffed.

"Why must you use that word? 'Okay.' What does it even mean? Yes of course. We are fine. We're not Jewish. They've no reason to question our sympathies."

I glanced at Rudi. He grinned. Some things, like my mother, never changed.

Fans caught wind of my arrival and gathered outside our hotel in Vienna to chant my name. My stay in Paris had made international headlines, so I went down two nights in a row to sign autographs. The attending press also snapped pictures, which reached the American press, which printed them under the caption "Marlene Defies Berlin."

It finally penetrated Mutti's reserve. On the morning she was scheduled to return to Berlin, as we prepared to accompany her to the train station, she motioned me aside and said in her most glacial tone, "I suppose you find these antics amusing."

"Antics?" Even as I feigned ignorance, my heart sank. I had forgotten Mercedes's advice.

"Yes. Entertaining that rabble with your disrespect for our führer. Or perhaps it's the fashion these days in Hollywood to show disdain for one's nation."

"Mutti, it's my job. My fans wanted to see me and——"

Her mouth thinned, in the same way it had when she'd caught me flubbing a chord on the violin. "You know exactly what I'm talking about. You might live too far away now, but Liesel, Willi, and myself—we do not. We are Germans. Would you have us put on some list because of this incessant attention grabbing for the press?"

"I am a German, too," I said angrily, but then I saw it, a fleeting moment of fear in her eyes. "Mutti, have they threatened you?"

She brushed her hands over her coat as if I'd sprayed crumbs while talking with my mouth full. "Of course not. They wouldn't dare. Our lineage goes further back than any Nazi's."

"So does the Wertheims' of the department store. Are they in business now?"

"They are Jews." She stepped past me to Rudi, holding her hand out to Heidede in her blue coat and matching cap. "Come, *mein Liebling*. Kiss your Oma good-bye."

"She's coming with us to the station," I said, wanting to make amends.

My mother shook her head. "I'd rather not. Your adoring fans will be waiting outside. I'd rather leave in privacy, without wondering if *my* photograph will end up in the newspapers."

Needless to say, she got her way.

ONBOARD THE *ÎLE DE FRANCE* on our way back to America, once I saw Heidede settled in our cabin and asleep, I donned one of my new Chanel white gowns and sauntered into the dining salon. I only intended to have an aperitif, still unsettled by Mutti's upbraiding and my farewell with Rudi, who told me not to fret, yet had upheld my mother's concerns.

"There's no reason to antagonize them, Marlene," he told me before he boarded his train. "Focus on your work and leave politics to others."

Although I hadn't said anything political out loud, I understood. I shouldn't have recorded the Jewish songs or let myself be photographed without setting foot in Berlin. I had allowed my rage against the Nazis to overcome my better judgment, and now sought distraction onboard, only every table but one was full—and everyone was staring—and the lone empty seat would have made me the thirteenth guest. It was bad luck on a crossing, so I retreated to the bar.

I had just ordered a cocktail diluted with soda water when a burly dark-haired man at a table pushed back his chair and made his way toward me. As he approached, his close-cropped black hair enhancing his strong-featured, florid face, thick eyebrows, and mustache, I set a hand high on my hip, a screen affectation, and braced for the inevitable come-on.

"I know you," he said with a disarmingly warm smile. "You're the Kraut."

I could tell he didn't mean to insult me, so I replied, "I am. And you are . . . ?"

"Hemingway." He thrust out his hand. "Ernest Hemingway. I'm a writer."

"I'm aware," I replied, for I was. "*The Sun Also Rises.*"

"You've read it?" He raised an eyebrow. "Or just the reviews?"

"I never read reviews if I can help it."

"Good for you. It's the one thing we can control: Don't ever let them see you sweat." He ordered a scotch. He reminded me in a way of Gary, with his masculine physique and directness, but also, strangely, of von Sternberg, like a man with something to prove.

"What brings you aboard this rust bucket?" he asked, looking into my eyes. With any other, I'd have interpreted this as the come-on. But it didn't strike me as his intent. He seemed more curious, as if he'd heard things about me that he had to ascertain for himself. "Wait. Don't tell me. Weren't you in Paris recently?"

I nodded. "And Vienna."

"Yeah, but I saw pictures of you in *Le Figaro,* wearing a suit and tie. My friend Gertrude Stein—do you know who she is?" When I assented, he went on, "Well, she thinks you're grand. She said you've got some serious cojones to walk around like that and not give a damn."

"I'm flattered. I understand Miss Stein doesn't lack for cojones herself."

"She sure doesn't." He laughed. "I admire a woman with balls. It's like I always say—"

"Never let 'em see you sweat?" I was thinking I'd like to see him do just that. In my bed.

"That, and—" He leaned close to me. "Don't do anything you sincerely don't want to do. Never confuse movement with action."

In that instant, I liked him very much. "A philosophy for life. I must remember it."

"Do so." He motioned at my glass. "Another?"

I drank down my cocktail in one gulp. "Why not?"

We didn't sleep together, but we closed the bar that night. By the end of the evening, during a lengthy stroll on the deck, I was calling him Papa and he never said my name.

I had made a lifelong friend.

VII

Upon my arrival in Los Angeles, I found out that von Sternberg's mysterious obligations had entailed a covert trip to Berlin to meet with the UFA, only to discover, as Lubitsch had assured me, that the studio had no wish to hire him.

"Those yellow-bellied swine," he raved before I'd even unpacked, waiting in my driveway with a pile of cigarette butts at his feet. "They think they can reject me because I'm a Jew. Without me, there would be no them! They'd be bankrupt, as everything that has kept them afloat came from *The Blue Angel*."

He exaggerated, but I served him cognac, soothing his anger while managing to finagle out of him that he'd hoped to shove Paramount, and Lubitsch in particular, into a corner once again by hanging a UFA offer over their heads.

"Cowards." He gulped down his cognac, then handed me his glass for a refill. "They acted as though they were doing me a favor by letting me through the back door. 'We're only seeing you because we hold you in such esteem, Herr von Sternberg, but we must abide by the new policy.' New policy," he spat out. "Kowtowing to Hitler and Goebbels and the rest of those idiots, as if the Nazis know anything about film or culture."

"They're burning our culture," I reminded him. "You might have spared yourself the indignity. You already knew Ernst wants us to work together."

"On a first-name basis with the new boss, I see." He scowled. "Of course he does. The man is a cretin, but he's not stupid. *The Song of Songs* was a vulgarity. Did you know the studio sent dozens of copies of that nude statue for display in the theater lobbies? It's a wonder the Hays Office didn't slap brown-bag wrappers on the lot and pull the picture for indecency."

I gave him an exasperated look. In light of his humiliation, of course he had to degrade the one picture I'd made without him. But I was glad he was here, relieved that he'd been allowed to leave Germany. "You were very reckless," I said. "You could have been arrested."

"For what? For bringing a script in my luggage?"

I paused. "You took a script to the UFA?"

"Well, I wasn't going to persuade them with my Yiddish charm, was I?"

"I see." I served him his third cognac. "And what is this script about?"

He turned vehement, as only he could be when possessed by a new idea. "A picture about Catherine the Great. All the studios are doing royals now: Kate Hepburn as Mary, Queen of Scots, Norma Shearer as Marie Antoinette, and Garbo as Queen Christina." He paused, anticipating my reaction to the news of MGM's queen playing a famous cross-dressing queen.

"Garbo in a doublet," I said dryly. "How original." I served myself a cognac, even if I had no intention of drinking at three in the afternoon. "Are you going to approach Ernst with it?"

"I already have. He loves it."

"He does?" Immediate suspicion overcame me. "Has he renewed your contract?"

"With absolute control. He also thought he was doing me a favor. And he has—because now we can do as we please, without the studio's interference."

As they said in America, I smelled a rat. He rarely had a full script before the first day of shooting, if then. He thrived on vagueness, on keeping everyone in suspense, so he could make it up as he went. It was part of his genius and the reason most actors detested him. Yet Lubitsch had granted him "absolute control." It seemed the height of folly. Or trust. I doubted the latter.

"I'd like to read this script," I said, bringing an immediate glower to his face.

"When have I ever led you astray?"

"How soon we forget," I replied, echoing his own past words to me.

He pulled out two crumpled pages from his pocket, flung them onto the sofa, and walked out, mumbling under his breath about ingratitude everywhere he turned.

It wasn't a script. Not even half a script.

I couldn't help but wonder if Lubitsch was more cunning than we knew.

IN A VOLUMINOUS VERMILION GOWN with skirts wide enough to house tribes, I felt like another candelabrum in von Sternberg's décor, his self-designed set drenched in baroque archways, Russian icons, and gargantuan doorways, the excessive tableaux better suited to the silent era.

"In this scene," he said, swiveling in his new director's chair, which was affixed to an ingenious platform that could be cranked upward for panoramic viewing, "you order the murder of your husband, the half-wit Grand Duke Peter."

"Yes." I lowered my eyes to the pages he'd left in my dressing room, trying to not dislodge my bejeweled wig. As expected, he revised the script daily, leaving me and hundreds of extras wondering what we would shoot that day. "About that. Must she be so evil?"

"He planned to kill her. She must have her revenge."

I was glad I'd kept Heidede off the set. She was almost eleven, old enough to join me at work after school. She'd made a brief cameo in the picture as Catherine's younger self, but then I left her in my dressing room, concerned she'd think these grotesqueries reflected my career.

"She seems to exact quite a lot of revenge. Without much in the way of words to go with it. Won't the audience lose sympathy for her if she doesn't explain her actions?"

"Who needs explanation when the mood will suffice?" He motioned brusquely with his white-gloved hand to the set, having reverted to his eccentric mode of apparel, sometimes bellowing instructions at the crew while brandishing his aviator goggles. "You've seen the rushes. It'll be sublime. A Catherine the Great unlike one that anyone has seen."

"That's what worries me," I muttered under my breath, but I took my mark.

By the time the shoot wrapped, I had no idea what we had made. After screening the unedited version, Lubitsch walked out. I knew then that my instincts had been correct.

"He led you by the nose," I told von Sternberg as he lay on my sofa with a damp cloth on his brow, exhausted by his creative mayhem. "He gave you full control and you ran with it."

"Did he say he hated it? Did he say he wouldn't release it or would make us reshoot?"

"No." I stood over him anxiously. "He said nothing. Isn't that enough?"

"He said nothing because he's a mediocre talent in a big office. He'll continue to say nothing, which is how I prefer him."

Perhaps, but I still made an appointment to see Lubitsch the next day. By the time we met, I was a bundle of nerves. "Well?" I said as soon as I sat before his desk.

He gave me a long look. "I apologize. I was beyond words. Like the picture itself."

I sank farther into my seat. "You think it's terrible."

"No. I think it's a masterpiece. But my opinion doesn't matter." He rounded his desk to take the chair beside me. A lifelong Berliner, he wasn't given to sympathetic gestures, but I had the feeling that if he were, he'd have patted my hand. "He can't restrain himself, Marlene. He's lost his perspective. A film like this is not salable to an American audience. They want reality now, not hyperbole. And he knows it. I'm afraid I'm not the only one he hates."

I jolted upright, scalded by the implication. "You cannot mean he hates me."

"He hates himself. From the moment he cast you as Lola-Lola, he surrendered his identity. He might declare to the press that he is Dietrich and Dietrich is him, but in his heart, he has always craved recognition in his own right. He deserves it. That is his tragedy."

"Will you tell him?" I was overcome by his perceptive appraisal of the man I had always sought to please with my performances but had often found incomprehensible off the set.

"What good would it do?" he said. "We'll release the picture as is, but one thing is clear: You must decide whether it's in your best interests to continue working with him."

I cringed at the notices. *Time* blasted it as "hyperbole in which von Sternberg buries Dietrich in a welter of gargoyles." Theaters balked at screening the picture, and word of mouth ran wild that the studio would pull it, finishing von Sternberg's and my collaboration.

Lubitsch confirmed it. "We have to do it for the sake of your career. We've a vested interest in retaining you. Not him."

"But you said—you told me it was my decision!"

"I thought it was. Corporate says otherwise. We can't afford it," he explained. "The truth is, von Sternberg never made us enough money to justify his expense."

"Our other pictures did well enough. You gave him control. You said he could make whatever he liked." I paused. "You knew this would happen," I breathed. "You *wanted* it."

Lubitsch lifted his palms in mock surrender. "He gave me no choice. He said it was his way or no way. He threatened to take you with him. Was I wrong in assuming he would have?"

"No. He couldn't. I'd already signed with the studio for two pictures."

"Then you have one more picture with him. Make it count."

*   *   *

VON STERNBERG TOOK THE NEWS IN STRIDE, which bewildered me—until he announced to the press that our next picture would be our last. *The Scarlet Empress* had been his revenge, a direct strike at Lubitsch, in the hope that, as with Schulberg, he could topple a rival. The realization undid me; I felt deceived, used by him in his self-destructive tangle. He had not spared a thought for how it might affect me, as long as he won his battle against Lubitsch.

I refused to answer his calls for weeks, despising his melancholic public assertion that the time had come for us to part, when he hadn't yet bothered to inform me in person. But when he finally came to my door, I had to open it.

"You did this to us," I said, barring his entry.

He gave a self-deprecatory shrug. "Lubitsch might be clever. I am wise."

"*Wise?*" I wanted to throttle him. "Paramount pulled the picture. We are finished."

"I am finished. Not you." He removed a bound sheaf of papers from his coat pocket, rolled up and crumpled, stinking of the half-smoked cigarettes he always kept about his person, as if he were a vagrant. "Read it. You'll see it's the best thing we have ever done."

"I've heard that before." But I was taken aback that this screenplay looked complete.

"My beloved." His voice turned disarmingly tender. "It had to end. I cannot—" He stopped himself. "Just read it. If you don't like it, I'll break my contract to spare you. I'll walk away and let the studio blame me. What can they do to me that they haven't done already?"

He set the script in my hand and returned to his car, his shoulders slumped. As I watched him depart, I suddenly understood. As Lubitsch had said, it was his way or no way. And as he couldn't find the key with which to unlock our chain, he had decided to sever it.

I sat down to read. When I was done, I did not move, my cigarette burning out in a column of ash. Sorrow overwhelmed me.

For our farewell, my exasperating director had offered me my favorite part.

VIII

She is every man's fantasy and every man's terror. Dandelion-speckled mantilla and lacquer *peineta*, riding in her balloon-festooned carriage through rainy Seville. She might be a factory worker by day, but at night, Concha Perez is desire incarnate. The young lieutenant who's been warned against her gazes in fascination as she passes, cruelty in her lace-masked eyes. She knows he will chase after her until he finds her invitation, inside a wind-up-toy box.

I wanted Concha to look Spanish. I was blond, blue-eyed. No matter how authentic my wardrobe might be, I did not resemble a woman from Seville. I'd heard of a doctor who assisted actors and paid him a visit. He prescribed two types of eyedrops, one to widen the pupils during shooting and the other to reduce them. I hid the bottles in my bag while I submitted to hours of special bronzing makeup to darken my complexion. Just before I went on set, I used the drops.

By the time I hit my mark, I was blind. Everything swam in a haze as I stumbled through my scene like a drunkard, until von Sternberg, furious at my inability to light a cigarette, strode over to me and hissed, "What the hell is wrong? The cigarette is right there—in your mouth."

I took one dazed look at him and started crying. He pulled me aside, out of earshot of the technicians. "What is it?" he demanded. "You're spoiling your makeup. Stop crying."

"I . . . I can't," I whispered, my eyes stinging from the drops. Collapsed on a crate in my ruffled flamenco garb, I buried my face in my hands and wept like a child. It all came erupting to the surface, the disappointment of fame and the terror of the future without him. I knew then, as I'd never known before, that I must love him more than any other man. Not carnally, not to play with in bed or flaunt on my arm; not like Rudi, who was my rock. But as the only person I'd ever trusted in this realm of make-believe.

He stood over me. When I finally spent myself, sniffling and wiping my nose with my sleeve, he said, "Marlene," and I looked up. He was still a blur. "What did you do?"

"I . . . I wanted black eyes. I used drops. With belladonna."

"If you wanted black eyes, why didn't you tell me? I can adjust the lighting, use postproduction touch-up." He sounded exasperated. "Have you lost your mind?"

I nodded, knowing my makeup was streaked and he'd have to delay the shoot. "See? You know everything. How—" My voice snagged in my throat. I, who rarely cried, found myself fighting back another onslaught of tears. "How will I survive without you?"

He crouched before me. "You will survive because you are the reason I can do this." There was no gentleness in his tone. He spoke as if he struggled against contempt; but I sat quiet, recognizing he was about to admit something he'd never say again. "I am the camera. The lenses. There isn't a thing I do that can't be done by another. Without you, there is nothing."

"That's not true—" I started to protest.

He cut me off. "It is." He came to his feet. "Now, go back to your dressing room and fix this mess. I'll call for an early lunch break, but afterward, we shoot this entire scene even if you have to use a guide dog."

I rose carefully. The crying had helped. At least I could see my way off the set.

"Belladonna," he muttered. "She poisons herself for me. If that's not love, what is?"

After that day, he became a monster, roaring like a lion—"Stop waving that fucking fan as if you have a fever! She's seducing him, not cooling off the olives. Again"—forcing me to bite back my own rage as he exacted take after punishing take. When the final scene was done, he flung aside his megaphone and thundered from the set, leaving me trembling, my Spanish comb, affixed with wires to my coiffure, bleeding into my scalp.

The studio executives mopped their foreheads at the preview. Lubitsch had not interfered, save to remind us of the odious Hays Office codes, which required that Concha not be seen accepting money for her favors, but perspiration dotted his upper lip. When *The Devil Is a Woman* opened in May 1935, his fears were justified. The critics hated it, warning audiences away, and the Spanish government, about to plunge into a savage civil war, warned that if Paramount did not pull the picture and destroy every print, they'd ban future movie exhibitions by the studio in Spain.

The executives complied. Von Sternberg called me to deliver the news. I was outraged, shouting that he'd again let us career into chaos.

He sighed. "If we had to fail," he said, "at least we did it magnificently. I kept an original print. I'll send it to you, in memory of our debacle."

He departed for New York the next day without another word.

That night, I shut myself in my bedroom and mourned like a widow.

I had worshipped and shunned him, embraced him and despaired over his tyranny. He had made me a star, lavishing upon me everything that haunted and excited him. He'd woven majesty in our name. Dietrich is me, he had said, and I am Dietrich.

My monster and creator, my angel and demon.

After six years of triumphs and defeats, he had left me alone.

THE HIGHEST PAID ACTRESS

1935–1940

"CAN YOU IMAGINE ANYONE CASTING
A SPELL OVER ME?"

I

With Paramount's contract renewal for two more pictures at $250,000 annually, I left my North Roxbury house for a palatial estate in Bel Air, west of Beverly Hills. Mercedes asked why I didn't purchase a house, seeing that I had no intention of returning to Germany while it was under Nazi sway. I replied that I enjoyed California, especially the climate, but I didn't consider America my home. "I'm an expatriate. We cannot grow roots in foreign soil."

"Especially when you pay for the roots of others," she said. "I know how much you give to every refugee who crosses your threshold."

By now, those refugees were legion, the finest talent in Germany, fleeing Hitler and his brutal reprisals. Mercedes's salon had proliferated; and the stories I heard there of persecution, of the Nuremberg laws depriving Jews of citizenship, and the Night of the Long Knives, during which Hitler had purged all opposition in his own party, made me dig my nails into my palms.

The land of my birth, of my first success, had become a place of unrelenting terror.

Supporting my fellow countrymen who came to Hollywood, with money, referrals to studios, and even a place to sleep, wasn't the right thing to do, it was the only thing I *could* do. I kept silent, conscious now of how dangerous my speaking out could be. I was detested in the fatherland, my pictures anathema, my image defaced, my very origins questioned by Goebbels, who published an article calling me the illegitimate daughter of a Russian. I could only imagine Mutti's outrage, but whenever I telephoned Uncle Willi, having made arrangements beforehand so she would be there, she invariably replied, "We have done nothing wrong. We joined the party as Hitler decreed. Why would they bother us?"

But they could. I feared they might, and Rudi assured me he'd not been denied permission from traveling to Germany and he would go visit my family to determine if Mutti spoke the truth. He went, reporting back that everything was as she claimed, although, he said, "You don't want to see it. The Berlin we knew is gone."

Meanwhile, I reunited with Gary for my next picture, *Desire*—an apt title, for as soon as we began shooting, we renewed our affair. He'd left Lupe or she'd left him—who could tell with them?—and was divorcing his wife. Now in his midthirties and a coveted leading man, he'd grown into his promise, more handsome than ever, and as skilled between the sheets.

Mercedes was miffed. She did not appreciate me sleeping with men, and while she and I remained occasional lovers, she returned full-time to Garbo. She even had a password she used over the phone with me— "*Occupée*"—whenever Garbo was in residence. I was tempted to drive to Santa Monica with Gary and park nearby, to catch a glimpse of my elusive rival, who, incredibly, I'd not yet seen in person.

"She's not all she's made out to be," Gary said. "You're much prettier, and," he added, working his way down to my navel, "tastier."

I cuffed him. "You never slept with her. She likes women. I have it on good authority."

"They say that about you." He licked me, making me shudder. "And look at you now."

DESIRE WAS A HIT, easing my heartache over the loss of von Sternberg. As the jewel thief Madeleine, I had all the sumptuous mink and allure the public expected, and the picture benefitted from my ripe banter with Gary's good-natured American, whom Madeleine embroils in her heist. It had a happy ending, too, like my romps with Gary, pleasing even the *New York Times*, which declared, "Freed from von Sternberg's bondage, Miss Dietrich recaptures her fresh spirit."

Lubitsch quickly assigned my next project, casting me as a chambermaid who falls for an army officer, played by the gallant French import Charles Boyer. The picture was supposed to do away with my glamorous image in favor of a more realistic approach, but the script wasn't ready by the third week of shooting. When word came that the corporate office, upset over the delay and Paramount's consistent loss of profit, had fired Lubitsch, I walked off the set in a fury.

I called Hemingway. We kept up regular contact, exchanging letters and phone calls, he sharing his adventures on safari or labors on his new novel, and me regaling him with Hollywood gossip and my adventures on and off the set.

"They got rid of him like they did von Sternberg. They hate us because we're German. Lubitsch supported me; he tried to give me choices for my career. Now, I have an unfinished picture and no idea what they plan to do with me next."

Papa chuckled. "Take a breath, Kraut. What did I tell you? Never do what you don't want to do. You don't like how your career is going? Don't bitch about it. Do something."

Tu etwas. My childhood motto.

And so I did. I hired a well-known Hollywood agent, Eddie Feldman, and had him haggle with Paramount. I'd fulfilled my contract; I couldn't be held accountable for script delays. Chastened, the studio shelved my unfinished picture, and while they sought a new West Coast chief, loaned me out for one picture to David O. Selznick International.

I was going back to the desert with my costar, Boyer.

WE SHOT *THE GARDEN OF ALLAH* in the Mohave near Yuba City. The scorpions that slinked into our trailers to nest in our shoes, the freezing nights and infernal sun by day, made the shoot torturous. In my swanky monochrome wardrobe draped like Grecian shrouds, I shed ten pounds and sweated out five more, and even once, to the cast's dismay, swooned from heatstroke.

Boyer was an affable companion, despite the temperature soaring past 135 degrees, but our roles were unsympathetic and the studio ploy to re-create the ambience of *Morocco* was incinerated by my anxiety over how Technicolor would render me.

I was thirty-four. In the mirror at night, I saw what makeup, lighting, and gauze filters concealed. I'd maintained my complexion by avoiding the sun, my closet full of flouncy hats and Savile Row umbrellas that I carried as other women did handbags. But I wasn't keen on the surgical remedies to which other aging stars resorted, relying on my healthy diet and an herbal moisturizer that Travis Banton—arbiter of all things beautiful—recommended.

Still, faint lines were materializing at my eyes and mouth—"laugh lines," Mercedes called them, "which prove you are human"—though to me, they were reminders of how the clock ticked much faster in Holly-wood. This picture was my first in Technicolor, and the vivid three-process palette exaggerated everything. Before I began shooting each day, I had a list of things to consult, from the position of the lights to the most benefi-cial camera angles for my face, enraging my director.

One afternoon as we prepared for a scene, the wind machines were gusting so hard that I felt sand grit lacerating my skin and Boyer's toupee came unglued, flapping over his forehead. I had to press my hands on my head to stop my hairstyle from going the way of my costar's as I called out angrily, "Turn off those machines. How can we see through all the dust?"

From his chair, the director snapped, "Even palm trees sway in the breeze. Surely a little reality will not spoil your timeless beauty."

I hated the script and the heat, but I hated him more. And the pic-ture did not do well at the box office, prompting me to reject another offer from Selznick—whom I didn't like anyway—to accept a personal one from Alexander Korda in England, with whom I'd made *A Modern Du*

Barry a decade before in Berlin. I was now eager to escape Hollywood and reinvent myself abroad.

Paramount vacillated until Eddie threatened them with my permanent departure. Korda was offering me $450,000 to play a Russian countess in his *Knight Without Armor.* To avoid defaulting on my contract, Paramount must agree and also pay the amount still owed to me for the aborted picture they'd shelved. Caught between two swords, the studio relented.

I pocketed a million dollars.

With Heidede and my new assistant, Betsy, I boarded the *Normandie* with the satisfaction of being proclaimed in the *Hollywood Reporter* as "the highest paid actress in the world."

Only I had begun to doubt if I still warranted being called an actress at all.

II

They're here again," said Betsy, coming into my dressing room at the studio outside London. "They've telephoned every day this week. Maybe you should see them?"

I saw myself grimace in the bulb-lit mirror, where I was applying eyeliner for my upcoming scene. Countess Alexandra was about to take a bath, frolicking among bubbles before her enraptured translator on the eve of the 1917 revolution. I intended to shoot the scene nude, though everyone expected me to wear the flesh-colored bathing suit provided by wardrobe. But the suit made my thighs bulge. Given the picture's portentous subject matter, with endless flights from rampaging Bolsheviks, a little reality, as my last director had claimed, was required.

Now wrapped in a fleece robe (the studio could have doubled as an icebox), I was in no humor for inopportune visitors, particularly ones from Germany. "Did you say I'm working?" I asked, as Betsy paused by the bathing suit on a chair. "I can't receive them now. Tell them—"

A knock came at the door, followed by a cheerful: "*Liebchen!* It's me, Leni. I know you're in there. Stop hiding. I won't bite."

"*Mein Gott.*" Horrified, I swiveled on my stool to Betsy. "Is that Leni Riefenstahl?"

She dangled the bathing suit between her fingers. "She didn't give her name. She only said you knew each other in Berlin and she's here on official business."

I hadn't seen or spoken to Leni in over ten years, but I'd heard from Anna May about how Leni had graduated from her Alpine epics, securing a contract to film the Nazi party rally in Nuremberg—a propaganda piece that made its way to America, in all its abhorrent display of faux-imperial grandeur, replete with strobe lights and a colonnaded stadium, with the only things missing being horse-drawn chariots and hungry lions to devour the Jews.

What on earth was she doing here now?

Motioning Betsy aside, I opened the door. My former Sister About Town greeted me with an effusive, perfumed embrace. "Darling Marlene. I thought you didn't like me anymore."

I drew back. I'd have been hard-pressed to recognize her, so sleek and manicured in her expensive sable, her hair bobbed and lacquered, doused in Chanel No. 5 and Nazi prestige.

"Why would you think that?" As I spoke, I saw a leather-coated man a few feet away, a German officer in civilian disguise, staring at me from under his cap, his face like a slab of rock.

Leni pushed past me. I shut the dressing room door on the officer and saw Betsy dive behind my dressing screen. "This is a surprise," I said. "I'm due on the set at any moment."

I wasn't rude, but not friendly, either. I suspected a setup, watching her take a seat on the chair, squashing my bathing suit and plucking a gold cigarette case from her fur-coat pocket. I almost expected her to pull out a camera and start taking candid photographs of me for delivery to Goebbels, who'd publish them in some Nazi magazine to prove I was one of them.

"Oh, I know how busy you are," said Leni. "I am, too. I'm only in London for a few days. I'm due back in Germany next week. The Olympic Summer Games are being held in Berlin this year, as you must know, and I've been hired to film them."

"How nice for you."

She lit her cigarette. I was on the verge of informing her that she needn't pretend; I knew she'd been pestering Betsy to see me, so she could forget the chitchat and just state why she was here. But I held back. I wanted to see how she played this out. She must have impressive credentials to bypass the studio security, and ever a performer, if rarely a good one, she never could resist drama. She might end up amusing me, though I doubted it.

"Is that your official business?" I asked, as she smoked with a pursed-lip affectation so as not to smudge her lipstick. "I can't imagine the Brits are keeping their athletes from you."

Her smile came out more like a sneer. "Marlene. Always so droll. You haven't changed a bit."

"Neither have you." I returned to my dressing table. "As I said, I don't have time now for a visit. If you want, you can tell me where you're staying and once I finish shooting, we'll—"

"This won't take long." She regarded me in the mirror. "I have an offer for you, a very lucrative one." As she saw me frown, she went on, "Herr Goebbels has read the notices for your last few pictures, darling. He knows things aren't going so well for you in America these days."

"Really? And here I thought Goebbels didn't fancy my work."

"You misunderstand. He likes it very much. So much, in fact, he's authorized me to offer you fifty thousand pounds to make a picture in Germany. You can hire any director you want."

Now, I had to laugh. "Leni, have you come all this way to *proposition* me?"

She went pale under her rouge. "Of course not. Heaven forbid." She tried to laugh herself, but her voice was shaky. "I'm booked solid. The Olympics and all."

"And if I were to name von Sternberg?" I asked. When she did not answer, I nodded. "I didn't think so."

"Marlene, really—"

I held up my hand. "As I said, this is a surprise. They want me to make a picture there? Last time I checked my notices in Germany, they were far worse than any in Hollywood."

"We promise an immediate reversal of the campaign against you, to prepare the public for your return." She leaned to me with a coy smile. "The führer wants to receive you personally. He's expressed great interest in meeting you. He has quite a way with the ladies."

She was wrong. I did understand. With Germany in the spotlight for the Summer Games, the Reich's brutality must be swept under the carpet until the games concluded. International tourists and delegates would attend; it would be inhospitable to offend foreign sensibilities with JUDEN VERBOTEN signage or the continued absence of Hollywood's highest-paid German actress.

As revulsion swept through me, I sweetened my voice. "Darling Leni, it really is so lovely of you to have come all this way. What a pity I cannot accept. I, too, am booked solid. I'm under contract for the next two years at Paramount, which brings us to the end of 1938. Then I've committed to other engagements. Can we possibly resume our little talk after, say, 1940?"

She froze. Then she ground out her cigarette on the floor. "It is a pity, to reject one's nation for dollars. It won't last. A woman of your age, no matter how well preserved—they don't appreciate maturity there like we do. And I fear 1940 will indeed be much too late."

"I'll take my chances." I didn't rise as she went to the door. She paused. "I'll be in London for another day or so should you happen to change your mind. My hotel is—"

"Have a safe trip home, Leni," I interrupted. "Give my regards to your führer."

She walked out, slamming the door behind her. From behind the dressing screen where she'd crouched, Betsy emerged. Meeting my eyes, she let out a giggle. "*Her* führer?"

"Yes," I said. "He certainly is not mine."

I ATTENDED MY PICTURE'S premiere clad in diamonds and silver lamé. At the studio after party, I was approached by the debonair actor Douglas Fairbanks Jr. Exceedingly handsome, he trailed after me like a puppy throughout the evening, until I invited him to my suite.

Unaware at first of our seven-year age difference, young Douglas was passionate and devoted, accompanying me to Paris to meet Rudi and Tamara, where he was surprised to learn I was married—apparently, he didn't read the press—but took pains to affect nonchalance.

Rudi gave me a mordant look—"Rather young, isn't he?"—which I ignored as we embarked for a monthlong family vacation in Switzerland.

During our stay in a rented château by Lake Lucerne, Douglas's nonchalance crumbled as he witnessed my arrangement with my husband and his mistress. We had no qualms about trotting around the grounds naked to take a dip in the pool, Rudi sunbathing and reading, while Tamara and I sat under a parasol and chatted about fashion or art. Tami was not well. She had developed a nervous condition, Rudi confided to me, exacerbated by the move to Paris. After having fled Russia, she was acutely sensitive to any change, sometimes falling into depressions that lasted for weeks. I was concerned for her and gave her extra attention, letting her wear my clothes and asking her to help me cook up meals in the kitchen. She was devoted to Rudi, more so than I'd ever been, and I did not want her to be unhappy.

"But he's your husband," Douglas said. "Yet she's his lover and your daughter calls her Auntie Tami. It's all so . . . irregular."

I slid my gaze over him. He was beautiful. Picture perfect, as Hollywood would say. But I was beginning to realize that he was indeed too young. He hadn't lived nearly long enough in Europe or anywhere else to develop that maturity I'd come to expect in a lover. "I told you that I'm not sleeping with him," I said. "What is the problem?"

He didn't reply. Until one morning after making love, when I left him to go sip hot chocolate and read the terrible notices for my new picture with Rudi and Tamara in their bed. Barging in on us, he took an outraged look at our chuckling, undressed trio—the reviews were so bad, we had to laugh—and cried out, "This is outrageous!"

"Outrageous," I said coldly, "is how you seem to have forgotten your manners."

I was obliged to escort him back to our room, sitting him down and informing him that I wasn't in the habit of being told what I could or could not do. "If you want us to continue," I warned, "you must stop behaving like a jealous spouse. I'm not interested in getting married again. One husband is enough."

He moped for a time but refrained from making another scene. Unfortunately, a more unpleasant situation caught me by surprise when Heidede, who'd gained so much weight that I chided her for eating herself out of her new clothes, bawled, "I don't care about your stupid dresses. I don't want to look like you. I don't want to be your little girl anymore."

Tamara went to comfort her, but I motioned her aside. In tears, Heidede said to me, "I want to stay with Papa in Paris. I hate America."

Belatedly recalling Gerda's words to me, of how miserable and homesick my daughter was, I knew this was my fault. I had ignored her feelings for too long. She was nearing adolescence; she needed more than a schedule and new clothes from me. I fought against the remorseful guilt that I'd not been a very good mother. I hadn't meant to neglect her, for I loved her so much, but I had done just that. I'd ignored her awkward entry into puberty and never solicited her opinions, afraid of her answers, which might mean I'd have to cease living my life my way. But she wasn't a child anymore; I could no longer treat her like my pretty doll. She was almost thirteen, with excess weight bloating her figure and an expression of utter misery.

"But, my darling, we've such a lovely home in America," I said, "and your school is there, with all your friends. Wouldn't you miss all your things?"

She glowered. "*Your* lovely home. *Your* friends. *Your* things. I never see anyone but the cook, the maid, or my bodyguard. The only friend I have is Judy at riding class, and she also works in pictures. Before she knew who I was, she asked me if I was your fat sister."

I regarded her in silence. Shame at my own behavior sharpened my voice. "You could try and make other friends besides that Garland girl."

"I don't want to. I hate Hollywood. I hate it all. Please, Mama, let me stay with Vati."

"Out of the question," I retorted, but after she staged morose defiance, refusing to leave her room, Rudi confronted me. "You have a contract to fulfill. You have to start working again sometime. I am here. Let her stay. You know it's for the best."

Under the circumstances, I couldn't justify forcing my daughter to return to Hollywood. If I wanted to prove to her that I cared, how could I refuse her request? Still, I resisted.

"To live with you in Paris?" I said. "Where you're working, too? And Tami, with her nerves? How can that be better for Heidede?"

Eventually, we agreed to enroll her in a prestigious Swiss boarding school, close enough that Rudi could visit on holidays but with a disciplined schedule that could help her shed some of her weight. Rudi also persuaded me before I left to put some of my more expensive jewels in a Swiss vault. I spent lavishly, on clothes, first-class travel, and hotel suites, and I never saved, as if disregarding any limitations would assure I had none.

"You must think ahead," Rudi said, fingering my jewels. "Putting these in safekeeping will give you something to fall back on, should you ever need it." He was worried for me, aware that my standing in Hollywood was precarious. "Paramount pays me a salary in Paris," he added, "and the studio supplements my rent. I don't need your support right now."

I did as he suggested. As for Heidede, she was so delighted with our new arrangement, she forgot to kiss me good-bye.

I returned to America with Douglas, fretful over my daughter's absence and the fact that my attempt to reinvent myself abroad had resulted in failure. It would take many years before I learned that my obsession with the latter was directly responsible for the former.

WITHIN WEEKS OF MY RETURN, Paramount lined up a picture for me—a potboiler called *Angel*, in which I played a diplomat's wife who drifts into an adulterous affair. I didn't want to make it; I found the plot as thin as my diaphanous gowns, and reviewers duly noted that "the lugubrious story comes to a stultifying halt every time Dietrich raises her elongated eyelids."

A few weeks after the lackluster premiere, my agent Eddie, an urbane man whose client list included other top stars, took me to lunch at the Brown Derby, that whimsical hat-shaped restaurant on Wilshire Boulevard that was considered the place to be seen.

His choice of locale was deliberate: public yet intimate, a celebrity watering hole where no one raised their voice, as I discovered after we ordered two Cobb salads. Unfolding the latest edition of the *Hollywood Reporter*, which only the previous year had lauded me as the highest-paid actress in the world, he slid it across the table.

"Now don't get upset. You'll see you are in excellent company."

I looked at the article he'd circled in red. There, in type that leaped out at me like a wolf with bared fangs, I read that the Independent Theater Owners of America had published the results of their annual audience poll. Bette Davis, Rosalind Russell, and Jean Arthur were the new popular favorites. Mae West, Joan Crawford, Kate Hepburn, and the sphinx herself, Garbo, along with myself, had been deemed "box-office poison."

I looked up in horror. "They're encouraging the studios to stop making pictures with us."

He nodded. "I'm afraid so."

"You're afraid so? Have you spoken to Paramount about it?"

He glanced around us. I knew at once that he was ascertaining whether anyone was eavesdropping, as Louella Parsons paid spies at the Brown Derby to pick up stray gossip. Then, as my chest tightened, he said quietly, "I have. They're very apologetic but given the situation, they regretfully cannot renew your contract. As I said, you're in good company. Garbo is there, too. This happens to some of the best talent."

I sat immobile, stunned. I couldn't have cared less if Garbo found herself in the same predicament; I had an expensive Swiss boarding school for my daughter, a house in Hollywood, a lifestyle to maintain. If the studio let me go, how was I going to afford it?

The waiter served the salads and asked if I wanted some grated cheese. When I failed to reply, he sniffed and retreated.

"The studio adores you," Eddie went on. "You're one of their favorites.

But with the state of the industry as it is, they can't afford to keep you. They wish you all the best."

A greeting-card sentiment, as though I'd been diagnosed with an inconvenient ailment. "All the best," I echoed. "That's it, after everything I've done for them?" My voice had grown shrill, bringing the waiter hurrying back to the table.

"Is everything to your satisfaction, Miss Dietrich?" he oozed.

"No." I glared at him. "It most certainly is not."

Eddie slipped the waiter a tip and sent him away. He regarded me in discomfort from across the table. "This isn't as bad as it seems. Think of it this way: You're now free to choose parts you want to do, not whatever the studio assigns. I'll put together a wonderful submission packet for you and—"

I raised my hand. "No," I whispered. "Please. No more."

He lowered his gaze. "I am sorry, Marlene. I realize this comes as a shock, but I represent you. My job as your agent is to look after your interests—"

I couldn't bear it. Coming abruptly to my feet, I retrieved my jacket from the coatroom and walked out into the blinding Los Angeles sunlight, calling for my car. By the time I reached my house, I was beyond tears. Beyond reason. Beyond despair.

I had fallen into an abyss of my own making.

THE STUDIO ISSUED MY FINAL PAYMENT FOR *ANGEL*. Infuriated by their abandonment, I flaunted my tarnished celebrity to the hilt, buying a new Cadillac and carrying on simultaneous affairs with Douglas, Gary, and Mercedes. My recklessness resulted in a nerve-wracking moment when, after accidentally overbooking myself, I ended up with Douglas at my door, shouting that we had reservations at the Cocoanut Grove, while Gary clambered half-dressed down the back stairs and Mercedes telephoned me in a snit because she had a salon waiting and I was nowhere in sight.

When I called her the next day to apologize, she berated me. "Really,

Marlene. *Two* men? And both such mediocre actors? I don't know whether to be more insulted by your relish for these imbroglios or your appalling taste in dick." She hung up on me.

Gary was more sanguine, remarking that I should hire a secretary to ensure I didn't end up with all three of them in my bed. Douglas wept. After demanding I give up the others and hearing my predictable answer, he ended our liaison. In turn, I left my house with its empty rooms—the studio was no longer paying for it—and rented a bungalow at the Beverly Hills Hotel, where I happened upon Cary Grant and Randolph Scott in the bar. They invited me to their Santa Monica cottage for coffee, after which I joined them for a walk along the beach with their terrier.

Touched by their kindness, I poured out my professional troubles. Cary shook his head sadly. "The studios own us. They control everything we do, vetting our scripts and choosing our parts, but then we get blamed when it doesn't work out."

Randolph took my hand, rubbing it as if I were an overwrought child. "But we think you're divine. I'll work with you on any picture. Just say the word."

They were so sweet to me, and so devoted to each other, I couldn't help but fear for them. If the studio had exiled me after a bad run, what might it do to them should the press discover that two of Hollywood's eligible bachelors did more than share a roof? Women who lived together were seen as a sorority, inoffensive and amusing, if they were discreet. But men doing the same—I had a feeling Cary and Randolph were in for a nasty upset of their own.

Nevertheless, I was adrift, without any prospects after eight years as a star. For Christmas 1938, to celebrate the holidays and my thirty-seventh birthday, I invited all my friends over for baked ham. Afterward, we sang carols and swam naked in the pool, with Gary and me diving into the deep end, in full view of the other hotel guests, gawking at us from their balconies.

After the festivities, I knew I couldn't go on this way, spending money I did not have. I called Eddie and gave my permission for him to submit me for hire. I couldn't bear to be idle another second. Without a place to go and work every day, I felt like a pariah.

"Sure thing," he said. "But it'll take some time. I have to negotiate terms and locate projects not yet assigned to contracted stars. I can do it, but can you manage until then?"

I looked about my bungalow, crammed with objects I couldn't bear to part with, my German clocks and paintings, my books and Dresden china. It didn't feel like home. My designation as box-office poison had accomplished the impossible: Dietrich the invincible, the Hollywood goddess of desire, had become an unemployed woman in a rented room.

"I think I'll go back to Europe," I told him. "I'll telephone you from there."

III

I returned to Paris in early 1939.

Worry over the rumors of impending war was my stated excuse; it was time to bring Heidede back with me. To pave the way before my departure, I applied for U.S. citizenship, claiming my family as dependents. The Nazi journal *Der Stürmer* promptly blasted me for betraying the Third Reich once again, my years of "living among Hollywood Jews" having rendered me "entirely un-German." I laughed off the accusation, faced with a more pressing threat: studio disinterest. Despite Eddie's offers to lower my salary, no one wanted to hire me.

Nevertheless, Paris weaved anew her spell. Under torrential downpours, I went out to dinner and the theater with the novelist Erich Maria Remarque, whose 1929 book, *All Quiet on the Western Front,* and its film adaptation had been massive successes, but were now banned by the Nazis, as was Remarque himself. I'd met him onboard during my crossing and was drawn by his fatalistic view of Germany's fiery course. Dour and in poor health, struggling to complete a new novel, he reminded me that as fellow Germans, we were as much scattered by Hitler as imprisoned by him, landless children forced to wander.

Remarque and I became lovers, though in truth he wasn't very amorous. He had suffered injuries during the Great War that he claimed had made him impotent. He wasn't, not entirely, but he tended to fatalism and needed some coaxing, both in and out of bed. It suited me to be seen about town with him, the German-born movie star with the celebrated exiled German novelist. I figured the press couldn't hurt, and I had nothing better to do with my time.

One evening after I'd given him feedback on his work, I arrived back in my suite at the Ritz, where I was ringing up a tab I could not pay, to find Rudi waiting for me. As I dripped rain on the carpet, he said, "Headlines again. You and Remarque, parading all over Paris. Why? Why did you come here?"

"I came," I said, pulling off my raincoat, "because I want to bring Heidede to America. And my parade, as you call it, is for publicity. I lost my contract. Maybe if I show I'm still newsworthy, someone will hire me. Besides," I went on, suppressing a twinge of guilt at my self-justification, "I thought we were past all this. We're still married. What more do you want?"

"Stop it. Stop lying to me. You only came here because at this particular moment, you have nowhere else to go."

He spoke without malice but his words stung. Lighting a cigarette, I paced to the window, smoking furiously as I gazed upon the rain-swept Place Vendôme. "Must you think so little of me?" I said.

"I don't. But I can expect more. You've cooked and cleaned for others. Everyone knows it: the movie goddess serving goulash to her lovers. Why not do it for me now? You've nothing left to prove. If Hollywood doesn't want you, I do. Stay and live with me, as married people should."

I snorted. "What about Tami? Have you asked her what she thinks about my moving in?"

"You are my wife. She has always understood that."

I couldn't look at him. How could I stare him in the face and admit what he clearly had not realized by now? I did care for him, more than he knew, but I found him tiresome, predictable; he was a good man who did his best and he must indeed love me to tolerate as much as he did, yet I couldn't imagine—indeed, had never been able to imagine—this life of compromise and bratwurst he cleaved to, this delusion that our marriage meant more than it did.

"You know I'm not made for exclusive engagements."

He sighed. It wasn't a sound of resignation. Rather, it was like the scrape of a dull scalpel across my back. When I finally turned around, he said, "Then why don't you divorce me? Why insist on this charade? I love you, Marlene. I always will. But you don't love or need me."

"I . . ." Without warning, I felt as though the floor had cracked open under my feet. "I do love you. And I need you, in my own way. Just not as you want."

I decided not to remind him that when we first met, I had wanted to need him. I'd wanted the security and shelter he had promised me. Only we chose another path; we put my career first. I found it demeaning that he'd reproach me now, when I was at my lowest point.

He shook his head. For an instant, I saw him as he'd been that evening at Das Silhouette, his eyes locked on mine as if I were all he could see, his hair slicked from his brow except for one careless lock. "You don't want a divorce because I am—how do the Americans put it?" A sour smile coiled his mouth. "Your golden parachute, in case all else fails."

I froze, my cigarette singeing my fingers. "That's a horrible thing to say."

His smile faded. "It is. But more than that, it's a sad thing to say. The very saddest any person can say to another. Because I may not be here in the end. I may leave you, instead."

"You won't." My retort was impetuous. "Who will pay the bills? You certainly can't; your job here barely feeds you. And Heidede—if you divorce me, you divorce her. I am her mother. I'll not stand for it. I will hire a hundred lawyers if need be to gain sole custody."

I meant to be cruel. To wound. To maim. In that terrible moment, he was everyone and everything that had forsaken me. He was von Sternberg and the studio, my mother and the past. He represented everything I had fought so tenaciously to overcome.

"No." His shoulders sagged. "You're right. I won't leave. But not," he added, as I raised my chin, "because I fear losing our daughter. I won't leave because I understand. Growing old alone is a punishment I'd never wish on anyone—especially you."

He turned and walked out, leaving me with ash filtering through my fingers.

The irony of it, that the one man I'd most neglected, not touched in years, could so unnervingly give voice to my deepest fear, one I'd not even recognized I harbored.

Solitude. Loneliness. An unacknowledged finale.

Where had it started? When had I started to believe that the only life worth living was one that was exalted, photographed and recorded? I could search for an answer, scavenge through memories of that little girl who lost her father too soon, the quick-witted student who hated school but was infatuated with her teacher, the ardent violinist without enough talent and the struggling cabaret performer. I had no idea. I didn't know who I was anymore. I couldn't reconcile the polished replica projected ten times her size on the screen with the stranger I'd become.

Who was I? What more did I want?

Dropping my cigarette, I squashed it into the carpet with my heel, grinding it into a mess of scorched tobacco, cinders, and nicotine stains.

I might never know, but I knew this much: I wasn't finished yet. Dead was dead, and there was nothing to do about it. While I was still alive, I would find some way to prevail.

MY PARISIAN HEADLINES REACHED HOLLYWOOD. Eddie telephoned me; there was interest from Universal, which had a Western comedy slated for the studio's male star James Stewart. The producer thought the supporting female role might be right for me. I asked to see the script, even as Eddie warned that it wasn't my usual fare and the pay was less than a sixth of my usual fee. "But it's a good project," he said, "and I think I can get them to offer a contract, if you agree."

"Then forget the usual," I replied. "Send it."

I loved the script. As Frenchy in *Destry Rides Again*, I would play a raucous saloon dame who falls for Stewart's prim, law-abiding hero. It was an all-American story, which might restore my career, show off my singing and bawdy humor. It certainly wasn't my usual fare; it parodied everything I'd cultivated—a vulgar woman down on her luck, entertaining riffraff in a dusty outpost. But the pay was indeed abysmal, so I cabled Eddie to negotiate a better salary and took advantage of the time before shooting was scheduled to embark on a holiday to southern France. I wanted to make amends to Rudi; I couldn't bear us quarreling, and he agreed, for, like me, he disliked it, too. Tamara also needed a respite, her moods having become more erratic. We went to pick up Heidede from her Swiss school; she was slimmer and more content than I'd seen her in years. Then, together with Remarque, who unlike Douglas before him, did not care if I was married, I traveled with my lover and my family and our mountain of luggage to a cliff-side villa in Antibes, which I rented with my customary disregard for the expense. I also sent word to Mutti to join us and, if she could, to bring Liesel with her. My mother returned word by telegram that she would "see," implying our last visit together remained a bone of contention.

That summer changed me. The British playwright Noël Coward was vacationing nearby and invited me to come see him; his wit and flamboyant flair, coupled with his astonishing talent, had me in awe. He treated us to cocktails at the Hôtel Cap du Roc. I ended up at the piano with him, his nimble fingers stroking the keys as I crooned his music in my smoke-infused voice, including my favorite song of his, "I'll See You Again."

"Darling, I had *no* idea you knew my tunes so well," he said, his beautifully shaped, expressive eyes and jutting ears giving him an elvish air.

I adored him. I knew he must be homosexual, though, like my uncle Willi, unwilling to openly acknowledge it; but he made it clear enough when he leaned to me and whispered, "There is someone here you must meet. A stunning Frenchman and, I believe, an admirer of yours—the actor Jean Gabin."

Rudi, Tami, and Heidede had gone to bed, tired from sun and frolic, while Remarque had disappeared, no doubt on one of his solitary walks to converse with the shadows in his mind.

"Gabin?" I breathed. I knew the name. His gangster picture *Pépé Le Moko* had been a smash hit in France and been remade in America as *Algiers*, with none other than my friend Charles Boyer. Gabin's rugged masculinity, unkempt thatch of dark blond hair, and sharp narrow blue eyes had attracted Hollywood notice, but he'd refused all offers and remained in France, collaborating with such distinguished French directors as Jean Renoir, son of the painter.

"I see you admire him, too." Coward pouted. "But you're so . . . overbooked," he said, alluding in his cunning way to Remarque. "However will you manage it?"

"I'll manage," I assured him, and with a gleeful clap of his hands, he arranged our introduction at his home, where, after drinks and a Mediterranean repast, he made himself scarce.

Gabin may have admired me, but he did not show it at first. With a hand-rolled cigarette dangling from his thin-lipped mouth—he told me tobacco should only be hand-rolled and set out to teach me how, resulting in a very misshapen lump—and his strong nose and that barrel chest under his striped sailor shirt, he resembled a working-class Parisian as he eyed me, seated with my legs crossed by the pool, before he said in his gravelly voice, "You should make pictures here. You speak excellent French, and the Americans—such expensive *merde* they churn out. You are not the same woman as you look on-screen."

I returned his stare. He reminded me of von Sternberg, telling me how terrible I was in my Berlin pictures, and how he could make me a star; but other than that, they were nothing alike. My director had been like a perverse housecat, eccentric and vicious with his claw swipes. Gabin was a lion, feral and blunt.

"Better? Or worse?" I asked him, peering at him from under my eyelashes.

He growled, "Don't play the coquette with me. What do you *think?*"

I took it as a compliment. "I think you're right. I'm not the woman that Hollywood pretends I am. I make bad pictures there for the money."

"Ah." He grunted. "Money. The scourge of the world."

He did not touch me until I was preparing to leave, already late to get back to my villa and my family. Mutti had sent word that she and Liesel would arrive the following week; I had to prepare their rooms and move Remarque into a hotel. He was drinking too much, obsessing over his languishing novel, and I'd rather not endure my mother's disapproval at finding my lover, my child, my husband, and his mistress all under the same roof.

Then, at the door, as Noël chuckled from wherever he was lurking, Gabin seized my waist in his hands, but did not yank me to him as I'd expected and hoped.

"*Vous êtes grande*, Marlene," he said, rolling the *r* in my name like a pebble.

"So are you," I replied. I meant it: He was grand, in every way a man could be, and so unmistakably French I could imagine the taste of the grime and allure of Paris on his tanned skin. "Shall we see each other again?"

He put his mouth closer to mine and murmured, "I think we must."

And so we did. I finagled afternoon escapes in the sweltering heat to take long drives along the coast, picnicking on liver pâté and smoked salmon sandwiches I made for us. He told me about growing up in a village north of Paris, the son of cabaret entertainers whose drunk of a father beat him. He attended a *lycée* but left his studies early to work as a laborer, until at nineteen, he entered show business with a bit part at the Folies-Bergère.

"I kept performing before I gave up and went into the military," he said. "I hated the Folies. But after my military service, I needed money and went back, taking whatever I could get in music halls and operettas, imitating Chevalier—though unlike you"—he grinned—"I have no musical talent. I eventually found work in pictures." He shrugged. "I started getting noticed. Then came *Maria Chapdelaine, La Grande Illusion,* and *Pépé Le Moko.* And voilà! Monsieur nobody was suddenly somebody. Ridiculous, yes?"

It echoed my rise in Berlin; in fact, we were the same age. But he spoke of filmmaking as if it were beneath him—"Not really work, is it?"—and he was deeply troubled by the growing political unrest. "You tell your mother and sister," he said, stabbing his finger at me, "to get out of Germany now. Hitler is a monster."

"You don't know my mother," I sighed, and he never did. He returned to Paris a few days before my family's arrival, without sleeping with me, as much as I tried. "You are married. I consider it a sacred vow," he said, with a shrug. "If you weren't . . ." Even though I assured him I did not think the same about marriage, at least not in that way, he did not change his mind.

After he left, I found myself thinking about him. He was rough-edged, unsure about being an actor, but I knew that feeling well; and he'd advised me to do the Western role when I described it to him. "Risk, Grande," he said, using his nickname for me. "Why not? The world could explode tomorrow."

The world at large did not explode, not yet, but mine did. Mutti arrived with Liesel, and I found my sister subdued, scarcely uttering a word, though I was happy to see her. Her husband, Georg Wills, on the other hand, was voluble, very pleased with himself, stout and rubicund, proclaiming he'd taken a job overseeing a chain of government-approved cinemas, as the Nazis had closed the Theater des Westens along with every other locale that reeked of decadence.

I was outraged when my sister's husband also conveyed another invitation from Goebbels. "He believes you were mistaken before," he said. "You'll be very welcome."

We sat at the dinner table. Delighted to see her aunt Liesel and Oma again, Heidede chattered away with them in German. As Rudi looked at me in warning and Tami kneaded her napkin, Mutti pretended to be deaf as I informed Georg tersely, "He is the one who is mistaken. I told his last envoy in London that I am not interested."

"That was then," said Georg. "You don't have a studio contract now."

"I have an offer." My voice rang out, despite my attempt to control it. I was suddenly trembling. "Even if I didn't, I'd rather wash floors in America than do anything for the Nazis."

The table went silent. Then Liesel ventured, "Lena, really. Georg is only doing what—"

"What Goebbels told him to," I said, cutting her off with an irate look. "No. And you obviously cannot stay there much longer, if they're asking you to bring me these invitations. It's not safe. I can arrange visas, I'm sure I can, for you and—"

"That is enough." Mutti's voice sliced through the tension. "Georg, please respect my daughter's decision," she said, glancing pointedly at him. "She does not want to return to Germany. That is her right." Before I could express my gratitude for her unexpected support, she went on: "But we, too, have the right to stay where we are. I will not hear another word about leaving," she said, looking directly at me. "We are Germans. We belong in our country."

The visit did not improve from there. We went to the beach and the casino, Rudi using his portable camera to take home movies of us, laughing and sharing family moments, but I refused to say more than absolutely necessary to Georg, and Liesel wilted, so dominated by him that she avoided any private time with me. Mutti ignored it all, devoting herself to Heidede. She left with Liesel and her husband just as she had arrived—without concessions.

After returning with Tamara and Rudi to Paris, I sought out Gabin. He was shooting a picture; we had only one evening to have dinner. When he pecked my cheek good-bye, wishing me *bonne chance* with the new film, I invited him to my hotel suite. Again, I was rebuffed—he said he was too tired—and I wondered at my persistence. For the first time since I'd met Rudi, I wanted a man more than he seemed to want me, and I found his refusal unsettling.

Heidede did not want to return to America and was sullen during the trip back on the *Queen Mary*. Remarque came with us. I enrolled her in high school, saw him settled into an adjoining hotel bungalow to write—our affair was practically over, if it could even be called that, but I believed in his talent and he had nowhere else to go—and then I signed my contract with Universal for the Western.

Only days before I began shooting *Destry Rides Again*, the news came that Hitler had invaded Poland. Rudi telephoned the studio switchboard in a panic. He feared the war would reach France and wanted to leave. I sent urgent word to the U.S. embassy in Paris, along with boat fare. My petition to claim him and Tamara as dependents was expedited; they took a ship from Calais to London and then on to New York, where I rented an apartment for them with my new salary. My subsequent telegrams to Berlin went unanswered until I eventually reached Uncle Willi at his store. He told me Mutti was still housekeeping, as unbelievable as it seemed; everyone was safe, he kept saying, but I detected a new wariness through the line.

"Let me help," I said. "I told Mutti I can claim you as dependents. Rudi and Tamara are here now, in New York. You can come, too."

"No." He lowered his voice until I barely heard him. "Please, Lena. Don't call again."

He hung up on me. I couldn't fault him for it, after I'd refused Goebbels twice, but I was upset. Getting my family to safety now, even if they were willing, would not be so easy with war breaking out, much as I wanted to demand their immediate evacuation on the next ship.

When *Destry Rides Again* premiered, it was a success, even against *The Grapes of Wrath* and *Gone with the Wind*. I had wonderful songs like "See What the Boys in the Back Room Will Have," in which I swaggered about in shoulder-baring feathers and disintegrating sequins.

Critics rhapsodized over my performance, exulting in my willingness to roll about in the muck. I gained a raise in my salary and another picture with Universal: the South Seas riot *Seven Sinners*, where I played the female lead, Bijou, opposite strapping John Wayne. I liked him almost as much as I liked Gary. Six feet of solid American beefcake, he was gorgeous, though, unlike Gary, disinclined to wit, though as ambitious and with as avid an eye for the ladies, despite his sulking backstage wife.

I invited him to my dressing room after our first week of shooting, greeting him in a sheer black peignoir. When I asked him the time and he mumbled that he had no idea, I lifted my hem to reveal a watch dangling from my garter. Setting my red-nailed fingers on his shoulders, which were broad enough to wrestle bulls, I said, "It's early. We have plenty of time."

He grinned and began tugging off his clothes.

But time was the one thing the world no longer had.

THE GOLDEN PANTHER

1942–1946

"I WANT A CHANCE TO REALLY SEE
A BIT OF LIFE BEFORE I DIE."

I

France surrendered to Hitler in June 1940. The fall of Paris sent shock waves throughout Europe and into America, bringing a new tide of refugees, now escaping the Nazis marching down the Champs-Élysées. I closed up my bungalow and rented a house in Brentwood, where I cooked after work and welcomed exiles. Soon, my house was full of wild-eyed French talent, stunned over their country's collapse. When the director Jean Renoir arrived with Gabin, both looking as if they hadn't slept in weeks, I nearly dropped my tray of roast beef and potatoes.

Gabin wept that night—angry, crunched-up tears—after everyone ate their fill, sang a rousing chorus of "La Marseillaise," and departed for their various beds on other people's sofas or floors. I offered him my spare bedroom, saying Heidede could sleep with me; he had a cheap hotel room he shared with Renoir and they were negotiating with the studios to make a picture here, but he didn't speak English well at all, and he was despondent. Making a movie seemed to be the last thing on his mind.

"Cowards," he said, his hand-rolled cigarette staining his fingers as he sat brooding, staring into the emptiness where the echo of the French anthem of independence lingered. "They gave in to Hitler. They let the monsters march right in. There's a new provisional government in Vichy,

agreeing to whatever they demand, dividing us up like a fucking quiche."
His cigarette ash trickled onto my carpet. "I wanted to stay and fight. But
Renoir said we had to leave, otherwise we'd be forced to make films for
them or end up arrested. I told him I'd come here but only to make money.
Once I do, I'm going back to kill Nazis."

"I'm so sorry." I touched his hunched shoulder, heartbroken for him. "I
know how it feels. I know how it is to lose one's country—"

He snorted. "You didn't lose Germany. You walked away to become
an American movie star. And Germany isn't being invaded. Everyone else
is being invaded by them."

I recoiled from him. "Don't be cruel. I *did* lose Germany. I'm losing it
more every day."

He frowned. Then his anger shifted into remorse. "I'm sorry, my
Grande. I am a beast. Pay no attention to what I say. I'm not myself."

He certainly was not, but I found that I liked him even more for it—
washed up on a foreign shore, alone and desperate, he needed my comfort.

"I could help you," I said. "Look over your contract, refer you to my
agent. Introduce you to people. Teach you English."

"With your German accent?" he said, but a smile teased the corners of
his craggy mouth. He contemplated me. "You would do it, wouldn't you?"
He spoke as if generosity from someone else was a revelation. "You would
do anything for me if I asked you."

I nodded. "Of course. Why shouldn't I? I also know what it is like to be
a European who comes to America and doesn't know anything about—"

I didn't have time to finish. He seized me, and finally did exactly what
I wanted. As his mouth crushed mine, he said, "Germany and France in
bed together. *À propos.*"

He was a rough lover, disinterested in refinements, but strong as a
ram and hungry for me, so hungry I imagined him ripping my flesh with
his teeth. I wanted to remain in control, but he refused to let me, hoisting
himself on top of me, blocking my sight so that all I could see was his
face, looming, leonine, as he whispered, "Show me who you are. Not her.
I want *you.*"

He unlocked me like a safe, dilating my pores with his tongue, his urgent thrust, his raw desire. Afterward, as I lay in a heap with our sweat still wet on my skin, he lit a cigarette and grinned. "That is how Frenchmen conquer," he said, and I gave a brittle laugh, the heat of his touch so thick, it felt tattooed like ink on my skin.

I knew then that he had breached something within me, a secret place that I had not let any man, not even Rudi, reach: that raw place where I'd hidden my vulnerability after my affair with Reitz in Weimar, all those years ago. Gabin had somehow, without even trying, sneaked past my defenses to show me how helpless falling in love could really be.

I asked him to stay. He sent for his few belongings; when I eyed a leather cylinder among his battered valises and an accordion case, of all things, he said, "Open it."

It held paintings, ripped from their frames: a Vlaminck, a Sisley, a Renoir, and a Matisse. Their pastel beauty, as iridescent as sunlit reflections on the Seine, glistened under my fingertips.

"Don't touch them," he said. "You'll taint the varnish. Just keep them here for me. I wasn't going to let the Nazis burn or steal them."

I had them reframed and hung in our bedroom. He began to learn English with a coach I hired for him, gaining enough of the language to start work in a picture called *Moontide*. To celebrate, I took him out, dressed in white tie, to the latest hot spot, the Mocambo, so we could be seen together and generate publicity for him. He hated the pretension of Hollywood nightlife; he preferred soda fountains and seedy diners, the Negro jazz clubs in back alleys where no one famous ever went. He was not interested in preparing for stardom, playing his accordion by the pool, where he often swam nude, or bicycling about Brentwood, marveling at what he called "*la putain* America," where people put out too much trash and no one seemed to care about the war raging in Europe.

I was shooting *Seven Sinners* with John Wayne. Gabin took an immediate dislike to him, glaring at John when he arrived in my Cadillac at the studio to pick me up and muttering under his breath, "Is that mule in your pants?"

"Not at the moment," I said, but I ended my dalliance with Wayne all the same, because Gabin had a black look in his eye that made me think he'd start a brawl. He didn't seem to mind about Remarque, however, who still toiled desultorily on his novel in the bungalow I'd rented for him. Perhaps because Remarque was an exile, like him, or, more likely, because I'd shared enough about Remarque's troubles in bed for Gabin to deem him not much of a threat.

One day I returned from the studio early to find Gabin pacing the garden in his undershorts, peering past the shrubbery and low brick wall that separated my house from the one beside it. "*Elle est folle*," he whispered to me as I came up beside him. "That woman next door, she's crazy. She watches me. Every afternoon at around four, I see her through the bushes. In a big hat and sunglasses. She stares at me."

"Does it surprise you?" I laughed. "You sit around naked, playing an accordion."

He gripped my arm. "No. I tell you, she knows something. What if she's a German spy?"

I hadn't bothered to find out who my neighbors were—the area was full of Hollywood people—so I telephoned my agent to inquire. It took him a few days but when Eddie called back, he said in a troubled voice, "That crazy lady next door, it's Garbo. That's one of her homes."

"Impossible," I exclaimed, but that very weekend at the appointed hour, I took a naked dip in the pool myself with Gabin and waited. To my disappointment, our peeping MGM queen, whom I'd not yet seen in person, failed to make an appearance. The following week, moving vans rolled up and away. The house next door was rented to someone else.

My infatuation with Gabin began to unnerve me. Gossip ran rife that we were lovers, which didn't bother me nearly as much as it did Eddie, who kept reminding me that everyone knew I was married. I was more disturbed by my own imperviousness, when I'd tried in the past to keep my liaisons, if not covert, at least discreet. It was a new sensation, this need for someone else and my willingness to indulge it. I'd been infatuated before, with Rudi before we married, and later, with von Sternberg as he crafted my ascent. But with Gabin, it was different, as though he'd mined a liquid force inside me that I couldn't contain, so that my insides quailed whenever he entered the room. I thought he must be my match, that twin soul that made movie fantasy so potent—the companion I could never dominate, as strong-willed as me yet also as vulnerable as an orphan. He roused in me imaginings of what it might be like to grow old together, when I'd never considered permanency with anyone but Rudi. And when I imagined telling Gabin that I longed to bear his child, I was appalled by my own delusion. It was the oldest trick in the world to hold on to a man, and I was past the age to become a mother again, even if it was possible—which, I told myself sternly, it was not. Not for me. One child was enough, considering how poorly I'd done with Heidede.

My husband sensed it when he called me from New York and I told him Gabin was living with me. There was a long silence before Rudi asked, "Are you in love with him?"

"I . . . I don't know," I said, hesitant to admit to the turmoil within me. "I might be. Or I could be, if I let myself."

Rudi sighed. "You will let me know if you do let yourself?" He sounded so resigned that I forced out a chuckle. "What? And give up my parachute?" I teased. "Besides, he wants to go fight the Nazis. Who knows how long we'll even last?"

Although I couldn't say it aloud, I wanted it to last. By day, Gabin was a thundercloud, storming off to the studio to work on a picture he detested; at night, he clung to me as if he sought to lose himself inside my ribs. I made him steak tartare and onion soup; I filled the house with fresh-cut gladioli and sang French songs so he could feel as though we were in Paris, that a little piece of his country was here, with us. I invited over his compatriots for dinner—Charles Boyer, the director René Clair, and gentle Renoir. We played cards, told dirty jokes, danced, and drank anisette. I showed off my talent on the musical saw, which made Gabin grimace. Boyer borrowed a violin, badly out of tune, from some movie set. I fixed it and regaled them with a fumbling rendition of Bach, which made Gabin smile.

Yet beneath my protective mantle, which I wrapped about us to shelter him from pain, Gabin seethed with fury—against the Nazis and his own cowardice for leaving his nation, for which he couldn't forgive himself; for the humiliation of France and his own humiliation, working for Hollywood in a role he did not want, in a country he found apathetic. His picture flopped, while my *Seven Seas* was successful, not as much as *Destry*, but enough to get me cast in *Manpower* as a hard-talking gun moll.

"What are we doing here?" he demanded, after he'd drunk more than he should and our guests had departed. "Playing silly games and making idiotic pictures when people are dying. We are cowards, too. All of us. We should be fighting, not filling the fat American wallet."

It was his litany. He railed against it but then he did the same, signing himself on for another picture, because, he said, he was saving up to join the cause. I had tried to convince myself that he'd never actually forsake the plenty of America for the terror of Europe and the war, but these rants of his were becoming more frequent, and though we lived together, he rarely shared the costs, so I had to wonder if perhaps I was deluding myself into thinking he cared about his personal safety more than he did.

"What else can we do?" I said. "We're not soldiers. I don't know how to shoot a gun."

"Neither does anyone who joins the resistance," he replied. "You don't need to be a soldier to learn to use a gun or stand up for what is right."

"Perhaps you don't, but I have a husband and daughter to support, and my family in Germany—"

"Bah." He cut me off with a snarl. "Your family in Germany are all Nazis by now, shouting '*Heil Hitler*' and watching the Jews be deported." He gulped down his whiskey; he liked Johnnie Walker. Too much, I thought. "I thought you were an American citizen now," he went on in a snide tone of voice. "Yet every time I bring up the war, you act as though you were forced out of Germany yesterday."

"I am an American citizen," I said, too tired from work and cooking for our friends to argue with him. He could be deliberately obtuse about the fact that I could consider myself both an American and a German and needn't choose one over the other. "America is not at war."

"Not yet." He banged his glass on the table. "But not for much longer. Go, then. Be a slut for Hollywood. But nothing will stop me." He went to the sofa and threw himself upon it. He'd stay out here tonight, drinking himself into a stupor. I was relieved. I found him exasperating at times like this, so I retreated to the bedroom, not wanting to argue, as Heidede could hear everything from her room. Lying awake, his snores reaching me from down the hall, I asked myself why I persisted. He was contrary and bellicose; he detested everything. He was turning my life upside down. How long would it take before he started hating me?

Or I started hating him?

The possibility terrified me. In the morning before I left for the studio, I made him breakfast and tidied up his clothes, which he habitually shed wherever he happened to be. He was asleep, exuding the stench of whiskey. He had finished off the Johnnie Walker. I resolved to not buy another bottle, as he might never manage to accomplish anything if he kept drinking at this rate. I had to shake him awake. Grumbling and with a hangover, he ignored my murmured endearments and plate of scrambled eggs to stagger off to the shower.

That night, I came home later than usual after visiting with Remarque, who was sunk in yet another depression. Gabin greeted me in a rage. "*Putain*," he yelled, flinging the contents of his glass at me. "All night I've been waiting, and you were—where? With that miserable German writer, I suppose. Or that American mule, Wayne, or God knows who else! *Assez!* I've had enough. Them or me. You decide."

I was so stunned by his assault, his alcohol soaking my cashmere coat, I didn't consider at the time that this had nothing to do with Wayne or Remarque. Infuriated by his boorishness, I shot back with the first thing that came to mind: "It's my house and my life. I'll see whomever I want."

His hand flew up. Before I could evade him, he slapped me. Stunned, I hit him back with my fist. Hard. He staggered backward and then, as he lunged toward me, his expression purple, Heidede screamed from her bedroom door—"No! Stop it!"—and Gabin froze.

I inched past him to rush to my seventeen-year-old daughter.

Gabin gazed at me as I clutched Heidede. With his hair tangled about his brow, his body coiled into itself, he looked like a bewildered child as he said in a desolate voice, "No more. I cannot . . . do this anymore. I—I must return to France."

My cheek was bruised. I could feel it throbbing. I would have to ice it, as I had a makeup call early in the morning. "Go," I retorted. "Start swimming to France. Now."

I herded Heidede into her bedroom and tried to calm her, assuring her I was fine, that it was just a fight and he was drunk. She was crying, however, and I was close to tears myself, a pit yawning inside me. The only man I'd ever struck before had been von Sternberg, and he would never have dared hit me back. I knew then that my relationship with Gabin had reached the end of its frayed tether. It had to stop, for both our sakes, and still I couldn't find it in myself to blame him. I blamed the war, the Nazis, his terrible frustration. When I heard him leave without a word, not even attempting an apology, a wail clawed at the back of my throat.

The next morning, I called in sick. Then I telephoned Jean Renoir and anyone else whom Gabin and I knew. He hadn't reported to his set but he showed up later at Renoir's apartment. Chastened and sober, he called me to beg my forgiveness, but said he would not move back in with me. He asked me to send over his belongings. I did, but I refused to part with his paintings and accordion. He chuckled sadly over the telephone. "My Grande. You must keep them. When we see each other again in a free Paris, you can return them to me."

To my horror, I heard myself whisper, "Please don't leave me."

"No," he said. "You don't mean it. You think this is what you want, but it isn't. We only hurt each other. I'm acting like my father, like a drunken brute. I was never a jealous man before. Not like this. I don't like who I am with you."

I wept. I begged. I lost all pride, my dignity. But he was stronger than me, and in the vast emptiness he left in my heart, I finally understood why I wanted him so much.

He was one of the few who could leave me.

The end of 1941 felt like the end of the world for me. Gabin was no longer mine; I missed him so much, I didn't even care that *Manpower* failed at the box office. Eddie nervously warned me that whatever I was offered next, I must carefully consider it, lest I ruined the waning glory of my performance in *Destry*. But I needed money; I'd spent too much on Gabin, was still supporting Remarque, Rudi, and Tamara, and after I'd asked her about her future plans for college, Heidede had informed me that she wanted to be an actress like me.

I nearly lost my composure, bursting with the furious urge to regale her with the reminder of what being an actress entailed. Had she not witnessed it herself, with her very own eyes? Had she not grown up practically without me, watching me toil for endless hours on a set and sacrificing personal fulfillment for my name in lights on a marquee? Acting was the last career I could ever wish for her—but I held my tongue, remembering my own determination at her age and how my mother's refusal to accommodate me had ended up alienating us from each other. I decided that if she was set on this path, let her experience some of its trials for herself. She would soon learn that acting was far more difficult than she envisioned. So I insisted she must study first to prepare, and enrolled her in the Jack Geller acting workshop and rented her a studio apartment nearby. Acting classes would dissuade her, I thought, teach her that nothing in this business was easy; but I now had to pay her expenses as well.

I accepted a loan-out for the comedy *The Lady Is Willing*, playing a stage actress who finds an abandoned baby. While on set, I tripped on a pile of wires and fractured my ankle. I had to finish the shoot in a cast, draped in a diaphanous white gown while lying on a couch. The news of my mishap made headlines, but the picture itself did not.

On December 7, the Japanese bombed Pearl Harbor—an act of unprecedented savagery that heralded the end of American apathy. It plunged me back into my childhood during the Great War, the tragedy and senseless loss, magnified now, spilling over everywhere to blacken the world.

I couldn't bear to look at a newspaper without wanting to scream, and I knew Gabin would not remain idle anymore, acting in pictures that meant nothing to him. I felt the same.

To economize and escape the memory of his absence, I left my house in Brentwood to return to my hotel bungalow. Remarque haunted my doorstep, morosely pleased that Gabin was gone and advising me on scripts I received. He tried to rekindle our flame, to no avail. I found him unappealing as a lover. He eventually drifted away, to finish his novel and meet the actress Paulette Goddard, whom he'd marry.

I was about to turn forty. Dietrich, carnal yet detached, whom I'd converted into a raucous dame with a tendency to rile up the boys, taunted me like a negative on the cutting-room floor. She could not save me—not from the realities of aging in a system that thrived on youth, or from wretched pictures, lackluster notices, and public indifference. Once again, I found myself treading the edge of an abyss, unsure of where to turn.

I heard Rudi, *Growing old alone is a punishment I'd never wish on anyone, especially you*—and I knew despair then as I never had before.

On New Year's Eve, I telephoned my husband in New York and wept. Rudi kept saying he loved me, over and over, but I couldn't feel it. I was hollow. Emptied. I could not look back and I dared not look ahead.

Loneliness was something I had never anticipated.

II

She had protuberant blue-gray eyes, sour nicotine breath, and the temperament of a dervish. I knew her by repute, though we'd not met until now. Thrusting out her hand, pumping my fingers as if I were a cash register, she said in her trademark clipped-glass voice, "I'm Bette Davis. I hear you hate the Krauts as much as I do. Is it true?"

It was 1942. I was on the set of *Pittsburgh*, my third picture with John Wayne, playing a woman caught between two coal miners, one of whom was Cary Grant's lover, my friend Randolph Scott. I'd taken the part to work with John, whose fame was skyrocketing, and also because the picture gave me the chance to do something patriotic, its plot highlighting Pittsburgh's steel production, part of America's war effort in the wake of Pearl Harbor.

My sorrow had not abated. Gabin had finally left for France by way of Morocco, to join the resistance. He took his Hollywood earnings. When he called to tell me, I asked to accompany him to New York. We had a week together, visiting the city and sharing a hotel room before I saw him off on his ship. I then went to cry on Rudi's shoulder. I still couldn't admit I was in love—I refused—but Rudi's lack of any inquiry made me think that, like Remarque, he was relieved. He might not ask, but my despair was enough for him to see that my infatuation might threaten our marriage, even if I already knew in my heart that Gabin and I weren't meant to be anything more. Tamara tiptoed around us, so as to not disturb, but I cut short my stay. She'd been suffering from anxiety again and I didn't want to aggravate her by monopolizing Rudi's attention.

By the time I returned to Los Angeles, Hollywood was in mourning for the actress Carole Lombard, wife of Clark Gable; she'd been killed in a plane crash during a war-bond tour. I'd met Carole at studio events and enjoyed her brash beauty, making a pass at her that she laughed off. "If I wanted a broad," she said, "you'd be my first choice." Gable was devastated; and as our first war casualty, her death proved that not even stars were immune to the cataclysm.

Now, here was Bette Davis, leading dramatic lady and first female president of the Academy of Motion Picture Arts and Sciences, whose highly publicized lawsuit to rid herself of her Warner Bros. contract, which she lost, had made her a beacon of hope to actresses everywhere and whose radical notions of equality churned corporate stomachs.

"I'm also a Kraut," I said. "I don't hate all my countrymen. Not all of us are Nazis."

She considered this, lighting her sixth cigarette in as many minutes. We sat in a fog of smoke; as I watched her puff away, I remembered hearing that when Bette had signed her first contract, she had to overcome the studio's assertion that she'd never be a leading lady. With her piquant features and bony figure, her incessant smoking—she made my own habit seem abstemious—parching her skin, she defied the idea of glamour as I knew it. But in her case, glamour was redundant. She had a quality many sought but few had: irresistible magnetism. Six years younger than me, she'd already won two Academy Awards. Her entire being was malleable, and she'd proved astute at avoiding typecasting, championing herself for challenging roles that I would never have dared test for.

"But you do hate the Nazis," she said at length, blinking rapidly. She spit out some tobacco from between her teeth. Definitely not a lady. I admired that. "I heard *mein* führer tried to entice you back to Germany with a huge salary and your choice of any director. You said no."

"He didn't offer," I said, succumbing to my own urge to smoke. Before I could reach for my Cartier lighter, a monogrammed gift from John, she snapped it up and lit my cigarette for me. "His propaganda minister did. And I did choose a director. They were not amused."

She guffawed. She had a raw laugh, husky from smoking and as strident as a gong. "Von Sternberg, I suppose?"

I smiled. "Who else?"

"Bastards. Between them and the Japs, we'll be wearing kimonos and kissing Hitler's ass if we don't get involved soon. Roosevelt has his hands full, but he can't ignore the war in Europe much longer. We've lost France, Poland, Czechoslovakia, Belgium, Norway, Greece, and Holland. The Nazis are bombing London and those Fascists in Italy and Spain are co-operating with them. Have you heard about the Jews?" she asked abruptly.

I swallowed. "I heard they were being deported to ghettoes."

"Not just ghettoes." Bette crushed out her cigarette and immediately lit another. "There are rumors of camps. But not like the ones we've set up to hold Japanese-Americans here, though that's bad enough." She scowled. "Theirs are actual work camps, where they use Jews as slave labor. The Free French have been broadcasting about it, trying to get word out, but no one's paying attention. Meanwhile, thousands are disappearing. It's an outrage."

I found myself biting my lower lip. "It is."

"You must *do* something." She hit her little fist on my dressing room table, making my makeup jars rattle. In the corner, Betsy muffled a laugh. She never ceased to find mirth in the grandiloquence of celebrities who came to visit me. "You're a German-American now. If we had you on our team, it would send a powerful message, show the world that Hollywood cares."

"Does Hollywood care?" I asked.

"Of course not. None of the studios will lift a finger to save a bunch of Jews. They're hiring those who make it here, to score pictures, to edit, write, or direct, but they're running their own kind of camp: Camp Get-A-Hebrew Cheap."

I had to chuckle. "And what would I do on your team, exactly?"

"Join our effort. I've organized a USO affiliate, the Hollywood Canteen, to entertain servicemen before they ship out. You could help us. Dorothy Lamour and Norma Shearer are doing it, so is that priss Claudette Colbert. Why don't you?" She paused, eyeing my lighter, which she still held. "Unless you're too busy making lousy pictures with that moron."

"John is hardly a—"

She waved her hand, spraying ashes. "Please. He can barely read a script. Everyone knows he's as dumb as an ox. But," she added lasciviously, "I hear he's hung like one, too."

"I wouldn't know," I demurred. "Should we ask him?"

She crowed again. "I like you. Hemingway said you were good stuff. I don't care who you screw—I should probably screw more of my leading men myself—but I want you on my team. What do I have to do to convince you?" Suddenly, her short-nailed hand with its smoldering cigarette was on my knee. "I'll do anything," she crooned.

I glanced at her fingers, then slowly lifted my gaze back to hers. "I don't think that will be necessary. Just tell me where and when."

She smiled. "Yeah. I'm no Garbo. But I'd have done you anyway."

I had no doubt. And if she'd been my type, I was sure she'd have been my best lover yet.

I REASONED THAT HELPING OUT at a celebrity canteen was safe enough. Many stars were doing it, either out of genuine concern or because the studios ordered them to (we couldn't appear to be oblivious) for extra publicity. I thought about telephoning Rudi to consult with him, then thought again. I didn't need permission to do what felt right.

Dressed in slacks and a plain white shirt, my hair under a scarf, and carrying grocery bags filled with hams and fresh-baked strudel from my bungalow oven, I arrived at the Hollywood Canteen at 1451 Cahuenga Boulevard.

Bette chortled. "Planning on a juggling act?"

"No," I said. "But I can play the musical saw. Will that do?"

"Go at it," she said, and I joined the others in the kitchens to cook meals.

The boys in uniform—for they were boys, so fresh faced and young I couldn't imagine them doing anything but chasing girls or one another—and servicewomen, as well, were so grateful and astonished to see me, Bette, Dorothy, Norma, Claudette, Mae West, and others serving at the tables that they lightened my heart. John joined us; so did Gary, Randolph, and Cary, and other top male stars. Bette had stormed the highest echelons, recruiting the most famous, her relentless optimism—"Go get 'em, boys!"—and consummate dedication making her heroic in my eyes. It was the role of a lifetime and she never wavered, working long hours to ensure our troops didn't leave without some love and glitz. Signed pictures of us were required; she distributed these so that every serviceman who came through the doors would have one.

One night after a performance by Rosalind Russell, the servicemen started banging their cutlery on the tables and chanting, "Marlene! Marlene!"

I was in the back, scrubbing pots with a breathtaking new contract player named Ava Gardner, whose green-eyed beauty was matched by her sailor's mouth. We were chuckling over MGM's choice for her first part, an unbilled socialite. "Now, they want to put me in a fucking musical, like Judy Garland. I can't sing like you gals," she said, unfazed. "I guess they'll have to dub me to make it look like I do. Pretty is as pretty does, right?" Then she paused. "Hey. Sounds like they're calling for you."

I went still, listening. Bette burst into the kitchen. "Take off that hairnet and get your ass out there. They want 'Falling in Love Again.'"

Ava rolled her eyes at me. "Can't escape that little ditty, can you?"

Jabbing her in the ribs as she laughed, I wrenched off my net and followed Bette. The explosion of shouts and applause brought me to a halt.

From the stage, clad in a silver gown that revealed her stellar legs, Rosalind crooked a finger at me and said into the microphone, "Ladies and gentlemen, your cook, Marlene Dietrich."

As I walked onto the stage with the yowls of servicemen deafening me, Rosalind said into my ear, "I've cued the band." She left me standing there, shirtsleeves rolled to my elbows and wispy curls flattened from my hairnet.

"Marlene! Marlene!"

"Hush, *Liebchens*," I whispered into the microphone. "You make a girl nervous." Then, as the music began, I called for a chair and one of the boys in the first row fell over his own feet to bring it to me. Straddling it, I pulled up my slacks to expose my calves. In the hush that fell, as their shining faces blurred into sudden tears I held back, I sang my heart out for them, following my signature number from *The Blue Angel* with songs from *Morocco*, *The Devil Is a Woman*, *Blonde Venus*, *Destry Rides Again*, and *Seven Sinners*. I used my scarf as my sole accessory, draping it about my head, shimmying it like a boa about my shoulders, and feeling as if I were bathed in glitter. When I was done, breathless and sweating, I paused, gazing out from beneath my lids at the multitude and spoke my favorite line from *Seven Sinners*: " 'Oh, look. The navy. Will someone please give me an American . . . cigarette?' "

The boys went wild. Dozens of cigarettes flew through the air to fall around me.

As I retrieved one, every man at the first twelve tables lunged forward with their lighters, flicking flames in the low-lit salon illuminating their ecstatic faces.

"God bless you, Miss Dietrich," I heard one whisper.

That night after the canteen closed and Bette held me, I wept. I didn't know why. Yes, I'd been moved by all those young men, all that ardent life, soon to be shipped off to fight and die just as German boys were. But I also wept for something else, an inchoate sundering inside me for which I had no name. It came flooding like a tide—the years of hope and disappointment, the highs and lows, Gabin and the entire silly carousel, as von Sternberg had called it.

"There now." Bette cradled me in her arms. "I had no idea you were such a natural. Those come-hither films of yours don't do you justice. You belong on the stage."

"You think so?" I looked up at her. It had been so long since I'd entertained like that, without costumes or accompaniment, without cameras or artifice, that I'd wondered if I sounded like Dietrich or a middle-aged Kraut with ham on her breath.

"Don't be coy. You heard their applause. No one could take their eyes off you." She chuckled. "Not even Rosalind, and believe me, she's not easily impressed." She paused. "Why don't you apply for a USO permit? Forget this racket. Go give our boys what they need. If I had what you do, I'd go," she added, lifting her skirt. "But who wants to see these chicken legs?"

It was my apotheosis. Though I was scheduled to be loaned out to MGM for an Arabian-themed extravaganza, from that moment I had only one ambition:

To support my adopted nation in whichever way I could.

III

Though it had taken Pearl Harbor to rally the nation, America had been providing military aid and reconnaissance since 1941, when Germany declared war on us. As part of the Allied strategy with Britain and Russia, the plans to defeat Hitler were as secret and dangerous as the mounting casualties, without any certainty if we would prevail.

I worried over potential repercussions in Berlin if I went out to entertain the troops. It was an overt declaration I'd not be able to rescind, even if I told myself that no one in my family had been arrested yet and I'd done plenty already to incite it. I couldn't hide away anymore, not with Hitler intent on ravaging Europe. Though I couldn't vanquish the fear that my actions might bring harm to my loved ones, I had to take a stand, both as a public personality and as a German. For years, I'd sought to protect my career and my family by remaining silent. I couldn't do it any longer. If I kept to the sidelines, I would be condoning the very thing I detested, participating in the carnage from afar because I was too frightened to do something.

In early 1944, I went to New York to submit my application for a formal United States Entertainment Organization (USO) permit, following an appearance before twelve hundred soldiers at Fort Meade. I'd finished *Kismet* for MGM, where I'd performed an unfathomable dance number—my first and last on film—layered in Arabian veils, braided headgear, and enough gilded spray paint to turn my legs green. I worked at the canteen in my costume; Bette scolded me. The fury of servicemen trying to dance with me brought the police in to accuse her of inciting a riot. I'd also taken part in Orson Welles's magic act for Universal's all-star picture revue *Follow the Boys*—a showcase featuring Hollywood talent, in which I did a mesmerizing act, was sawed in half by Orson, and the studio pocketed the screening profits.

Bette fumed. "Those greedy motherfuckers. When the history of this town is written, they're going down as collaborators. They'd exploit Hitler himself if they could sign him."

I doubted anyone would bother with how terribly the studios behaved, but I was also so disgusted by the flagrant money grab that it sealed my decision to go off on my own, with Bette's encouragement and Orson's blessing to steal his mesmerizing act. Packing up three flesh-colored net gowns designed to be both provocative and practical (no ironing), I went on the road to dazzle soldiers waiting to deploy, their rousing cheers buoying me all the way to Manhattan.

At home, travails with my daughter had resulted in her own departure to live with Rudi and pursue her acting career. Despite my determination to be more attentive and my hope that studying acting would dampen her enthusiasm for it, my long days on the set and nights at the canteen had left me unaware of her precipitous affair with a fellow student until she proclaimed her engagement. Nothing I said made a difference; they went ahead despite my protests, though I deemed him a mediocre talent with no future and doubted Heidede truly loved him. She seemed lost, confused; again, I blamed myself. But she was obstinate, like me; and on principle alone, Rudi and I did not attend the wedding. I did go to their apartment after they left on their honeymoon, however, ordering some of my furniture brought from storage (I still lived in my crammed bungalow) and arranging it after I scrubbed everything from windowsills to floors. In my apron and scarf, without makeup, the building manager thought I was a maid and gave me a two-dollar tip, suggesting I could find extra work with the other tenants. I thought Mutti would be proud that I'd apparently not forgotten how to properly wax a floor.

Six months later, Heidede, or Maria, as she now wanted to be called, rejecting her childhood name, admitted her marriage had been a mistake. She petitioned for a divorce; when I questioned her, she said flatly, "I don't want to talk about it. It never happened."

Rudi and I encouraged her to pursue her studies in New York. She'd never escape my shadow in Hollywood, and stage training, we told her, was essential to the rigors of the craft, even if we both had our misgivings over her hopes for a career in the midst of a world war.

But I understood her silence, because the reason I hadn't taken to Broadway was something *I* didn't want to talk about. The offer to star in a play titled *One Touch of Venus* should have filled me with joy. The producers courted me; Kurt Weill, he of the gloomy disposition in Paris but now happily employed in America, was the composer. The role was ideal—a statue of Venus comes to life, only to discover that mortal life isn't what she envisioned. Weill was enthusiastic during the visit to woo me. Everything had been conceived with my talents in mind. "You never recorded what I wrote for you in Paris," he said. "But now, you'll have many songs and will be the toast of Broadway."

Many songs, I learned, were too many. I knew it the moment I attempted the score. In addition to mastering Weill's convoluted music, I'd not been on an actual stage in fifteen years, and the part required a vocal range I'd never had. It was also too seductive, even for me. I wasn't Lola-Lola anymore, much as I might feign otherwise. Weill was enraged. I insisted I had a war duty to undertake, and they hired Mary Martin instead, who brought down the house.

I didn't regret it. While waiting for FBI clearance on my USO assignment, I received a telegram from Gabin. He was in Algiers, his passage to France delayed. He'd joined a tank regiment of the Free French of course; Nazi tanks were prized Allied targets. "Grande," he wired, "I am happy." I had no way to send word back to him, his wire routed through several clearances so that it had taken weeks to reach me, but I was elated that he had thought of me.

I stayed with Rudi and Tamara, saw Maria settled in her new academy, and, buoyed by the news from Gabin, began rehearsals with my accompanist, Danny Thomas, a comedian from the nightclub circuit. He taught me how to engage a temperamental audience; how to make the material seem spontaneous; and, most important, how to perform without cameras and lights. Broadway might have been too challenging but I'd been playing Dietrich all my life. As for the act itself, composed of my greatest hits, all I had to do was remember Bette's canteen.

On April 2, 1944 (under the designation Major Dietrich in the unlikely case I was captured and required military treatment), my troupe boarded a C-54 transport with a platoon of new soldiers. It was the first aircraft I'd been on; not until we were aloft was our destination disclosed.

We were going to Casablanca, in Morocco.

I considered it a good omen.

IV

Electrical storms jolting the plane caused my troupe to cluster in misery, while the soldiers suddenly looked as if they wished they'd never enlisted. I'd packed a flask of cognac to keep warm, having been forewarned that the plane would be cold. Danny puked it up, but I got pleasantly drunk and distracted the soldiers with tales of my days in Berlin, singing for them as the plane veered and swooped, and anything not strapped down slid across the floor. Twenty-two hours later, after two fueling stops in Greenland and the Azores, we touched down on a pitch-black tarmac in pitch-black Casablanca, where Allied forces fought off Nazi air raids.

Slight chaos ensued when the officers in charge discovered who we were. A mistake in USO scheduling meant there was no place to lodge us. After hurried consultations on the tarmac as Danny and I nervously eyed the bomb strikes flashing on the horizon, we were escorted to a nearby empty barracks, closer to the soldiers than was permitted by regulations.

Our accommodation was a pit—dirty, smelly, with bunk beds as hard as planks, and no latrine. My troupe, composed of Danny, an accordionist, and a piano player, was wretched, exhausted from the trip and clearly wondering what kind of hell we'd signed up for. I tidied the place, took a bunk, and used my satchel packed with my gowns and makeup case as a pillow.

I was so excited, I couldn't sleep. At last, I was about to do something worthwhile.

The next day, bouncing around in a Red Cross convoy truck, we drove along pitted, dust-choked roads to Rabat and Tangiers, where we did two shows a day for weary masses of men. We were a hit; they'd not seen anything like me before, with my sequined gowns and quick banter, but Danny warned that we shouldn't rest on our laurels.

"These are the reserves. The guys are so bored, they'd cheer King Kong. Wait until Algiers. We're scheduled to perform in the opera house there before over a thousand Allied soldiers, and I hear they're a tough crowd. They threw frankfurters at Josephine Baker."

Frankfurters and sauerkraut, I discovered, along with some unidentifiable canned meat, were the cuisine of choice when we could get it. Otherwise, it was gruel and soda crackers.

In Algiers, which was partially submerged in rubble, the shell-pocked opera house was packed to the rafters with men from all the Allied nations—soldiers who had fought, suffered losses, and were very demanding of suitable entertainment.

Danny and I had spruced up the act to include an element of surprise. But when he first bounded onto the stage in his rumpled tuxedo, two thousand angry voices derided him for not wearing a uniform. "Uniform?" he quipped. "Are you nuts? Haven't you heard there's a *war*?"

He broke the tension. As laughter erupted, he went on, "Marlene Dietrich was supposed to be here tonight, but an American officer pulled rank for her . . . services."

The sudden silence confirmed that the men had no idea who'd been scheduled. Then, as more jeering boos were flung at Danny, I cried out from the back, "No. Wait. I'm here," and I ran down the aisle in my military uniform, fleece-lined cap on my head and suitcase in hand. Onstage, I removed one of my gowns from the suitcase and began to undress.

The boys howled. Yanking me behind a tattered screen, Danny made suggestive eyes at the panting audience until I emerged minutes later in my gown.

Their cheering must have echoed all the way to Berlin.

I launched into "See What the Boys in the Back Room Will Have." As I sang, I felt them, all of them, leaning hungrily toward me in their seats. That surge of warmth, of raw adulation, was so tangible, so intoxicating, it was unlike anything I'd felt before. After four songs, playing my Viennese saw, and another costume change, I had them shouting and whistling in cacophonous rapture, and my voice was hoarse. Twice, an air-raid siren sent everyone hurtling to the ground, with Danny throwing himself so forcefully on top of me to shield me from the expected blast that I hissed, "Stop protecting me. You're going to chip my teeth."

Our mesmerizing act was a mess. The boys kept yelling at me to sing more until I finally went down among them, ignoring Danny's worried attempt to keep me onstage. Sidling along the jammed aisles and pausing now and then to meet a pair of lustful eyes, I sang "Falling in Love Again," my voice breaking, my own eyes spilling over with unabashed emotion.

I was falling in love again, for the fourth and most enduring time in my life.

I fell in love with legions I'd never met, flung across trenches and the pillaged cities of Europe, with their courage and strength, their indefatigable resolve to rid us of peril.

And they must fall in love with me.

Hours later, after signing autographs, giving lipstick-smeared kisses, lifting my gown to display my legs while posing with GIs who smothered me in their arms for candid shots, I returned to my lodgings, as limp as a wet rag, every nerve in my body pulsating.

Danny remarked, "I guess that went better than I thought."

It was the understatement of the year.

The next morning, a general accompanied me to visit the infirmary. On endless rows of cots, I beheld such a horror of missing limbs, blinded eyes, wounds, and putrefaction that I nearly gagged. But the gratitude and feeble joy I found in those pain-twisted faces, the clasping of my hand as I leaned over them to hear them whisper, "Are you the real Marlene

Dietrich?" filled me with equal anguish and resolve. These boys were dying for us. They were our saviors. What I'd endured, what I thought had been hardship—I had no idea.

Then one of them, a cherubic Brit whose left forearm had been blown off, told me, "Go over there, in the back ward. They're Nazis and you speak German. I bet they'd like to see you."

I froze for a moment. Then as I looked up at the general, he said, "Prisoners of war and in no better shape. You don't have to, Miss Dietrich. Your convoy is due to leave in an hour."

"No," I said, surprising myself. "I . . . I want to see them."

What did I expect to find? Monsters with skulls on their caps, leering from black sheets? I couldn't say, but as I neared the ward separating them from the others, guarded by soldiers with guns, I found more boys—pale, wasted boys with shocking white bandages covering severed arms and legs, masking burnt faces and clutching, scarred hands.

I stopped by a cot. The Nazi looking up at me couldn't have been older than nineteen.

"What is your name?" I asked, hearing those nearby struggling upright to stare.

"Hans," he said faintly. The entire right side of his face was mangled; morphine dripped into his arm, but he was coherent, aware of me. I detected fear, as any German soldier must feel, but also his ragged humanity, the bewilderment of a young man ordered to fight for country and honor, without understanding what that fight would entail.

"Hello, Hans." I touched his hand. "*Ich bin* Marlene."

"The actress?" piped up a voice from a cot behind me. I turned to him—dark haired, with a rash of pimples on his cheeks, sad green eyes, and both legs amputated above the knees. The long tube dripping blood into his arm was brutally red against his pallor.

I nodded.

All of a sudden, he began to warble. I recognized the lyrics at once, from the first war—a song about a soldier yearning for his lost love:

344   C. W. GORTNER

"Outside the barracks, by the corner light,
I'll always stand and wait for you at night.
We will create a world for two.
I'll wait for you, the whole night through,
Lili Marleen. For you, Lili Marleen . . ."

And as the boy's voice faded, the echo of the lyrics moved through me, and his haunted green eyes met mine as he said, "They told us we couldn't sing it anymore. After Stalingrad, Goebbels declared it unpatriotic." He smiled wistfully. "But I always liked it. And the Allies . . . I think they might like it, too, fräulein."

I managed to whisper, "Yes. I believe they would."

At our next stop, in Tunis, I sang "Lili Marleen" for the first time.

I would continue to sing it until we were free.

V

While waiting to cross into Italy, a detachment of tanks run by the Free French rumbled onto the dock. I heard men talking in French and bounded from my jeep, wildly searching the stolid iron monsters around me. "Gabin?" I asked every man I saw. "Is the actor Jean Gabin here?"

Finally, one of them pointed. "Over there, mademoiselle," and I saw him, clambering out of his tank. I ran toward him. As I neared, he called out, "*What* are you doing here?"

"I'm going to war like you," I cried back. "I want to kiss you."

He laughed as I plunged into his arms. "*Ma* Grande," he murmured, stroking my matted hair under my cap. "You are insane. Where are my paintings and my accordion?"

"In storage." I drew back, staring into his eyes. He looked exhausted, battle worn, but he looked like himself again, too. "If you ever want to see them again, you must kiss me first."

He hesitated, until the men surrounding us started to cheer, and then he did kiss me—a quick, hard kiss on the lips.

"I think we must," he said, and I caressed his face. "Yes, we must."

We had an hour together before he departed. He held my hand and we sat quietly by his tank, the coalescing of our fingers enough to keep his curious comrades from approaching, although throughout my tour, soldiers had delighted in showing me photographs of their sweethearts back home, tattered shots of pretty girls that they carried around like shields. When we said good-bye, Gabin embraced me, still without a word. As I watched the huge landing ship swallow up his tanks like a whale and churn out to sea, I whispered a prayer for his safety.

I didn't know if I would ever see him again. But somehow, it no longer mattered.

We had both found a cause more important than ourselves.

IT WAS MUD SWAMPED or arid, freezing cold and blazing hot, bloody and harsh, cruel and remorseless. It was not limousines or red carpets or shrieking fans. It was not anything any human being or animal should ever endure. I determined to never complain.

I had to abandon my luggage and makeup case, leaving them behind as our struggle to traverse Italy crammed us into ever-smaller trucks. I tore one of my gowns during a performance and left it hanging, like a flag, on an ashen tree. I caught dysentery from putrid water and found lice crawling in my pubic hair; a GI gave me a stinging antiseptic lotion and advised me to shave.

In Naples, we had a brief respite. On the balcony of a house commandeered for me, I reclined naked to sunbathe. I was later told that soldiers raced to every available rooftop in the area, braving sniper fire to catch a glimpse of me. Had I known, I would have stood up.

Near the medieval city of Cassino, we got separated from our convoy. We drove around for hours, lost in a scorched landscape punctured by back roads and dead livestock. As night fell over a nectarine sky torched by the Allied onslaught against the Nazis holed up in a monastic enclosure, refusing to surrender, we camped. Huddled together for warmth and scraping our tins for whatever we could ingest, afterward we went in pairs behind the thornbushes to empty our watery bowels. In the distance, we could hear the booming of a 240-millimeter howitzer mobile gun pulverizing the monastery and most of the adjoining city.

"The most effective diet I've been on," I told Danny as he groaned, crouching beside me. "I'll be a sylph for my next picture."

"God, Marlene." He winced. "How can you joke at a time like this?"

"What else is there to do? If I start crying, I might never stop."

A detachment of French soldiers found us the next morning. As they rattled up in their battered truck and surrounded us, guns at the ready, I called out, "*Je suis Marlene Dietrich.*"

One of the soldiers chortled, "If you're Marlene Dietrich, I'm General Eisenhower."

Striding to him with a flashlight, I shone it under my chin, sucking in my cheekbones and arching my eyebrow. The effect must have been skeletal, as I'd lost so much weight, but he turned white. "*Mon Dieu, c'est vrai.*"

"Of course it's true," I retorted. "And you stink."

"*Ah. Excusez-moi.*" He swept into a clumsy bow. "Last night I slept beside the corpse of a Senegalese soldier. I wish I'd been at the Ritz, instead—with you."

I burst out laughing.

They helped us locate our American convoy, which was most displeased by our night-long absence. The major in charge scolded us. I shrugged. "I'm a major, too. You can't put me in lockup." That very night, without a microphone or a gown, illuminated only by flashlights held by the soldiers and dressed in my soiled fatigues, I sang as Cassino fell to the Allies. I figured if they didn't like my performance, they just had to turn off their lights.

They demanded an encore.

With charcoal from the campfires, the men drafted leggy sketches of me on roadsides and tree trunks, pointing the way for those behind as we straggled toward Rome. Halfway there, I developed a persistent fever and a gurgle in my chest. Within hours, I was delirious. Five days later, I awoke disorientated in a camp infirmary to find Danny at my side. He hadn't left me for a moment; I was suffering from pneumonia and severe dehydration. The doctor had injected me with a few precious doses of a new drug called penicillin, reserved for soldiers.

Without it, I would have died.

"Did the boys miss me?" I croaked.

Danny chortled. "They did. And you've a lot more to entertain, my golden panther. The forces ahead of us have broken into Rome. And we've just received word that a combined Allied force of over a hundred and fifty thousand is landing in Normandy."

I cried then. I cried until I had no more tears left.

IN ROME, THE NAZIS WERE STILL ENTRENCHED, bolstered by Italian sympathizers. There was brutal fighting near the Forum and Trajan's Column. With the rattle of gunfire and bombs exploding overhead, we helped ferry the injured on stretchers into a vacant palazzo. Amid peeling frescoes and looted tapestries, I sang for those who weren't dead or undergoing surgery, threading back and forth among the makeshift cots and ignoring a resurgence of my fever.

Danny finally brought a halt to it. "Our ten weeks are up. We have to go home."

"No." In bed with a compress on my throat and another dose of penicillin in my veins, I was in no position to defy anyone. "I want to stay. They need us. And I—"

"I know." He squeezed my hand. "You need them. But you're going to die if you keep this up. You need to rest and recover. We're returning to New York. Don't even think of trying to stop me. I'll carry you onto the airplane if I have to."

He ended up carrying me anyway, as I was too weak to stand.

WHEN WE ARRIVED IN AMERICA, reporters and photographers clamored. I'd performed more shows in more war-torn areas than any USO performer before me. After granting several interviews, swaying against Danny's shoulder, I took to my bed in Rudi's apartment, where Tamara fussed over me. When I felt better, I phoned my agent.

Hollywood had ignored me. My last picture, the Arabian fiasco *Kismet*, had tanked in national previews. While MGM insisted that I must attend the official premiere and still held the option on my contract, the studio had no current plan to feature me in anything.

"You should come anyway," Eddie said. "You're getting amazing coverage for your USO tour. I'm sure they'll reconsider once they know you're back and ready to work."

"Let me think about it," I replied, and as soon as I hung up, I telephoned Danny, who sighed. "I adore you, Marlene. But I can't go back. I have a family to feed."

So did I, but mine was eating well enough without me. Ignoring the studio mandate since Carole Lombard's death that stars under contract could not travel by airplane, I flew to Hollywood. After attending the premiere, I spent a few nights at the canteen with Bette, who kissed me fervently and roused the entire assembly to a "Lili Marleen" serenade. Eddie wanted to schedule rounds for me at the studio, saying I looked incredible.

"Eating nothing but wieners does wonders for the figure," I said, adding that I couldn't stay. I had to return to New York to spend time with my daughter but would call him soon.

The moment I landed in Manhattan, I filed for another USO tour of duty.

In late August, soon after the joyous liberation of Paris, I headed out to entertain troops in Labrador, Greenland, and Iceland before visiting England and France.

Unbeknownst to me, the worst lay ahead.

VI

Guts and Bones" his men called him, but I felt it wasn't a fair description. Oh, he was impressive—a harsh-featured raptor of a man in polished cavalry boots, with old-fashioned pistols at his belt. Yet he also had a big laugh, a bigger appetite, and a surprisingly delicate touch.

I was presented to General George S. Patton at 50 Grosvenor Square during a reception hosted by the Supreme Headquarters, Allied Expeditionary Forces, a branch of which oversaw high-brass requests for entertainers on tour. I was actively courting them in the hope of obtaining engagement at the front. To my frustration, the USO was no longer willing to risk sending its contracted entertainers into active war zones. With Germany cornered but defiant, the fight to capture Hitler and destroy the last vestiges of his power had turned the front into a charnel ground. Losing Paris had struck a fatal blow to the Reich; enraged, Hitler had ordered all of the city's bridges packed with explosives and detonated, only his commander had hesitated, allowing the Americans enough time to cede liberation of the city to General de Gaulle. Now, the Nazis vowed to fight to the death in their own rubble and the USO warned me via their London office that I'd been declared a wanted enemy of the Reich. There was a price on my head; the USO could not be responsible for any danger befalling me.

"How much are they asking for my head?" I said, and the London office refused to accept my calls again.

Their refusal wasn't about to deter me. In London, I reunited with Douglas Fairbanks Jr., who was scheduled to shoot a much-delayed picture. We didn't resume our affair—I wasn't about to tolerate his jealous tirades again—but he proved a delightful entrée into the high military circles of the Allied forces, which were organizing a strategy to free those parts of Europe still under attack, where I wanted to be: with the boys. I also wanted to discover as much as I could about the Allied plans for Germany, as my recent attempts to contact my family had failed, the telephone lines dead and my wires gone unanswered, as if a wall had barricaded my country.

"I'm told you like to sunbathe nude," Patton said moments after we'd been introduced. Outside the salon, London was knee-deep in the debris of the Blitz, sirens wailing as the dead and injured were unearthed, but indoors champagne flowed and everyone seemed optimistic.

I sipped from my glass. "We're at war, General. You can't believe everything you hear."

"Oh, I think this particular rumor must be true." His small blue-gray eyes scoured me in my tailored military jacket and gored knee-length skirt. "Soldiers never lie."

"Neither do majors," I said. He was quite a few years older than me; with the exception of his height, he wasn't the type of man I usually gravitated to. He had something of the stern uncle in him, a dictatorial authority that made those under his command trust him with their lives, even if the look he now gave me was anything but familial. "But," I went on, "if I did sunbathe nude, would it be enough of a qualification to get me to the front?"

He went silent for a moment. "I'd have to see it for myself."

"The front?"

"No." He refilled my glass. "The sunbathing."

HE WAS A NO-FRILLS LOVER, which was fine. It was a no-frills situation. Afterward, as I smoked and he palmed his prized mother-of-pearl inlaid

Colt .45s, replicas of those belonging to some long-dead general he admired, he said, "So, do you really want to go to the front?"

"Yes," I said, turning to him eagerly.

He grimaced. He did not like me smoking in bed. "It could be arranged. You can travel with my unit to Paris and then on to eastern France and Belgium, but"—he chuckled as he fended off my kisses—"only if you tell me why you truly want to go."

"Why?" I paused in astonishment. "Why else? I'm an entertainer. I came here to entertain. Surely your boys deserve to see Marlene Dietrich after everything they have done."

"And continue to do." His weathered face turned somber. "It's dangerous, more than you seem to think. This is not a Hollywood premiere. No one can guarantee your safety."

"I survived the war in Italy. I'm sure I can survive a few shows at the front. And I don't expect you to guarantee anything. I know what I signed up for."

"Do you?" He went silent, chewing on his lower lip before he broke his own rule and retrieved his disgusting, half-smoked cigar from the bedside ashtray. He clamped it between his teeth; when I made to reach for my lighter, he shook his head, gnawing the cigar as he eyed me. "I think you have another reason besides this patriotic duty to show us your legs. Not that my boys would mind; I certainly don't. But in war, mistakes are often made by those on the same side. I can't afford to have you be my mistake."

I went still. Should I confide in him? I only hesitated because of who I was—an American citizen, yes, hailed by my adopted country, if not the studio heads, but still with the blood of the enemy in my veins, no matter how much I might declare my abhorrence of Hitler.

"It's Germany, isn't it?" he said, surprising me with his insight. It shouldn't have; he was revered for his tactical brilliance. "You want to get in there. It's why you agreed to do the wireless program with the American Broadcast System, singing 'Lili Marleen' and giving rousing speeches that they broadcast into occupied territories. What did you say in that last one?"

"That all my songs are dedicated to the Allied soldiers of course."

"'Who are about to meet up with you boys and destroy your thousand-year Reich,'" he added wryly. "Hardly music to Hitler's ears. You must know by now how much he hates you, the homegrown star turned Allied pet. If you're ever captured, they'll make an example of you. Hitler will have you shot in front of the Brandenburg Gate."

"And Goebbels, too," I said. "Don't forget that he hates me even more."

"It's not a joke, Marlene. If you're captured, we can't do anything about it. We can't risk our entire operation for one person, as admirable as you may be."

"So, there *is* an operation."

"That's classified. But you've just answered my question."

I smoked, watching him in silence before I said, "I have family there. My mother, my sister, and my uncle . . . they're not Nazis."

"You don't know that. You don't know anything. That's my point."

"I still have to find out if they're . . ." Suddenly, I couldn't say the words. Was my family still alive? Or had this horrendous war killed them like so many others? My mother had said they were safe, good Germans, protected by their loyalty as long as they kept their heads down. But everything had changed. The Reich was crumbling. I'd humiliated Goebbels by turning down his proposals, filing for U.S. citizenship, and flinging my contempt in his face. The Nazis knew what I'd done in Italy; they must hear me now, singing my defiance over the wireless. I couldn't expect my family to have escaped. But I needed to see for myself. I had to know.

Patton handed me one of his revolvers. "I'm going to teach you how to shoot. And when you've learned, I'm going to give these to you. I want you to carry them with you at all times. If there ever comes a time, God forbid, I want you to use them. Can you do that?"

I closed my fingers around the gun, warm from his touch. I understood what he was saying. Suicide was preferable. "Yes," I whispered. "I can."

"Good. Because if you'd said no, the only place you'd be showing off your legs is Piccadilly Circus."

✻   ✻   ✻

PARIS.

What can I say about my return to the city I'd come to love, that alabaster muse whose crowded garrets had housed some of the most daring artists of our time? She wasn't the same. She might look the same, if a bit ragged after the deprivations of occupation, but she felt different. Tense. Like a hunted animal being lured into a snare, waiting for the Free French to haul her before their pitiless tribunals.

The savage purge had begun. Suspected collaborators, including women left to fend for themselves while the Nazis held sway, were being prosecuted, their hair shorn before they were taken through the streets in a public procession, stones and filth flung at them, with not a few spontaneous executions by the mobs, resulting in corpses in tattered negligees dangling from lampposts.

Chanel was gone, her boutique shuttered. Others had fled, as well—anyone with a reason to fear the liberators would prove more punitive than the oppressors. But in the bar at the Ritz, I found an unexpected friend: Papa Hemingway, sousing it up with fellow reporters who'd raced to the city with the Allied forces to document Paris's liberation. Papa had also participated in D-day, flying missions with the RAF, combat being his preferred aphrodisiac.

"Kraut!" he boomed, grabbing me in his bearlike embrace. "Of all the women in the world, I should have known you'd be the only one to walk into this joint—and with pistols at your belt, too."

The pistols might be unique, but I wasn't the only woman. Seated at the bar next to his stool was a petite, scowling brunette. I might have told her she needn't look so unhappy, I wasn't competition, not with Hemingway, but her terse nod when he introduced us, "Kraut, meet Mary Welsh. She writes for the *Daily Express*," made me think twice.

I saw it at once in her sharp appraisal that no matter what I said, I was unwelcome. Papa was still married to his second wife, Martha Gellhorn, also a journalist, but I knew from his letters that the marriage was over. Mary Welsh must be angling to pounce as soon as he got divorced, although I'd advised him that his penchant for marriage was unhealthy, seeing that he couldn't maintain it.

However, after a stormy Channel crossing on a U-boat and a jarring ride through the bomb-torn countryside to Paris, I was in need of some amusement. Smiling at her as I linked my arm in Papa's, I asked, "And Martha? Is she here?"

"She was." He pinched my underarm, apprised of my wiles. "But she left to file her report in London. She'll be back. She won't be able to stay away."

"I see." I didn't take my gaze from Mary, who sat so erect on her stool her spine might have been made of brass. "Well, then. How lovely to see a few friendly faces."

Mary had gone pale at the mention of Papa's wife. "Come, dear." I glided to her, taking Papa's stool. "I'm desperate for information."

"Information?" She frowned at me. "I can't divulge my sources."

"Even on where I might find hair bleach and razors?" I leaned closer to her, but not so close that Papa would fail to overhear. "I've just been with General Patton on the filthiest U-boat you can imagine. I made the mistake of visiting the latrines and caught a little—how shall I put it? A teensy bug problem? Oh, nothing to worry about," I said. "Or at least nothing a shave and delousing powder won't solve. Only, I forgot to pack a razor, and on top of it, my roots are starting to show. See?" I bent my head, feeling her recoil as if my little problem might leap out and infest her. "I'd be so grateful. There must be some contraband here?"

Behind me, Papa roared with laughter and bellowed at the bartender, "A drink for Miss Dietrich. The best whiskey in the house."

Mary Welsh glowered.

What could she do? She found my razor and bleach on the black market, and I made a point of attaching myself to them. I joined Papa in the bathroom as he shaved, perched on the toilet as he regaled me with news about the war from his sources. He insisted on my company at the Allied parties, saying that whenever I showed up in my khakis, with my

356 C. W. GORTNER

skirt hiked several inches above regulation requirements and sporting my newly dyed coiffure, "Somehow, like the miracle of the loaves and the fishes, caviar and liquor follow."

Mary eventually warmed to me, a fellow woman in a male-dominated arena. One night as we applied lipstick together, she suddenly giggled. "He proposed to me. As soon as he's rid of that bitch Gellhorn, we're going to get married." She eyed me in the mirror. "She's no good for him. Too ambitious. She competes with him for everything. She thinks she's the better writer."

"Perhaps she is." I returned her stare. "Women often do things better than men, but we also often have to go to extra lengths to prove it."

Before I departed for my engagement with the troops, I offered her and Papa my bed, as I had a full in my suite and they were sleeping in twins. Mary was so delighted with my evident acceptance of their engagement, over the Ritz manager's protests she helped me haul the entire bedstead to their room. Papa never slept in my bed, however, as he'd left the night before to report from the eastern front.

I couldn't help but smile as I drove out with Patton the next day, wondering how Mary Welsh would enjoy the surprise I'd deliberately left for her, crawling within my sheets.

Perhaps a teensy bug problem of her own would teach her that if screwing another woman's husband was acceptable, conniving to break up his marriage was not.

VII

If Italy had been purgatory, Belgium was hell.

It was one of the coldest winters on record, a fanged wind spitting sleet and snow, biting through my layers of wool and droopy fleece long johns. I caught lice, and had dysentery and frostbite; I performed for the boys in my spangled gowns and left the stage with my feet turning blue in my high heels and my teeth chattering so much, I couldn't speak. Patton had a charcoal stove installed in my tent; he had one in his, too, which I preferred to share. Everyone knew we were lovers, and the boys only liked me more because of it. "Legs," they dubbed me, which was also the official password Patton gave me, Legs Marlene, and their joy in seeing me singing my heart out every night before they went out to risk their lives made every discomfort bearable.

But the frostbite nearly cost me one of my toes and an incipient infection in my jaw forced me to return to Paris for treatment. Once I recovered, I joined Noël Coward and Maurice Chevalier for a musical performance, but as soon as I could, I went back to the front in early February, following the epic lightning strike of the Battle of the Bulge. Patton was now in Aachen, the first German city to fall en route to Berlin, which the Soviets had encircled. In Aachen, I did another show, only this time I sat squeezed between two bodyguards, my pistols at my hips as I rode in Patton's open-air jeep at the head of the Third Army. As the German people who'd survived the Allied bombardment gathered at the roadside in freezing temperatures, I called out my name through a megaphone, requesting immediate evacuation of the streets so our tanks could pass.

No one fired a shot at me. Regardless of the USO warning that I had a bounty on my head or Patton's advice that Germans reviled me for my stance, I found only limpid acceptance in those with whom I stopped to speak, the hunger and fear scoring their faces turning to befuddled awe when they realized who I was.

"Lola-Lola," one woman whispered. "You're the Blue Angel."

No one denounced me. No one shook their fist or turned their back. Regardless of the bile Goebbels had spewed, it seemed not everyone had been hoodwinked into thinking I was the enemy. Still, when a reporter for the International News Service asked me what I thought about the destruction, compared with my life in Hollywood, I had to blink back sudden tears.

"I'm not thinking about the movies," I replied. "I may never think about movies again. As for all this"—I gazed at the wreckage, the toppled buildings and rubble-piled avenues, the charred parks, the destitute scavenging for anything to eat or drink—"I hate to see it, but I guess Germany deserves everything that's coming to her."

My declaration was printed in newspapers across the globe. "If they weren't running away to escape us"—Patton grinned—"they'd be hunting you down now for sure."

"Let them try," I said, and I continued to perform for the troops in half-collapsed theaters or on makeshift stages in frozen fields. When not regaling the boys, I combed my pubic hair for crabs and assumed duties as a translator and goodwill ambassador to the dazed German populace along the way, all of whom acquiesced in the concerted effort to bring down the Reich around their ears. In private with Patton, I railed, "They're like sheep! If they had any character at all, they would fight us. This is who they are: Germans to their bones, who obeyed even a lunatic."

"The lunatic isn't dead yet," Patton grimly said. "He's still their führer."

But after April 30, 1945, he no longer was. After forcing an army of children to defend Berlin while the Soviets hammered the city with rockets and grenades, Adolf Hitler cowered in his underground bunker and swallowed a lethal dose of cyanide that he first had tested on his elderly dog. He took his wife, Eva Braun, with him. Goebbels followed suit. On May 8, Germany surrendered. The way to Berlin cracked open, albeit through colossal wreckage from the Allied assault.

My country had fallen. The Third Reich was over.

I had no idea if anyone in my family had survived it.

IN MUNICH, I tried to recover from my exhaustion, dehydration, and a severe lice infestation that required me to stand under a scalding shower and shave off every last bit of hair I had except what was on my head, which I would not sacrifice, submitting instead to a stinging delousing solution that turned my scalp crimson and my short locks a pale greenish hue.

Munich looked no better. That beautiful city, ancient citadel of the Bavarian dukes, where Hitler first attempted to seize power, had fallen to seventy-one separate air raids—a jagged heap, where even the rats were starving and disease festered. The stink was atrocious. I couldn't step outside my tent in the U.S. Army headquarters on the edge of the city without breathing in a toxic miasma of chemical fumes and human putrefaction, thousands of corpses rotting under still-smoldering rubble.

Horrifying news had been filtering into the headquarters for weeks, as Allied troops swept eastward and uncovered the abomination beneath Hitler's bombast: his Final Solution, exposed in his *Konzentrationslager*, or "concentration camps," where his right-hand henchman Himmler had devised vast complexes, with specially designed gas chambers and crematoria, to dispose of millions of Jews.

At first, I couldn't believe it. Hitler had been insane, obsessed by his hatred of the Jews. But wholesale decimation of an entire people? It was unimaginable. Reports had it that Germany itself was riddled with these camps; regardless of the Nazis' stranglehold, surely my own people had not condoned such savagery? Surely someone, somewhere, had tried to stop it? Yet Bette's prophetic words, *"Thousands are disappearing,"* returned to me as the liberations of Dachau, Buchenwald, Flossenbürg, Ravensbrück, and other camps forced me into recognizing that what had happened in Germany went beyond anything I could ever have imagined.

Still, I clung to denial when word came that in Bergen-Belsen near Hannover, a camp recently liberated by the British, a woman claiming to be my sister had been found.

"Impossible," I told Patton. He was with General Omar Bradley, a stalwart man who'd also performed miracles during the Battle of the Bulge, that monthlong offensive launched by Hitler to recapture Antwerp, which had caught the Allies off guard. Like Patton, Bradley had lost thousands in the battle. Nonetheless, they were more rivals than friends (similar to movie stars, I had discovered, generals competed for acclaim), although Patton, due to leave for engagement in the Pacific, had instructed Bradley to assume charge of me.

With a concerned frown, Bradley handed me the wire. "She says she's Elisabeth Felsing Wills. That's the name you gave us. You requested that we look into her and your mother Josephine Felsing Dietrich's whereabouts."

"She can say whatever she likes," I said, ignoring the wire. "She can't possibly be my sister. Liesel lives in Berlin. Her husband was managing a chain of kinos there—"

"Kinos?" asked Patton.

"Picture houses," I explained. "He oversaw government-approved cinemas. He told me himself the last time I saw him. He wouldn't have been sent to this camp unless . . ." My indignation faded as I recalled my refusal to accept Goebbels's second invitation, sent through Georg. I had no idea where my brother-in-law worked. I'd assumed he and Liesel remained in Berlin, but now a dark wave of fear pushed through me. What if the Nazis had arrested my family? What if they'd all ended up in a camp because of me? It wasn't impossible. Nothing was impossible anymore, not where Hitler was concerned.

Patton said quietly, "Is it possible, Marlene?"

I nodded, swallowing. "Yes. I suppose it is." I searched their faces. "What should I do?" I asked at length, my voice subdued.

Patton glanced at Bradley, who said, "We think you should see this woman for yourself. It's the first lead we've had regarding your family. We can arrange air transport."

I found myself wanting to refuse. I didn't want to go. I didn't even want to contemplate it, though he was right. It was the first lead we'd had, though it couldn't be true. It had to be a mix-up, a bureaucratic mistake. People had been flung everywhere since Hitler plunged us into disaster. Identities had been stolen, papers and passports forged. Perhaps this woman was using Liesel's name. Perhaps she might know where my sister actually was. In any event, I was the only person who could confirm or deny her claim.

"Fine." I tossed the wire back on the desk with an umbrage I no longer felt. "But you won't stop searching in Berlin. You'll keep inquiring there?"

Patton nodded. "We're doing everything we can. But it's very chaotic; there have been thousands of casualties. I wouldn't get my hopes up. The city is in ruins."

I came to my feet, clutching the side of the desk. "My mother is stronger than you think. She made it through the first war. If she made it through this one, she's there. She must be."

Bradley went quiet as Patton reminded me, "I did warn you. I told you, this isn't a movie. There is no script. No happy ending."

"I remember," I said. "How could I forget? No movie could be this horrible."

GENERAL BRADLEY BRIEFED ME before I departed from Munich. Bergen-Belsen was one of the last camps to be forsaken by its Nazi overseers—a detention center where wealthy Jews coming in from France and Holland had waited for transport to Poland. Soviet prisoners of war had also been held there, in exchange for German POWs taken by the Allies. As British-Canadian forces neared the camp, a typhus epidemic swept the compound. Years later, I would learn that a Jewish girl named Anne Frank had died in that epidemic, along with many others.

"They left corpses everywhere," said Bradley. "You'll be taken to the former Wehrmacht headquarters, which the Brits use as their command post. Captain Arnold Horwell is in charge and will receive you. But you mustn't ask to tour the camp itself. Just meet this woman to see if she's your sister. We need the airplane back. One day, Marlene. It's all you have."

I agreed, but as my plane touched down on a tiny airfield in Fassberg and an army escort drove me to Bergen-Belsen, I found myself suddenly longing to see. I had to fight against the overwhelming *need* to see. I'd heard enough by now to know that the horror unleashed by the Nazis would haunt me forever, ravaging the last shred of hope I had for my nation. Yet I had an obligation to bear witness to the carnage waged in our name, if only to prove to the world, and myself, that not every German was capable of looking the other way.

Then I sensed it—not a stench, precisely, though there was that. Most of the dead had already been bulldozed into pits, while the worst areas had been cordoned off to contain the spread of disease. The survivors were sequestered in hastily erected infirmaries, where they continued to die; but I could still feel it, an indefinable thickness in the air, like a miasma, that made breathing difficult and raised the hairs on my neck. As we approached a disconcertingly banal spread of brick buildings and wooden barracks, I beheld miles of electrified wire fencing.

Despair, I realized. This was what I felt. The entire place exuded human despair.

The corporal who'd driven me had to assist me from the jeep. My knees were wobbling; I focused on putting one booted foot before the other, staring straight ahead as he led me toward the Wehrmacht headquarters, still adorned with a swastika over its entryway. Then I glanced to my left, through the sagging fence, my attention caught by the sound of a truck coughing exhaust and men speaking in clipped British accents: "Careful, now. It's heavy."

Soldiers. Hauling a load of what looked like kindling.

"Major Dietrich." The corporal, an exhausted-looking Canadian, touched my sleeve. "Please. This way."

My soul curdled. Not kindling. Not wood. Legs and arms and skeletal ankles, jutting in a pyramid of bones from the truck's rear compartment.

"Dear God," I whispered. "What have we done . . . ?"

"Please." The corporal propelled me inside, but I kept looking over my shoulder as the truck lumbered toward a distant field from where I could discern the grinding of heavy machinery, of tractors and other equipment, so loud I had to resist putting my hands over my ears and nose, as if I stood on the edge of whatever was there, choking on putrid dust.

A gateway tilted near the field, bearing an askew sign: KINDERGARTEN.

All of a sudden, I wanted to scream. Was Liesel here, a victim of this hell on earth?

"Do—do you have a cigarette?" I searched the pockets of my fatigues but did not feel anything, my fingers numb. I was so light-headed, I thought I might faint.

He extracted one from a pack, flicked his butane lighter. As I drew in acrid smoke—army-issued cigarettes made me rasp—and the nicotine jolted my blood, he said, "Wait here. I need to alert Captain Horwell that you've arrived." He paused, his gaze tender, so understanding that I could only meet it and let him see my anguish, my helpless disbelief drowning me as he repeated, "Wait here, please. I'll be back in a moment, Major."

He proceeded down the corridor as I stood under a framed portrait of Hitler on the wall, dressed in his tan uniform, with his protuberant eyes and pursed mouth under that ridiculous block mustache. I wondered why his picture was still here. Why hadn't they torn it down? I couldn't understand any of it, how anyone could have taken such a ludicrous man seriously enough to commit mass murder. It was like the movie Patton had assured me it was not, only nothing a studio contrived could equal this inhumanity, executed for maximum impact. We would never outlive it. We must all bear the shame and the world's condemnation for it.

In those endless seconds as I waited to be summoned, I lost whatever remained of my hope. I surrendered it. Never again would I regard my country with anything but contempt. Never again would I take pride in calling myself a German.

I could not. I refused.

The corporal reappeared, beckoning me. Crushing my cigarette under my heel, I picked up the butt and flung it at the portrait. "Monster," I whispered.

And I went down the hall to face my own monsters.

VIII

He spoke German. That was the first thing he told me after I saluted him in an office that had sheltered the SS command. Mounds of dossiers and other files littered the desk, some bearing the red eagle stamp of the Reich. As he saw me staring at them, he said, "They destroyed a lot of records before they left. But what is here—it's more than enough."

"I know." Squaring my shoulders, I said, "I saw. Outside. I want to see everything."

"Major Dietrich." He sighed. He was a diminutive man with a receding hairline and a weary face; had we been anywhere else, at any other time, I'd have mistaken him for a studio accountant. "I don't believe you do." He lit a cigarette, offering me one. I declined. Beyond his narrow window, which allowed a circumscribed view of the camp, thick smoke was roiling from that field. Were they incinerating the corpses?

"We found evidence of cannibalism," he said, wrenching my gaze back to him. "That's the least of it. They cut off the water and access to supplies; bolted the gates behind them and left the prisoners to endure as best they could. Women and children. Entire families. Entire generations. Gone. You don't want to see it. Trust me, no one should ever have to see it."

Without requesting leave, though he was my superior according to military protocol, I sank onto the chair before his desk. I couldn't breathe. I had to sink my face in my hands, clamping back a howl, until I felt him come around and awkwardly pat my shoulder. "Chin up, Major. Yes?"

I raised my eyes to him.

He offered me a cigarette again. This time, I took it. As I smoked anxiously, he returned to his papers. "Is Elisabeth Felsing Wills your sister?"

I hesitated. "That is her name. But I . . . I'd have to see her."

"Well, she is here. Until recently, she was in our infirmary, in fact."

"Infirmary?" My heart started to pound. "Is she sick?"

"A mild case of influenza. Nothing serious. According to her husband, Herr"—he consulted the dossier in hand—"Wills, they were only doing as directed. It's a common refrain, I'm afraid. They all say that. They were all just obeying orders."

The office seemed to shrink, closing in around me. "Orders?" I echoed. My voice sounded remote, not mine at all. "Aren't they prisoners?"

He looked at me. "No. Or they weren't when the camp was under German command. Now . . . well, I'm afraid it's not so simple."

I whispered, "What do you mean?"

He set the dossier aside. "First, let me tell you that I have lost loved ones. My actual surname is Horowitz. I am a Jew. I fled Berlin in '38 and was fortunate to find a post in the British army, though I had to lose my 'witz.'" His smile was brief. "I have a doctorate in economics and of course speak fluent German, so men like me were vital to the cause. But others in my family weren't so fortunate. My parents died in Czechoslovakia, in Theresienstadt. Some of my other relatives were gassed in Treblinka."

I wanted to offer my condolences, but it seemed so futile, unworthy of the enormity of his loss. Instead, I heard myself utter, "I don't understand."

"No, you wouldn't. Forgive me."

I sat immobile. "What aren't you telling me? If this woman who claims to be my sister and her husband weren't prisoners, why are they here?"

He went quiet, meeting my eyes. Then he said, "They were assigned here. Georg Wills was a Special Services officer, appointed to run the canteen for the SS. He also managed a nearby cinema in Fallingbostel for the troops. He was well compensated. They had private accommodations in town, ample rations, hot water, and a bedroom for their son—"

"Son?" I bolted to my feet. "Then she can't be Liesel."

"No?" He frowned, reaching for the dossier.

"I never heard that she gave birth," I said. "I spoke with my uncle in Berlin. He never mentioned it."

"Recently?" he asked, and when he took in my silence, he added, "If it was more than six years ago, you may not have known. The boy is five, according to these records."

"It can't be her. I'm sorry to have wasted your time." I had started to turn to the door, desperate now to escape, when I heard him say, "You still must see her. I insist. When we found them hiding, Herr Wills declared that his wife had an important family member with the Americans, one of considerable propaganda value. He said this relation could vouchsafe for them. We didn't know whom he meant at first, until further questioning of Frau Wills in the infirmary revealed your name. That's why I telegraphed Munich. Those who were involved, in whatever capacity, will say anything now to avoid repercussions. We need to confirm their identities before we can file the appropriate paperwork." He paused. "Their ultimate fate rests with the military governor. I'm not here to exact revenge. I understand that ordinary people, placed in extraordinary circumstances, will do whatever they think is necessary to survive."

"Never." I stared at him over my shoulder. "I will never vouchsafe for a Nazi."

He motioned to my vacant chair. "Major, if you please. A minute or two of your time is all I require. Frau Wills has already been told you are here. She's on her way as we speak."

I inched to the chair but didn't sit. Squashing my cigarette in his over-flowing ashtray, I waited with him in silence until I heard footsteps coming down the hallway.

Bracing myself, I turned to the door.

When she walked in, the sight of her knocked the air from my lungs.

She wore a straw hat, which she pushed back hastily, revealing her wan face. She wasn't emaciated. Not even too thin. While more slender than the last time I'd seen her, what now seemed a lifetime ago, she was still Liesel, still my sister, in her faded coat and rumpled wool stockings, her gasp of recognition followed by a fervent embrace that froze me where I stood.

"Lena." She clutched me. "I knew you'd come. Oh, it's been awful. Dreadful. These nice people"—she drew back to cast a strained smile at Horwell—"they seem to think we're somehow responsible for all this. But we're not. Tell them, Lena. Tell them who I am."

As she spoke, she looked fretfully to the doorway, as if she expected someone else to enter. Horwell said, "Your husband, Herr Wills, will not be joining us. This is a private meeting. I didn't want Major Dietrich to be overwhelmed. She's been very worried for your safety and seeing as you were recently ill—"

"Major!" Liesel returned her surprised gaze to me. She had been ill, I could see it now. She still had a low-grade fever, a slight heat coming off her. But it wasn't typhus or starvation, I found myself thinking. Not anything like what those around her had suffered. "You're a major now?" She pouted. "No one told me."

"Yes. It seems no one told either one of us a great many things." I let my implication sink in, her eyes narrowing as I added, "I hear you have a son."

She nodded. "Oh, Lena, he's so afraid. My Hans doesn't understand why we're being held like this. Like hostages. They separated us from Georg and he misses his father so. It's all a terrible mistake. Can't you just tell this lovely gentleman who we are, so we can go home?"

"Home? I thought that's where you were. This is—or was—your home."

"You sound angry." She made a distasteful moue. "Honestly, Lena, if you've come all this way to reproach us for—"

"Cigarette, Frau Wills?" Horwell interrupted, proffering his case.

She simpered and took one, but when he made to light it, she shook her head. "Thank you but I don't smoke."

"Then why did you take it?" I snarled.

She gave me an astonished look. "Because one does not refuse a cigarette from a British officer. It would be impolite."

Impolite? She was citing propriety to me, after what *she* had done? I clenched my hands at my sides, overcome by the urge to smack that genteel, chiding smile from her face. Through my teeth, I managed to say, "Where is Mutti?"

"In Berlin." She tucked the cigarette into her pocket. "She was fine the last time we saw her. There were shortages of course, and no work, but Uncle Willi was looking after her. We tried to telephone his store. The call didn't go through," she said, with a shrug. "Something to do with the lines, I suppose. There had been a lot of power outages and—"

"Berlin has been destroyed." Rage ran molten in my veins. I had to step back, had to put some distance between us lest I wrapped my hands around her throat. "The entire city has fallen to the Allies. Hitler is dead. The Reich is dead. And so are all the people they sent to this camp, where you and Georg . . . where you—" A furious sob cut off my voice.

She cocked her head, the veneer slipping, betraying her awareness of not only her circumstances but of those around her. She was feigning ignorance, terrified for herself, for her husband and their son. They had participated. They'd screened films for the Nazis and gone home to their private accommodations, their hot water and ample rations, while just beyond the fences, thousands perished. While *I* had worried and struggled to find my conscience, keeping my mouth shut for too long, out of fear of endangering our family.

Horwell cleared his throat. "Major Dietrich. For the record, please, is this woman known as Elisabeth Felsing Wills your sister?"

She was looking anxiously at me in a silent plea.

"No." I turned to him. "She is not."

"Lena! How can you say that? I am. I am her sister. I'm—"

"*No.*" I whirled to her. The fury in my voice drained the sparse hue from her cheeks, so that her rouge stood out like ghastly spots. "I have no sister. I don't know who this woman is."

"She's lying." Clasping her hands, Liesel directed herself to Horwell. "I am Elisabeth Felsing Wills, daughter of Wilhelmina Josephine Felsing and Lieutenant Louis Otto Dietrich. My husband is Georg Wills. We showed you our identification papers." Her words tumbled out, in an earnest rehearsed rush. "We are not to blame. We were given this assignment but we didn't hurt anyone. Georg saved a Jewish actor named Karel Stepanek. He hid him in the Berlin theater he was managing before they closed it and helped him escape to London. Herr Stepanek is in your country. Ask him if you don't believe me."

"I certainly will." Horwell made an annotation in the dossier.

With a satisfied lift of her chin, Liesel went on, "And she is my sister. She is Marlene Dietrich, the Hollywood star. If you harm me or my husband in any way, the world will know."

Horwell gave her a contemplative look. "I'll keep that under advisement, as well. Major Dietrich, will that be all?"

I nodded, my gaze on Liesel as he instructed the corporal outside to escort her out.

"The world *will* know," she said again, this time flinging her words at me. "We did nothing wrong. We obeyed orders. We had no choice. None of us had a choice. We're not you. We're not all famous and rich enough to thumb our noses at our country and get away with it."

I didn't say a word. The moment the door closed behind her, the air in the office thickened, as if the monstrosities outside seeped through the walls to invade this sterile space.

Horwell gave me a few moments to gather myself before he said, "She's right, you know. You do realize that? They didn't hurt anyone."

"No," I replied. "They just showed movies while everyone died."

He lit another cigarette, exhaled smoke pensively. "I understand how difficult this must be, but my job here is difficult enough. The military governor wants every camp survivor identified to the best of my abilities and repatriated to their countries of origin. Besides Dutch citizens, we have Austrians, Hungarians, French, Czechs, Russians, and Poles. It's the same dilemma everywhere we turn; we've documented over two hundred of these camps to date. We have countless dead, but also survivors, whom no one knows what to do with. Do you see my dilemma?"

When I gave uncertain assent, he said, "They're from the very countries whose regimes, either by force or voluntarily, allowed them to be deported. There's nothing left in Europe for them, and at this time, no Allied nation is willing to accept them. I'm working to have the repatriation orders revoked so these people can have a say in where they go, seeing as they were given none when they were taken. What Frau Wills and her husband did or did not do means little to me. They'll not be prosecuted. They were indeed only obeying orders, like so many others. Their punishment will not atone for the loss of life or help those who are left."

"But she—she saw this," I whispered. "She *knew*. She knew and she did nothing."

"Perhaps there was nothing she could do. You might consider that Frau Wills was correct in her assertion: Not everyone is you. I don't agree with her morally, but she's neither unique nor remarkable. She is everyone who did what they felt they had to do to get through this war."

"Are you suggesting I forgive her?" I said in disbelief.

"That is not my place. I am suggesting, however, that being who you are, you should take into account the consequences should her husband's role here become public knowledge. There will be press. Unpleasant questions. Do you want to deal with that?"

"Unpleasant questions do not scare me. Not after what has happened."

"I admire your courage." He slid his cigarette case to me, watched me retrieve one with a trembling hand. "But I still think you should consider it. Like I said, it is unlikely charges will be filed against them. Our tribunals are overwhelmed. We have high-ranking officers and other prominent members of the Reich to locate. They're scurrying for cover, and apprehending them is our top priority. The architects of this machine, the engineers and planners, the actual hands who set it in motion—those are the ones we want, not the menials who greased the wheels. Were it otherwise, I'm afraid we'd have to arrest practically every soul in Germany."

"You should." I couldn't light the cigarette. I couldn't even smoke. Placing it on the desk with a lipstick smear on it, I said, "What do you want me to do, Captain?"

"Acknowledge her identity and allow me to proceed. Herr Wills will be questioned again, but he's already told us everything he knows. He gave us the names of his superiors. I suspect he and Frau Wills will eventually be released and sent home to Berlin with their son."

I held his gaze for a moment before I nodded. "Very well. She is my sister."

"Thank you, Major."

I murmured, "You are an exceptionally kind man."

"For a Jew," he quipped, and as I winced, he softened his tone. "As I said, I'm not in the business of revenge. But believe me, plenty of others are. They will see those responsible brought to justice. The world will indeed know what has been done."

I extended my hand. He held it. "If you would allow me one more request?" he asked.

"Of course. Anything." I waited as he looked at our twined hands. "I feel rather foolish asking, after the day you've just had. But," he said, "might you give me an autograph for my wife? She adores your work. She's seen all your films. She'd be so delighted."

A quavering laugh escaped me. "Do you have anything I can sign?"

He withdrew a leather-bound notebook from his inside pocket, along with a silver fountain pen. As I scrawled my name, I thought he carried the accessories of civilization even here in this desolate place, like talismans, perhaps, to remind him that beyond Bergen-Belsen, beyond the darkness, a more congenial world still existed.

On impulse, beside my autograph, I wrote a message and left a lipstick kiss. He took the notebook and read aloud, " 'Dear Mrs. Horwell, I've met many brave men in this war, but none as gallant as your husband.' " He inclined his head, murmuring, "You do me too much honor. I'm a soldier, like you, trying to find purpose in the incomprehensible. I'm no better than anyone else."

"You may be a soldier," I said quietly. "But you are not like anyone else."

He saw me back to the airfield, where General Bradley's plane waited. He made it so that I didn't witness any other barbarity, taking me out another way to the jeep and chatting about inconsequential things until we said good-bye and I boarded the aircraft.

It wasn't until I was on my way back to Munich that I realized not once had Captain Horwell used the term "Nazi." It was the ultimate irony—a consummate German gentleman, survivor of the very people they'd tried to exterminate, now in charge of cleaning up their mess.

As for Liesel, I would never forgive. I could never forget. During the two-hour plane ride, I was visited by memories of our childhood, of her wheezing bronchial tubes and other unspecified ailments, of the procession of governesses and Mutti clucking over her; and of that evening in Schöneberg when our mother and I had played music while she reclined on the sofa, a pale vision of dutiful obedience.

She had always done her duty. Mutti trained her to it. Duty, above all else.

But I meant what I said.

As far as I was concerned, I no longer had a sister.

IX

The Soviet forces had invaded Berlin, or what was left of it, fighting with the Americans like curs over a pile of scorched bones. I had no word about my mother or Uncle Willi; I now had to accept the likelihood that they probably were dead, like so many others. I grieved and avoided the wrecked city to resume my tour, traveling to liberated parts of the country to entertain troops.

From Munich to Frankfurt, Dresden, and Cologne, I sang beside ditches and in bombed-out movie palaces, on decrepit stages in rubble-strewn halls. I played my musical saw, that oddity I'd learned in Vienna, sitting on a stool with the blade between my legs and coaxing Roma refrains from it, old beer-garden tunes, and other relics from our imploded past. I always finished my performances with "Lili Marleen," rousing the boys to sing along with me, to lend them strength as they navigated a decimated land where sudden death by a buried mine or toppling building, by a lone sniper clinging to his Nazi armband, were now as much a reality as our lost millions, vanished without a gravestone to mark their passage.

Finally, my strength gave out. The infection in my jaw, never fully cured, surged anew. In blinding pain, I submitted to hasty medical intervention in Paris before taking flight to New York. I'd outstayed my USO engagement by three months. I had left as a star, eager to show my patriotism, but also eager for the attention it brought. I returned as someone different—forged in fire, in the blood of the battlefield, and by the specter of a ravaged nation I'd resolved to disown.

Photographers and reporters thronged my arrival; this time, I gave no interviews. Customs confiscated my revolvers, despite my protest that they were a gift from General Patton. Looking grayer and more stooped, Rudi collected me in a car and rushed me to the hospital, where I remained for two weeks while my jaw was hollowed out, treated, and repaired.

I convalesced in his apartment. Maria wasn't there; she'd followed my example and departed on her own USO tour, though she stayed out of Germany at Rudi's request. Our daughter was too obvious a target, even with the Reich destroyed.

When I felt human again, the swelling in my jaw having eased enough that I could talk, I called my agent. I had no intention of staying in my husband's home any longer than necessary. I needed money for a hotel suite and, if possible, a job. Sooner rather than later. The Ritz in Paris had footed my tab, waving aside my assurance of future payment, but I owed them. I also had an enormous hospital bill and didn't like leaving debts in my wake.

Eddie did not mince words. "You left on a soldier's salary, which isn't much. The rent on Rudi's flat, Maria's tuition, storage for your belongings from the bungalow, not to mention installments on your back taxes—it's eaten up whatever savings you had. I'm still owed my commission on your last two pictures. And I'm sorry to say this, but the studios have gotten used to you being away. I'll make the rounds, but I can't guarantee anyone will take my calls."

"But MGM held the option on my contract," I said, dismayed. "When I was last there, you told me I looked terrific. You were sure they'd line up another picture for me."

"That option expired. And you did look terrific. Do you still look terrific now? Because you sound awful."

I glanced into the bedroom mirror, the phone crooked at my ear. I looked . . . old. Exhausted. Thin and unkempt, my jaw bruised and still misshapen. I looked like what I was—a forty-three-year-old former movie star who'd trudged through hell. I could get it all back, I had no doubt. But I needed time. And the bills wouldn't wait.

"I left some jewelry in a deposit box in Switzerland," I said. "My emeralds and diamonds. I can have it appraised and sell whatever I need to."

"Sure, but hold off on the emeralds, okay? I'll do my best to get your name out there. It's changing here, you know. Since the war, there are new opportunities, independent producers and directors. Stars are beginning to challenge the system, and you're getting a ton of fan mail. I've a pile of cards and letters from wives and sweethearts of GIs who saw you at the front, all thanking you for helping their men. America loves you, Marlene. I just need to prove it to the studios."

I didn't like the idea of him wielding fan mail as my entrée back into the very world I'd deserted. Unlike other stars, who'd done what they must to support the effort but never at the risk of their bankability on-screen, I'd walked away to plunge into the only cause that mattered to me. And although I'd not seen much since my return, I did not find America changed. That was the most disconcerting part; to my eyes, not much had changed at all. The war seemed distant here, among the skyscrapers and bustle, its tragedies reduced to newspaper headlines. Soldiers were being shipped home in body bags or clinging to life without limbs, blinded by tear gas and deaf from the bombings. No one seemed to care. The bars and restaurants were overflowing. Plays were still being staged on Broadway. Movies were still being made, even as Europe moaned under the wreckage and Japan cowered in the atomic fallout of Hiroshima.

On August 15, 1945, Japan surrendered. The Second World War came to its crushing finale. New York exploded with streamers, champagne, and jubilation in the streets. From Rudi's apartment terrace, I stood in my bathrobe and thought it looked like a scene from one of my pictures with von Sternberg—a celebratory rampage, careening into an all-week-long debauchery, without anyone having the faintest idea of the toll this war had taken.

I realized then that my own personal battle had just begun.

As I'd felt that day in Paris when Rudi confronted me, I didn't know who I was.

"You should go back for a visit," Rudi advised. I'd been finagling my way into beauty parlors, plying my name in lieu of cash. Eddie had not exaggerated my appeal. I found a host of experts more than willing to tone and groom me back into Dietrich. I'd gained a few pounds, which I needed, submitted to rigorous tonic cleansings and countless facials. I was starting to look like myself again, despite the crow's-feet at my eyes and the new lines on my forehead. Makeup could disguise that. A face-lift could eliminate it. A cosmetic surgeon in New York, referred by my jaw doctor, had offered to perform the lift for free, asking in return that I provide his name to other Hollywood women. At the moment, I was undecided, having seen enough of surgical knives and hospitals for the time being.

"Eddie hasn't sent word that anyone wants to see me," I said, as Tamara emptied my ashtray and gave me a look. She was on medication to deal with her nerves; whatever she was taking had caused her to stop smoking, not that she'd ever smoked as much as me or Rudi. Besides, my jaw surgeon had advised me to quit, saying it had contributed to the infection and damage. "I don't see why I should humiliate myself by going somewhere I'm not welcome."

Rudi sighed. "You can't sit here for the rest of your life. I know you're afraid, but—"

"I'm not afraid," I interrupted sharply. "I'm just not ready to keep every eyelash straight. Hollywood never knew what to do with me. Every risk I've taken, I took on my own. And don't forget, I'm still German. No one wants to see movies with a German femme fatale."

"Are you telling that to them or to yourself?" asked Rudi, making me scowl. I despised the fact that he could still see through me. "You've done more for morale with your USO tour than any other performer. You're a war hero. That must count for something. You could stay with Orson Welles. He sent you a personal invitation, offering his home for as long as you like. He's directing his own films; his wife, Rita Hayworth, is one of Columbia Pictures' biggest commodities. They'll introduce you to everyone. It could be the start of a brand-new career—one you're finally in control of."

I laughed and lit another cigarette, ignoring Tamara's disapproving snort. "When has anyone who signed a contract been in control of their career?"

Yet his words stayed with me. He was right. I couldn't hide away and hope they came to me. They wouldn't. I'd made them a lot of money once, but as Eddie said, things changed. Or not, as the case might be. In Hollywood, we were only as important as we made ourselves appear. I'd been out of the limelight for too long to hope an amazing part would drop into my lap. I'd have to go to them. I'd have to go and look irresistible. I would have to smile and pose and genuflect, demonstrate I had value, that my name could still attract an audience.

But I seemed to have lost the will. All I could think of was Paris, where people I knew, like Gabin, now worked to revive the stagnant film industry, offering up their talents in partnership with destitute European studios to make films that depicted the realities of today—gritty stories without sequins, about how we lived now. I could find work there; Paris was where I belonged. Without ever having acknowledged it, Paris felt like home.

I'd already decided to book a ticket back to Europe when unexpected word came from an attaché of General Bradley, who'd not forgotten his promise to me.

My mother had been found in Berlin. Alive.

I traveled to Paris to apply for the necessary permits to enter Germany. While I waited, I reunited with Gabin, who'd returned to his beloved Paris after having endured his own harrowing battles during the advance to liberate the city. His hair had gone silver; he was weatherbeaten and careworn, aged beyond his years, but still magnetic. He took me to bed, chided me about his beloved paintings, which remained in my storage, before he talked about us working together. He had a script he felt I'd be perfect for; he would play the lead opposite me. France needed to restore her culture, and he'd always thought I should act there. Why not now?

I wanted to do it, but asked for time while the army processed my application to travel to Germany. The Allied tug-of-war over the country, with the Soviets staking their claim to the east, meant every applicant was scrutinized, run through multiple security checks to ensure they had a valid reason for entering enemy territory. Contraband, racketeering, and the occasional Nazi stowaway were rife. Nothing and no one was safe. I had to be patient to get into Berlin.

I'd charmed my way into more perilous engagements. A telegram to Bradley himself, reminding him that I was a major, finally secured my authorization, albeit with the caveat that I was under duty to report when summoned. They even provided me with an official plane, which I accessorized by wearing my military uniform—khaki jacket, gored skirt, tie, and cap.

When I landed at the Tempelhof airfield, international news photographers blinded me with their flashbulbs. Word had leaked out, but this was an event I wanted them to record. It suited me to be seen reuniting with the woman who'd given birth to me and outlived two wars.

She was on the airfield with the army-assigned chauffeur. As I dodged past the airplane propellers, their wind shearing at my cap, I took one look at her spare, brittle form—so small now, so aged, when once she'd seemed immutable, like the Brandenburg Gate—and threw my arms around her. She stiffened; and then, as we went to the waiting car, she cast a censorious glance at the cameras and said, "You're too thin. You'll look like a bean stalk on the front page."

I wanted to clutch her veined hand when we settled in the car. But she tucked her fingers into her lap and, as we drove into the city, she remarked, "You'll find everything changed."

She had a way of making it seem as though the streets had been re-paved, her expression detached as I melted in disbelief at the window, staring out at the wasteland my city had become. I didn't recognize a thing. There was nothing to recognize. Berlin was a husk, a burnt-out shell. It was already a ghost, a lost memory.

"Wait," I started to tell the driver. "This can't be the way to Kaiserallee . . ."

Mutti sniffed. "My flat was bombed. The area is a shambles. Good thing I wasn't there. Those endless ration lines people complained about? Standing in one saved my life."

"I thought you were dead." I was doing everything I could to contain myself, knowing she'd not approve of histrionics. It did not fail to strike me that within minutes of our reunion, I'd reverted to the daughter she'd raised, wanting to please, to make her proud and avoid censure.

"Then we both thought the same." She met my eyes. "I heard you singing over the wireless. And your speeches." Her voice tightened, though I couldn't tell if she approved of my defiance or considered it an intolerable breach of etiquette. "Later, they declared that London had been destroyed and came to my door—I was still at the flat—to inform me that you had died in the Blitz. An enemy of the Reich, they said, who has paid the price. *Heil Hitler.*"

"But I was with the Americans," I exclaimed. "I had everyone searching for you."

"Is that so? They didn't search very well. I've been here the entire time."

I almost laughed. She wasn't saying it to disparage the soldiers who had located her. She simply stated a fact. No one disliked incompetence more than Josephine Felsing.

By the time we arrived at her new home in the Fregestrasse, a neutral suburb between the Soviet- and American-occupied areas, I could see she was weary. She had trouble climbing the flight of stairs, and once we entered her dimly lit flat, which consisted of a sparsely furnished living room, adjoining kitchenette, and closetlike bedroom, she sighed.

"If you need to use the WC, it's down the hall. The entire floor shares it."

I made her a cup of tea, noting she had army rations and whispering a word of gratitude to General Bradley. Then, as she sat on the lumpy sofa, I rolled up my sleeves and went to work, tidying up whatever I could until she said irritably, "You needn't prove you can still keep house. I cleaned the apartment myself when they told me you were coming. Sit with me."

Perching beside her, I didn't know what to say. I could now clearly see how much the war had wrought on her. She wasn't only underweight; her entire being seemed diminished, that unquenchable force within her ebbing like water from a ruptured pipe.

"Mutti, are you sick? You don't look well."

She set her cup on the table. "It's Berlin. No one looks well. We've lost another war. Only this time, we'll pay for it more harshly. Between your Americans and the Reds, they'll see us penned up like beasts in a stockade." She paused, glancing askance at the apartment, which contained none of her prized possessions, all lost in the bombing. "I'm a stranger in my own city. I don't understand how any of this could have happened."

It was the first allusion she'd made to the catastrophe, the first time I could recall her revealing a vulnerability that made her question her unswerving belief in the proper order.

"It happened," I said softly, "because we let it happen."

She sighed again. "I suppose that's as reasonable an explanation as any." She twined her fingers together; she still wore her wedding band, though it now hung loose on her knuckle, like someone else's memento. "Your uncle Willi is dead."

I gasped. "No. How? When?"

"Must be over a year now. A heart attack, poor man. Like your father. One minute he was at the store, doing whatever he could to keep it afloat— business was hopeless, like everything else, and his insistence on retaining that imperial patent on the wall didn't help—and the next, he dropped dead. A mercy. He never liked the situation. Toward the end, he was selling engagement rings at a discount to Wehrmacht officers who wanted to marry their girlfriends before they went to die at the front. I had him buried in the Wilmersdorf chapel. He would have liked the service, I think, though no one we knew was there. You were gone, and Liesel—"

She caught herself, looking sidelong at me before she went on: "He bequeathed everything to me in his will. It isn't much. The store was heavily damaged by the bombings. But whatever is left will be yours and your sister's when I'm gone. If the Russians don't take it first."

"Mutti, let's not talk about this now." I started to reach for her hand, overcome by sorrow that my beloved uncle, with his fancy mustache and elegance, was no more. "It's not necessary. You are tired and—"

"No." She grasped my fingers. "Listen to me. I am an old woman who has seen too much. I don't want to live in a world where I don't exist, where the country I love, that I've called my home, no longer exists. It's not a tragedy. Not like what has happened. It is God's will. We live as best we can, and if we're lucky, we die in our own bed. So many have not had that privilege. But you mustn't let our name disappear. You must fight for what remains. You are our heir. You alone can save what we fought for so long to build."

"Mutti." My voice quavered. "I'm an actress. I'm not anyone."

"You're more than that. You are my daughter. My child. You are not Liesel; you have proved that much. I want you to promise that no matter what, you'll do everything you can to restore our name. We—we did not do this," she whispered. "We are not responsible. We are good Germans. Some of us have always been good Germans."

Her eyes and voice were fervent. It had been eating at her, consuming her strength, this terrible guilt and fear that we'd be held culpable for the actions of a madman. I wanted to tell her what I'd seen in Bergen-Belsen, what the world was now seeing—the evidence that even if we'd not personally drawn up the lists or herded them onto the trains like cattle, we were still to blame because we had done nothing to stop it. We had turned away and refused to look.

But I held back. She was indeed an old woman now. Not the dragon anymore, not the mother I'd fought and rebelled against, her demands too stringent to include in my life. She was a survivor, who had earned the right to dictate her own epitaph.

I nodded. "I promise I will do whatever I can."

"Good." Her fingers unraveled from mine. "I must rest awhile. Are you staying long?"

"As long as you need me," I said. "Or as long as the army will let me."

She smiled vaguely, motioning to a rickety credenza. "There are some calling cards for you. A few of your fellow students from that academy and friends who didn't leave or were taken away. They've been coming by, wanting to know if you are really alive."

I started, turning to look at where she pointed before returning my bewildered gaze to her. "But you . . . I thought they told you I was dead."

"They did." She harrumphed. "But who could believe anything those criminals said? I suspected you might not be. You always were stubborn. I preferred to think you were dead until you came to me. I wasn't certain you would. These days, it's easier not to hope."

She retreated to the lone bedroom, clicking the warped door shut.

Alone on the sofa, I let tears slip down my cheeks. So much time lost, so much we could have shared, if only we'd found common ground. The war had taken everything from her.

But it had brought us together.

XI

They came on rickety bicycles and on foot, haggard and swathed in an assortment of mismatched clothes—frayed scarves, moth-holed caps, and ill-fitting coats that barely protected against the chill. November had fallen upon Berlin like a fist. It would be another long winter and few in the city had the means to withstand it. There was a shortage of everything: food, fuel for transport, kerosene, coal, and apparel. While the Allies haggled over the nation's fate, those who had withstood the Nazis and the resultant reprisals now faced rampant hunger and destitution.

I was overjoyed to see them—these people whose faces I did not remember, acquaintances from our champagne-and-opium-infused heyday, when Berlin bloomed with postwar intoxication, the future unclear yet, had we only known it, full of misguided hope. Looking back as I greeted them and they filled Mutti's apartment—she'd gone next door to stay the night with her widowed neighbor—whisking contraband Russian vodka and British gin from their pockets and settling on the sofa, the chairs, and the floor, I marveled at our lost innocence. We had believed we were invincible. We'd boozed, smoked, and slept with one another like pagans; but to see us now, a threadbare collection of pinched cheeks and bruised eyes, was to realize we'd experienced a time that would never come again—a glorious pageant of protest and perversity, squashed under intolerance and coils of barbed wire.

Then Camilla Horn, my rival-friend from the boardinghouse, walked through the door.

I fell apart.

She engulfed me in her arms. She looked the same in her squirrel-trimmed coat and chic beret, bleached curls peeping out to frame her narrow, still arresting face, an unexpected vision from the past, though as she whispered, kissing my cheek, "Not so young anymore."

"But more blond," I said, wiping my tears. "Weren't you a redhead?"

"You set the trend. I only copy it." She swept her feline stare over the others, nodding to those she knew. "I need a drink." One of the men, an actor I vaguely recalled from our Reinhardt days, rushed to pour vodka for her into one of the army-issue tin glasses.

"*Danke.*" As he flushed and backed away, she said to me, "I heard you were here, so I made a special trip from Vienna. How long has it been?"

"Too long." Hooking my arm in hers, I drew her into a corner. "How did you . . . ?"

"Survive?" She downed her vodka. "Not easily. Certainly not like Leni." She grimaced. "You know she made propaganda films for them?"

I nodded. "I saw one. *Triumph of the Will,* I think it was called."

"Atrocious, wasn't it? Like a bad DeMille epic. Leni always did tend to the garish." She made an irritated sound. "She used inmates from detention centers as extras, then watched them being loaded onto the death trains to Poland. She escaped Berlin, but the Americans captured her as she fled over the Alps. They're holding her for questioning, using her own propaganda to identify missing officials. I hope they hang her. She was fucking Goebbels, a miserable failed novelist, just as she failed as an actress. A party of losers. Who would have thought?"

I had to agree. Leni Riefenstahl deserved whatever was coming to her. She had not been an innocent caught up in the maelstrom; she had actively participated, helping to whip the maelstrom into murderous frenzy with her overwrought paeans to the Reich.

"Do you know anything about Gerda?" I asked, bracing myself. I'd not heard from her since our falling-out over the kidnapping threat. She'd taken her final paycheck, which I'd left as promised, and disappeared. I assumed she'd returned to Europe. Where else would she have gone?

"Not lately," said Camilla. "Last I heard, she was in Austria. She wrote for a Viennese newspaper—Nazi approved of course. Guess she had to make a living. Then, because of her connection to you, she was hired by Goebbels to write a series of articles about your life in Hollywood. They weren't exactly flattering, but they probably saved her."

"Is she alive?" I said. "She wasn't arrested or gone missing?"

"Not that I'm aware of. Word traveled fast when people were taken. Like I said, knowing you must have saved her. The Nazis may have declared you a traitor in public but in private they couldn't get enough of you. Leni told me after she saw you in London, Goebbels was furious that you'd refused their offer. Hitler was a fan; he'd seen all your pictures, even those they banned, and he wanted to make you his mistress. Just think," she said wryly. "You might have helped us win the war if only you'd agreed to come here and screw the führer."

I closed my eyes for a moment, in gratitude that Gerda had survived. Then I looked at Camilla and said, "Will you tell her I asked about her if you see her?"

"Of course. But Gerda never liked our circle much, as you know. It's unlikely I'll run into her anytime soon." She paused. "Do you want to know how I made it through?"

I assented, prepared for the worst. Those who were still here—despite their forlorn appearance, they must have done something. No one could be entirely without blame, if only for their silence. And Camilla had always been an opportunist.

"Well, in case you're wondering," she said, "I never fucked one. I should have; it might have made things more tolerable. Instead, I was arrested twice, first for refusing to salute some SS pig and then on suspicion of working for the resistance. I wasn't a spy, so they convicted me of traveling without a permit. I spent three months at the women's prison in Vechta."

She shrugged. "It could have been worse. I could have been Leni. I knew they'd be watching me, so when I was released, I went to Italy and made a few pictures there. Now I'm back and looking for work. Not that there's any to be found. Vienna is no better off than Berlin or Rome. The world may have gone up in flames, but unemployed actresses are as plentiful as ever."

Relief flooded me. "I can't believe you're here," I said, as she thrust out her glass and her hovering admirer hastened to refill it. "After all this time, I thought—"

Her ironic laugh cut me off. "You never thought of me. You were too busy being famous. I understand. Life goes on. We leave some behind." She paused. "Still married to Rudi?"

"Yes. He's living in New York with our daughter."

Her smile widened. "He was quite the prize. I hated you for that."

I chose not to tell her that the prize wasn't all he'd been made out to be. As we sat together reminiscing, I learned that others we had known were missing and presumed dead.

"Trude died of a stroke," Camilla said. "She never saw the worst of it. But Karl Huszár-Puffy, remember him, who played the publican in *The Blue Angel*? And Gerron, who played the magician: both sent to the camps. And the girls of Das Silhouette went to Dachau. That's where they sent all the degenerates. So much talent," she mused. "We'll never be the same."

Fury gripped me. Friends and colleagues, the most vibrant and daring, who'd infused Berlin with her sparkle—gone. I might have suffered the same, had I not gone abroad. Or perhaps later, if I'd returned to Berlin. Hitler's admiration had not precluded killing his own.

Biting back futile tears, I turned to regard our companions, lubricated on cheap alcohol and engaged in fierce debate. "We'll become something different," I said vehemently, as if I was trying to convince myself. "Nothing can stop artists from creating."

"When there's no other choice, what else can we do?" Camilla reached for the vodka. "I certainly intend to keep on acting. We've hit the bottom of the heap—and this bottle, too, by the looks of it—so we must start over. Germany is a phoenix. She will rise from the ashes."

I gave her a contemplative look. "Will she?"

"We can always hope." She clinked her glass against mine. "To absent friends."

I proceeded to get drunk. At one point, someone cited a producer I'd known from the Nelson revue, who was now staging an Allied-approved version of Weill's *The Threepenny Opera*, and I shot to my feet, sloshing gin as I cried out, "I'll buy a theater. I'll repair it, and Camilla and I will star in a revival of *Two Bow Ties*. Everyone here will have a job!"

Everyone there applauded. Only, when I swerved to Camilla, she regarded me archly and demurred, saying, "Aren't we rather long in the tooth to play showgirls?"

Gulping down the rest of my drink, I staggered into the kitchenette to prepare *Ersatzkaffee*, offering up my carton of American cigarettes and doling out advice on how all of us, together, could re-create the acerbic joy of our Weimar days until most of them passed out.

Although she'd imbibed more than me, Camilla remained sober. When I escorted her to the door to say good night, she abruptly pressed her gin-soaked lips to mine. Then she pulled away with a sly look. "We never did get our chance together. I hated you for that, too."

"Stay, then." I caressed her wrist. "Mutti is sleeping next door. Stay with me tonight."

"Oh, no. We're also rather long in the tooth for that. Let it remain something you never wanted and something I can always desire. We've too little left to sacrifice our regrets."

I never saw her again.

But as she tugged up her collar and vanished into the night, I knew she would live. She would continue to survive. A woman like her could never be defeated.

She was one of our good Germans.

THE FOLLOWING WEEK while I undertook a short military tour outside Berlin, Mutti died. It was November 6, a few days before her sixty-ninth birthday. As with Uncle Willi and my father, her heart stopped. It was sudden. Painless. As she would have said, it was God's will.

The Wilmersdorf cemetery where she'd laid my uncle to rest had been destroyed, so in an adjacent lot covered in slush and cinders, I had a hole dug and buried her in a makeshift coffin built from discarded school desks. Several GIs volunteered to assist me; as they lowered her into her grave, in my grief I thought of what Camilla had said.

There was indeed too little left to sacrifice our regrets.

Not having had more time with my mother was mine. She'd been my final link to my homeland, the last person to remind me of who I was. Our Felsing store was lost. Despite my promise, I couldn't save it. The Russians had served me with an impossible bill. Either I repaired the wreckage or the store would be torn down. Already, they were bulldozing half the city, hauling out its ravaged past to make room for their steel-and-concrete future. I didn't have the money to satisfy their demands; even if I had, there was no point. What Mutti most feared had already come to pass. Our name was lost. All I could do was ensure I didn't bring it more dishonor.

And under a glacial rain powdered with snow, I crumbled a handful of dirt over her and recited the poem she'd once embroidered on a panel and hung above our mantel:

> "'O love, while it's still yours to love!
> O love, while love you still may keep!
> The hour will come, the hour will come,
> When you shall stand by graves and weep.'"

I must say good-bye. There was nothing for me here. I had left Germany long ago.

But as I turned around to depart, as the GIs shoveled sodden earth upon her casket, I heard my mother's voice, as clearly as if she were still beside me.

"*Tu etwas*, Lena. *Do* something."

XII

I thought of selling my saw, my gowns and stockings, pawning the rest of my stashed jewelry in Switzerland and turning my back on Hollywood. I could live in Paris. Germany was not my country anymore, and America certainly wasn't the place where I wanted to die. I didn't even own a bed there to die in.

But I had my husband to support, and once I returned to New York, I found Rudi's health had declined. He had a persistent lung ailment that had Tamara in a constant state of worry. Like me, he'd been advised to stop smoking. Like me, he refused.

"I'll have to go back," I said to Tamara. "I need work to pay the bills."

She was helping me unpack in the spare bedroom; she said, "Do you want to?"

I sighed from where I sat on the edge of the bed. "I don't want to do anything but sleep. So, for now, that's what I'll do. Then we'll see what tomorrow brings."

"Very Scarlett O'Hara of you. Maybe they can remake *Gone With the Wind*. You can play a woman who must rebuild her bombed-out cabaret. It would fit the times, don't you think?"

I laughed. I also slept, for twelve hours straight, so exhausted by my travels and my grief over my mother that the world went dark. When I awoke, my neck sore from the soft heap of pillows, Tamara was standing at my bedside with a coffee cup and a telegram.

"From Mr. Welles. He's holding a soirée at his house next month. All the big names, the studio heads and important pretty people, will be there. You're invited."

"A Hollywood party?" I groaned, seizing the cup from her. "I'm in no mood."

"No?" She crossed her arms at her chest, the telegram between her fingers. "Then I suppose you don't care that the queen herself has announced her retirement and is scheduled to make her final appearance at the party."

I burned my lips on the coffee. "Garbo will be there?"

Tamara nodded. "In the flesh. Shall I start packing your bag?"

IT WAS SURREAL.

Chinese-style lanterns dangled over the illuminated flagstone terrace and pool; buffet tables draped in pristine linen were heaped with hors d'oeuvres. As a small orchestra played the latest tunes in the background, handsome waiters in short white jackets and crisp trousers circulated with platters and chilled champagne. The war seemed even more remote here than in New York, with only a few familiar faces to ease my discomfort: Bette in a hideous taffeta gown and slash of lipstick. Gary with his silvering temples and satisfied smile (he'd won an Academy Award for his role in *Sergeant York*). John Wayne, who copped a feel when no one was looking. And Mercedes, who murmured, "They've been dying to see you. No one thought you'd come. But I knew you would. The Venus from Berlin doesn't hide from battle. She greets her enemies in full bugle beads, with a Viennese saw between her thighs."

"Are they my enemies?" I accepted a flute of champagne from a waiter and wished there was something stronger. "I thought we were among friends here."

Mercedes clucked her tongue. "It's Los Angeles. Even our friends are enemies."

Truer words had rarely been spoken.

I'd arrived here the previous week, and Orson and his wife took me under their wing. Rita had become an international sensation, adored by the public and criticized by the censors for her performance as the temptress Gilda—a part I'd have undergone two face-lifts to play—with her taunting black-satin shimmy and lush red mane. But at heart, she was a generous, simple girl who loved to dance and yearned for a family, her Spanish heritage imbuing her with a penchant for domesticity that ill-suited Orson's wandering eye. She'd confided to me one evening that she knew he was unfaithful. When I replied that infidelity didn't signify a lack of love, she retorted, "But refusing to buy me a house does. All this, you see, it's rented. Even the furniture. He says he doesn't want the responsibility because it interferes with his freedom." Rita pouted. "Why marry at all if you don't want to be responsible about it?"

I didn't comment. I was hardly an example, although in her naiveté, Rita seemed to think Rudi and I were the perfect couple.

"So many years together," she sighed as she helped me apply my makeup that night, having plucked my hairline to broaden my forehead—"A studio trick," she said, showing me her own heightened brow—and scoring the lower rims of my eyes with a white pencil, "to enhance their luster." She even applied false eyelashes she'd trimmed to a feathery texture, as I'd come woefully unprepared, and loaned me her own shade of crimson lipstick.

After she finished and I cocked my hip in my azure satin gown with its diamanté-clasp straps, she applauded. "Stunning. They'll be green with envy to see you so beautiful."

"Envious enough to offer me a job?" I checked in the mirror for lipstick stains on my teeth. "I'm considered rather an old warhorse these days."

"You are not." She was indignant. "Women like you don't get old. You ripen like wine."

I hugged her. "You're the wine, *Liebchen*. I'm just an aperitif."

She took me downstairs, her hand clasping my elbow. "Now remember what they say," she whispered as I paused at the terrace entrance, overwhelmed. I'd had no fear of prancing onto creaking stages that threatened to collapse underneath me, and singing amid exploding shrapnel and the rattle of gunfire, but the predatory glances already turning my way, the quick incline of heads to share whispers, made me want to flee.

This was a mistake. I should not have returned here.

"What . . . do they say?" I quavered.

"'Never let them see you sweat.'" Rita smiled at my startled expression. "Papa stayed with us once. He adores you, his Kraut. He couldn't be here tonight, but he said to remind you if you ever showed up."

"Did he?" I said, and I tossed my recently bleached-and-waved hair before I strode into the arena. Mistake or not, I would not let them see it.

Now, I stood with Mercedes, surrounded by people who knew me, who'd seen my pictures or heard of my war efforts, and I'd never felt so isolated. Bette had hissed that she wanted us to visit together "as soon as this kiss-ass fest is over," but aside from her, no one appeared too excited to welcome me. Some of the younger actresses, whose names I didn't know, gauged me as if I might steal a coveted role from under their upturned noses. Things had indeed changed. Yet everything remained the same. At forty-four years of age, I reasoned I should take solace in the fact that I was still impressive enough to be seen as competition.

"Is she here?" I finally asked Mercedes, who of course knew to whom I referred.

"Not yet. Unlike you, she does prefer to hide. Why? Do you want to meet her?"

I shrugged. "If she's going to be here, why not?"

Mercedes lifted an eyebrow. "After all this time, you still carry a torch. I believe you're as curious about her as she is about you."

"She is?" I forgot my nonchalant stance. "Has she ever said anything about me to you?"

"Marlene." She sighed. "Why ask?"

Two hours later, I was ready to call it a night. Rita had introduced me to Harry Cohn, the production head of Columbia Pictures who'd launched her career. He was surprisingly young and dapper, kissing my cheek and expressing his delight, but I didn't get the impression his enthusiasm would yield an offer. He wasn't interested in building his own talent, Orson had warned me. Rita was an exception, but Cohn was one of the new breed who preferred to hire actors on loan from other studios, thereby attracting a presold audience. I wasn't under contract and had no presale appeal. I hadn't made a picture in over two years, and my last one, *Kismet,* had been consigned to oblivion, where it belonged.

Still, before Harry Cohn went off to engage a group of simpering starlets, he handed me his card. "Tell your agent to call me," he said. "We should talk."

Rita was enthused, even if she muttered under her breath, "He's a devil. He'll want to buy your soul. And he can afford it. He's a Jew."

I recoiled, casting a sharp glance at her.

"Not that I care," she added hastily. "I like Jews. But after the war, and with you being German . . . Still, he'd be an idiot not to sign you."

He wouldn't. I returned to Mercedes, smoked two cigarettes, and then, just as I decided I might as well retreat upstairs and peel off my false lashes, which were fluttering at the edges of my eyes like moribund butterflies, an excited murmur rippled through the crowd.

Mercedes straightened from her slouch. Her face took on a peculiar sheen. Before I even followed her unblinking stare, I knew what I would see.

Garbo had arrived.

I had never forgotten that night Anna May, Leni, and I went to see her in Pabst's *The Joyless Street* and how I'd wept at her preternatural presence. I didn't expect to encounter the same woman. Like me, Garbo was past her prime; like mine, her career had had its ups and downs. After three Academy Award nominations and stupendous critical acclaim, encroaching age and a dimming box office had precipitated her decision to leave it all behind, to retreat into privacy and her much-vaunted need for solitude.

Still, I found myself standing on tiptoe to peer over the crowd, everything fading around me as Orson in his tuxedo escorted her onto the terrace. The stars parted before her like an awestruck firmament. As she neared and her pale eyes caught sight of Mercedes, I saw a flicker of recognition in her gaze that she immediately smothered.

Beautiful did not begin to describe her.

She was tall for a woman yet also, paradoxically, smaller than I'd imagined. But then, weren't we all like that, fashioned by nature to be enlarged, blown up to deified proportions? Despite her height, her features were fragile perfections, with those sculpted cheeks and regal nose, that extraordinary mouth and severe countenance, which could be so still, so enigmatic, that audiences etched their dreams upon it, like drawing upon pure white sand, until her private lagoon seeped forth to wash the shore blank again.

Caught in a whirlpool of emotions, elation vying with disbelief that she was here at last, the icon I'd been told I resembled, had been styled to emulate, her trajectory blazing like a sister comet next to mine but never coinciding, I dropped my gaze to her feet.

She might be perfect everywhere else, but Garbo had the feet of a peasant.

Orson snapped his fingers at a gawking waiter, bringing up my startled gaze. Champagne was offered. She shook her head. Clad in a simple black dress that draped her in mystique, she whispered to Orson, who nodded, turning toward—

Me.

Mercedes's mirth purred in her throat. "See? She is indeed curious. Go."

I stumbled forth. I lost all sense of time. As I took the few steps to where she stood waiting, I saw myself in a dizzying rush of transformation—the besotted schoolgirl with an oversize bow and soggy marzipan in her fist; the rebellious adolescent with her dedication to the violin, splaying her thighs, open for adventure; the monocle-eyed doyenne of the cabaret, sauntering through sawdust to a movie set, where her frilled underpants would kindle an obsession. I saw the protective mother with her child, the daring seductress and neglectful wife; I saw the star catapulted to adoration on anonymous desire; and then, as I came before her and reached out, I saw the battle-worn major in an infirmary, clasping a dying Nazi's hand.

I wanted to ask her if she had spied on Gabin when he swam naked in my pool. Instead, I heard myself say in a tremulous voice, "I am Marlene Dietrich."

And as I felt her touch, so cool and dry, Garbo replied, "I know."

AFTERWORD

In 1946, Marlene returned to France to shoot *Martin Roumagnac* with Jean Gabin. The picture was unsuccessful, and their relationship ended on a bitter note. A heavily censored release of the film in the United States also seemed to confirm her end as a Hollywood star.

Undeterred, she went on to make fourteen more pictures, including Hitchcock's *Stage Fright* (1950), Billy Wilder's *Witness for the Prosecution* (1957), a cameo in Orson Welles's *A Touch of Evil* (1958), and Stanley Kramer's *Judgment at Nuremberg* (1961), in which she took on the challenging role of a German widow, whose husband, a Nazi officer, was executed for war crimes. She proved in these roles that she had more in her arsenal than legs and glamour, but she was never again nominated for an Academy Award.

In 1950, France awarded her the Légion d'honneur for her valor during the war; she was later promoted to the title of officer. Belgium, Israel, and the United States also honored her with Medals of Freedom. Soon after, Marlene embarked on a bold new chapter in her career, returning to her cabaret roots as a solo performer at the Hotel Sahara in Las Vegas. Her engagement was so successful that she took her show on the road, selling out venues in Paris, London, Moscow, and other cities throughout the world.

Her songs "Falling in Love Again," "Allein," and "Lili Marleen" were staples of her shows.

Marlene returned to perform in Berlin in 1960. Her appearance was embroiled in acrimony, with protesters picketing outside the theater against her wartime exploits, but she won over her audience and the critics. Throughout her life, she remained defiant in her contempt for Nazism and Germany's role in the war, though she admitted that in her heart, she would always be German. She also refused to publicly admit her sister's existence, though Liesel, working as a schoolteacher, resided in Berlin with her husband. Despite the damage between them, the Dietrich sisters maintained sporadic contact until Liesel's death in 1973.

Marlene later acknowledged that she was at her best on the stage. "In every single bar of my music, every single light that hits me," she said, "I know and can control it. In films, there are too many intangibles." And as a stage performer, she proved immensely popular, entrancing her public with her nude-spangled gowns, sumptuous white furs, and husky voice. Recordings attest to her consummate showmanship, yet with Marlene, the voice is only half the appeal.

In 1963, she appeared with the Beatles at the London Palladium. Her stage career was waning but the quartet who revolutionized music declared her "the most elegant woman in the world." She finally performed on Broadway from 1967 to 1968, for which she won a special Tony Award.

Josef von Sternberg continued to work in Hollywood until 1953, often as an unbilled assistant director. In his later years, he taught film aesthetics at UCLA, citing in his classes much of his oeuvre with Marlene. He also wrote an autobiography. He died in 1969, at the age of seventy-five. Marlene was devastated by his passing, although in a classic example of their oft-contentious relationship, when once asked by a student if he ever heard from her, von Sternberg retorted, "Only when she *needs* something."

In between the engagements in her hectic schedule—a notorious perfectionist, she oversaw every aspect of her performances—Marlene engaged in a robust personal life while also devoting time to her family, a doting grandmother to her daughter's two sons. She stayed married to Rudi Sieber until his death from cancer in 1976. His mistress, Tamara Matul, had died years before in a California residential facility after a debilitating battle with mental illness. As she'd done throughout their marriage, Marlene assumed the costs for Tamara's and Rudi's care. After her daughter, he was the constant in her life, the husband she could always turn to in times of tribulation. Friends who knew her well remarked that she never fully recovered from his loss.

She did not marry again.

Marlene retired in 1975. A fall during a show in Wiesbaden that resulted in a broken collarbone was followed by a more severe thigh fracture in Sydney, Australia, revealing a legacy of brittle bones from her war-deprived childhood that would eventually confine her to a wheelchair. Following successful radiotherapy for cervical cancer, her remarkable stamina had begun to ebb and she sought a private existence, out of the public eye.

Leaving her apartment in New York, she took up residence on the exclusive Avenue Montaigne in Paris. A 1984 documentary about her life by actor/director Maximilian Schell was nominated for an Academy Award; Marlene collaborated but refused to be filmed for it. Her last on-camera appearance was a small, highly billed role in 1978's *Just a Gigolo* with David Bowie, which she agreed to do for the salary and the film's decadent prewar-Berlin theme.

Reclusive and dependent on painkillers in her final years, Marlene maintained contact with the outside world through prolific letters and telephone calls, still politically active and allegedly on friendly terms with such world leaders as Reagan and Gorbachev. Though she avoided any public engagements, in 1989 she spoke via telephone on French television about the fall of the Berlin Wall. She sounded elated.

Marlene Dietrich died of renal failure on May 7, 1992. She was ninety years old. Her funeral was held at La Madeleine in Paris and attended by over a thousand mourners, including ambassadors from Germany, the United States, the United Kingdom, Russia, and Israel. Her closed casket was draped in the tricolor French flag and adorned with white wildflowers and roses from President Mitterrand. Her three medals were displayed, military-style, at the foot of the casket. During the eulogy, the priest said, "She lived like a soldier and would like to be buried as a soldier."

Though a report in the *New York Times* stated that Marlene had instructed in her will that she wished to be buried near her family, her actual testament held no such provision. Nevertheless, on May 16, her body was flown to Germany and interred in the Städtischer Friedhof III, Berlin-Schöneberg cemetery, next to her mother's grave. In 1992, a plaque was unveiled at her birth site, Leberstrasse 65. Despite the controversy in her homeland over her stance during World War II, the Marlene Dietrich–Platz in Berlin was inaugurated in 1997, along with a commemorative postage stamp. She was made an honorary citizen in 2002. A significant portion of her estate became part of the exhibition at the Filmmuseum Berlin, including her film and stage costumes, over a thousand items from her personal wardrobe, photographs, posters, and portions of her voluminous correspondence, which she'd requested should not be published.

The American Film Institute has named Marlene Dietrich the ninth-greatest female star of all time.

As with every book I've written, my passion for my subject inevitably collided with a finite word count. Having been a fan of Marlene since my teens (the first film I saw of hers was *Morocco*), I knew it would be impossible to portray her entire life in a single novel. I chose to focus on her youth and career in Hollywood, selecting events that I thought best encapsulate her, but I'm well aware that I've had to leave out as much as I included. I can only hope my admiration for her shines through, and that in my small way, I've done her spirit justice.

To those unaware of every detail about her, I wish to say that while the time line has been altered on occasion to facilitate the plot, everyone in this book actually lived and I strove to be as faithful to their documented personalities as possible. Likewise, every major event occurred, albeit re-interpreted here through invented dialogue and my protagonist's impressions. Marlene wrote her memoirs but wasn't often forthcoming—and in some instances, she wasn't forthcoming at all. Fictionalizing her required a touch of deduction, a dash of gut instinct, a strong dose of courage, and meticulous consultation of other sources.

My fascination with celebrity and the struggle to obtain and maintain it are personified by Marlene Dietrich, whose seemingly meteoric rise was actually the result of years of perseverance, often at the cost of her personal fulfillment. In the years since her death, Dietrich's enduring myth proves she became an expert at cultivating her image, even if in some respects she became famous in spite of herself, her unconventional choices at odds with the system she worked under and the morality of her times. That said, I'm honored to have had the privilege of living through her eyes. Of all the characters I've written, Marlene has been one of my most joyous experiences.

ACKNOWLEDGMENTS

I owe this experience to many people, starting with my editor Rachel Kahan, whose citing of Marlene's cameo appearance in my novel *Mademoiselle Chanel* (she ended up on the editing-room floor) lit the spark. My publishing team at William Morrow supports me with enthusiasm; I'm grateful for all their efforts. The ladies of the Jean V. Naggar Literary Agency, Inc., in particular, my agent Jennifer Weltz, are my champions. Not every writer is as fortunate to have such fearless advocates at their side.

My husband supports all my endeavors, sustaining me through the long hours at my desk and the ups and downs of being a writer. He reminds me to eat and rest. He takes me away to warm oceans and keeps our life in order, as I can become distracted when possessed by a character. My cats, Boy and Mommy, give me comfort and love; their presence is one of companionship interspersed with daily belly rubs. My friends Sarah Johnson, Linda Dolan, Michelle Moran, Robin Maxwell, Margaret George, M. J. Rose, Kris Waldherr, Tasha Alexander, Heather Webb, and Donna Russo-Morin are always there for laughter and kvetching. I also appreciate my Facebook community for their wit and support. Social media is my watercooler, where I can join in conversations about more than my current work in progress.

Most important, I thank you, my reader.

As a storyteller, I cannot do this without you.

SOURCES

I consulted too many sources to list here. From film archives to newspaper clippings, newsreels, blogs, Web sites, and piles of books, Marlene has such a devoted fan base that I think wherever she is, she must be singing "Falling in Love Again." I relied most consistently on the following volumes. Please note, this list does not represent a full bibliography:

Bach, Steven. *Marlene Dietrich: Life and Legend*. New York: William Morrow, 1992.

Bruno, Michael. *Venus in Hollywood*. New York: Lyle Stuart, 1970.

Chandler, Charlotte. *Marlene: A Personal Biography*. New York: Simon & Schuster, 2011.

Dickens, Homer. *The Films of Marlene Dietrich*. New Jersey: Citadel Press, 1973.

Dietrich, Marlene. *Marlene*. New York: Grove Press, 1989.

Frewin, Leslie. *Dietrich*. New York: Stein and Day, 1967.

Friedric, Otto. *Before the Deluge: A Portrait of Berlin in the 1920s*. New York: Harper & Row, 1972.

Higham, Charles. *Marlene*. New York: Norton, 1977.

Sarris, Andrew. *The Films of Josef von Sternberg*. New York: Museum of Modern Art/Doubleday, 1966.

Spoto, Donald. *Blue Angel: The Life of Marlene Dietrich.* New York: Doubleday, 1992.

Swindell, Larry. *The Last Hero: A Biography of Gary Cooper.* New York: Doubleday, 1980.

Walker, Alexander. *Marlene Dietrich.* New York: Applause Books, 1999.

Wood, Ean. *Dietrich: A Biography.* London: Sanctuary Publishing, 2002.